Bourgeois Morality

Bourgeois Morality

Maria Ossowska

Translated from the Polish by
G. L. Campbell

Routledge & Kegan Paul
London and New York

First published as Moralność mieszczańska for the Societas Scientiarum Lodziensis by
Ossolineum Publishers (Wroclaw), Łódź, 1956

This edition first published in 1986
by Routledge & Kegan Paul plc

11 New Fetter Lane, London EC4P 4EE

Published in the USA by
Routledge & Kegan Paul Inc.
in association with Methuen Inc.
29 West 35th Street, New York, NY 10001

Phototypeset in Linotron Bembo, 11 on 12 pt
by Input Typesetting Ltd, London
and printed in Great Britain
by St Edmundsbury Press
Bury St. Edmunds, Suffolk

Library of Congress Cataloging in Publication Data

Ossowska, Maria.

Bourgeois morality.
Translation of: Moralność mieszczańska.
1. Middle classes. 2. Social ethics. 3. Middle
classes—Europe—History. 4. Middle classes—
United States—History. 5. Europe—Moral conditions.
6. United States—Moral conditions. I. Title.
HT684.O813 1986   305.5'5'094   86-3211

British Library CIP Data available

ISBN 0-7100-9782-4

Contents

Plates

Preface

In my book *Podstawy nauki o moralności* ('The Foundations of the Study of Morality'), which I wrote before the war, I distinguished three main groups of problems which arise in the systematic and scientific study of morality. These are: (1) the analysis of moral evaluations and moral norms; (2) the psychology of morality; and (3) the sociology of morality. It was then my intention to devote a book to each of these three fields. Thus, *Podstawy nauki o moralności* was connected with the first group of problems, and my later book *Motywy postępowania* ('Motives of Action') took up questions arising from the second. The present book, *Moralność mieszczańska* ('Bourgeois Morality'), was conceived as an introduction to the problems connected with the third group; and here my intention was to try to convince those who still feel able to speak of 'morality', in the singular and in the abstract, that even when we limit ourselves to a given place and a given time, any society with a complex class structure will be found to possess not one morality but a plurality of moralities.

I had long been interested in courtly and chivalrous traits in morality, and had tried to trace these, starting from the *Iliad* and proceeding through the courtly romances of late French feudalism and Castiglione's courtiers, down to the European nobility of the nineteenth century. The material I had collected on this theme was destroyed in the war. When I returned to the subject after the war, I decided to postpone treatment of the courtly traits in morality, and to deal instead with bourgeois morality, the development of which, it seemed to me, raised more interesting questions. My approach to the subject was analytic rather than historical, in that I was mainly concerned with isolating and identifying certain classical variants of class morality. In this way I hoped to be better able to reconstruct a specific moral climate, the moral facts of a given case, and to provide a fund of comparative material – the sort of thing which is indispensable if any of those interdependencies and relationships are to be established for which every researcher is on the look-out. The book is therefore designed to be a systematic study, based on concrete historical facts. In the presentation of this material – e.g. in my sketches of the views of Defoe, Franklin and Volney – I have referred to historical events and processes only in so far as these are necessary for an understanding of these men as writers. I have assumed that the readers at whom my book is aimed are not unfamiliar with these matters. The realm of facts I deal with is one that is amply covered in standard textbooks, and accordingly I saw no need for superfluous recapitulation.

The researcher accustomed to working on purely philosophical themes in which conceptual analysis has a crucial role to play if the product is to be a genuine contribution to philosophy, is bound to feel daunted when confronted with the limitless sea of facts which go to form the history of human culture. As one burrows one's way into philosophical theories and concepts one feels – perhaps mistakenly – that one is in control of the material, and that it can be interpreted with some degree of precision. Not so here: the deeper one penetrates into the subject, the more one is convinced that some facts are escaping, eluding one's grasp; or that the very next source to be explored will force revaluation of one's whole carefully constructed picture of reality. We can never have the satisfaction of knowing that the ground has been covered, the material exhausted. At a certain point the researcher feels that he has lost the thread, that the continuity has been broken, and that he is following a completely new tack; but later study often shows that what seemed to be a lacuna in reality was in fact a lacuna in his own mental equipment. I am only too well aware of the imperfections in this book, but I take comfort in the thought that others working in this field will be able to assess my findings by placing them in a wider and more thoroughly researched background. Someone has to take the first step.

Acknowledgments

Plates are reproduced courtesy of the following: BBC Hulton Picture Library for Plate 7; Biblioteka Narodowa, Warsaw, for Plate 2; Bibliothèque Nationale, Paris, for Plates 10 and 11; Mansell Collection for Plates 3, 4, 6 and 8; Phaidon Press for Plate 5; Victoria and Albert Museum for Plates 1, 9 and 12 (photographer John Campbell).

The poem on pp. 27–9, 'On Trash' by Mayakovsky, is reprinted from *Mayakovsky: Poems*, translated and edited by Herbert Marshall, by permission of Dobson Books.

Acknowledgements

Chapter 1

Introduction

1 What does 'bourgeois morality' mean?

The statement that a set of moral directives and attitudes is 'bourgeois' in character can be interpreted in more than one way. It may be a genetic description, asserting simply that the set of attitudes in question arose in a bourgeois milieu. Then again, it may mean that the bourgeoisie by and large acknowledges and accepts these directives, even though they have been generated in a non-bourgeois setting. Each of these definitions identifies certain directives as 'bourgeois' without going into their content. Examination of the content provides us with two further definitions. The first of these states that directives which serve bourgeois interests can be described as 'bourgeois'. The second identifies a directive or a doctrine as 'bourgeois' if it reflects bourgeois principles or expresses a bourgeois frame of mind. Although the rise and spread of a doctrine in any given social setting may fairly be taken as evidence that the doctrine serves the interests of that setting, the converse proposition is not always true. As we all know, a given doctrine may well suit a class and serve its so-called objective interests even though it was neither created by that class nor, owing to what is known as 'a lack of due awareness', enjoys popular recognition and approval within it.

The course of history presents us with various 'bourgeois moralities' under each of these headings. So, when we speak of 'bourgeois morality' in the singular, we have to be cautious: exactly which bourgeoisie do we have in mind? When and where did it flourish? But, in general, when people speak of 'bourgeois morality' without specifying spatio-

1

temporal indices, they have in mind nothing more than a generalised set of attitudes and views which they take to be characteristic of the bourgeoisie of their own time and place.

In this sense, the term 'bourgeois morality' can be usefully compared with the term 'Christian morality'. To speak of 'Christian morality' in the singular, as sometimes happens, is obviously the result of faulty and unhistorical thinking: faulty because the morality of St Francis of Assisi, on the one hand, and that of St Ignatius Loyola or Alfonso da Liguori, on the other, can hardly be grouped under one common denominator – to say nothing of the profound differences between Catholicism and the various branches of Protestantism. As a homogeneous historical entity 'Christian morality' does not exist; it cannot be detected even in the Gospels. Those who speak of Christian morality in the singular are usually thinking of a certain specific type of morality which came to be associated with the behaviour of Christians at a certain time and in a certain place: usually a morality in which such 'soft' virtues as sympathy, compassion, humility and patience predominated – the brand of Christian morality which was attacked by Nietzsche. Again, it is with such an interpretation as this in mind that people look for analogies between Christianity and Buddhism. In this sense, 'Christian morality' is ascribed to the meek in spirit, even if the meek in spirit subscribe to no article of Christian dogma. In short, 'Christian morality' as thus interpreted is not necessarily 'the morality of Christians'.

Similarly, those who speak of 'Puritan morality' have a certain type of morality in mind. They are not thinking of the morality preached and practised by certain sects at a certain historical moment in Western European countries and in the United States. Doctrinally, these sects differed rather widely, but they are all lumped together under the heading 'Puritan' because of certain similarities in their life-styles. 'Puritan morality' is thus a collocation of certain recurrent factors occurring in the ethical attitudes of differing – often, indeed, mutually hostile – sects: such factors as a distinctive attitude to sex, and a hostility to every form of pleasure and pleasure-seeking. Defined in such reductionist terms,

'Puritan morality' may well be sought and found among many primitive tribes.

That this typological conception of bourgeois morality has been prevalent in Poland and elsewhere, at least from the middle of the last century to the present day, is incontestable. Wherever thrift, providence, orderliness and an aptitude for arithmetical reckoning and accountancy are identified as 'bourgeois' virtues, no need is felt to pinpoint, in terms of space or time, the morality thus defined. Thus, for example, Jan Kott in his discussion of Z. Urbanowska's novel *Księżniczka* ('The Princess'), speaks of the 'cardinal bourgeois virtues' and the 'bourgeois catechism'.[1] It is in this sense that bourgeois morality is ascribed to the well-paid, highly skilled worker in the Anglo-Saxon countries, and it is in this sense that the working class is elsewhere warned not to let itself be infected by this 'bourgeois' attitude. With this interpretation in mind, it can be argued, aptly or inaptly but in any case reasonably, that the morality endorsed in the European fable from Aesop to La Fontaine is bourgeois in character. Speaking of 'bourgeois morality' we have here a certain delimited quality in mind; just as when speaking of 'bourgeois interiors' we have a mental picture of opulently massed furniture in protective covers, with artificial flowers or palm-trees, and a canary in its cage.

The bourgeois morality which we propose to study in the present work is more precisely a set of moral directives regarded as typical of the bourgeoisie in various European centres between the mid-nineteenth and the mid-twentieth century. Both the literature and the journalism of the period familiarised their readers with a certain concept of bourgeois morality in a certain modality; and in Chapter 2 I shall try to illustrate the role played by this concept in the given period – the role, that is to say, of a specific typological unit.

More than once, Engels used examples drawn from the history of France to elucidate this point: for example, 'The centre of feudalism in the Middle Ages, the model country of unified monarchy, resting on estates, since the Renaissance, France demolished feudalism in the Great Revolution, and established the unalloyed rule of the bourgeoisie in a classical purity, unequalled by any other European land.'[2] The

quotation shows very well how admirably Engels understood the value of formative paradigms for the purposes of
theoretical study. Here, France serves as a paradigm both of
feudalism and of bourgeois supremacy in its classical form
after its victorious revolution. Any attempt to establish laws
in the field of the social sciences necessarily involves
comparisons, and every researcher knows that in order to
make such comparisons he must select and retain as 'typical'
certain facets of his subject. It is a point to which we shall
have occasion to return in the final chapter.

2   'Bourgeoisie' and 'petty bourgeoisie'

We are mainly concerned with bourgeois morality as a
generic whole in the sense defined above; nevertheless, we
shall often find ourselves speaking of bourgeois morality as
the morality of the bourgeoisie or of the petty bourgeoisie
– as, for example, when we inquire whether 'bourgeois
morality' is, typically, the morality of the bourgeoisie. This
is analogous to asking whether 'proletarian morality' is in
fact the morality of the proletariat. So it may be as well to say
a few words in this introductory section on the difficulties
associated with the concepts of 'bourgeoisie', 'petty bourgeoisie' and 'middle class'. In pre-war England, as the
authors of a recent monograph on the English middle class[3]
facetiously remark, the middle class could be defined as being
composed of those people who used napkin rings, since the
upper class changed their napkins with every meal, while
the lower class had no napkins at all. Alas, the war obliterated
these distinctions, thus robbing the researcher of a valuable
criterion.

As regards the literature on the bourgeoisie produced in
the capitalist countries, it is often difficult to decide on the
basis of a title alone exactly what we can expect from the
text. As I have already pointed out elsewhere,[4] some authors
when they speak of the 'bourgeoisie' mean a class, equipped
with certain rights, which is distinct from the nobility, from
the clergy and from the urban commonality. It is in this
sense that the word is used with reference to the bourgeois

in the Middle Ages, or the triumph of the bourgeoisie in Cromwell's time or in the French Revolution.

Other writers – for example, those dealing with rustic themes – contrast the bourgeois world with the rural world, the village and the countryside, and usually understand by 'bourgeoisie' the totality of those living in towns. That is to say, the group is defined from an ecological standpoint. It is this approach that we find for example in J. Ptaśnik's well-known monograph, *Miasta i Mieszczaństwo w dawnej Polsce* ('Towns and Town-dwellers in Old Poland').

In his celebrated work on the bourgeois (*Der Bourgeois*) which we shall be looking at in more detail later, Werner Sombart takes a rather different standpoint. For him, the bourgeois is *Homo oeconomicus* dwelling in a town; and the bourgeoisie is a group defined, as a whole, by ecological factors and by its participation in the production and/or exchange of material goods, particularly in the capitalist era. This definition turns out, however, to be too wide for the actual content of the book. In practice, Sombart deals with the bourgeoisie, as thus defined, only in the countries of Western Europe; and he fails to take into account the Jews resident there (although he did devote a special monograph to them). There are other restrictions: for example, ethnic minorities are ignored, the field of research is limited to those of Christian persuasion; and these restrictions are tacitly assumed, rather than explicitly set out. So, not every *Homo oeconomicus* dwelling in a town falls within the purview of Sombart's argument. The need for closer differentiation within this broad group – a need which became at least partially clear to Sombart himself – will be discussed below.

In the analysis of the French bourgeoisie at the end of the nineteenth century offered by the French authority on the bourgeois, E. Goblot, in his book *La Barrière et le niveau*, we find a group selected by totally different criteria.[5] Goblot's bourgeoisie is a group forming a sort of clique in an urban setting, whose members do not belong to the aristocracy. This group is not closed: it is open to new recruits, and members can opt out. Adherence to it is determined by a certain level of education and by a certain life-style. It is, accordingly, a group defined by criteria similar to those employed by J. Chaɫasiński in his work on the Polish intelligentsia.

It is at just such a social group that Gabriela Zapolska's critique of bourgeois morality is directed. It does not cover artisans and shopkeepers. In Zapolska's stories we are introduced first and foremost to professional men such as lawyers and doctors, or the proprietors of blocks of flats. These belong to bourgeois society in terms of Chaɫasiński's criteria. I realise that, in speaking of 'society' in the singular, I am not being strictly accurate: there existed, at least in the larger towns, a whole hierarchy of social groups, a ladder whose ascent was often seen as the main object in life. But there is no need to go into this further complication in the present context.

Again, it is precisely the group of shopkeepers, artisans and petty officials, not social spheres, that S. Ranulf has in mind in his book *Moral Indignation and Middle Class Psychology*.[6] The criteria based on property used to define this group are somewhat vague. Failure to provide rigorous definition of his criteria tends to vitiate Ranulf's thesis, a point which we shall take up in due course.

Examples could be multiplied. From what has been said, however, it should be clear that any work on the 'bourgeoisie' should first of all answer the question: who or what served as model for the study? The range of models is much greater than our brief selection suggests. Thus, for example, if we wish to trace the variations in the range of meaning, the content and the emotional colouring of the word 'bourgeois' on French territory alone, it is worth our while to study R. Johannet's book *Eloge du bourgeois français*.[7] At the time, this pro-Fascist French writer was under the spell of Mussolini's march on Rome. He would have liked to see the French bourgeoisie undertake something similar, and his book is aimed at the putative leader of such an exploit. His attempt to rouse the bourgeoisie by reminding it of its past achievements was also designed as a counter-attack against its latter-day critics, whose views will be the subject of Chapter 2 of the present work. In the many French texts cited by this author from various periods of French history we find not one or two but literally dozens of meanings of the word 'bourgeois'. In some of these sources, merchants do not belong to the bourgeoisie, nor do artisans; in others again, these are the quintessential bourgeoisie. Sometimes the word is associated with comfortable living and enjoying oneself; at other times with unrelenting labour and self-denial. Often it is difficult to discern any socially conditioned continuity or regularity in the historical development of the concept. 'Bourgeois', says one of the authors quoted by Johannet, 'is there in our language a more elastic word, a word which lends itself to so many different uses imposed upon it by any and every variation in the circumstances surrounding it? The term changes its meaning depending on the status, the calling, the traditions and the prejudices of the person using it. It can sound respectful, solemn, pompous or grotesque. It can be applied to the hero and to the snob. Often it is a polite term, even an obsequious one; often again it is an insult. As social circumstances change it may denote a state of affluence, well-fed obtuseness, a fat paunch or a heavy head.'[8]

In this context we have to remember that, as it entered the lexicon of various languages, the French word *bourgeoisie* took on a new meaning under the influence of the Marxist classics. As used by Marx and Engels, the word usually refers to the body of privileged persons as opposed to the proletariat. Deviating here from its etymological sense (*bourg* = town) it includes the landed gentry as well. At the same time, however, we find the term used by these writers in a narrower sense: e.g. when landed proprietors are mentioned alongside the bourgeoisie. In Engels's preface to the *Communist Manifesto* of 1883, the bourgeoisie is opposed to the proletariat as the class of exploiters and oppressors. Similarly in the introduction to the English edition of 1888. In *Ludwig Feuerbach*, however, Engels speaks of the struggle between landed proprietors and the bourgeoisie.[9]

The word 'bourgeoisie' is used then to refer to different categories. But even when it is applied more rigorously to one category alone, this category itself can vary strikingly from one country to another. In the well-known letter to Ernst, written in 1890, Engels stresses how markedly the 'bourgeoisie' varies in different countries, and warns Ernst

not to expect the Norwegian bourgeoisie to be anything like
the German model. The German bourgeoisie had tried its
hand at revolution and had failed. The Thirty Years War
and its aftermath must be blamed for the timidity, helplessness and lack of initiative displayed by the German bourgeoisie. The English or French petty bourgeois is not at all
like his German counterpart, who amounts to a caricature.
The same goes for the Norwegian bourgeois, who has a
very different history behind him. The Norwegian peasant
never experienced serfdom, and when he joins the ranks of
the petty bourgeoisie he confers upon his new status a
character quite different from that found in Germany.

Aware of the difficulties bound up with the concepts of
'middle class' and 'bourgeoisie', writers in capitalist countries
have often tried to analyse these concepts into more homogeneous groupings. Thus, bipartite and tripartite divisions
of the middle class have been variously proposed. The most
usual bipartite division distinguishes an upper and lower
middle class (*haute et petite bourgeoisie*) – categories based on
property criteria which are not rigorously specified.

The tripartite division runs along similar lines. In his paper
entitled 'Ideology and Class Consciousness in the Middle
Class', Gerard Degré uses what he calls 'class attitudes' to
distinguish the following groupings within the middle class
(whose existence as a separate entity he accepts as a datum):
those who feel themselves linked to the proletariat (including
the so-called 'white collar workers'), the proletariat intelligentsia; secondly, those who are trying to make their way
into the upper classes by appropriating upper-class
consciousness and ideology; and, finally, those who
represent the middle class in its undiluted form. Degré does
not specify the economic criteria which he uses to identify
the 'middle class': but he describes it as non-homogeneous
as regards its affiliations, for part of it adheres to what is
below it and part to what is above it. The middle class
proper will be distinguished by its property status and by its
class consciousness.[10]

Other authors use a variety of criteria to make a tripartite
division along rather different lines. (a) The petty bourgeoisie
is characterised (reference here is mainly to France before the

First World War) by a primary education and a modest standard of possessions sufficient to give a man who works hard, some degree of stability during his working life and a measure of security against the future; in the best case, a petty bourgeois family may employ a general servant – usually a daily help. This category includes shopkeepers, artisans, petty officials and small farmers.

(b) The bourgeois middle class comprises, according to this classification, people who have had secondary education at least, and who enjoy a moderate standard of possessions, which does not, however, exempt them from having to earn their living in one of the professions. They can afford one or two servants but do not possess their own means of transport. In addition, this group includes those who own nothing but who are linked to the main core of the group by reason of kinship or by social and cultural tastes.

(c) Finally, the highest stratum includes those people who have university degrees or, at least, a secondary education. They have sufficiently ample means to permit a life-style of some luxury, they have a staff of servants and their own carriage or car.[11]

As we see, the criteria used here are very diverse: financial circumstances, number of servants, possession of one's own means of transport (serving as an index of financial standing), education, and, finally, the feeling of belonging to a certain grouping. This last factor affects poor relations, retired people, and so on. Such palpable indices of membership of a certain category as number of servants or ownership of a car, have the advantage of being simple and readily identifiable. At the same time, however, they are valid for a given country only, and, as social, political and economic conditions change, they have to be revised every few years.

If classifications such as these and the criteria they are based on are viewed unfavourably in the literature of Western Europe and the United States, this is for reasons bound up with the concept of class. The authors of the 1949 work on the English middle class quoted above adopt the standpoint that in deciding to which class (as they understand the word) an individual belongs, we have to consider his origins, his calling, the way he talks, how he spends his money, his recreations, the way he dresses, his education, his morals, his personal degree of culture – always bearing in mind that belonging to a class is not an individual but a family matter. In these circumstances, it is not easy to use the concept of 'class'.

The difficulty is bound up with non-Marxist ideas of social class. Using Marxist analysis, particularly the Marxist concept of class, we get a different social structure in which the middle class as hitherto understood disappears, and the petty bourgeoisie emerges as an intermediate class between the bourgeoisie proper and the proletariat. This way of construing social structure is based on two basic factors, in comparison with which all other factors are of secondary or derivative nature: these factors are the possession or non-possession of the means of production, and the employment or non-employment of wage-earners. When these criteria are applied, the petty bourgeoisie is revealed as that class of persons who do indeed own certain means of production but who, instead of employing wage-earners, work for themselves on their own premises.

Whatever criteria are used to bracket off the petty bourgeoisie as a separate class, the variety of callings and occupations it pursues forms a very heterogeneous collection.[12] Speaking of the petty bourgeoisie, both Marxist and non-Marxist analysts have usually had shopkeepers and artisans in mind. It is these above all who are threatened by the growth of large-scale capitalism. Working on their own, they are not well suited to team-work or corporate effort; in their dislike of high taxation, they have anarchic tendencies.

The situation of the wide stratum of petty officials is quite different. As wage-earners, they can be seen as a section of the proletariat. To speak of them as 'the proletariat in white collars' is not inappropriate, although as a group in the capitalist countries, they feel as a rule no solidarity at all with the proletariat. The French official calls his pay '*traitements*', the English official calls it 'salary'; but in each case the class distance dividing those paid monthly from manual labourers who are paid by the week is maintained. In France, weekly pay is called '*salaires*', in England 'wages'.

As Meusel points out, however,[13] in the capitalist countries the group of clerical workers requires further differentiation. The situation of the civil servant – the functionary in a ministry, for example, or in municipal public service – is one thing, the situation of the clerical worker in a private enterprise is quite another. The civil servant's position has always been relatively stable and assured, and he was insured against old age at a time when the clerical worker in a private enterprise was not. The civil servant felt loyalty towards the state, a loyalty which he clung to as something above and beyond the class struggle. Not so in the case of the clerical workers in private enterprises. Where the civil servant lost out on armaments and wars, clerical workers and officials in private industry, which thrived on both, seized the opportunity to feather their own nests. Civil servants had an interest in high taxation; people in private enterprises, like merchants, liked taxation to be as low as possible.

The teaching profession forms a third grouping of the petty bourgeoisie. This is also a group of wage-earners, the great majority of whom are, in so far as their relationship to the means of production is concerned, in the same situation as the proletariat. It was long ago pointed out that the university professor in his college is really working in a large factory where student raw material is processed into graduates equipped with first and second degrees, in much the same way as a baker turns dough into rolls and loaves of a prescribed shape. When Goblot first made this comparison in 1925, people took it as some sort of joke. But today, when university personnel talk about 'productive' staff conferences, student selection, etc. – when terminology derived from the factory or the farm is transferred to the academic sphere – no one finds it in the least surprising. Those who object to the inclusion of wide sectors of the teaching profession in the proletariat, preferring to classify them with the petty bourgeoisie, are either defining 'production' in such a way as to exclude education from it, or are guided by non-economic criteria which they do not bother to specify.

Apart from the shopkeeper, the artisan, the petty functionary and the teacher, the rank-and-file soldier, i.e. the lowest rank in the military hierarchy, has to be mentioned as the representative of another large grouping which it is best to include within the petty bourgeoisie. In the capitalist countries the military establishment has its own peculiar physiognomy. On the basis of its allegedly non-party character, servicemen are held to be 'outside politics' and were not even allowed to vote in general elections. If the shopkeepers formed a pacifist element, the military were not averse to war, which confers exceptional national importance upon the soldier, and offers possibilities of rapid promotion.

Clergy with modest stipends formed yet another grouping within the petty bourgeoisie. Their situation was not unlike that of teachers and they were treated in much the same way. As dispensers of religious comfort they too could be viewed as people performing a service, and they formed quite a large group within the ranks of the petty bourgeoisie.

In general, then, all these groups, heterogeneous as they are, are held to be petty bourgeois in character. To them, if we are to adhere to principles so far adopted only by Marxism, we must add the figure of the peasant cultivating his plot with his own hands, helped only by his own family.

Finally, we come to the professions – doctors, lawyers, journalists, artists, etc. And here we run up against the difficulties connected with the concept of the 'intelligentsia' or the so-called 'working intelligentsia', which includes certain other categories mentioned above. The difficulty of squaring these concepts up with the concept of the petty bourgeoisie is notorious. As Lenin wrote:

> No one will venture to deny that the intelligentsia, as a special stratum of modern capitalist society, is characterised, by and large, precisely by individualism and incapacity for discipline and organisation (cf. for example, Kautsky's well-known articles on the intelligentsia). This incidentally is a feature which unfavourably distinguishes this social stratum from the proletariat; it is one of the reasons for the flabbiness and instability of the intellectual, which the proletariat so often feels; and this trait of the intelligentsia is intimately bound up with its customary mode of life, its mode of earning a livelihood, which in a great many respects

approximates to the petty-bourgeois mode of existence. (Lenin, *One Step Forwards, Two Steps Back*, in *Selected Works in Three Volumes*, Moscow, 1967, vol. 1, p. 314)

According to Lenin, then, their 'mode of life' is enough to ensure that the intelligentsia is brought, willy-nilly, into close contact with the petty bourgeoisie. But over and over again the intelligentsia has shown that it is ready to put itself at the service of the ruling class and liaise with it in its own interests. Hence, if solidarity of interest is to be our main criterion in the allocation of people to different classes, the intelligentsia should be linked with the bourgeoisie. But clearly we have to bear in mind that the intelligentsia has never formed a homogeneous unity, and that it has been known to provide revolutionary movements with their leaders. So any description claiming to treat the intelligentsia as a homogeneous unity must be viewed with the utmost caution.

Fortunately, our immediate task does not require us to tackle all of these problems. It will be enough if we can distinguish between those who serve as models for the descriptions of the petty bourgeoisie with which we shall be concerned, and those to whom they do not apply.

3 A note on the growth of this study

It was during the German occupation of Poland that I began to study the problem of bourgeois morality; and my intention was to demonstrate the class character of morality to those who still believed it to be homogeneous and above class. As my starting point I took Benjamin Franklin, and the first edition of the present work opened with my discussion of this writer. In the course of further study, however, it became clear that this particular choice was prompted by a subconscious conviction that I already knew what bourgeois morality was. Faced with a wide range of moralists of bourgeois provenance, why had I chosen Franklin to illustrate bourgeois morality? It could only be because in my mind's eye he already figured as the embodiment of it. Which in turn suggested that, if Franklin could figure as its paradigm, a preconceived notion of bourgeois morality was already present in my mind. And no doubt all those who had accepted Franklinism as a model of philistinism had followed the same mental path.

So how had I acquired my preconceived idea of bourgeois morality? Today I do not doubt that what played a large part here was the criticism levelled at the unhappy bourgeois from many quarters in several countries in the second half of the nineteenth century and the first quarter of the twentieth. The image of bourgeois morality as a certain genetic whole, an image which in the heat of battle often took on the lineaments of caricature, took shape at a time when the bourgeoisie was already on the defensive.

Given this historical background, there seemed to be no good reason why the new edition of the text should not take it into account. To this end, the order of the chapters has been altered, and a new section is devoted to the attack on the bourgeoisie. Indeed, this theme deserved broader treatment, since it reflects a social factor of no little consequence in the development of morality. The attack on bourgeois morality was launched from three quarters simultaneously: first by the Left as a whole in the name of the new, superior morality of the proletariat; secondly, by the aristocracy in defence of privileges allegedly theirs by virtue of their status and position; and thirdly by the artistic world, the *vie de bohème*. Clearly, these three groups are not of equal status. The first two acted from specific class positions; the third represented no one social class. To this point we shall return in due course. For the present, the facts can be allowed to speak for themselves. In what follows, we shall take each of the three criticisms in turn, and use them to fill in our picture of bourgeois morality. Once this is done, we shall be in a better position to ask ourselves whether it is fitting to link this picture with the middle class – and, if so, with exactly *which* middle class.

A few general misunderstandings remain to be cleared up. Whenever the question of criticism of bourgeois morality comes up, people keep on reminding me about Balzac, and seem surprised to find that his strictures are missing from my account. We are all familiar with Balzac's accounts of bourgeois greed and miserliness, of struggle for advancement by fair means or foul. However, our theme in what follows will be an ideological critique rather than a critique of practice. I am not concerned with exposing bourgeois egoism or bourgeois brutality. 'Criticism of bourgeois morality' is not equivalent to damning the bourgeois for all his faults, which, be it noted, are not always his alone. If one bourgeois bullies his children as in Gorky's *Smug Citizens*, if another makes life in the office hell for his subordinates, our distaste is aroused: but this distaste is not an expression of the sort of criticism I have in mind. What I am concerned with is a critique of slogans, and of the human postures which are sanctioned, sanctified, by these slogans. Zapolska's criticism of the sex life of the scions of bourgeois families who only marry when they have gained the proper 'position' in life, having meanwhile seduced the servant-girls, is a critique of bourgeois morality in my sense of the word; for such practices were sanctioned by, accepted by, a bourgeois society which was scandalised at the very idea of two young people marrying if the husband could offer his wife no more than he could get with his bare hands. This sort of attitude to sex and marriage falls within our terms of reference, just as slogans about thrift and industriousness do.

In connection with the production of Stefan Żeromski's *History of a Sin* the Polish press had much to say on the critique of bourgeois morality contained in this work. Let us recapitulate: the fact that a rich old woman should try to get the man she has fallen in love with, at whatever cost – and that, when she fails, she should seek to prevent his marriage with the woman to whom he is emotionally drawn – is not specific either to bourgeois morality of a given time or place, or to bourgeois morality as a genetic whole. And, even if it were specific in this sense, it would belong not to the category of recommended actions, but to the category of actions which take place but are *not* approved. Zofia Parmen's actions would find no approbation in her milieu: which would, on the other hand, find it perfectly natural that a man should be unwilling to marry a woman with no dowry.

I am well aware that there is a close connection between

what people say and what they actually do – in other words, between the slogan and the practice – and that the habitual performance of certain actions in defiance of slogans is not without effect on these slogans. The slogans may continue to be reiterated in a hypocritical attempt to cover up what is actually going on: but gradually the facts transform the slogans and force them to take notice of reality. Thus, eighteenth-century condemnation of the merchant who tried to undercut his competitors was to disappear from the lexicon of commercial moralities under the influence of the triumphant demand of the clientele for free competition. So, bearing in mind these mutually interacting influences, we can try to differentiate between ideology and practice, between slogan and performance. As I said, the bourgeois morality with which we are here concerned is primarily a corpus of directives and of those actions alone which are sanctioned by these directives. It is in a critique of these directives that the clash between different outlooks on life makes itself most obvious.

This brings us to another stipulation that must be made at the outset. In our portrayal of bourgeois morality as a certain type of morality, we shall from time to time find ourselves associating with this type not only traits susceptible of moral evaluation but also certain traits which rate as morally neutral ground, in so far as these are bound up with the former and help to colour the picture as a whole. It was in an effort to identify such a comprehensive whole that several researchers in this field were led to speak of a petty bourgeois *ethos*, an ethos connected with different religions. What they described was wider than morality: it was a way of life in which morality was indeed a weighty component, but one set in a wider background. This concept of ethos will prove useful to us too; it is not helpful to subtract morality from this wider background. Accordingly, I take over the concept of ethos without further explanation, in the belief that this will in no way jeopardise understanding between author and reader.

Chapter 2

Bourgeois morality on the defensive

J'appelle 'bourgeois' tout ce qui pense bassement.
(Flaubert)

1 Left-wing criticism of bourgeois morality

The attack on the bourgeoisie which we shall now consider
will help to fill out our picture of bourgeois morality as a
generic whole. What is here pilloried is not the morality of
the grande bourgeoisie; in one or another of its three forms,
this attack was launched primarily against the petty bourgeoisie. As Engels said in the passage I quoted earlier, the
lineaments of the petty bourgeois vary from one country to
another. However, most of the characteristics we are about
to list will not be limited to any one country at a given
moment of time. This widening of our field of inquiry is
justified by the invariant character of certain petty bourgeois
traits. These invariant traits derive from the essential locus
of the petty bourgeoisie within the social structure – a locus
common to petty bourgeois wherever they exist, since this,
after all, is what makes them what they are. Where relevant,
I shall also classify as 'petty bourgeois' those who go along
with, who act in solidarity with the petty bourgeoisie as thus
defined. 'Just as little must one imagine', wrote Marx when
discussing the representatives of the petty bourgeoisie, 'that
the democratic representatives are indeed all shopkeepers or
enthusiastic champions of shopkeepers. According to their
education and their individual position, they may be as far
apart as heaven from earth. What makes them representative
of the petty bourgeoisie is the fact that in their minds they

17

do not get beyond the limits which the latter do not get beyond in life, that they are consequently driven, theoretically, to the problems and solutions to which material interest and social position drive the latter practically. This is, in general, the relationship between the political and literary representatives of a class and the class they represent.'[1]

In many countries this class is numerous and influential. Marx and Engels emphasised the numbers of the *Kleinbürgerei* in Germany. Nor did Lenin underestimate its role in Russia; more than once, when drawing up his plan of action, he urged his comrades-in-arms to bear its representatives constantly in mind, to keep an eye on them and seek to awaken their political awareness, as an ally which must be taken into account.[2] And the way to do this was to convince the petty bourgeoisie that their only chance of standing up to the bourgeoisie proper lay in their gaining the support of the proletariat.

As the Marxist classics make plain, the key factor in the formation of the petty bourgeois mentality and way of life lies in its obliquity, its intermediate position. 'Suspended' between the bourgeoisie proper and the proletariat, the petty bourgeoisie is in a state of unstable equilibrium.

Plainly, it was not only conditions in Russia that Lenin had in mind when he wrote in *Lessons of the Revolution*: 'everybody of course has seen the small owner bend every effort and strain every nerve to "get on in the world", to become a real master, to rise to the position of a "strong" employer, to the position of a bourgeois'. A member of this class has the choice 'either to raise himself to the capitalist level (which is possible in the best case for one small owner in a hundred), or drop to the level of a ruined small-holder/owner, to semi-proletariat status and finally to forming part of the proletariat'.[3] The risk of becoming a *déclassé* is always real: the craftsman's skills are devalued as new methods of production come into use, small-scale capital is helpless against large-scale, wars and crises strike above all at the petty bourgeois.[4] They are supported, on the other hand by the existence of the bureaucratic and military apparatus which provides the highest strata of peasants, small artisans, merchants, etc., with relatively comfortable and secure jobs carrying some prestige which places those holding them over the common run of the people.[5]

(a) Contradictions in the petty bourgeois psyche; its instability

Connected with the indeterminate, vacillating status of the petty bourgeoisie is a series of traits which we shall now consider in turn. Falling between two stools, as it were, and trying to place itself first on one and then on the other, the petty bourgeoisie could hardly fail to present a sorry picture of inconsistency and contradiction. 'In an advanced society, the petty bourgeois necessarily becomes from his very position a socialist on the one side and an economist on the other: that is to say, he is dazed by the magnificence of the big bourgeoisie and has sympathy for the sufferings of the people.'[6] And, adducing Proudhon's petty bourgeois origins as the reason for his fondness for 'dialectics', Marx writes: 'The petty bourgeois is composed of . . . "on the one hand" and "on the other hand". This is so in his economic interests and therefore in his politics, in his scientific, religious and artistic views. It is so in his morals, in everything. He is a living contradiction.'[7] And again we read in Marx's Letter to Annenkov: 'A petty bourgeois of this type glorifies contradiction because contradiction is the quintessence of his being. He is himself nothing but social contradiction in action.'

Instability is an unavoidable concomitant of contradiction. As a class, wrote Engels in *Revolution and Counter-Revolution in Germany*, the petty bourgeoisie is highly unstable in its views: 'Humble and crouchingly submissive under a powerful feudal or monarchical government, it turns to the side of liberalism when the middle class is in the ascendant: it becomes seized with violent democratic fits as soon as the middle class has secured its own supremacy, but falls back into the abject despondency of fear as soon as the class below itself, the proletarians, attempts an independent movement.'[8] Proudhon (whom Marx described as 'petit bourgeois tout pur') 'wants to soar as the man of science above the bourgeois and the proletarians; he is merely the petty bourgeois, continually tossed back and forth between capital and labour, political economy and communism'.[9]

(b) The fundamentally reactionary nature of the petty bourgeoisie

Prone as it is to alternating transports of joy and bouts of blackest despair, the petty bourgeoisie is basically closest to the bourgeoisie proper. 'The petty bourgeoisie are in real life dependent upon the bourgeoisie, for they live like masters and not like proletarians (from the point of view of their place in social production) and follow the bourgeoisie in their outlook.'[10] When they oppose the bourgeoisie which threatens their existence, when they demand that the stranglehold of large-scale capital be curbed – even then they achieve no more than the semblance of a revolutionary stance. 'The lower middle class, the small manufacturer, the shopkeeper, the artisan, the peasant, all these fight against the bourgeoisie to save from extinction their existence as fractions of the middle class. They are therefore not revolutionary but conservative. Nay more, they are reactionary, for they try to roll back the wheel of history. If by chance they are revolutionary they are so only in view of their impending transfer into the proletariat.'[11]

(c) Alleged classlessness

Another trait characteristic of petty bourgeois mentality, as portrayed in the Marxist classics, is the fond illusion that it belongs to no class. Writing in *The Eighteenth Brumaire of Louis Bonaparte* on French democracy as representative of the interests of the petty bourgeoisie, Marx says: 'but the democrat, because he represents the petty bourgeois, that is, a transition class, in which the interests of two classes are simultaneously mutually blunted, imagines himself elevated above class antagonism generally. The democrats concede that a privileged class confronts them but they, along with all the rest of the nation, form the people. What they represent is the *people's rights*: what interests them is the *people's interests*.'[12] And elsewhere: the French petty bourgeois 'inwardly flatters himself that he is impartial, and has found the right equilibrium which claims to be different from mediocrity (*le juste milieu*)'.[13]

(d) Individualism; tendency towards anarchism

Working for oneself in one's own workship is socially divisive rather than unifying. The Marxist classics are correspondingly rich in examples of the individualism of small owners, their sad lack of discipline and team spirit, their atomisation, their jealous defence of their privacy. The nature of their work and the form their property takes go to explain why 'revolution' in the mouths of petty bourgeois smells of anarchism, an anarchism further fuelled by the petty bourgeois dislike of paying taxes. For these reasons, the petty bourgeois is incapable of uniting with his fellows and acting together in a coordinated fashion.[14] And this is why Lenin saw in the lip service paid by the petty bourgeoisie to revolution one of Communism's main enemies.

(e) Peace at any price; the quest for safety

Probably because it is the petty bourgeois who stands to lose most heavily in crises of whatever sort, the Marxist classics tend to portray him as timid, apprehensive and avid for peace at any price. It is the petty bourgeois who is most likely to take one step forwards and two steps back.

In general, the petty bourgeois prefers not to think about class warfare. Where, however, class warfare is unmistakably present for all to see, he does his best to hush it up: 'after all, we all want the same thing; all the differences rest on mere misunderstandings' – the 'favourite phrase' which Engels puts in the mouth of the democratic petty bourgeois.[15] For the petty bourgeois, class warfare is something undesirable and 'vulgar'. He is guided by 'a genuine love for humanity' and empty phrases about 'justice'. The ideal of the petty bourgeoisie – at least of the petty bourgeoisie contemporary with Marx – is, as Marx put it in words which have become proverbial, 'mediocrity, moral sensitivity and business as usual'.

The petty bourgeois likes peaceful solutions. Where he

opts for socialism, he wants it without revolution. When it is a question of redressing social ills, he indulges in illusions which are often held in all honesty. He wishes to 'perfect' imperialism by 'reforming' it. 'Pure Philistine obscurantism' – thus Marx dismisses Proudhon's suggestion that the abolition of interest could provide a basis for social reconstruction.[16] Failing to recognise that 'the state is the organ of the rule of a certain class', the petty bourgeois would like to reconcile classes through the state.[17]

The desire for peace at any price ties up with a need for security. In *The Holy Family* Marx criticises Eugène Sue's sentimental 'petty-bourgeois social fantasy' *Les Mystères de Paris*, and ridicules the hero Rudolphe who tries to convert Chourineur the butcher to bourgeois ways – to become 'a quiet cautious man who behaves according to the rules of fear and worldly wisdom'.[18] And elsewhere Marx writes of 'safety' – a police concept – as the highest social concept of bourgeois society: 'the whole of bourgeois society lives by ensuring the personal safety, and the inviolability of the rights and of the property of each of its members'.

Describing the petty bourgeois spirit in his *Materials Towards a Theory of the Proletariat*, Georges Sorel said that the middle class was the ideal class in the eyes of an ineffectual government, since it was the most easily led. Its highest stratum which wants to 'jouer aux bourgeois' and whose main aim in life is to have a servant, is the darling of moralists (whom it never shocks), of philanthropists (of whom it asks nothing) and of economists (who esteem it highly). It is a factor making for peace. Infection of the worker by its spirit is the surest way of rendering him harmless.

(f) Thrift; doing without for the sake of having

In the 'Economic and Philosophical Manuscripts' of 1844 Marx wrote:

> Political economy, this science of wealth, is therefore at the same time the science of denial, of starvation, of saving, and it actually goes so far as to save man the need for fresh air or physical exercise. This science . . . is at

the same time the science of asceticism, and its true ideal
is the ascetic but rapacious skinflint and the ascetic but
productive slave. Its moral ideal is the worker who puts
a part of his wages into savings . . . it is therefore – for
all its worldly and debauched appearance – a truly moral
science, the most moral science of all. Self-denial
(*Selbstentsagung*), the denial of life and of all human needs,
is its principal doctrine. The less you eat, drink, buy
books, go to the theatre, go dancing, go drinking, think,
love, theorize, sing, paint, fence, etc., the more you
save and the greater will become that treasure which
neither moths nor maggots can consume – your capital.
The less you are, the less you give expression to your
life, the more you have, the greater is your alienated
life and the more you store up of your estranged life.
Everything which the political economist takes from
you in terms of life and humanity, he restores to you in
the form of money and wealth, and everything which
you are unable to do, your money can do for you . . .
and you must not only be parsimonious in gratifying
your immediate senses. You must also be chary of
participating in affairs of general interest, showing
sympathy and trust, etc.[19]

In the end, it comes down to this: 'in order to live, you have
to give up all the things that make life worth living (*propter
vitam vivendi perdere causas*)'.[20]

(g) The cult of money; thinking in terms of money

The political economy of the capitalist countries takes the
view that all human passion and all human activity necessarily centre on the desire for possessions: 'the morality of
political economy is gain (*der Erwerb*), labour and thrift,
sobriety'.[21] The worth of a man is measured in money. 'What
I am is by no means determined by my individuality . . .
that which I can pay for, i.e. which money can buy, that
am I, the possessor of the money. I am a wicked, dishonest,
unscrupulous and stupid individual, but money is respected,
and so also is its owner. I am ugly but I can buy the most

beautiful woman. Which means to say that I am not ugly, for the effect of ugliness, its repelling power, is destroyed by money.'[22] This way of evaluating people by the extent of their wealth recalls the well-known French proverb: 'Un idiot pauvre c'est un idiot; un idiot riche, c'est un riche.'

(h) Egoism and selfishness

'Petty-bourgeois selfishness' is a phrase that occurs fairly often in Lenin's works. According to Lenin, the small owner's viewpoint can be summed up as: 'As long as I get as much out of it as possible, the rest doesn't concern me.'[23] When the petty bourgeoisie does battle with large-scale capital, it is for reasons consistent with its own interests – as Marx points out in *The Class Struggles in France*. It demands, for example, graduated taxes, limitations on inheritance; and it expects the state to be responsible for carrying out major capital investment works. These demands are, of course, not specific to the petty bourgeoisie, any more than are those mentioned above. As the *Communist Manifesto* says, all that is left to mankind in bourgeois society is naked self-interest, and society is guided by self-interest alone. The desire for 'safety' in a bourgeois society is the desire to safeguard one's own selfish interests.

(i) Mediocritas

We return now to those traits which are specific to the petty bourgeois. One such trait is mediocrity, a particular source of irritation to the artistic world when it is fighting the petty bourgeoisie under the banner of romanticism. The petty bourgeois likes everything to be 'middling'. Thus, in Gorky's *Smug Citizens* Tieterev says to Bezsemionov: 'I like you too . . . you've got just the right amount of brains and the right amount of stupidity. You're middling good and middling bad, middling honest and middling crooked, middling cowardly and middling brave. In fact, you're a model petty bourgeois. You're just about as trivial as you could be . . . and triviality, now, that's what defeats heroes, survives and triumphs.'

(j) Respect for social hierarchy

Describing Proudhon (whom he regards as the typical bour-geois), Marx jeers at his servility to those placed above him in the bureaucratic hierarchy[24] (the reference is to Councillor Dunoyer).

In his description of the French petty bourgeoisie, Sorel seizes upon the same trait. As he sees it, the petty bourgeois can be very easily led by the nose if he thinks he has a chance of being admitted to polite society. The true petty bourgeois is instantly won over by an invitation to call upon his betters. Sorel has a witty description of such a 'grooming' manoeuvre on the part of President Millerand. Asked to a reception given by Millerand, the petty bourgeois goes overboard completely at such an honour and does not fail to tell the janitor all about it – after all, the janitor's opinion plays a crucial role in his life.[25] (See Plate 10.)

(k) Sentimentalism

Again we find the Marxist classics agreed on attributing to the petty bourgeois a maudlin sentimentality. The sentimental Eugène Sue, who is pilloried in *The Holy Family*, and the sentimental Proudhon, appear as the archetypal French petty bourgeois. In Germany, the petty bourgeoisie is offered that brand of socialism which the *Manifesto* ironically dubs 'true'. The pretentious garb in which its 'eternal truths' were presented was put together from 'speculative cobwebs, embroidered with flowers of rhetoric, steeped in the dew of sickly sentiment'. Even the idealist Hegel made fun of Schiller's unattainable ideals.[26]

(l) Philistinism

'That class alone', wrote Lenin, in a greeting to Hungarian workers, can get something done 'whose finest members are full of hatred and contempt for everything petty-bourgeois and philistine, for the qualities which flourish so profusely among the petty bourgeoisie, the minor employees and the "intellectuals".'[27]

As a matter of fact, the concept of the 'Philistine' and related ideas play a rather large part in criticism of the petty bourgeois ethos. Lenin makes wide use of them, and the anonymous translator who translated the *Selected Works* of Lenin into Polish used the words *filisterstwo* and *filisterski* both for the equivalent Russian words and for the words *obyvatel'shchina* and *obyvatel'skij* which also appear in Lenin's text. Thus, the *obyvatel'skaya* point of view comes out in Polish as the *filisterskie* point of view. As a rule, of course, the word *filister* suggests to the Polish reader someone who is smugly shut up in his own little world, oblivious of communal life and of any reason why he should take part in it. The *filister* sees himself as apolitical, and instinctively recoils from anything that seems to threaten his internal comfort: 'Leave me alone and let me live my life my own way' – thus Gorky sums up the petty bourgeois.[28]

In *One Step Forwards, Two Steps Back* Lenin contrasts the Philistine point of view with the party ethic.[29] The party ethic is concerned with the good of a cause, with ensuring its successful outcome; the Philistine is concerned with seeing that no one is aggrieved or offended. For Lenin here, Philistinism is the transfer to the political arena of customs taken over from social life and the life of entertainment – one more variant of a somewhat elusive concept whose content is sometimes diluted to the point where very little recrimination is left in it.

The philistinism for which the petty bourgeois is castigated is usually a characteristic of those who are financially secure, satisfied, who guard their peace and quiet jealously while enjoying the good things of this world. Clearly, the description fits the well-to-do petty bourgeoisie and those immediately above them, rather than those who have to live in austerity and do without to make ends meet. The Polish word *koltun* means something else. Usually it refers to the lower strata of the petty bourgeoisie, that is, to people whose mental horizons have not been widened by education. Like the Philistine, the *koltun* is enclosed in the world of his own interests and impervious to public affairs; but he is stupid into the bargain. His thinking runs along habitual lines: it does not change any more than do the habits of mosquitoes, frogs or cockroaches.[30] It reacts to novelty in scandalised horror and amazement; which, of course, plays into the hands of those who like to *épater les bourgeois*. The Philistine may well grasp the desirability, the aptness of certain social reforms, even though he may instinctively oppose them. The *kołtun*, cannot even understand them. His conservatism is a product of stupidity rather than of complacency; and he looks after his own interests out of egocentrism rather than out of egoism. Anyway, we have to agree with Mayakovsky:

> Creeps –
> they come in all sizes
> all sizes
> and shades.
> A reward
> for him
> who sorts them all out.[31]

In his work on Feuerbach, Engels discerns 'the Philistine's pigtail' ('*ein Stück Philisterzopfes*') even in such major figures as Goethe and Hegel. The fact that the word 'Philistine' can be used here, whereas use of the word *kołtun* is simply inconceivable, underlines the reality of our distinction between two concepts which are often used indiscriminately.[32]

As a whole, the characteristics we have been describing exhibit great tenacity and tend to crop up even in conditions which might at first sight seem less than favourable.

Let us quote Mayakovsky on 'trash':

On Trash

Glory, glory, glory to the heroes!!!

Incidentally,
for them
enough tribute's been stashed.
Now
let's thrash out
about trash.

In revolutionary laps the storm is hardly heard.

It's surfaced with a Soviet mish-mash of slime.
And emerging
from behind the back of the USSR
purred
the Philistines.

(Don't take me literally,
It's not against the petty-bourgeoisie I'm rising.
It's the Philistines,
whatever their class or estate,
I'm eulogising.)

From all the boundlessness of Russia they gathered,
from the very first day of our Soviet Constitution,
they poured in,
quick-changing their feathers,
and ensconced themselves in every institution.

Callousing their behinds from five-year sittings,
shiny-hard as washbasin toilets,
they live till now –
quiet as water flitting.
In cosy parlours and comfy bedrooms coiling.

And in the evening
mean and nasty,
they watch the wife, –
piano-learning's the fashion –
and say to her,
by the samovar basking:
'Comrade Natasha!
Got an anniversary rise –
24 thousand.
The Official Tariff.
Hey,
I'll order a pair of breeches,
Pacific-ocean wide,
out of them
I'll rear
like a coral reef!'
Then Natasha:
'And for me a dress with emblems displayed.

Without hammers and sickles one can't appear at all!
For how else
today
could I figure
at the RevMilSoviet Ball?'
On the wall Marx,
in a red, red frame.
On *Izvestia* a cat preens, staring.
And hanging from the ceiling
chirrups inane
a moulting canary.

Marx from the wall looked on appalled . . .
Then suddenly
opened his mouth
and bawled:
'The Revolution by Philistine meshes entangled.
A Philistine-existence's more terrible than Wrangel.
Hurry!
Wring that damned canary's neck –
So that Communism
by canaries won't be wrecked!'[33]

We may recall Katayev's play *Squaring the Circle*. Two
young married couples are living in one room which is
divided into two halves: each couple goes its own way, with
the wife in each case furnishing her half of the room in the
style she wants. In one half reigns bleakest austerity, along
with a total dedication to non-personal matters. In the other
half, there are curtains on the window, pictures on the walls
– and there is a canary. A canary, artificial flowers or palms,
and loose covers on the furniture are essential ingredients in
our stereotyped image of petty bourgeois interior decoration.

These are some of the main traits which the political left
and the Marxist classics are agreed on ascribing to the petty
bourgeoisie. To this list, a few writers add smugness and a
tendency towards nationalist megalomania. As I have already
pointed out, these traits struck the critics we have quoted as
being of more than purely local cogency. When Lenin
warned the Hungarian workers to beware of the petty bourgeoisie, he was guided by the premise that Hungarian

workers were being threatened from a quarter which also threatened workers in Russia. The same traits crop up again and again in criticism of the petty bourgeoisie in various countries. They are not simply local phenomena since, as I said, they are closely bound up with the locus of the petty bourgeoisie in the social structure, a locus which in fact identifies the petty bourgeois as such. Not all of these traits have proved to be equally durable, however. Thus, the 'peace at any price' component was discarded by the German petty bourgeoisie during the Nazi period. It is none the less a fact that the classic research of the Lynds on the American petty bourgeoisie – forming part of our next chapter – confirms our list of petty bourgeois qualities.

In Chapter 1, I mentioned the heterogeneity of the petty bourgeoisie. This heterogeneity helps to explain why not every characteristic of the petty bourgeois will fit every member of this composite whole. The instability attributed to the petty bourgeoisie is mainly bound up with his vacillation between two antagonistic classes and also with the fact that he fears both of them – capitalists and proletariat alike. This is unreservedly true of the petty entrepreneur or craftsman, but rather less so of the smallholder cultivating his ground with his own hands, the minor official or the lower echelons of career servicemen. The lack of corporate spirit evinced by the craftsman, the shopkeeper or the smallholder cultivating his own soil is readily understandable when one considers the sort of work they do and the fact that any profit they make is at the expense of their competitors. But the civil servant, the white-collar worker, comes under a completely different heading. His earnings do not depend on the success or failure of his colleagues. Civil servants work together in the sense that, as in a factory, the work done by one meshes with and is coordinated with the work done by others. This goes also for the work of the teaching staff in schools; and career servicemen are uniformly trained to take joint action. So, either the lack of team spirit is not common to the whole corpus of the petty bourgeoisie and some differentiation will have to be recognised; or, if indeed it is common to the whole grouping, then it must be conditioned by some additional factor or factors which we have to identify. The respect for the social hierarchy which is strongly marked among the petty bourgeoisie should then be a characteristic primarily of those of its constituent groups which are, in fact, structured in hierarchic fashion, e.g. career servicemen or civil servants. 'The trait that best exhibits the insipidness of this miserable lot', wrote Balzac, with reference to civil servants, 'is a sort of involuntary, mechanical, instinctive respect for that Great Bonze in every ministry, who is known to the staff from his illegible signature as "His Excellency the Minister".'[34]

We can check the adequacy of our definitions of the petty bourgeoisie by applying them to various models. We also have to ask ourselves whether or not the intelligentsia fits into the framework of the petty bourgeoisie. In countries where the intelligentsia is strongly influenced by the aristocratic style of life, it may not exhibit certain traits which are typical of the petty bourgeoisie in general. And even if these traits are exhibited, they may be due to a completely different set of causes. The individualism of the intellectual does not come from the same source as the individualism of the shopkeeper; and if the intellectual persists in the delusion that he is outside and above the class struggle, it is in his case a delusion which does not derive simply from the fact that in him the contradictory interests of the class above him and the class below him cancel each other out. It may also derive from his reading which gives him vicarious possession of the class attitudes of many times and places.

If anything has brought a certain homogeneity into the make-up of that motley patchwork, the petty bourgeoisie, it is woman. As Lenin saw her, she was still a domestic slave, 'in spite of all the laws emancipating woman' for she was crushed, strangled and degraded by the petty business of housekeeping; shackled to crockery and nappies, she wasted her labour on a barbarously unproductive, narrow, enervating, stultifying and stupefying drudgery.[35] Whether she was the wife of a shopkeeper or a craftsman, a minor official, a serviceman or a teacher, the housewife's lot was the same. Her share in shaping the petty bourgeois way of life deserves further study.

2   The aristocratic view of bourgeois morality

So far, we have examined left-wing criticism of bourgeois *mores*, most of it drawn from the Marxist classics. We now turn to criticism emanating from the Polish nobility.

The nobleman's view of bourgeois morality does not seem to have changed very much since the sixteenth century. In his book *Miasta i mieszczaństwo w dawnej Polsce* ('Towns and Town-dwellers in Old Poland'), published in Warsaw in 1949, J. Ptaśnik draws attention to the increasingly contemptuous attitude of the sixteenth-century Polish nobility towards trade and handicrafts.[36] As supporting evidence for his thesis, the author points to the fact that social advancement and elevation to the ranks of the gentry, both of which had been relatively easy for the bourgeois, became progressively more difficult.

The deterioration in relations between the nobility and the bourgeoisie in the sixteenth century is also recorded – with regret – by W. A. Maciejowski in his work *Polska aż do pierwszej połowy XVII wieku pod względem obyczajów i zwyczajów* ('Customs and Manners in Poland up to the First Half of the Seventeenth Century', Warsaw, 1842).

Outstanding among the writers who were at that time deeply preoccupied with Aristotle's *Politics* is Stanisław Orzechowski. In his book,[37] as in the works of other aristocratic writers of the period, we find a deep conviction that 'nobleness' inheres in the nobility and is inherited along with rank. The state is similar to a well-run household. It has to have a master, a mistress and servants. The master commands his children as a king, his servants as their lord, 'ruling his servant and his servant's thoughts as a vessel for the use of the lord; for the servant is not his own master, he is entirely his lord's man, having no free will of his own' (p. 14). It is up to everyone in the household to look after his post of duty, and 'what the servant is in the household, the commonalty is in the kingdom' (p. 17). The family consists solely of the master, the mistress, his wife and their children; in the same way, the polity consists solely of the king, the council and the knighthood (p. 20; in later pages, the priest is added to this list). Ploughmen, artisans and merchants are not members of the kingdom of Poland. They are its 'fortuitous parts' (*partes accidentales*). They are not free men. 'The merchant . . . could not well serve at one and the same time his own profit and the common weal, he has to limit himself to serving one of these; over and above this, the merchant is not concerned in his trading with living a good and virtuous life, it is enough for him if he stays alive. Nor can the craftsman and the merchant lead good and virtuous lives . . . for neither craft nor commerce can exist without deception; the merchant lauds what he sells, ignoring what he knows to be the truth. In the same way, the mean drudgery by which the artisan earns his living does not befit a worthy man. Take into your hands anything he makes, you will find nothing that could occupy any man in worthy fashion' (p. 20). And elsewhere: 'truth and commerce cannot live together, for God says: *non potestis Deo servire et mamonae*; to wit, it is impossible for you to serve God, that is to serve the truth, and be a merchant . . . Therefore, Polish law forbids the nobility to engage in commerce in towns on pain of loss of status, for the nobleman sets all on truth, which cannot coexist with trade' (p. 23).

Truth and faith 'abhor whatever monies accrue from trade'. Monetary gain is evil. The feel of money awakens in us 'an antipathy to concupiscence for money'. This is incompatible with nobility of spirit, on which are based 'wisdom, justice, courage, integrity' (p. 24). Poland depends on those who are concerned solely with virtue. 'But to those who chase after a groat, who measure an ell but give a quarter, who make things, who take payment, or who are bound by the plough to another' – to these Poland has allotted a subservient role, 'for to all such, gain tastes better than virtue' (p. 28). Wherever there is greed for gain, there is deceit. Associating with mean things, they have mean thoughts. Poland wants to have pure noble blood and 'abhors the burgher'. It spurns adulteration with 'business' blood. 'In Poland, we call those well-born, neither of whose parents was ever in thrall to a craft or a trade' but directed such activities and sat in judgment over them.

In the main, Orzechowski follows Aristotle's partition, but in some respects he modifies it and illustrates it with his own examples. He divides craftsmen into four categories, progressively decreasing in respectability. The first of these comprises carpenters, tailors, masons and weavers. To the second category belong those who 'defile' their bodies, such as shoemakers, furriers, blacksmiths and tanners. The third comprises the menial occupations in which 'the body itself does all', and includes porters, potters, diggers, sawyers. 'The fourth category is of those artisans who in order to do their work have no need of virtue, such as dog-catchers, executioners, prosecutors and informers who are very necessary for and very similar to the prosecutor; for just as the whore lives by her dirty carcass so does the informer by his snout, for he sells his tongue to everybody' (p. 24). As we see, Orzechowski's three categories are differentiated in considerable detail: the dirtier (literally) it is, the less one has to think while doing the work, the lower it is in Orzechowski's estimation and the dirtier it is in a figurative sense.

Like handicrafts, trade too comes in for varied treatment. Here again, Orzechowski distinguishes four categories. The first comprises those who are concerned with foodstuffs 'consisting of those things which are native to us here in Poland, (the produce of) pasture and arable land, water, game . . . It (i.e. the first category) is honoured among merchants, and (as a vocation) it is held to be pious and worthy of decent men' (p. 25). To the second category belong those who buy and transport surplus goods, and bring in things which are in short supply and which people need. 'Such merchants are like bees which come from various directions and fill their hives with the honey which is useful to us.' The third group comprises those who provide goods which are not necessary and which serve only for luxury and debauchery. They deserve the gallows. In his last category Orzechowski puts those who use money to make money, providing nothing in exchange in the shape of goods, after the manner of the Jews. Speculation and usury come in for Orzechowski's total condemnation; he uses arguments similar to those used by Aristotle in the *Politics*. According to Aristotle (*Politics*, book I) money was created to facilitate the exchange of goods, and not for the purpose of generating more money, which is contrary to nature. Following Aristotle Orzechowski recommends heavier penalties for the usurer than for the thief.

I have quoted rather extensively from Orzechowski so as to let the privileged classes put their typical views in their own blunt and classic Polish. We find a contemporary of Orzechowski's, Łukasz Górnicki, agreeing very explicitly with the participant in the dialogue in his *Dworzanin* ('Courtier'), who asserts that there have indeed been nobles who led shameful lives, and that 'often in people of low estate we behold great and superior inborn gifts'.[38] Nevertheless, he clings to a belief in the inherited nature of nobility: 'for a raven has never produced a swan, nor has a jackdaw ever mothered a thrush'. 'But in battle or in places where men may gain honour,' we read in *Dworzanin*, 'the nobleman will do better than the commoner and excel over him; for in all things nature has sown that secret seed which passes on the properties and powers which it had from its first ancestral seed to the seed which it engenders from itself and which will make its progeny the same as itself. The which we see not only in herds of horses and other animals, but also in trees . . .' In the same way, Mikołaj Sęp-Szarzyński gives the nobility a monopoly of nobleness of character, which is passed from father to son: for 'the brave eagle does not beget a dove, nor does the abject hare issue from the mighty lion'.[39] For Starowolski, as for his predecessors, the word 'trade' is properly accompanied by the adjective 'foul'; and 'trade', 'craft' is usually 'stinking'. As Starowolski sees it, it is not for the nobleman to go about the market-place among vendors and pedlars lest he be defiled by that 'lust for gain'. It was not for nothing that the Greeks placed their market-places outside the city.[40]

Thus did the nobleman continue to view the bourgeois. Even for Henryk Rzewuski, social man's prosperity depends not on the material forms of government – the mistake, in his opinion, made in the eighteenth century – but on the moral disposition of the members of society;[41] and for Rzewuski moral superiority is the exclusive privilege of the nobility. 'Even in the aberrations of the superior caste, something of dignity remains.' The lower orders never attain to this level of behaviour, although the times now are such that 'blackguardly plebeians behave as though bent on impudently mimicking men whose very faults they are unable to copy'.[42] Since noblemen alone are endowed with dignity and honour, they alone have the right to fight duels. In any case, 'the working man, the artisan, whose health is the sole asset he possesses for the support of himself and his family, guards it therefore and is careful not to expose it to danger for the sake of an opinion, however strongly held. In his case, a monetary settlement will always seem more satisfactory than the doubtful outcome of a duel.'[43] Inborn qualities are compounded by calling: 'among the people, all of whom are bent on speculation and trading, rickets makes the children look like cripples'.[44] Rzewuski's racism is reinforced by his doctrine of the inheritability of traits acquired in the pursuit of a calling; and this acts as an additional barrier against any attempt to cross class divisions. 'He who is scandalized', he writes, 'by the fact that the son of an illustrious general takes more readily to his (military) calling than does the son of an obscure parent, is gainsaying natural law, the law of necessary consequence.' This champion of the social hierarchy (whose apex, of course, he himself adorns), this opponent of equality in the eyes of the law, makes short work of democrats. In the case of inveterate democrats, he says that 'the arena of argument is not the proper place, the house of correction is the only answer they deserve'.[45] His antipathy to all who offend against the faith and tradition extends even to Socrates: 'And although here death became, as it were, the emblem of philosophy, I would not take it upon myself to assert that it was not well deserved.'[46]

The belief that healthy social relations depend exclusively on the moral standards of the citizens – the standards in question being, of course, the sole privilege of the class to which Rzewuski belongs – turns up again and again in various formulations. 'People who fail to observe propriety in their speech, their dress and their manners are, for the most part, base and stupid.' This calls to mind Lenin's very differently angled comment in *A Great Beginning*: 'a person of ordinary common sense and experience when glancing at the irreproachably "polished" features and immaculate appearance of the "fain fellow, dontcher know" immediately and unerringly puts him down as "in all probability a scoundrel!"'[47] *Parti pris* in both cases – from very different angles!

From Starowolski, who thought that the nobility should not work, and who was above all concerned that they should not let themselves be 'infected' with the desire for gain, Rzewuski is already divided by an age which respected work and money-making. 'There can be no doubt', Rzewuski acknowledges, 'that money is the most powerful instrument both for all manner of good and for all manner of evil.' And elsewhere: 'One must value money and efforts to put it to use, so that by being capitalised it may increase public resources,'[48] though it should not be idolised. Among Rzewuski's most acute observations – which are here of more than purely historical interest – is his division of people into types according to their attitude to money. Here, Rzewuski's psychological insights are very much to the point and could well be drawn on by anyone interested in the ramifications of what is commonly called 'economic motivation'.

Henryk Sienkiewicz's attitude to the bourgeoisie, expressed mainly in his novels of manners, hardly differs, if at all, from the views of the aristocratic writers I have quoted. Noblemen are not interested in money, nor are they motivated by desire for gain. Such things should be left to the bourgeoisie. 'Out of the blue,' we read in *Bez Dogmatu* ('Without Dogma'), 'there arises from time to time an aristocratic speculator, and from time to time it even happens that blind fortune favours him at the outset and he is soon a rich man. . . . But I have not seen one who has not been bankrupted before death.' Stressing aristocratic indifference to monetary gain, Płoszowski recalls the nobleman 'who, having extensive estates of the best land, tilled only as much as "the dog could bark at"'. Of himself, Płoszowski says: 'Money has never played any part in my life, whether as means or as end; I regard myself as unfit to handle such a weapon; I know how degrading it would be for Anielka and me to use such a thing in our relationship, and it would cause me . . . unspeakable moral abhorrence.' It might be objected here that in the figure of Płoszowski, Sienkiewicz is depicting a degenerate who is not necessarily the mouthpiece of the author's own views. However, one can hardly doubt Sienkiewicz's feelings on this score. It is the detestable figure of the upstart Kromicki who is motivated by desire for gain, while Połaniecki, the positive hero, who has to overcome aristocratic opposition to the thought of earning one's living by trading in grain or muslin, is convinced that taking part in economic matters has something unclean about it, and he never talks about money in his family circle.[49] 'His nature as a Połaniecki', says Waśkowski about him, 'is incapable of applying itself wholeheartedly to the business of making money.' This is not the attitude of the bourgeois characters in Sienkiewicz's book. In Gastein, Płoszowski brusquely summons a doctor for Anielka. The doctor assures him that it is nothing more than a slight nervous upset. 'For these words,' says Płoszowski, delighted with the news, 'I filled his pockets to such an extent that he didn't put his hat on till he was outside the villa gate.' It is my opinion that if the scorn expressed in these words went against the grain with Sienkiewicz, he would not have put them in the mouth of Płoszowski. It is true that Płoszowski praises the sons of the impoverished merchant Chwastowski for getting down to earning their bread in the town; and he regards it as a promising sign 'that there are people in this country who can turn their hand to something, and who form a healthy intermediate link between over-sophistication in the nation and barbarism'. But even here, in his relationship to the Chwastowskis, there is a hint that he remains aware of his own superiority. It is the relationship of a man who is proud of his sleepless nights, to someone who has only to lay his head on the pillow to snore peacefully till morning.

His veneration for the aristocratic ethos leads Sienkiewicz to endorse the nobleman's failure to pay any attention to appointments or time-limits, nor does it bother him that the nobleman cannot be held to his word. These little shortcomings are justified by the nobility's relationship with the soil. '*Chez nous* it was the Jews who looked after trade, and they couldn't teach us to be accurate; after all, the peasant has to be unreliable, because the earth is unbelievably unreliable, and he cannot be tied down to time-limits, because the earth cannot.'

In spite of these foibles, however, it is the nobility in Sienkiewicz's works that is typically called upon to play the leading or controlling part in relation to the bourgeoisie. So it turns out in the partnership between Poľaniecki and Bigiel. 'The partners complemented each other perfectly. Poľaniecki, incomparably more competent and more enterprising, had more ideas and was better at seeing things as a whole; Bigiel was better at getting things done. Where energy was called for, or someone had to be driven into a corner, Poľaniecki was in his element; where patient supervision of a dozen different things at once was called for, Bigiel came into his own.' Poľaniecki as director and Bigiel as manager of the planned muslin factory formed the perfect combination. When Poľaniecki first acquaints his partner with his brilliant idea for a grain business which would prosper on hunger, Bigiel is initially shocked – not because of the immorality of the scheme, but because of its verve and dash.[50] 'Bigiel took fright – but that was his reaction to any and every business venture.' Timidity along with common sense, solidity, moderation, patience, industry – the whole repertory of bourgeois virtues is present in this portrait. Nor is the proverbial sentimentality lacking: in the evenings Bigiel plays Schumann's 'Träumerei' on his violin, with his eyes closed or fixed in rapture on the moon.

Sienkiewicz's attitude to the grocer is expressed through Pľoszowski when the latter says, as he ponders over Anielka's feelings: 'Women of little spirit often refuse to yield because of a certain philistinism of virtue. They are chiefly interested in having their account books in order, just like any shopkeeper. They are afraid of love in the same way as a grocer is afraid of rowdiness in the street, afraid of big words, impassioned words, bold thoughts, daring ideas and enterprises. Peace above all things! Because it is only in peace that one's true and positive interests can flourish. Anything that oversteps the everyday, sensible and commonplace tenor of life is bad, and deserves the contempt of sensible people.' 'Perhaps', thinks Pľoszowski to himself in a moment of despair over Anielka, 'her soul is just not capable of rising above the boredom of household accounts.'

Here enshrined, as it were, is the whole stereotype of the

bourgeois ethos. To round it off *vis-à-vis* the aristocratic ethos, we have lastly to mention the aesthetic factor in bourgeois morality. More than once, Płoszowski stresses the part this plays in his moral attitudes. 'There are many things I wouldn't do,' he says, 'not because they are bad but because they are ugly.'

It is scarcely necessary to remind ourselves that not every Polish nobleman adopted the attitudes we have been describing, *vis-à-vis* the bourgeoisie; my selection has been drawn exclusively from the ranks of the conservative Polish nobility. Few would deny, however, that conservatism was typical of the Polish aristocracy in general. Our review leaves us with a rather scanty harvest of commonplace observations. The nobleman is above the common run of humanity: his birth guarantees this. He is aloof from economic matters, allegedly indifferent to monetary gain, and he does not bother to keep accounts; on the plus side, he has spirit and dash, he takes risks, he is open-handed and courageous in battle. The bourgeois – seen usually in Poland as someone with a drop of foreign blood in his veins, mainly German or Czech (Bigiel) – is someone of mean birth. He is out for money; he is calculating, apprehensive and a man of peace. In very much the same terms did that ancient country squire Xenophon in his day describe the merchant and artisan in the *Oikonomikos*.

3   The Young Poland attack on bourgeois morality

Similar difficulties await us when we try to identify exactly who (in terms of class affiliation) launched the attack on bourgeois morality from within the Young Poland movement, and on what precise grounds. The attacks on the petty bourgeoisie which we have so far considered, and which contributed to producing a certain stereotyped picture of bourgeois morality, were all launched by people representing the interests of certain social classes. We turn now to criticism expressed by a group delineated by totally different criteria; and its collocation with the preceding groups may seem incongruous to the reader. Whatever their due place within the social spectrum, however, we have to thank the

Bohemians – as they liked to be called – for the most potent and deadly criticism of bourgeois morals at the end of the nineteenth and in the first decades of the twentieth century, a criticism which, not only in Poland, often ran parallel to the criticism expressed by the left in general. As an example of a Polish writer who attacked on both of these fronts, we may take Wacław Nałkowski.

As is well known, the concept of the *vie de bohème* was shaped by the pen of Henry Murger in his book *Scènes de la vie de bohème*. The work appeared in parts in one of the Paris dailies in 1846–49, before its publication in book form. Although Murger himself in his introduction traces the ancestry of the social 'bohemian' back to ancient Greece, there can be little doubt that the *vie de bohème* as we understand it today first took shape against the background of nineteenth-century democracy. It was then that artists freed themselves from patronage, both royal and aristocratic, and struck out on their own in an act of 'private initiative'. 'Henceforth . . . Balzac', writes Tadeusz Boy-Żeleński, 'has only his pen to serve him both as weapon and as hope.'[51] These were the peculiar conditions, in Boy's opinion, that went to creating the Bohemian – 'this king without a country, drawing his torn cloak proudly about him as though it were a regal mantle. The realisation that talent, and talent alone, decides his worth, breeds in the artist a contempt for social ethics *vis-à-vis* the townspeople, the middle classes (philistines, soap-boilers, as they used to be called in Poland) whom they regard as the representatives of a hostile race. Instability of income, the discrepancy between their material state and their spiritual tension, some acquaintance with the world of luxury – these factors generate that particular form of economic management in which the fruits of several months of work are consumed in a few hours, and the artist is faced next morning with starting all over again that life of penury, that life of contrasts which yet befits the artist more than controlled moderation.'[52] When they have money, Murger writes in his preface, 'they ride bareback on insatiable fantasy, embracing whatever is youngest and most beautiful, drinking what is best and sweetest, throwing their money out of every window.' They share irregularity of income and budgetary chaos with the lumpenproletariat.

We have no space here to go into detail concerning the historical vicissitudes of this group. Murger regarded them as being perpetually with us, but they are in fact connected with a particular historical period, and in Poland they belong to the past. Their heyday in Poland coincided with the activities of the group which A. Gorski called 'Young Poland'. In 1898, Stanisław Przybyszewski arrived in Kraków, armed with the slogans of the Norwegian and German Bohemians. In Norway, the circle round the well-known painter Edvard Munch had created, to quote Przybyszewski, 'a world of its own, a world for itself which terrified ordinary people. . . . This circle unleashed a savage attack on "polite" society. It tore off the hypocritical mask with which polite society covers its ulcers; things which hitherto could only be whispered in the ear were shouted by young people at every street corner. . . . There was a lot of shouting and arguing, and polite society was forced to defend itself. . . . There were day-long sittings in cafés, the old "prejudices" were dissected and derided – and oh what a lot we drank!'[53]

In his book *Znasz-li ten kraj?* ('Knowest Thou the Land?') Boy-Żeleński draws an affectionate picture of the Bohemian circle of Kraków. The café atmosphere was saturated not so much with cigarette smoke as with intensity of thought. The people who met each other there had a surprising breadth of education, gained solely within the café walls. The ancient Greeks knew how to value their street philosophers, and perhaps we ought to pay more attention to these apparently unproductive sages. 'More than once,' Boy-Żeleński recalls, 'I pondered on the role of the unproductive, a role so much more important than appears at first sight. They are the bearers of the pollen of intelligence. They imbibe thought and digest it for others, they help it to circulate. Often it may be said they read for those who . . . write. Writers, as a rule, read far less than is commonly supposed, they instinctively defend themselves against too much print. Reading and writing – perhaps one can't do both.'[54]

(a) Mediocrity of bourgeois aspirations

So, what sort of reproaches did our café Bohemians level at the bourgeoisie, as they talked and wrote? The first thing that came in for attack was the mediocrity of bourgeois aspirations, their making-do with a humdrum average, their idea of happiness as a state of satiety, stabilisation and stagnation. In contrast to this stagnation, the Bohemians offered a spiritual elitism, an exclusivity, a dynamic and violent cult of life, the cult of eternally unsatisfied youth, of suffering and eternal longing.

'The collective spirit,' wrote Przybyszewski, 'sluggish and domesticated, comfortably settled on its evolutionary rung' abhors the spirit of the 'eternal revolutionary' and hurls abuse at whatever transcends the accepted norm.[55] But under that which 'to the pitiable brain of the bourgeois appears to be the most laughable idiocy, depths of intensity are always hidden'.[56] Old Poland 'smiled benignly at the childish exuberance and excesses of young people whose romantic fervour would soon blow itself out, as the God of "profit" allows a goodly harvest to be garnered and the money-bags fill up'.[57] But 'the norm is foolishness – degeneracy is genius'.[58] And elsewhere: 'The bourgeois brain exhausted itself in the effort to create the laws and conditions for a contented life. But these laws are veritable saturnalia of foolishness. The bourgeois ethic, the doctrine of a happy and harmonious life, is the only genuine, the only authentic "Communist manifesto" of today's plebs.'[59]

'Drop in on the family circle: what happiness, what a lot of shining, well-fed faces . . . drop in on the Christian working-men's clubs, what an absolute harmony reigns there between capital and labour.'[60] And again: 'in the radiance of blind faith – faith in profit and sheepfarmer's wits – all is harmony and serenity, all contradictions are evened out'.[61] This last salvo may seem to bespeak Marxist attitudes but the analogy is deceptive: the struggles and contradictions to which Przybyszewski is referring are personal rather than social.

I have already referred elsewhere to Leopold Staff's attack on this bourgeois concept of happiness:

We do not seek happiness in bloody battle,
Brothers! Let us leave happiness to little people,
We are going to face up to immense anxieties.[62]

And Jerzy in Jan August Kisielewski's well-known play *W sieci* ('In the Net') regards happiness as 'an empty Philistine term'. 'Happiness, as I understand it, is Christ in action, that strange uneasiness of the soul consumed by a lust for mighty action, for glorious creation.'

(b) There's always something to worry about!

Another criticism levelled by Young Poland and the naturalist novel of their time at bourgeois attitudes lies in their assertion that the bourgeois simply do not know how to relax and enjoy themselves. The contrast between those who can enjoy the moment in happy unconcern and those who are always worrying about something, always being cautious, always prevented from giving free rein to their personalities – this is one of the main themes in Gabriela Zapolska's *Sezonowa miłość* ('Seasonal Love'). Here, Zapolska contrasts Tuśka, the wife of a minor Warsaw civil servant, with the light-hearted world of the stage which the author sentimentally endows with all the merits which were, at the time, denied it, such as moral scruples and a fondness for family life.

For the first time in her life, Tuśka is in the Tatra Mountains, but she seems quite unable to relax and benefit from the experience. She eats sparingly so as to look her best. She cannot go out to have a look at the mountains as walking might spoil her new shoes. Since childhood, her daughter Pita has been kept on apron-strings. 'You can walk round the house,' says her mother to her, 'but don't walk in the sun, and take care of your shoes. Don't forget your gloves . . . and breathe through your mouth, not through your nose, this air is costing enough!.'

One of Tuśka's main worries, one which unfailingly inhibits any spontaneous reaction she might feel, is concern about her social position. She cannot allow herself to be less well housed than Councillor Warchlakowski's wife, who lives next door. The first time the two neighbours meet 'they took stock of each other's clothes, hands, hats, teeth, character, probable income, quickness of wits; and they identified certain blemishes, blackheads on their noses, number of freckles, gold fillings and gaps in intelligence'. No end of things one must remember to do (or not to do). Pita must be perpetually on guard against sunburn. Women's ideas changed when they went on holiday, though not sufficiently to obliterate class distinction. True, it was mainly the gentry who went to take the waters and they who set the tone, but they had to take good care to keep their hands and faces white, otherwise they would be indistinguishable from sunburnt peasants. This behavioural pattern went into reverse when urban life began to impose its own standards: then one would hold one's face up to the sun in obligatory ecstasy, because, upon return to the town, a bronzed visage would help you to stand out from the urban proletariat who did not have the time even to be aware of the sun or of country greenery.

One might well point out here that Zapolska is giving the bourgeoisie a monopoly of traits which are by no means exclusive to them. Thus, as regards the first meeting between Tuśka and Madame Warchlakowska, it is quite normal for people to set about establishing 'pecking order' when they first meet. Who is to be first in line, who pecks, who is pecked – this is the customary trial of strength we observe in the world of birds, whence the expression has been borrowed to describe, very aptly, the world of humans. There is nothing unusual in the fact that Tuśka and Madame Warchlakowska fix on a pecking order; what *is* of interest is the weaponry they choose, the relative values to which they appeal. In different social circles these factors change significantly, thus disclosing the hierarchy of values deemed to be of importance in that society.

(c) The role of money

After birth and behaviour, the strongest card in the social hand is money, with all that money can buy. The malicious and prying eye which is a constant factor in the further development of relations between Tuśka and her neighbour, never fails to spot a shortfall in Tuśka's budget. Tuśka does what she can to cover up. Dulska also spends a lot to keep up appearances, but when no one is watching her she skimps on every penny, cuts down on newspapers (which she can in any case borrow) and tells her son to sit hunched up in the tram so as to look younger than he is and not have to pay.

Here the bourgeoisie is vividly contrasted with the Bohemians who never miss a chance of demonstrating what little store they lay on money, who never put a price on anything but flaunt their poverty and act the poor man even if, in actual fact, they are not so poor.[63] In this bravado, some critics see a compensation for economic weakness – making a virtue of necessity, an attempt to ridicule something one is unable to get for oneself. No doubt there is some truth in this, but it is certainly not the only factor that goes to ensure that those living under the sign of the muses should have a very different system of values.

(d) 'They've no eye for beauty'

'Beauty means nothing to them' jeered Young Poland: an attack on people without art launched by people whose lives were ruled by art. The man in the street cannot hope to grasp art, writes Przybyszewski, since he is guided by 'utilitarian and money-grubbing instincts'. Not only does he not understand art; still less can he be expected to make anything of the slogan 'Art for art's sake' as promulgated by Young Poland. Julka, Councillor Chomiński's tomboy daughter who wants to become a painter (in Kisielewski's *W sieci*) cannot count on any support from her family. 'But can you tell me', says her mother to the writer Jerzy, 'what are we going to get out of all this painting? Can't the world do without masterpieces of painting? Anyway, is it going to make her happy? Is it suitable for a young girl?' To say nothing of the fact that Julka is painting nudes – which threatens her sisters' chances of marriage. 'Go to Paris – to Australia – to an exhibition in Paris,' says her mother to Julka. 'Go! Perhaps girls there are in the habit of painting such masterpieces, but, as for you, be good enough to remember that you have a family, that you have four sisters, and that your good name is all you've got.'

The artificial palms with which Zapolska adorns Dulska's parlour are not so much a sign of a fondness for durable things, of reluctance to spend money on short-lived things, as of a lack of aesthetic sensibility; and the same goes for the fake Japanese dishes and the imitation pottery which Zapolska hangs on the walls of the same interior. 'Secession rubbish and don't forget the loose covers,' says Boy-Żeleński in his instructions to the stage-manager on how to furnish Dulska's drawing room. A portrait of Kosciuszko was also desirable.[64] The loose covers also figure in the Chomiński drawing-room in Kisielewski's book. 'And of course a piano – that goes without saying.'

Perhaps the most memorable catalogue of bourgeois hideosities is that given by Tuwim in his well-known poem 'Mieszkańcy' ('The Inmates'):

Horrible dwellings. In horrible dwellings horribly dwell the horrible dwellers.
Along the walls wintry horror and dark agony crawl with soot and mildew.

From early morning, a mumbling. They mumble and drivel that it's raining, that life is expensive, that this and that. They walk for a while and sit down for a while, all is ghostly and spectral.

They check their pockets, they check the time, they brush their ties and smooth down their lapels. With measured tread they step out from their dwellings on to an earth that is so familiarly round.

And now they proceed, hermetically buttoned up, they look right and left, and as they look they see everything *separately*: the house . . . Stan . . . a horse . . . a tree.

They finger newspapers like a lump of dough and chew them into a thick porridge, till they are at their swollen wits' end, puffed up with paper-cake.

And then they mouth again: that Ford . . . the cinema

. . . and God . . . and Russia . . . radio, sport and war
. . . layer upon layer the ghastly drivel piles up and drifts
phantom-like through the jungle of events.

Blindly they dangle their swollen heads, hanging heavier
and heavier towards nightfall. They crawl under the bed
to sniff out miscreants, and bang their crowns on the
chamber-pot.

Once more they check their pockets, receipts, trousers
darned on the seat, their revered property and sacred
purchases – their own, exclusive, hard-earned.

And then they pray: '. . . from sudden death . . . from
war . . . from hunger . . . eternal rest . . .' and fall
asleep, snout on chest, the horrible dwellers in their
horrible dwellings.

We need not attempt to analyse the poem: it can speak for
itself. In it, the reader will recognise many of the traits we
have already mentioned. The bourgeoisie as incorporated in
Dulska, wrote Boy-Żeleński 'must and ought to perish
because it is abominably ugly. How to put it to death
without bloodshed – this is the task to which we must all
contribute whatever is in our power.'[65]
The world of the bourgeoisie is also accused of being
prosaic. This is a reproach in which aesthetic disapproval
plays a key part. In this prosaic setting Tuśka struggles and
frets, once she has come to know a new life in the world of
the stage. In her new mood, the following letter from her
husband is not likely to be well received:

My dear wife!
I am very pleased to be able to send you another two
hundred roubles. I beg you, stay a bit longer; since the
holiday is doing you good, go on enjoying the air with
Pita, and take care to get well so that at least this expense
is not in vain. I was able to get this money and I still
have fifty roubles but that's really all I could get. I'll try
to repay it. Try to spend as little as possible so that you
can stay there as long as possible. I had to change my
restaurant as they started giving me very poor food to

eat. For the most part, I eat broth and a piece of meat, as they can't poison me with that. I have been suffering continuously with my stomach and I no longer eat supper. I take something home from the butcher's, and the caretaker makes me some hot tea. It's a pity you locked everything up, I've just got the one glass for tea and for washing my mouth out. It's the same with the towels. The boys are well but they've made holes in their shoes and I had to send them something from Warsaw. . . . The palms still have insects on them, and tobacco doesn't seem to help. I'm having the mattresses taken out to the balcony and laid in the sun because the sun kills bacteria. I enclose two hundred roubles. The rate at the moment is 126½ – be sure they don't shortchange you. Have a look at the newspapers. I have nothing more to tell you at present. I kiss you and Pita.

Your devoted husband, Walery

I have given a fair amount of space to this letter as it is an excellent example of what is meant by bourgeois prosaicness. This letter is prosaic in that it is completely taken up with economic trivia, the petty details of housekeeping. It is the combination of Walery's stomach pains, the holes in the boys' shoes, and lice in the palms that generates the ugliness of this preoccupation with trivia. If Walery had written about his lung infection, about his worry over his continuing high temperature, he might strike the reader as a man who is preoccupied with his health – but his letter would not necessarily be prosaic. What fixes this letter as prosaic once and for all is the fact that there is nothing else in it. 'I have nothing more to tell you at present' – these words settle it. Contempt for a preoccupation with everyday and household trivia may be felt by any member of the privileged classes who does not have to be aware of such things in the ordinary course of events. Contempt for someone who cannot think of anything else, however, may be felt even by those with holes in their pockets.

(e) The bourgeois attitude to sex and family life

From Norway and Germany, Przybyszewski brought revolt against the bourgeois attitude to sex. In Bohemian circles abroad, he wrote, very different ways of conducting one's sex life were openly discussed. The new tenets of free love and sexual equality drove some people to suicide, and some women in Bohemian circles became prostitutes; for them, promiscuity was an act, not of love but of protest against 'respectable' people.[66] We know how vehemently Zapolska fought against the sexual conventionalities of her milieu. She attacked the convention that men should not marry until they were in a position to support their wives – which meant, of course, that up to their wedding day they seduced the servant girls (Kaśka Kariatyda, *Moralność pani Dulskiej* ['The Morality of Mrs Dulska']), and preyed on poor girls who tried to get on to the stage (*Panna Maliczewska* ['Miss Maliczewska']), and ended up, worn out and often ill, trying to run a family (*O czym się nie mówi, O czym się nawet myśleć nie chce* ['What One Doesn't Speak About, What One Doesn't Even Want to Think About']). Kisielewski's Julka has to marry an aged suitor because her father is in debt to him. 'They sold me like a sick heifer! For seventy-five florins!'

   For both husband and wife marriage is a sort of burial, the final collapse under the burden of the conventions and trivialities of the milieu. 'From the day of my marriage I slept the sleep of the comatose, the sleep of the glutton, the sleep of the German manufacturer beside his German wife – the whole world around me has, you might say, dropped off in my own image – I travelled round relations, doctors, shops, and since a child was going to be born to me, I thought of a wet-nurse.' Zygmunt Krasiński could still write like this in his *Nieboska Komedia* ('The Un-Divine Comedy'). Thus did our writers from the Romantics to Dr Judym view marriage. 'You'll darn socks and fill an armchair,' says one of Kisielewski's characters to Julka, sketching her connubial future. The bourgeois family is not a field where values likely to appeal to Young Poland are nurtured; a colleague advised Julka to 'kick the whole bloody lot out'.

The family, as seen by Young Poland, lives incarcerated in its own interests and in preoccupation with social advancement – in pursuit of which the wife is tireless. 'Father took the easiest way out,' says Zbyszko about Felicjan Dulski. 'Mamma elbows her way through the world for him, and he follows her.' As a whole, the bourgeois family is concerned about its good name and steers clear of scandal. This is the 'waterproof' family, as Stanisław Brzozowski says in *Legenda Młodej Polski* ('The Legend of Young Poland').

(f) Bourgeois and Philistine

What threatens a man after marriage? Boorishness and Philistinism – twin concepts which Young Poland critics used as unsparingly as did the left wing. Zapolska calls her *Moralność pani Dulskiej* a tragi-comedy of Philistinism. 'The Philistine is zero, nothing, null . . .,' writes Kisielewski in the above-quoted play. 'It's something that doesn't exist but it moves.' There is a *philister domesticus*; there is a super-Philistine. 'The Philistines . . . I'd murder them, roast them alive, break them on the wheel, impale them, flog them, slice, sting, gnaw, spit them out,' says Jerzy, the writer, in the same play. 'You're dividing the whole of humanity into Philistines and artists,' answers Madame Chomińska, not altogether inaptly one feels.

Our contemporary historians of literature have very properly pointed out that Young Poland's battle with the Philistines was a battle with a certain psychological type (some would say, with a certain psycho-biological type), whose social parameters were not closely identified, and against whom struggle was not explicitly recognised as class struggle. As K. Wyka has observed, as long as the word 'Philistine' denoted overfed complacency and insensitivity to any new idea, and, therefore, by definition, to new movements in art, criticism of the Philistine was, to a certain degree, anti-capitalist criticism. As time went on, however, the word came to be used more and more of the man who can make nothing of art for art's sake.[67]

We can take it that the word 'Philistine' did not mean one

and the same thing for all the writers we have quoted. It meant one thing to Przybyszewski, for whom 'art for art's sake' was something fundamental, and something else to Zapolska, whom he loathed and for whom the Philistine's reaction to art was in no sense a cardinal issue. But quite apart from these minor variations in meaning, which we need not go into here, the anti-philistine campaign was not waged in terms of class warfare.

In Berlin, Przybyszewski had been the editor of the journal *Die rote Fahne* ('The Red Flag'), and he arrived in Poland deeply imbued with socialist ideas. For some time he edited the *Gazeta Robotnicza* ('Workers' Gazette'), in whose pages the *Złota Książeczka* ('Little Golden Book') of Piotr Ściegenny made its first appearance in Polish. Concerning the 'noble order, decency and universal justice' which, according to the bourgeoisie, ruled all around, Przybyszewski wrote: 'And what does it matter if millions of hands are raised in anguished supplication for bread? In no way does that disturb social harmony: *"Ecrasez l'infâme"*.'[68] But an occasional outburst of this sort, the kind of thing which had appeared earlier in other texts we have quoted, does not alter the fact that it was not in the social arena that Przybyszewski's contest with philistinism was waged. For Przybyszewski, the struggle took on the contours of simple dichotomies: artist/rabble, chosen spirit/plebeian world: dichotomies in which the second term – rabble, plebeian world – does not constitute a social class. The rich Philistine too belongs to the rabble, the proletarian who is susceptible to beauty may be recruited into the world of the elite. 'Elite' in this context is a Nietzschean concept, as long as we understand by this Nietzsche's original concept, not its subsequent deformation under Hitler. It is for this elite and for it alone, in Przybyszewski's opinion, that art exists. 'Art for the people – that is an abominable and insipid banalisation of the means which the artist uses, a vulgar hand-out of something which by its very nature is rare and arcane.'[69] In *Współczesna powieść w Polsce* ('The Contemporary Novel in Poland') Brzozowski draws our attention to the fact that Przybyszewski treats society as if it were something other than a human creation.

'Something terrible is happening with and around me, something I neither acknowledge nor want, and yet something in which in spite of everything I take part' – these are the words which Brzozowski uses to characterise Przybyszewski's attitude to society.[70] His writings and his published letters have much to tell us about his satanic personal struggles. If we can believe Boy-Żeleński's testimony regarding Przybyszewski (see *Znasz-li ten kraj?*), these attitudes were connected with Przybyszewski's naive and trusting outlook in his personal relations.

The opposition of an elite – an intellectual if not an aristocratic elite – to the 'rabble' was not without its influence on criticism levelled at the bourgeoisie by contemporary writers on social questions. For example, Nalkowski's typology: on one side a highly-strung elite; on the other side, blockheads, brutes, swine. These are psycho-biological categories, and the victory of the highly strung is not the victory of the proletariat.[71]

Of all the attacks on the bourgeois ethos carried out by Polish writers, it is Kasprowicz's 'Modlitwa Episjera' ('The Grocer's Prayer') that shows particular receptiveness to the way in which certain social factors operate. Let me conclude my survey of the criticism expressed by Young Poland and the contemporary naturalist novel by quoting a few passages from it:

The Grocer's Prayer

For fifteen hundred years and more, O God, Thou hast protected priests and marquises . . .

But the humiliation of the people is over; their heads have fallen under the sword of Justice, and in the Place de la Bastille where man's dignity died in madness, a noble veteran today opens a small door leading to the interior of the July Column . . .

I know, Lord God, that in these days of anger and vengeance we did Thee most grievous wrong: Thou hast been shamefully cast forth from Notre Dame . . .

But time is a wonderful healer; from all of this Thou hast recovered, and Thou hast pardoned all, for to whom is the power of forgiveness given if not to Thee,

O Lord, Thou the incarnation of all perfect attributes
. . .

But if Thy benevolence is limitless, then let it be so that my neighbour Monsieur Rabattet may strike a bargain as quickly as possible with Monsieur le Comte de Contrexeville, wind up his liquor business and settle himself comfortably in the country. I understand that, being fed-up with Sunday drives in a hired cab to the Bois, he wants to have his own horses and a park in which trespassers will be prosecuted.

A ruthless and dangerous competitor: his vodka undercuts my wine; I offered him a partnership but he refused. He secured the help of the Cartesians,* they gave him sole rights of representation on the Continent, and it is his boast that he sometimes sat on the same bench as Combes.

He takes part in the annual ordination of the clerics, and assures enemies of the Church under his breath that this is so that he can convince himself that his abhorrence of Prejudice has in no way diminished: 'anyway,' he adds, 'I enjoy a good show, at the opera or in the Cathedral, for me there is no difference.'

Let the wells flame in Baku – the struggle for freedom is always sacred – and in the Borysławski basin, in a country of half-savage, rather stupid barbarians, please let the oil flow abundantly . . .

Lord! I confess openly: I wished to turn away from Thee, for I see Thee not and it does not become a progressive man to transgress the boundaries of perception.

And yet in our hearts there is a secret something, a mysterious trepidation which whispers to us that all is not over at death.

. . . they tell me to wait for the Légion d'honneur; who will give me patience if not Thy all-embracing patience?

I wish to put forward my candidature; where, in these times of confusion of concepts and tendencies, can I

---

* Translator's note: The Polish text of Kasprowicz's Collected Works has 'Cartesians', but presumably 'Carthusians' is meant.

find a glimmer of enlightenment except in Thy perfect
wisdom?

Who will deflect mishap from my poor, miserable
vineyard except Thy omnipotence? . . .

Let the multitude not look upon me with hate because
I have an extra morsel of bread – for I too am of the
people, and I understand who are the people, and who
are the scum and dregs of society.

Let my fellow republicans not suspect me of treachery
to my upright republican convictions, because I am
giving my dearest child, my only daughter, into the
hands of a scion of those ancient and honourable knights
who once went hence to do battle with pagans for the
grave of Thine Only-begotten and Beloved Son . . .

Long live France! Long live the Republic ! Long live
democracy! Amen.[72]

Here, Kasprowicz has scored a bull's-eye. In this prayer
of a French bourgeois, slogans of the bourgeois revolution
are wittily interwoven with much solicitude for his own
private well-being and with concern that his daughter should
marry a titled person; while God is given the job of ruining
his business competitors. And indeed we find closely analogous themes in manuals devoted to the behaviour of a good
citizen, contemporary with Kasprowicz and destined to be
used in French elementary schools.

4   The social background of Young Poland's attack on the bourgeoisie

In this *aperçu* of the attack on bourgeois values as contained
in Polish literature during the second half of the nineteenth
and the first half of the twentieth century, I have stressed
certain qualities, alleged to be characteristic of the bourgeoisie, which had some influence on its moral attitudes. If
I have discounted purely personal opinions and some exaggerated accounts of bourgeois hypocrisy, this is partly
because hypocrisy is not peculiar to the bourgeoisie alone,
but mainly because hypocrisy does not in itself contribute
to the formation of moral attitudes: rather, it is a subterfuge

serving to disguise an inner nonconformity with moral precepts publicly professed by the individual or by the milieu. On the basis of her moral principles, Dulska should evict the prostitute who rents the annexe – but she is keen to get more rent out of her; and she justifies her actions with the thought that the money which her lodger earns in somewhat questionable fashion loses its taint as Dulska pockets it. After all, she is not going to use it for any personal needs but merely to pay her taxes.

We can now look at the social role played by this criticism. In Poland, criticism of this type coincides with the era of imperialism, though at first sight its connection with the economic basis of imperialism may not be obvious. After all, the criticism is aimed not at large-scale capitalism, at monopolies or cartels, but at the petty bourgeoisie. It is for this reason that K. Wyka writes: 'Instead of attacking the capitalist structure and the *grande bourgeoisie*, the naturalists at best attack the petty bourgeois, thereby displacing the whole contest, or they attack the artistic philistine.'[73] And further, when discussing Zapolska as a creative artist: 'The naturalist attack on the petty bourgeoisie was a substitute attack . . . which concealed and obscured the main conflict between the bourgeoisie and the proletariat. Again, it was a misplaced attack in the sense that the petty bourgeoisie bore far less responsibility for the crimes and contradictions of capitalism as discerned by the naturalist eye, than the *grande bourgeoisie*: and far less responsibility than the naturalist school would have us believe. Especially in the ensuing epoch of imperialism, when the concentration of financial capital struck at the property, the position and the independence of the petty bourgeoisie in equal measure, it is rather mystifying why all the blame should be placed on their shoulders, and why the hysterical fads of petty officials and their bored wives should be seen as the main enemies of progress.'[74] J. Z. Jakubowski takes Zapolska to task for giving us a critique of bourgeois customs rather than of the capitalist structure. 'In Zapolska's works,' he writes, 'what is primarily reflected is a doubtless wretched philistinism and a feeble petty bourgeoisie which was never called upon to perform any great historical tasks.' Zapolska's criticism led to figures of the Daum and Dulska sort achieving mythological dimensions. Grundyism was seen as a powerful social force, and the class nature of morality was ignored.[75] K. Wyka, whom I have already quoted, admits that even with their shortcomings the strictures of Zapolska and Kisielewski had some positive effect, while Przybyszewski's revolt was on balance – to quote Jakubowski – 'objectively reactionary' and counterproductive. After the 1905 revolution, anti-middle-class satire gathered strength 'on the crest of a wave of post-revolutionary disenchantment with the bourgeoisie in general'. The proletarian revolution had its influence on the contents of the 'Grocer's Prayer' which Wyka treats as an anomaly in the generally reactionary writings of Kasprowicz.

As I said, the criticism voiced by Young Poland and the naturalist school has been blamed for not attacking what really should have been attacked, if Przybyszewski and Zapolska had recognised the laws of social development as formulated by Marxism, and if they had wanted to contribute to the building of socialism. This is no doubt true; but the next question – why their criticism should have taken this direction in preference to any other – remains puzzling. And vague talk about 'substitute attacks' and 'mystification' does nothing to make things any clearer.

At the same time, it is not easy to pinpoint the social bases of this criticism in a country like Poland where Western European trends were rapidly grafted on to a keenly receptive native intelligentsia, though these trends were the product of conditions differing widely from those obtaining in such an economically backward terrain. Similarly just before the last war, there were Polish writers who saw fit to fulminate against the excessive technicalisation and mechanisation of life, in the wake of such writers as Irving Babbitt in the very different setting of the United States. As was appropriately pointed out at the time, this amounted to giving Poles injections for a disease which people were suffering from in America.

Polish Neo-romanticism inherited much from Romanticism, sharing with it, for example, a pronounced aversion to the mediocre, the prosaic. It is noteworthy that this aversion which in Neo-romanticism is aimed primarily at the petty bourgeoisie, had no such class adversary in Romanticism. For the Romantics, there were those whose heads were in the clouds and those whose feet were planted firmly on the ground, but this division is not yet the division into artists and bourgeois boors. We may recall Mickiewicz's poem 'Zaloty' ('Courtship'):

> When I sing the charms of the daughter,
> Mamma listens, Uncle reads;
> But when I sigh for her heart and hand,
> I listen, and the whole family quizzes me.
>
> Mamma runs on about hamlets and souls,
> Uncle about rank and income.
>
> Mamma, Uncle! I have only one soul,
> And I have estates in Parnassus.
> I have to earn my income with my pen,
> And my rank is in the hands of posterity.

In Krasiński's *Nieboska Komedia*, Henryk groans under the burden of matrimonial boredom and prosaicness – which is, however, not quite the same thing as the prosaicness of the middle class. Krasiński himself explained in a letter to Reeves that he was not marrying Henrietta in order to avoid the commonplace dullness of life, a dullness which he sees most clearly in his own social class. Clearly, what is wanted here is closer study by competent literary historians; but at first glance it looks as though the tendency to offload on to the shoulders of the bourgeoisie everything that the Romantics disapproved of, is a later development in Polish literature and one especially characteristic of the Young Poland Neo-romantics.

If the attack on the bourgeoisie was a local phenomenon in Poland, we may take it that its intensification in a country deprived for so long of an influential third estate, was partly due to the influence of the aristocracy on the Polish intelligentsia. It should not be forgotten, however, that an anti-bourgeois wave was at the same time sweeping across Europe, reaching its climax – oddly enough – in bourgeois France. Hardly had the bourgeois established himself in France and consolidated his rule than Balzac laid bare his shortcomings and pilloried the hideousness of his dwelling-places (see, for example, the description of Madame Vauquer's dining room in the first few pages of *Le Père Goriot*). Almost at once, the literary champions of '*l'art pour l'art*' in France were repudiating moderation in any shape or form, and refusing to accept utility as the sole criterion of value. The graphic arts followed suit. Paul Gavarni (1804–66) and Honoré Daumier (1808–66) poke fun at the learned professions as well as at the grocers on whom, in his short stories, Maupassant was to vent all his ferocity. Probably at no time up to the outbreak of the Second World War is the French grocer not in the pillory, not only for his own but for others' faults as well. It would be difficult to find a more gruesome Chamber of petty bourgeois Horrors than the one round which the doctor conducts us in Céline's *Voyage au bout de la nuit*. In some countries, music was also brought into the attack: thus, Schumann founded the *Davidsbündler* for the struggle against the Philistines. Various members of the society are portrayed in *Carnaval*, in the last section of which the *Davidsbündler* march against the Philistines.

Not only literature and art, but almost all important socio-political currents at the end of the nineteenth and in the first decades of the twentieth century view whatever can be called bourgeois with deep disfavour. Of course, the nature of this criticism varies, depending on the nature of the base from which the attack is launched and on the remedy suggested. But as far as the general picture of bourgeois narrow-mindedness is concerned, there is fairly general agreement; that is to say, 'bourgeois morality' is presented as a generic whole – as we have seen, a somewhat questionable stereotype.

It is well known that both Fascism and Hitlerism depended on the petty bourgeoisie: which did not prevent Fascist and National Socialist theoreticians from giving voice to anti-bourgeois sentiments.[76] From Ciano's diaries we learn that Mussolini spoke with contempt of the bourgeois ethos. Hitler had to overcome bourgeois pacifism, and his SS men were called upon to stamp out bourgeois sentimentalism among their subordinates. In his memoirs, Goebbels uses the word 'bourgeois' pejoratively. According to the memoirs of Rudolf Hoess, Eicke, who was in charge of the concentration camps, meted out his most savage punishments to those – including some of his own officers – who rebelled against the atrocities they were ordered to commit. Such insubordination showed, as he saw it, that the culprits 'had not got over their old bourgeois attitudes which had been rendered entirely obsolete by the revolution carried out by Adolf Hitler. These views are evidence of a softness, a flabbiness unworthy of SS officers, which could even become dangerous.'[77] Max Scheler, whose views were rather close to Hitlerism in its advanced stages, could not stand bourgeois attitudes; and Eduard Spranger, whose articles were printed in *Das Reich*, described *Homo oeconomicus* with outspoken aversion. (To *Homo oeconomicus* we shall shortly return.) In fact, the petty bourgeois came in for a drubbing from all sides. It was not enough that he was called upon to bear the cost of the wars, that devaluation was aimed precisely at him; he was attacked by both Right and Left as well. Hitler urged him to be stern and hard like the Prussian knights of old, and punished him when he flagged; while those who had to flee Hitlerism hated him all the more because he had allowed himself to be seduced by dreams of power. The German refugee Erich Fromm saw one reason for middle-class readiness to go along with Hitler in the mentality of the petty bourgeois. The petty bourgeois, he wrote, are attracted to power and they hate weakness: they are small-minded, full of petty hatreds, tight-fisted in expenditure, whether of money or of feelings. 'Their outlook on life was narrow, they suspected and hated the stranger, and they were curious and envious of their acquaintances, rationalizing their envy as moral indignation: their whole life was based on the principle of scarcity.'[78] So Fromm too uses the ready-made stereotype which until very recently kept on turning up in scientific literature.

In this book, I am not primarily concerned with the *sources* of the attack on the petty bourgeoisie which pervades the literature and art of Europe through the second half of the nineteenth and, especially, the first quarter of the twentieth century. What matters is that the attack took place at all, and that it gave rise to a stock view of bourgeois morality.

However, certain aspects of this attack may be briefly mentioned as of interest to students of the sociology of literature. In several European countries, Parnassian movements of various types entered the lists against the ethos of the petty bourgeoisie – movements which liked to see themselves as elites, aloof from the growing and increasingly insistent mass of the proletariat. Matthew Arnold (1822–88), who fought the 'Philistines' in England under the banner of an elitist culture, was deeply alarmed (as we learn from the Preface to the 1925 edition of his works) when the great English Reform Bill of 1867 extended the right to vote to almost a million members of the English and Welsh working class. It seems very likely that it was precisely this fear of reform, reinforced perhaps by the Chartist movement, which led Arnold to preach the importance of perfecting oneself, and the construing of culture as 'the effort towards this perfection'. To similar sources we may well trace Arnold's exhortations to break with all practical and political considerations which might restrict the free play of pure thought. The fact that Arnold's escapism is obvious even to those who are not normally inclined to think in terms of class warfare does not, however, guarantee that this explanation can be applied to any and every *odi profanum vulgus*. In the case of Arnold – and in many similar cases – the question remains: given a situation where an author has every reason to fear and despise the proletariat, why should he wage war on the bourgeois Philistine? Arnold defines the 'Philistines' as those who devote their lives to lining their own pockets. They think about nothing else. They are 'stiff-necked', stubbornly opposed to whatever is new, and they are recruited from the ranks of the Puritan and Old Testament-ridden middle class – a class which the author would like to draw away from Israel and restore to the influences of Hellas. For Arnold, Franklin with his 'imperturbable common sense' is a representative of the philistinism which is, in general, characteristic of the development of the United States.[79]

Pitfalls await those who try to explain such elitist slogans as '*l'art pour l'art*' and 'ivory towers' by appealing to variant social backgrounds. But even greater difficulties seem to beset those critics of bourgeois morality who attack on a general front in the manner of Maupassant and Zapolska. Setting their criticism and that of the Parnassians against the background of local social conditions, the literary sociologist must try to ascertain what literature and art had to offer in preference to the ways of the bourgeois money-grubber, on whom they had declared war. Przybyszewski returned from Norway intoxicated with the works of the sculptor Wiegeland; but the world which Przybyszewski opposes to the world of the 'soap-boiler' is quite different from that of Wiegeland: Wiegeland's work exhales a healthy and joyous eroticism whereas Przybyszewski's world smells of rottenness. Even within the confines of the Young Poland movement, the Philistine was portrayed in one way by Przybyszewski's followers, and in quite another way by those who looked to the people and national tradition for spiritual rebirth. The effect of local social factors must never be forgotten; but equally we must remember that the battle with the Philistines is a clash between two hierarchical systems of value as old as the hills. These systems collided in the shape of Socrates and his judges, and in the shape of Spinoza and his parents, who wanted him to be a merchant; and they are incarnated in the figures of Thomas Buddenbrook and his son who preferred to compose fugues rather than interest himself in the contents of the family warehouses.

Chapter 3

The classical model of bourgeois morality: Benjamin Franklin

... heard a good sermon of Mr. Gifford's at our church upon 'Seek ye first the Kingdom of Heaven and its righteousness, and all these things shall be added to you'. A very excellent and persuasive, good and moral sermon. Shewed, like a wise man, that righteousness is a surer moral way of being rich, than sin and villainy.

(Diary of Samuel Pepys, 23 August 1668)

1 Franklin's life and moral precepts

It was said of him that he deprived the tyrant of his sceptre and God of his thunder; but the name of Benjamin Franklin, the great spokesman of nascent capitalism in the United States and Europe, the first bourgeois (as one of his biographers calls him), does not figure in any history of ethics known to me. Not because he does not fit into the history of ethics (indeed, Franklin's thought is closely bound up with the mainstream of moral philosophy), but rather because the selection of authors for treatment in histories of ethics largely reflects academic philosophy. What socially minded writers and novelists, even the most influential of them, have to say on these matters is ignored to make room for the far from original and often obscure utterances on ethics made by the philosophers canonised by the textbooks. Enshrined in this neglect is a certain attitude to ethics and the history of ethics. The history of ethics was supposed to be the history of a science systematically approaching ever closer to the truth: a system in which incidental reflections on moral themes had no place. But this criterion has not been consistently applied: La Rochefoucauld, for example, and Nietzsche, regularly figure in the history of ethics. This lack of consistency is hardly surprising, for the dividing line between the moralist and the ethical philosopher is very elusive. On the one hand, 'ethical systems', so-called, are not, as a rule, systems at all; while, on the other hand, writers with something to say on moral issues often express themselves far more systematically and succinctly than do the alleged specialists in ethics. Whether this is so or not, a history of moral thought giving due consideration to those thinkers who played a genuine part in the major crises of social morals has still to be written. In such a history, Franklin will certainly find his due place as the classic example of bourgeois morality in the sense defined above. So far, we have been looking at a caricature of bourgeois morality; it is now time to see it in the true lineaments of its apostles.

Franklin's family had long been resident in the village of Ecton in Northamptonshire. The family was Protestant. Under the Catholic monarchs it had been called upon more than once to put the strength of its convictions to the severest of tests. The Bible which was read in secret was strapped to the underside of the table top, which could be quickly reversed when the children posted at the door as lookouts gave the alarm. Franklin's father was a Presbyterian Nonconformist, and his maternal grandfather had written in defence of Baptists and Quakers. About the year 1682, Franklin's father, attracted by the prospect of religious freedom, emigrated to New England. In his home town he had worked as a dyer. As there was little demand for this trade in Boston – at that time still a small town – he turned his attention to the manufacture of candles and soap. It was in Boston that Benjamin Franklin was born, in 1706, one of the youngest of a very numerous family. At an early age he was taken in hand by his father for training in the family business, but the work did not appeal to the boy. He was a voracious reader, and this led his father to send him to learn printing. In 1702, one of the elder Franklin brothers started publishing one of the first newspapers to appear in what was to become the United States. Benjamin worked on the paper as a printer and wrote occasional articles under a pseudonym. However, disagreement with his brother led Benjamin to leave his job, and at the age of seventeen he launched out on the independent life of the classical 'self-made man'. He tried his luck first in New York and then in Philadelphia. He had to suffer poverty, failure and disappointment. His restless spirit drove him to England, at that time by no means an everyday journey. On the way, he fell in with a travelling companion who assured him that his poetic talents would be appreciated in England. Franklin was only eighteen years of age when he reached his ancestral homeland, and his eighteen-month stay in England had a great effect on his mental development. At that time, cultural life in England was very lively indeed, printers were kept busy, and Franklin was able to find well-paid work in his trade. The theatres drew the crowds, and in the eating houses lively discussion was the order of the day. It was in the 'Horns' ale-house that Franklin made the acquaintance of Bernard Mandeville, the author of the *Fable of the Bees*, whom he found 'a most facetious, entertaining companion'.[1] A proposed meeting with Newton in another inn fell through. Even before coming to England, Franklin had learned much of the *Spectator* off by heart, with a view to modelling his style on it. He drank deeply at the sources of Whig liberalism, and played a part in the birth of freemasonry.

Upon his return to America, Franklin settled in Pennsylvania, attracted there by friendly Quakers. In Philadelphia, he opened a shop selling writing materials and books. At the same time he began to take more and more interest and play an active part in public affairs. The urge to improve both himself and his environment, which is such a striking trait in Franklin's character, led him to open a club on the lines of the English masonic lodges. As a meeting-place for small traders and artisans, this club was nicknamed 'the leather-apron club' by the big merchants of the town. Admittance to a genuine masonic lodge, founded in Philadelphia in 1727, gained Franklin access to more influential business circles. In the next few years we see Franklin as the founder of the first lending library, as the editor of an independent newspaper, as the founder of an Academy which formed the nucleus for the future University of Pennsylvania, as the organiser of the first learned society in the colony, and as the publisher of a celebrated Almanac which ran for about twenty-five years in what was for the time an exceptional number of copies and which was translated into various languages. From 1748 onwards, Franklin was carrying out his famous experiments with electricity. In about 1754 he began to step up his political activity. From 1764 to 1775 he represented Pennsylvania, Georgia and Massachusetts in England. To begin with, he adopted a conciliatory policy which laid him open to the charge that he was too English in America and too American in England. Gradually, disillusionment with English policies set in, and his tone grew more caustic. When America threw off the English yoke, Franklin was sent to France as the first accredited representative of the United States in Paris. He stayed in France from 1776 to 1785 and gained wide popularity, so much so that his face was jokingly said to be as familiar as that of the moon. Making skilful use of Anglo-French rivalry he obtained a treaty with France which was very favourable from the American point of view. His last political act was to sign a petition for the abolition of slavery. He died in 1790.

Any attempt to assess Franklin's life runs up against an immediate difficulty – what to leave out. Few life stories offer such a wealth of interest, as Franklin changes before our eyes from the young apprentice, eager for knowledge, to the great statesman and sage of the Paris salons.

Franklin was continuously and obsessively interested in improving himself and his environment. For any and every scrap of theoretical knowledge he would at once seek a practical application. When the stove smoked, he tried to find out why. Seeing streets full of litter in London, he came up with a practical way of keeping them swept; travelling by sea to France, he composed a memorandum on ways of perfecting navigation. The waste of artificial light which he noticed in Paris inspired his 'Economical Project' which he sent to the editor of a newspaper, and which sets out in mathematical form the amount of money Parisians would save on candles if they all got up at sunrise. Franklin's celebrated experiments on electricity resulted in such practical devices as the lightning conductor and the condenser.

His ability to take a broad view of things did not mean that he lost sight of even the most minute detail. In his last will and testament he justifies his decision to bequeath large sums to public projects, not to his family, on the grounds that he himself never inherited anything from his own family. But while allocating his wealth to grandiose projects he could still take the trouble to specify that the marble tablet over his grave should be six feet long and four feet wide; and he himself jotted down the terse epitaph.

The most complete editions of Franklin's works are in ten volumes. They include: the Autobiography (particularly valuable for our present purposes, though regrettably it does not go beyond the year 1757), political papers, economic projects, moral tracts, suggestions of a practical and rationalising nature on production processes of every kind, and hundreds of letters. The fund of letters was further increased by the researches of B. Fay, whose monograph on Franklin, published in 1929, is based in part on newly discovered correspondence. Fay was French, which underlines the undiminished interest in Franklin felt in France. The autobiography itself actually appeared for the first time in Paris, and only later in the United States, the country which Franklin helped to shape by taking an active part in drawing up its constitution and by providing it with his 'self-made man' as a model to aim at.

Franklin himself made no secret of his petty bourgeois origins, and indeed paraded them in his practical counsels. In contrast to François Arouet, who took the name 'de Voltaire', Franklin never showed the slightest inclination for this sort of social advancement, and to the end of his life he took pride in the fact that his father had been a candlemaker. 'The simple ploughman', we read in the Almanac, 'is worth more than the vicious prince.' When they asked him in Paris how he wished to be addressed, he said he would prefer to be treated as a scholar and addressed as 'Doctor' – a choice which speaks volumes for his scale of values. He frequently voiced his disapproval of inherited privileges and honours. Social position, according to Franklin and other bourgeois writers, must be won through personal endeavour and personal merit. If glory is to accrue to any member of a family, it should be to the parents; for, if a child goes on to achieve something to be proud of, the glory is theirs for having reared him. Franklin's open-mindedness to progressive thought is revealed in his patronage of Tom Paine, a facet which Howard Fast takes up in his book on Paine. And indeed in Franklin's correspondence we find letters warmly recommending the author of the pamphlet *Common Sense* to American relatives and acquaintances as 'an ingenious, worthy young man'.[2] In some quarters, indeed, Franklin was for some time regarded as the author of the book. More than once, Marx pays tribute to Franklin as a pioneer and innovator, and asserts that Malthus profited from Franklin's ideas. Again according to Marx, Franklin was one of the first after William Petty to discern the true nature of value, and to state that 'the best way to assess the value of anything is' to assess the labour that went into making it'.[3] Finally, Marx attributes to Franklin the very apt definition of man as 'a tool-making animal'.[4]

Let us now consider the main features of that social paradigm which Franklin urged his compatriots to copy.

The man who has only himself to thank for all he has achieved is characterised by two traits in particular – worldly ambition and sobriety. His eyes are not on the world beyond. He does not work for it, nor does he expect help from it. 'God helps those who help themselves; forewarned is forearmed': aphorisms like these adorn the pages of Franklin's Almanac. Success has to be won here on earth; and if a man can forge his own destiny, helped by no form of inherited privilege, this should give him very special satisfaction.

Virtue is to be measured by its utility. We can all do very well without self-denial and ascetic practices which avail us nothing. Here we seem to hear the voice of David Hume, who had hard words for asceticism in all its forms, which, he said, did nothing for us except sour our nature. In a lecture which he delivered in a masonic lodge in 1735, entitled 'Self-denial not the Essence of Virtue', Franklin argued that merit is not diminished if we do something without effort, and that justice, compassion and restraint are and remain virtues, irrespective of whether they are exercised in tune with or counter to one's inclinations. He who does foolish things, says Franklin with reference to ascetic practices, just because they are against his nature and inclination, is a madman.[5] This is the path which Helvétius was later to take in his attempt to sever the connection between virtue and self-denial, and to base virtue on the human passions, in the conviction that virtue based on self-denial can never be reliable; for if we are continually called upon to get the better of ourselves, there is always the danger that we might lose the battle.[6] A completely different approach to this question is to be found in the work of that representative of the German *Aufklärung*, Immanuel Kant; though, like Franklin, Kant too came from a strict sectarian background (Kant's family was Pietist). In Kant's view, if an action is morally praiseworthy it is precisely because it represents a victory over a certain inner resistance – and we are then close to what Franklin dubbed a 'state of madness'. In Franklin, the man of the *Aufklärung* and the businessman have overcome the Puritan.

Franklin's intention, as he tells us in the Autobiography, was to explain and propagate the idea that 'certain actions are not bad because they are forbidden, but forbidden because they are bad for us'; and that it is accordingly in the best interests of everyone who wants to be happy in this world to be virtuous.[7] 'Honesty is the best policy' had to be the war-cry of all those who like Franklin felt themselves called upon to educate the masses in virtue.

The same utilitarianism which Franklin introduced into moral practice can be seen in his views on religion. As he tells us in the Autobiography, he was only fifteen when he broke with religion. There are, however, certain beliefs which help people to live in this world: and these, he advises, should be retained. Thus, though he did not deny that the materialist standpoint was probably the true one, he deemed it useful and profitable (in line, here, with contemporary Deist thought) to believe in the immortality of the soul and even in God who looks after the world, and rewards or punishes people during their lifetime or after death. Franklin himself took no part in religious practices of any sort, and he did not shrink from jeering at the clergy. From the letters which he wrote from England to his daughter, it is clear that he regarded religious practices as something better left to women – indeed, he even advised women to occupy themselves with such things. We shall come back to this subject.[8]

When Marx observes in *Capital* that credit can be treated as an economic-political evaluation of a man's morality, he hits on an essential trait of that human exemplar which Franklin urges us to imitate. In Franklin's scheme of things credit can be taken as the yardstick of virtue, and the allegation that Franklin's ideal is the man of good credit, is not wide of the mark.

While running his stationery business, Franklin conducted himself as he describes in his own words:

In order to secure my credit and character as a tradesman, I took care not only to be in reality industrious and frugal, but to avoid all appearances to the contrary. I drest plainly: I was seen at no place of idle diversion. I never went out a-fishing or shooting: a book, indeed, sometimes debauched me from my work, but that was seldom, snug and gave no scandal; and, to show that I was not above my business, I sometimes brought home the paper I purchased at the stores through the streets on a wheelbarrow. Thus being esteemed an industrious thriving young man, and paying duly for what I bought, the merchants who imported stationery solicited my custom; others proposed supplying me with books, and I went on swimmingly.[9]

And in the *Advice to a Young Merchant* (1748) we read:

Remember this saying, The good paymaster is lord of another man's purse. He that is known to pay punctually and exactly to the time he promises, may at any time, and on any occasion, raise all the money his friends can spare. This is sometimes of great use. After industry and frugality, nothing contributes more to the raising of a young man in the world than punctuality and justice in all his dealings; therefore never keep borrowed money an hour beyond the time you promised, lest a disappointment shut up your friend's purse for ever.

The most trifling actions that affect a man's credit are to be regarded. The sound of your hammer at five in the morning, or nine at night, heard by a creditor, makes him easy six months longer; but if he sees you at a billiard-table, or hears your voice at a tavern, when you should be at work, he sends for his money the next day; demands it, before he can receive it, in a lump.

It shows besides, that you are mindful of what you owe; it makes you appear a careful as well as an honest man, and that still increases your credit.[10]

As malicious critics of Franklin were not slow to point out, the man of good credit may well rest content with the semblance of virtue rather than try to be virtuous himself. But if success was to be achieved, appearances were certainly not enough. Only once in the Autobiography does Franklin admit to contenting himself with appearances – in the case of the virtue of modesty; though he also asserts that it pays to relinquish small vanities or conceits because 'assumed Feathers' will be restored to you.

So, it is three virtues above all others that ensure a man's credit: industriousness, the punctilious discharge of one's monetary obligations, and frugality.

Both the Autobiography and the Almanac swarm with aphorisms enjoining diligence on the reader. If you are diligent, so Franklin's father taught him, you will find yourself among kings – which is in fact what happened, as Franklin's diplomatic missions gave him repeated access to these exalted regions. How much time do we spend lying in bed, forgetting that a sleeping fox catches no chickens! Work pays off debts, despair and sloth compound them. Laziness is like rust which destroys things more effectively than use. The key which is always in use is bright and shining. By dint of work and patience, the mouse gnaws through the thickest rope; small repeated blows bring down the giant oak, etc., etc.[11]

In the Middle Ages, people made holiday on the slightest of pretexts. It simply never entered pre-capitalist man's head to work all day long. Attendance at court, military service, inheritance, usury, alchemy – such were the things that occurred to a man if he thought about getting some money. We shall search the moral codes of the nobility in vain for any mention of 'industriousness'. On the contrary, it was *de rigueur* not only to be idle, but – much more important – to be seen to be idle. In his well-known book *The Leisure Class*[12] Thorstein Veblen coined what is now the accepted term in sociological literature for this phenomenon: 'conspicuous leisure'. One had to loaf conspicuously, for that was essentially what distinguished the upper class from others. Even if someone belonging to the upper classes was not himself an idler, he had to support people who were and who lived as parasites – a pampered wife, a scattering of servants yawning in corridors and decked out in a livery proclaiming their status as members of his retinue. If their lord and master failed to be fittingly idle, they took care of his image as a conspicuous wastrel.

Among the nobility, the custom of giving a pledge which, once given, had to be honoured irrespective of the sacrifices entailed or the dangers involved (cf. the Polish folk-tale of Podbipięta, who had to remain a virgin for many years before he was able to cut off the heads of three pagans with one stroke of his sword) – this custom was not linked to monetary considerations unless these involved so-called debts of honour. However, monetary obligations were not as a rule binding within the framework of one's own class. When the Polish gentry flocked to the capital at carnival time to exhibit their daughters at balls and get them married off, they usually left behind them a great many unpaid bills – money owed to tailors, barbers and lady teachers who brushed up a girl's French. It was all right to welsh on those who did not belong to your own class. The inviolability of the nobleman's pledged word had nothing in common with bourgeois dependability in a business deal, which was an exercise in virtues alien to those interested above all in personal distinction.

Among the privileged classes parsimony was something to be ashamed of, which, if practised at all, had to be studiously disguised. In his memoirs, Franklin, however, stresses how modestly he and his wife lived, even at a time when they were fairly prosperous; and he recalls that it was a long time before they allowed themselves the luxury of eating off china. In a letter to his wife written when Franklin was his new country's representative in England, he enjoins her not to spend much even on their daughter's wedding – an unnecessary reminder, it seems, as Mrs Franklin was stingy even by Franklin's own standards. He who cares naught for a penny – to quote the Franklin Almanac – is not worth a penny. It is by thrift and work that people get rich. And again: the fatter the kitchen, the leaner the last will and testament; what you have to eat today, save it for tomorrow; what you have to do tomorrow, do it today; if you buy what you don't need, you will soon have to sell what you do need. Such are the maxims which, if not actually produced by Franklin, were certainly popularised by him and have passed verbatim into the anonymous repertory of bourgeois folklore.

Thrift was bound up with the cult of the balanced budget, something remote from the nobleman's creed – wager the lot and cut a dash. When you know how to spend less than you earn, wrote Franklin, you have gained possession of the philosopher's stone.[13] The moral flavour of the balance between 'credit' and 'debit' is something which we shall come back to in due course.

Living with pencil in hand means being methodical, planning ahead. 'Give everything its proper place,' Franklin exhorted, 'do everything at the proper time.' In his own life, precise times were fixed for sleep, work, rest and recreation.[14] Methodically he went to work on himself: he directed his self-improvement methodically, and equally methodically he worked on his moral standards. As we have seen, it was not for nothing that the Methodist sect which took shape in eighteenth-century England, and which drew its membership from the middle classes, was so called. This methodicalness may well be linked with certain religious tenets. The Catholic church, which offered its adherents absolution from sin through confession, never required them to keep constant watch over themselves in the same degree. It was otherwise in those Christian persuasions which offered no such easy cleansing from sin: here, a constant measure of self-control was necessary.[15] But even if this factor did play a certain part, it was, in my own opinion, of secondary importance. The Catholic church also requires its faithful to examine their consciences daily; and we find 'methodicalness' as recommended by Franklin in the Polish Catholic artisan who also applies it primarily to gaining his own ends – i.e. doing well for himself.

A good example of Franklin's methodical approach is the table of sins and virtues which he prepared to assist him in the daily exercise of self-examination. Here we have an inventory of the virtues which Franklin promised himself he would acquire. They are thirteen in number, and are as follows:

> (1) Temperance; (2) Silence (avoid trifling Conversation); (3) Order; (4) Resolution (perform without fail what you resolve); (5) Frugality; (6) Industry; (7) Sincerity (use no hurtful Deceit); (8) Justice; (9) Moderation; (10) Cleanliness (in Body, Cloaths or Habitation); (11) Tranquility (Be not disturbed at Trifles, or at Accidents common or unavoidable); (12) Chastity; (13) Humility.[16]

Week by week, Franklin concentrated his attention on one or another of these virtues. For this purpose, he had a sort of rota in grid form with the days of the week down the left-hand side and the thirteen virtues along the top. In the squares thus formed he would each day mark those virtues which he had in some way failed to observe. Particular attention was paid to the 'set virtue' for that week. The ideal was to achieve a whole week consisting of nothing but blank squares. The same process was repeated each week, with one or another of the virtues forming the centrepiece – though never to the total exclusion of the other twelve.[17]

There is no doubt that in every social class people are to be found who set about doing whatever it is they want to do in orderly and programmed fashion. Even among the nobility, the heirs to knightly tradition, examples are to be found of individuals who led lives systematically governed by rules they themselves had laid down. The difference is that methodicalness as practised by the bearers of knightly traditions was not promulgated by them in the form of slogans, nor did it set the tone for the behaviour of a group.

I have set out this list of virtues in illustration of that methodicalness which Franklin wanted to instil in others and cultivate in himself. Not all of them actually enter into the make-up of that personal exemplar which Franklin promotes in his Almanac, and it is these excluded items that we shall now consider. Franklin's personal directives are of interest to us in so far as they are not limited to his own personal case. In turn, we shall limit ourselves to those points which seem to be of particular significance and importance for this way of life.

One of the key points is Franklin's attitude to money. In *Advice to a Young Merchant* he wrote:

Remember that time is money. He that can earn ten shillings a day by his labour, and goes abroad, or sits idle, one half of that day, though he spends but sixpence during his diversion or idleness, ought not to reckon that the only expense: he has really spent, or rather thrown away, five shillings besides.

Remember that credit is money. If a man lets his money lie in my hands after it is due, he gives me the interest, or so much as I can make of it during that time. This amounts to a considerable sum where a man has good and large credit, and makes good use of it.

Remember that money is of the prolific, generating nature. Money can beget money, and its offspring can beget more, and so on. Five shillings turned is six, turned again it is seven and three-pence, and so on till it becomes an hundred pounds. The more there is of it, the more it produces every turning, so that the profits rise quicker and quicker. He that kills a breeding sow, destroys all her offspring to the thousandth generation. He that murders a crown, destroys all that it might have produced, even scores of pounds.[18]

And in *Necessary Hints to Those that would be Rich* we read:

For £6 a year you may have the Use of £100 if you are a Man of known Prudence and Honesty. He that spends a Groat a day idly, spends idly above £6 a year, which is the Price of using £100.

He that wastes idly a Groat's worth of his Time per Day, one Day with another, wastes the Privilege of using £100 each Day.

He that idly loses 5s. worth of time, loses 5s. and might as prudently throw 5s. in the River.

He that loses 5s. not only loses that Sum, but all the Advantage that might be made by turning it in Dealing, which, by the time that a young Man becomes old, amounts to a comfortable Bag of Money.[19]

There could be no more telling assertion of the creative and generative power of money, or a more peremptory reminder for the reader than the maxim 'Time is money'. What Franklin is advocating here is not the money-grubbing of the rentier but the investment of capital for profit, a key factor in nascent capitalism. Franklin was by no means the first man to believe in the value of making money (we shall return to this point in due course), but the conversion of time into money, the insistence that not a moment is to be lost, and the urge to make this style of life universal – these are new elements which go to form the ethos which was to distinguish Europe and America so sharply from the cultures of Asia.

Not a few of Franklin's commentators have grossly distorted his views; and it is worthwhile pausing here to consider these views in their historical perspective, as a certain stage in the everyday wisdom of capitalism. As in ancient times, here too what matters is to gain independence. The Stoics sought and gained independence by denying the value of everything except their own moral standards: the Epicureans by eschewing constraints and giving themselves over to the pleasures of the mind. Neither of these forms of independence was accessible to any but exceptional men. The Stoic sage was as rare as the phoenix. Capitalism when it came on the scene offered people an incomparably more democratic form of independence: an independence gained by money. Franklin's own career was in itself proof that here indeed was a way open to everyone. In an item entitled

'How one may always have money in one's pocket' in the Polish version of *Poor Richard's Almanac* we read: 'Let decency be, as it were, the soul of your soul, and never forget to keep a few pence from your wages for the reckoning and settlement of all expenses; you will then reach the apex of happiness, and independence will be your shield and buckler, your helmet and your crown.'[20] So much for so little![21]

The extracts from Franklin which we have quoted above were used by Max Weber to illustrate his thesis that in a moral code developed from Puritanism, making money became a *calling* – which it is argued distinguishes this particular ethos from the slogan '*enrichissez-vous*' as promulgated in post-Revolutionary France. We shall come back to this thesis of Weber's shortly. Franklin being what he was, a man of good humour and kindliness of spirit, there is not a shadow of rigorism or religious bombast in his slogans; but it remains nevertheless an undeniable fact that in his view virtue was dependent on making money. About his Almanac he wrote:

> I therefore filled all the little Spaces that occur'd between the Remarkable Days in the Calendar with Proverbial Sentences, chiefly such as inculcated Industry and Frugality and thereby securing Virtue, it being more difficult for a Man in Want to act always honestly as (to use here one of these Proverbs) it is hard for an empty Sack to stand upright.[22]

It is a thought that recurs again and again in Franklin's writings, in many guises: 'He who is badly dressed is devoid of virtue' we read in the Almanac for 1736. To money we are indebted not only for our virtues: it determines our social position as well. 'Now that I have flocks and cattle, everyone greets me, everyone bids me "good morning!",' says old Maciej to the people assembled in the small-town market-place. (In the Polish translation, old Maciej is the equivalent of Abraham's father in the original.) 'You would gladly be convinced, my friends, of the power of money. Go and try to borrow some, for going after a loan is like trying to recover a debt – you're landing yourself in trouble.' And although Franklin was already aware that the business world was a hard world (as he wrote in the 1736 Almanac: 'Bargaining has neither friends nor relations') yet he says explicitly that this is a price worth paying for economic success, for 'nothing but money is sweeter than honey'.

The link between money and virtue may remind us of Aristotle, who asserts (in the *Politics*) that virtue is neither gained nor retained by means of external goods, but that external goods are gained through virtue; while, according to the doctrine of the mean, virtue is best served by a medium degree of affluence. The rule of the best is not the rule of the richest; for the best men have as a rule only moderate resources.[23] Aristotle's *kalokagathos* shows moderation in his attitude to wealth, but, obviously, he cannot do things in style unless he has adequate resources, just as he cannot attain to this happy state without having free time at his disposal; as contemplation is, in Aristotle's view, an important element in happiness.

In such aristocratic ethical systems, virtue is not directly but indirectly linked to property status. Nobleness is something which is inherited; and inheritance, it goes without saying, is bound up with a certain property level.

The aristocratic ethos did not tolerate an obsession with money; Franklin's ethos not only tolerated it but actually urged that time be reckoned in terms of money. Both in the Autobiography and in his letters, Franklin is much taken up with prices. Recalling how his household slowly acquired china dishes, he is careful to add the figures which reflect the amount of china they now own. Sending his wife some English silk for a dress as a present on the occasion of a diplomatic success scored on the colonial issue, he does not forget to mention how much a yard he paid for it. During his first stay in England, Franklin became friendly with a young poet and his sweetheart. When the poet had to absent himself for a while, leaving the lady in Franklin's care, Franklin threw himself into the business of looking after the forlorn beauty so enthusiastically that the friendship could hardly survive. 'So I found', writes Franklin sadly, 'I was never to expect his Repaying me what I lent him or advanc'd for him.'[24] An obsessive interest in monetary matters may indeed be characteristic of the life-style advocated by

Franklin, but this is not to say that money did not also play an important role in the ranks of the hereditary nobility. In many respects there is little difference. The crucial difference, however, lies in the fact that in aristocratic circles money and housekeeping were things that one did not mention; one might very well be attracted to the idea of making money, but it was something one did not talk about, much less boast about. In Franklin's world, no one is ashamed to talk about money; if you are filling your coffers you can shout it from the housetops. One goes patiently on, remembering that many a mickle makes a muckle: but cautiously, not forgetting that 'big ships can sail in deep waters, but little boats must stay close to the shore'.[25]

If a methodical life is to be led, formidable forces have to be controlled, forces which may at any moment threaten the self-imposed discipline. So, when drawing up his list of the thirteen desirable virtues, Franklin advised his readers to make love rarely and only in so far as requisite for health reasons and for the purpose of bringing offspring into the world: never to the point of exhaustion or stupefaction, and never to the detriment of one's own or another's peace or reputation. It must be admitted straight away that Franklin himself fell short of these standards. Even as an old man he was still very susceptible to women, and this led him to do things which he described in the Autobiography as 'the errata in my life'. When he opened his stationery shop in Philadelphia, the neighbours set about pairing him off with a kinswoman of theirs. In these circumstances Franklin adhered to the first part of the adage he was later to insert in the Almanac: 'Have your eyes wide open before marriage, and closed thereafter'. When the girl's family proved unwilling to part with the dowry requested by Franklin (£100 to cover his debts) he backed out, suspecting that he was supposed to yield under emotional pressure. Franklin finally married the woman to whom he had promised marriage while still a youth, thus making up for his long neglect of her. As part of his marriage portion he brought to his wife the illegitimate son born from an earlier clandestine liaison. Deborah Franklin was a faithful wife, thrifty and a good housekeeper, but the gap between her and her husband was considerable, which probably meant that if domestic harmony was to be preserved he had to keep his eyes closed after marriage. Things were helped, of course, by the fact that for long periods Franklin was away from home. After the death of his wife, Franklin, now over seventy but undeterred, married Helvétius's widow in Paris, and had a half-erotic, half-paternal affair with Madame Brillon de Jouy. His own very full sexual experience must underlie his warning in the Almanac: 'where there is marriage without love, there will be love without marriage'.

The effect of his last years in Paris doubtless changed Franklin's earlier attitude to women and modified the role he had allotted to them in his model society. In his earlier scheme of things, women were allowed a rather narrow range of activities, being preordained to work in the house and bring up children. In a letter to his daughter written in 1764, Franklin urges her to go regularly and faithfully to church – although he did not do so himself. He also advised her to study arithmetic and book-keeping, to be good and prudent and to love her mother. A rather limited programme!

Since the bourgeois attitude to art was a main target in the criticism of the bourgeoisie launched from artistic circles, we may close this section with a few words on this subject. In his young days, Franklin had dabbled in poetry but – as he relates in the Autobiography – his father had dissuaded him, assuring him that poets were no more than paupers. Later, Benjamin himself was to write: 'I approved the amusing one's self with poetry now and then, so far as to improve one's language, but no further.'[26] As Franklin's cultural horizons widened, his attitude to art changed somewhat, and the same development may be traced in his correspondence. In the Almanac, however, Franklin maintained his father's standpoint: 'Poverty, poetry and new titles of honour make men ridiculous' we read in the 1736 issue.

2   Franklin's self-made man: the sequel

Franklin's teaching was addressed to the petty bourgeoisie and served their interests. In Pennsylvania, Franklin maintained good relations with the bourgeoisie as its members grew in power and wealth, though, as we have seen, they called the club he founded 'the leather-apron club' – a rather derogatory reference to its artisan character. Are we now to accept that the Franklinesque slogans were really identical with those slogans which were under attack from the mid-nineteenth century onwards (see Chapter 2)? If so, this is to admit that bourgeois morality, as a certain type, is historically incorporated in the morality of the Western European and American petty bourgeoisie: a morality explicitly crystallised in the eighteenth century which proceeded to gain ever-widening circles of support in the age of liberalism, from the ranks of the small capitalists on the one hand, and from the top stratum of workers in the developed countries on the other.

It would take several volumes to trace the history of Franklinism in the USA and in Europe. Here we can do no more than take a few examples from certain typical periods of history. In the case of the USA, we pass over the nineteenth century and concentrate on the period of imperialism, to see whether the Franklinesque paradigm survived the economic transformation which divides the America of Sinclair Lewis and Theodore Dreiser from that of Mark Twain. In Europe, we shall glance at economically backward Poland and the gradual establishment there of Franklinesque morality, in the nineteenth century, as a morality answering the demands of 'sound progress' (see p. 97 below): in the period, that is, immediately preceding the rejection of this morality by the Young Poland critics and by Polish naturalism.

Two centuries after Franklin's Almanac, there appeared in America the Lynds' classic studies on a typical American township – an 'inland city', to which the Lynds gave the fictional name of 'Middletown'. They began their research in 1920, and their book appeared in 1929. The further development of the town up to 1935 was then pursued in the book *Middletown in Transition*, which was published in 1937.[27] When the authors began their study, the town had about 37,000 inhabitants; when they returned to it, the population had risen to 48,000.

Middletown took its tone from the petty bourgeoisie.

From the outset, it was an industrial town, though in its early stages it lacked large industrial enterprises. It was seen by its inhabitants, very properly as a town of small businesses. In this phase of its development, it was possible, according to the authors, to distinguish two classes only – the business class and the working class. The workers were weakly organised. No attention was paid to class warfare, any symptom of which was in any case carefully hushed up by a press which represented business interests only. Misfortune at working-class level was regarded as *individual* misfortune. Out of about 13,000 people who could be regarded as belonging to the working class in 1929, only 900 were in any way organised. By 1934 the figure had risen to 2,800, only to fall the following year to 1,000 (p. 27).[28] When the Lynds published their second book, Middletown had gone through some six years of economic depression. As a result, it was possible to discern signs of incipient class solidarity among the workers; basically however, they still failed to see any real difference between themselves and the businessmen, and continued to accept the life-style and attitudes of the latter as models to aim at (pp. 447–8). The town presented, then, a homogeneous life-style which the authors call 'the Middletown spirit'; and it was equipped with a system of axioms which, given the absence of nonconformist media, went unchallenged, allowing the younger generation to be reared in a climate governed by business interests, and conventionalist to a degree unimaginable in the cities of capitalist Europe. On the basis of verbal testimony, questionnaires, leading articles in the local press, occasional speeches, club rules, etc., the authors gradually lay bare the corpus of convictions accepted 'of course' by the average citizen as self-evident. A large part of the catechism set out on pp. 403–18 of *Middletown in Transition* consists of quotations garnered from various sources. In what follows, I give a summary of this catechism.[29] It covers not only moral issues but also the basic elements of the average Middletownman's world-view, the backcloth against which the moral issues must be seen. They cannot be treated in isolation. Moral comportment is in stylistic harmony with its setting.

The citizen of Middletown is convinced that it is his duty

to make money, to get rich. This is self-evident; there can be no question about it. It is a duty to oneself, to one's family and to society. For those who are unable, for one reason or another, to live up to this duty (only thus can such aberrations as choosing to be a teacher or a clergyman be explained) one feels contemptuous forbearance. In the business of getting rich you are on your own; God helps those who help themselves. For those who are industrious and thrifty, the way to the top is open. It is the American way, today as yesterday: 'from poor boy to President'. According to the Middletown catechism, America is the place where, sooner or later, everyone gets what he deserves.

The principle of 'each for himself' is the definitive rule governing the world of business affairs which gets along best when the government does not meddle in its running. Economic development proceeds in obedience to a certain natural order which man-made laws must not be allowed to hamper. 'More business in government and less government in business' – that's how things should be. Within this natural order of things economic depressions may naturally intervene. But when that happens 'it's like it is with feelings – one day a guy feels good, another day he feels real bad'. Depressions pass, and the pendulum swings 'our way' again. The Middletown code denies the very existence of such things as class warfare. Basically, capital and workers have the same interests. Employers pay as much as they can, and can be relied on to raise wages just as soon as that is possible. 'You can take it for sure that if the average worker and the employer sat down together to discuss their differences, that would get rid of difficulties far more quickly than politics or extremists on either side.' Reaching an understanding with the employer is the right way to go about things, not organising trade unions, which lays the workers open to manipulation by 'outsiders'. Like strikes, trade unions are organised by trouble-makers who lead workers astray. 'We condemn agitators who pretend to be idealists under the protection of our constitution. We demand the expulsion of foreign communists and anarchists.'

Middletown man is content with his country and with his home-town. Life in a big city does not attract him. American democracy is the best form of government and the Americans are the freest people on earth. In America, the newspapers give 'the facts'. 'American business will always lead the world. . . . In the USA like nowhere else, big businesses exist side by side with little businesses, and that shows us how healthy the American way of life is.' 'The small businessman is the backbone of American industry.' Most foreigners are a pretty poor lot. The slogan 'America first and foremost' is simply a matter of sound common sense. His satisfaction with things the way they are makes the citizen of Middletown lose his temper with those who criticise basic American institutions, those who want to bring about change, particularly violent change, and a planned society, which wouldn't work anyway. Schoolteachers ought to remember that it is dangerous to put ideas in children's heads that call basic things in question.

If you are to make something of your life, you must be practical, enterprising, industrious and thrifty. Hard work is the key to success. If a man is not to jeopardise his family financially, he should not allow himself to indulge in foolish speculation or 'isms'. Too much education and contact with books, it is felt, makes a man incapable for practical life. Character is more important than intellect. Society need not pamper a man who neither works nor saves – if he hasn't done well for himself, it's his own fault.

The citizen of Middletown does not want to be conspicuously different from others – one should be like other folks. In the long run it's those who take the middle way who turn out to be the wisest: it's best to go slow and avoid extremes. It is perfectly reasonable to distrust 'others'. The Middletown citizen is opposed to all nonconformist types of personality, especially those who are not suitably optimistic. Equally, he is against loners, ill-disposed or pretentious people. Nor does he care much for those who are too brainy. 'A few cultural deviants tend to be tolerated', as the Lynds put it in *Middletown in Transition*. In the event, Middletown may even be proud of them – but does not want too many of them. Certain eccentricities may, however, be permitted in someone who has done particularly well in business: after all, the very fact that he has done so well for himself is proof that deep down he must be OK.

In personal relationships, one must be straight, a good neighbour, 'a good guy', and have community spirit. One should encourage others. One should be a good partner, and try to have good relations with one's competitors. Away from business, it's best to praise folks rather than find fault with them. If you're too clever or too critical you'll spoil the fun. *Vis-à-vis* other citizens, Middletown recommends solidarity. You should buy things locally, in Middletown, in conformity with the slogan 'Buy where you earn'.

For the citizen of Middletown, the family is a sacred and fundamental social institution. The married woman's place is primarily in the home and everything else must take second place to the cardinal necessity of providing a good home for her husband and her children. A woman should not be too brainy, nor should she be independently minded and aggressive, critical and nonconformist. She should not think of having a career and competing with men; rather, it is up to her to support her menfolk in their undertakings. Few women understand public affairs as well as men do; and men are more practical and work better than women. It is in the subtleties and the moral finesse of social life that women come into their own. Men are apt to be tactless in personal relations; women understand these things better. Culture and so forth is for women rather than for men, and anyway, women are more virtuous than men.

When we come to discuss (Chapter 6) the significance of puritanism for the man of affairs, we shall see that puritanism has never been able completely to settle the conflict between a Christian upbringing and the urge to 'get on'. From what the Lynds have to say about the Middletown catechism, it is clear that in this respect the American businessman is guided by two separate moralities. There is nothing in the business rule book that requires a man to have consideration for others, even if 'fair play' suggests he should. Outside the sphere of business interests, however, consideration for others is obligatory (p. 242). As the Lynds say: 'There is no personal trait – unless it be honesty – of which Middletown is prouder than its friendliness' (p. 440). Returning home, the businessman casts off his business morality as one might lay aside an overall, and adopts a second morality suitable for neighbourly and amicable relations, a morality of mutual help and friendliness which is not only recommended but very much practised. If the catechism regards woman as the more virtuous sex, this is probably because, as someone not harnessed to business interests, she can permit herself the luxury of living continuously on this moral plane of comparative goodwill.

In religious matters, the Middletown citizen is not exactly zealous. It doesn't much matter what you believe; what matters is who you are. At times it may be a bit of a bore having to go to church, but no one would want to live in a society without churches, so everybody should support the church. As it is simply unthinkable that folks should just die and that's the end of it, there must be a life beyond the grave. Middletown religion, to judge from the Lynds' catechism, is a rather cosy and easy-going affair. It makes few demands, and provides ready-made solace in case of need. The idea that the soul is immortal is attractive enough to command belief (p. 416) but it is linked less and less with possible retribution as a corollary. The Middletown citizen makes little distinction between the various Protestant denominations, but he is in no doubt that Protestantism is always better than Catholicism, and that no Catholic should ever be elected President of the United States.

Obviously, the Middletown citizen's beliefs underwent a certain change in the Great Depression. After 1933, the slogan 'More business in government and less government in business' began to appear more and more questionable in the eyes of the less affluent. Workers began to doubt whether, in fact, the man who really wanted work could always find it. Not everyone, it now seemed, was your buddy. Broadmindedness, formerly widespread, was now confined to situations where it was either unavoidable or didn't much matter. Nationalism and a dislike of foreigners grew apace. Probably the feeling of increasing insecurity had a dampening effect also on that optimism which had been such a salient feature of the Middletown citizen's code – an optimism not unlike that which had inspired the bourgeoisie

indeed presumed by the either/or argumentation of the type described above. Here it is useful to refer back to the comments made in the preceding chapters of this book: in so far as the material conditions and relations refer to products of historical-social activity they always and with necessity appear in the context of specific 'ideal' or meaningful orientations. Even the historical-social conflict between the human being and nature is inexorably dependent on such 'ideal' mediations. A variant of the well-known Marxian statement would be that this material reality also exists only as one 'inverted in the human mind', therefore it is *also* ideal. In principle we should be led astray, or into fruitless scholasticism, if we enquire into the possible interrelationship between the previously isolated material and ideal aspects of social practice. If the material (i.e. economic) base of human practice is indeed of an entirely different order to the 'ideological superstructure', it would be hard to explain why this base should universally (and indeed even in socialist societies) be in need of this superstructure and how a 'mediation', indeed the closest involvement, between the two essentially different spheres could be possible. In fact, the 'ideological' interpretations (that is to say, in the narrower sense of religious interpretations) should regularly connect with the 'ideal' bases of a specific mode of production, and vice versa, either by enhancing or destroying it, and not with anything 'purely material' (i.e. physical or concrete).

Considerations of the latter type explain why Weber's first essay on the sociology of religion focusses on the interrelationship between a specific religious 'ethic' and the *'spirit* of capitalism' and why even in the remainder of his writings on the sociology of religion in so far as they concern the problem area addressed here, he always initially thematised the interrelationship between religious-ethical ideas and 'economic *views*', or 'economic *ethics*'.[6] The assertion occasionally still made amongst Marxist critics (e.g. Kuznecov, 1975, 14 ff.), that Weber had attempted to explain modern capitalism as a whole and particularly its material aspect in the narrower sense (in other words, for example, mineral reserves, machines, means and modes of communication etc.) as direct consequences of specific religious-ethical ideas, is therefore based (and this applies to their own position too) on ill-considered reflection.

In contrast, an adequate interpretation is provided above all by Neusychin who also supplies by far the most detailed description of the Weberian argumentation (1974, 422–44).[7] Neusychin observes that Weber had been seeking to clarify the aspect of the sociology of religion in the grounding and justification of those 'norms', or that 'economic ideology', which had guided capitalist management in its development (1974, 445, 446).[8] Certainly Neusychin still distinguishes between this 'ideal' side of the capitalist mode of production and the material preconditions in the narrower sense (original accumulation, availability of free labour, etc.) on which Marx concentrated in his analysis of the historical process, though by no means strictly limiting his attention to this.[9] However, he does not consider it necessary to derive in turn the capitalist economic ideology from *these* material conditions.[10]

Similarly another objection to Weber's sociology of religion in general or *The Protestant Ethic* in particular, which is obviously held to be particularly crucial by other Marxist critics, cannot be found in Neusychin. This objection is that Weber dispenses with an explanation of the *essence* of religion and indeed is forced to in the face of the limited scientific possibility of his argumentation: 'The question concerning the nature and essence of religion . . . is lost' (Kuznecov, 1975, 20; similarly, e.g., Bel'cer, 1973, 145 and Horn, 1958, 131).[11] This is an entirely appropriate observation, but the question is whether, or under what circumstances, this observation can be used critically against Weber.

The 'question concerning the nature and essence of religion' aims at discovering what religion (*all* religion) really is. For Marxist theorists the question concerning the essence of religion is identical with the question concerning its 'truth', so far as religions first and foremost represent systems of ideas or statements about the world (as a whole) and about the final determination of man. In the view of these theorists, but also according to the conceptions of both the radical non-Marxist critique of religion (such as that by Feuerbach and Nietzsche) and specific non-Marxist sociological conceptions (e.g. those of Durkheim, Freud and major parts of systems theory), the general and definitive answer to this question resides in the statement of social and/or psychological origins or functions of those types of statement systems. In contrast Weber did not believe that even the most thorough analyses in empirical science on the social determination and ideological function of religious interpretations of the world could ever lead to a situation in which their importance would be *exhausted* in any particular social or psychological function. Such an assertion can even less be made *a priori*, i.e. without a most thorough examination of the contents of such systems of interpretation and the grounds of validity claimed by them. Weber's reservations about a systematic social science, or psychological 'reduction', or 'deduction' of religious contents of meaning (cf., for example, *PE*, 277 f.), arose from his conception that an empirical form *sui generis* is documented in religions whose own legitimacy cannot in principle be disputed within the potentialities given to empirical science research.[12] Accordingly Weber thought that the analyses in the sociology of religion could only marginally touch on what is 'valuable' to the theologian (cf. *PE I*, 28; *PE II*, 345).

The Weberian conception cannot of course be interpreted as an attempt to provide in a way *ex nativo* 'scientific existential proof for the primacy of religion' with which Bosse reproaches Weber within the framework of a moderate Marxist argumentation (Bosse, 1970, 99). On the other hand, the same author at another point criticises Weber's *dispensation* with an answer to the question concerning truth (*op. cit.*, 138). The self-defined limits of empirical science research that Weber advocated apply on both sides,[13] and Marxist theorists should set out subjecting their continued claims to a more detailed examination and grounding. Firstly, the widespread deduction of the specific social functions of religion to its 'essence' is convincing neither in its structuralist-functionalist nor, which applies to Marx himself, materialist form.[14] Secondly, causal explanations could only be interpreted as explanations of essence if they were able to state the adequate empirical conditions of not only the emergence, but also the meaningful contents, of each religious system of interpretation, including the relevant grounds of validity claimed. One cannot assert that this task is generally recognised in its full complexity, let alone that it has already been largely accomplished.

Weber's enquiries in the sociology of religion show how much (causal) significance he attached in many contexts to economic, political and socio-cultural conditions and 'interests' in the emergence and development of religious ideas, and indeed this penetrated even the explanation of *specific* meaningful contents and their grounding. This, of course, applies to his explanation of the decline in religious interpretations of the world in the course of the growing 'disenchantment' (*Entzauberung*) and 'rationalis-ation' of the relationships between man and nature and the historical-social world. However, analyses that are oriented in this way, and not only the special theses of *The Protestant Ethic*, are to be counted as the much cited 'Positive Critique of the Materialist Conception of History'.[15] At least this is the case if one links the materialist conception of history to the dual assumption that religious ideas should, 'in the final analysis', always and in every way be explained in terms of economic interests or relations[16] and that this form of explanation at the same time provides a definition of the essence of religion in so far as it specifies its necessary and appropriate conditions.[17]

If this dual assumption is a hallmark only of the 'vulgar materialist' form of Marxism (with which, according to popular opinion, Weber was primarily concerned), then Weber's 'positive' critique, i.e. that based on empirical analysis, cannot be used as evidence of his fundamental anti-Marxism. In this respect it is most remarkable that the two Marxist theorists, Bukharin and Kautsky, who are usually characterised as particularly undialectical and 'mechanistic', seem obviously more able to comply with Weber's differentiated argument than many of their more recent Marxist critics. As Neusychin also observed, this may be due to the fact that Weber's analyses and theses gain greater persuasive power to the extent they are judged from the perspective of empirical science or history, rather than that of a world view.

5.2 Class and status

Weber explicitly emphasised that the explanatory direction he pursued in *The Protestant Ethic* was one-sided (cf., for example, *PE*, 26, 284; *PE II*, 47). However, this is by no means characteristic of his sociology of religion and certainly not of his work as a whole. The cited critique of the particular manifest forms of material 'deduction' or 'reduction' did not stop him from enquiring into the causal importance of economic, or socio-economic, conditions to an extent quite exceptional for a non-Marxist theorist.[18] Class-theoretical assumptions in particular play an enormous role in Weber's entire historical and sociological work – from the essays on agricultural relations in antiquity to the enquiry into the situation of the agricultural workers east of the Elbe, from the analyses of the *Wirtschaftsethik der Weltreligion* to *Economy and Society* – that any special reference is quite unnecessary.[19] It is striking that this very important aspect of the Weberian mode of explanation is hardly noted in the Marxist reception of his work, nor is it discussed in any great detail. We do not go so far as to suggest that the Marxist tradition exercised a 'dominant influence' on Weber in this respect (as did Adler, 1964, III, 35, with reference to Weber's concept of class), but we might well assume its influence to be more complex and indirect (cf. particularly Roth, 1971).[20] At any rate the actual affinity of broad passages in Weber's historical social science analyses with a 'materialist' perspective would seem to urge an argument and critique of these. Here too we can only suspect that the overwhelming, probably politically motivated, desire by many Marxist theorists for clearly defined boundaries may well have reduced their willingness to attend to and discuss this aspect of Weber's work.[21] A more detailed critical treatment of this aspect would certainly have led to *one* result: the popular schematisations, especially the inevitable dichotomy of materialism/idealism applied to determine the class of 'bourgeois ideologues', would have proven to be absolutely useless. Similarly, the specific theses of the type that Weber, in the sociology of religion, had, in the final analysis, replaced an explanation in terms of 'concrete class situations' with an appeal to the 'metaphysical needs of the mind' (Weber) (Bel'cer, 1974, 88),[22] should very rapidly have proven untenable.

Where Marxist authors concern themselves with Weber's conception of class they primarily refer to the conceptual definitions in *Economy and Society* rather than Weber's application of this conceptual set of tools in his empirical, historical essays.[23] There is therefore no discussion of the usefulness of the distinctions proposed by Weber. Rather, the critique by these authors is directed at the very fundamental inadequacies in the theory or philosophy of science (including logic) supposedly apparent in Weber's conceptual definitions.

The first of these objections, presented by Herkommer, has already been mentioned in another context. It is: 'Weberian social science research on the stratification of the population into classes, status groups, strata and other groups does not seem to rise beyond definition while it reduces historical material to a mere example.' The concepts attained in this way would 'no longer be understood as historical ones', but they would take priority, 'in poor abstractness' over 'historically changing social relations' (Herkommer, 1975, 128). To the extent that the fundamental problem of the relationship between conceptual-theoretical, abstraction and historical analysis is addressed here, I refer the reader to the above discussion. This critique by no means affects the status and function of the theoretical concepts of class and structure in Weber's work. Obviously Herkommer interprets the necessarily 'abstract' conceptual clarifications in *Economy and Society*, which nonetheless incorporate a large number of historical aspects, not as the means, but the ends of social science. This is a notion that is utterly incompatible with Weber's own conception and research practice. But if his objection is directed at Weber's endeavours for definition as such, it is to be observed that, firstly, the materialist theoretical tradition by all means possesses and requires a conceptual apparatus of similar, if not higher, abstraction. Secondly, some conceptual clarification and precision is most desirable precisely within the range of materialist class theory. Thirdly, the terminology used in class theory in particular has led quite a number of Marxist authors to attach over much schematic importance to 'historical material' and to use it for the purpose of mere exemplification. This tendency seems to have contributed greatly to the underdeveloped state of concepts in class theory.

This state of affairs, then, should provide some impetus to subject Weber's proposals to closer scrutiny.

A far more crucial objection, which is much more closely related to the distinctiveness of the Marxist concept of class, is that Weber's definition of 'class' and 'class situation' restricts itself to the sphere of distribution while disregarding the sphere of production. It is true in fact that Weber defined class situations in terms of their typical probability for '(1) procuring goods, (2) gaining a position in life and (3) finding inner satisfactions'. The most important distinction – that between the *property* class' and *commercial* class' – relates in the first case to 'property differences' as such, while in the second case, it is 'the marketability of goods and services' that 'primarily determines' class situations (*ES*, 302 – Weber's emphases). In a broader sense, according to Weber, it can be said for both classes that the 'class situation . . . is ultimately market situation' (*ES*, 928). This in turn does not imply that the class situation is in every respect and in a like manner *determined* by the market (*RS I*, 1974). Evidently Weber is consistent in his perspective when he terms the class conflict between acquisition classes as the 'price struggle' (*Preiskampf*) (*WL*, 528; cf. *MSS*, 36) or the 'price struggle' *or* 'competitive struggle' respectively (*ES*, 927). However, Weber clearly had no wish for this definition to be taken as being strictly distinct from the sphere of production, as can be seen by his observation that: 'Classes are stratified according to their relations to the production and the acquisition of goods' (*ES*, 937).

Braunreuther labels Weber's form and level of definition as 'economistic' and associates it with the 'idealistic' perspective governing *Economy and Society* as a whole (1964, 102 f.).[24] Nor does he elaborate on the objection beyond establishing that it is the sphere of production that is the 'primary social determinant'. This is not the place to engage in the drawn out and unresolved internal Marxist debate on the relationship between the spheres of production and distribution. But I take the liberty to speculate that the two spheres – particularly within the framework of the capitalist mode of production – are so closely interrelated that the dispute about the primacy of one or the other is purely scholastic in nature.[25] The question alone of interest here is (a) whether Weber's procedure leads to essentially different outcomes (i.e. conceptual definitions) from the approach based on the sphere of production and (b) what could be said in support of this procedure. In this case the restriction to the two chief classes of the capitalist social formation is necessary.

It seems to me that the first part of this question has to be answered essentially in the negative. A glance at the pertinent definitions in Marx and Engels, for example, should suffice as evidence. Throughout the capitalist class is primarily defined in terms of the ownership of capital or the means of production, and the possibility based upon it to buy and exploit labour in the form of 'free wage labour' in the market place (cf., e.g., Marx, *Das Kapital*, Vol. 3, 750; Engels, *MEW*, German edition, Vol. 21, 462). Engels' definition of the 'proletariat' that correlates with this reads: 'By proletariat we understand the class of modern wage labourers who, since they do not own any means of production, are forced to sell their labour power in order to live' (*ibid.*). These definitions thus refer essentially to the ownership of capital/means of production, or 'mere labour power' respectively, and the interlinked possibility/compulsion to buy or sell.

As a matter of fact, Weber's definitions, more decisively than those of Marx and Engels, focus on showing how the different classes or class situations appear in social reality, not least in their latent or overt conflicting nature (i.e. as class *conflict*). Accordingly for him the most important question (though by no means the only one) is how class situations and possibilities of action defined by them, can be or are experienced by the members of classes. This could perhaps also give rise to the interpretation that Weber's definitions are even more definitely linked to the perspective of empirical social science research than the traditional Marxist concepts. If this is an accurate observation it is logically possible that even fundamental assumptions enter into class-*theoretical* analyses on the processes operating in the sphere of production; for example, the assumption that the classes of capitalist society and their conflicts are constantly reproduced through the effect of the 'law of value'.[26] It would be worth considering though how far such assumptions relate to laws that are built into the capitalist processes of production (and exchange), and determine them to a large extent in certain circumstances without in turn being a product of historical-social activity.[27] In this respect Weber's reservations about the sphere of production (in the Marxist sense) may possibly be due to his binding the definitional efforts in *Economy and Society* to the social dimension in the narrower sense.[28] We may criticise this, but not his alleged 'subjectivism' or 'idealism'. But in that case we would have to consider Weber's explicit motives for such distinctions, as outlined in the last chapter in more detail.

In this context the final objection aims at the fact that Weber operates with a fundamental distinction of classes, on the one hand, and status groups, on the other, thereby assigning primarily non-economic characteristics and causes to vertical social status differentiation. Of course Marx too occasionally referred to the relative autonomy of status differentials, but in his view this differentiation arises from economic causes 'in the final analysis' and, besides totally submerges in the class structure in capitalist conditions.[29] That Weber in contrast created a separate category for the 'status group' may similarly be linked to his decided social science orientation. The systematic tendency to attach separate importance to genuine social or socio-cultural factors certainly arises from this orientation. Moreover it is an empirical question whether the status structure, i.e. the structure according to 'life-style', 'hereditary or occupational prestige', 'formal education' (ES, 305), and possibly also 'monopolistic approbation of economic opportunities' (RS I, 274; ES, 306), can in all cases be reduced to differentiation by primarily economically determined (i.e. class) factors. This question will not, of course, be discussed in the present context.[30] But the question that is worth asking is what we could hold against a systematic consideration of the possibility that there are heterogeneous sources of social structure. The available empirical evidence seems to support this possibility. The cohesion and closedness of a theory (in this case, the materialist class theory) is not of 'value in itself'. It does not justify sacrificing an eye for a possible and perhaps considerable advance in knowledge, especially if this advance in knowledge has crucial implications for political practice (for example, with regard to political practice in tendentially *class*less societies).

One last note to conclude these brief considerations. Weber's conceptual-theoretical and empirical analyses should be seen as more worthy of discussion the more Marxists distance themselves from any hypostatising or even metaphysical interpretation, particularly in relation to the class situation and class consciousness of the workers (cf. the discussion on Lukács above). There are many signs that something like this is happening.[31] The general reason for this process could reside in the differentiated nature of these definitions and analyses and the degree to which they have substance in reality. Moreover the sobriety with which Weber analysed the categories with a particularly strong political nuance, 'class interest', and 'class action' (cf., e.g., ES, 928 and 848 ff.), would seem to have gained some persuasive power by now.

5.3 The city

Weber's essay on the city holds a special position in the history of the Marxist reception of his work in so far as it is the only part that has attracted perhaps greater and earlier attention and appreciation amongst Marxists, rather than non-Marxists. In the Soviet

Union, Neusychin[32] and Stoklickaja-Tereškovič (1925) published extensive review articles soon after the Russian translation (1923, edited by Kareev, a non-Marxist social scientist from Petersburg) had appeared. Moreover briefer, and consistently positive, references can be found in, e.g. Wittfogel (1924), Kautsky (1927, 303 f.) and Kapeljuš (1931, 274 ff.). This reception has not been continued and developed further in more recent times though. However, apart from the references in Anderson (1978, 1979) there are several comments on the 'admirable developments on the city in *Economy and Society*' in a more recent Marxist work (Vincent, 1973, 75; cf. the interpretations on 150 ff.).

It is easy to understand why particularly the essay on the city aroused such strong and positive interest among Marxist researchers and, at the same time, why the decline in this interest has had some very negative effects. *The City* is an historical-sociological analysis that (a) belongs to the range of problems also investigated in *The Protestant Ethic* (the conditions of emergence of 'modern capitalism' as well as the 'modern State' (Roth, in *ES*, ECIII), but at the same time it also (b) systematically tackles those factors and dimensions of reality (economic and political interests, class situations and class conflict) whose elimination in *The Protestant Ethic* to a large extent facilitated the standard schematising critique of Weber.

Thus Stoklickaja-Tereškovič notes that the 'presuppositions of the philosophy of history' held by Weber, who was 'by no means a representative of the materialist conception of history' (1925, 116), had not prevented him from emphasising the crucial role of economic factors throughout the essay (especially in the section on the Plebeian city) and accordingly furnishing his ideal-types with 'contents of a predominantly economic form' (*ibid.*, 117). But even the central thesis of the sociology of religion in the essay on the city (as an element of a complex, multi-factorial, historical-sociological analysis) does not seem unacceptable to any of the Marxist critics. The fact that Weber attributed 'great significance' to the Christian community as 'a confessional association of individual believers, not a ritual association of kinship groups' particularly in the foundation of the association of the medieval city (on the basis of a *conjuratio* of individuals), according to Kapeljuš, merely confirms the Marxist characterisation of Christianity as a 'cult of the abstract human being' (1931, 274).

In the opinion of Neusychin and Stoklickaja-Tereškovič (the latter also originally a historian), the main strength of Weber's essay is rooted in his reluctance to engage in any hasty construction of concepts and theory or the deduction of social historical conditions and processes, whether of idealist, materialist or any

95

other origin. Rather, these authors think that it is the combination of a highly differentiated, multi-dimensional and highly documented (and therefore in fact at times hardly surveyable) historical enquiry, endeavouring conceptual clarification and theoretical abstraction at the level of historical-sociological typologies, that establishes the persuasive power and exemplary significance of the essay. Both authors attach their very detailed and entirely affirmative[33] description of the substance of Weber's analyses to some comprehensive considerations on his method.[34] Regarding their evaluation of Weber's sociological achievement in the narrower sense there are, of course, marked differences between Weber's and the authors' own conception of science.

In Weber's ideal-typical construction of the economic policy of the medieval city Stoklickaja-Tereškovič sees a 'persistent scientific property' and an exemplary use of the 'organising role of sociological enquiry' for historical research (1925, 113). Thus, she holds that 'this marks one of the cardinal methods of making the complexity of historical events manageable', even though large parts of the essay still lack a corresponding sociological thoroughness. 'The ordering function of the ideal-type cannot achieve its full impact and many historical moments from the life of the city remain isolated links which are not integrated into a higher synthesis.' (*Ibid.*, 118.)[35]

In comparison, Neusychin, who even more firmly emphasises the primacy of historical research (and the instrumental function of sociological abstraction), highlights the appropriateness of Weber's way of dealing with conceptual-theoretical abstractions in this essay and favourably contrasts this practice with many sociologists' far-reaching (and above all rash) ambitions for generalisation. In this context he also makes several critical remarks (as again in the essay of 1927)[36] on the introductory 'theoretical' parts of *Economy and Society* (*op. cit.*, 496).[37] He observes that the method actually practised by Weber from the perspective of historical research also constituted an essential prerequisite for an appropriate 'concrete' handling of materialist 'monism', i.e. the materialist theory of history as a dialectical development of productive forces, relations of production and 'superstructure'. Neusychin continues that when Weber referred to the role of economic, military-political, social, legal and even religious processes in the development of the city, he was not offering a 'theory of the reciprocal action of factors', which was unsatisfactory at this stage of research. Rather, Weber had presented a 'history of the reciprocal action of complex phenomena, that reciprocally penetrate each other, combine with one another, oppose each other and conflict with each other' (*ibid.*, 499).

Neusychin does not consider this 'pluralism' eclectic and incapable of explanation, but necessary, making the 'mechanism of that complex reciprocal action' concrete by means of justifiable simplifications and thus preparing the ground for a 'sociological construction'. He believes that Weber's essay on the city was not only a 'valuable historical enquiry', but was of 'enormous value' as a sociological study, precisely because it did not lay down the universal laws of all events, but instead sought to make 'the first step on the path towards a sociological illumination of historical phenomena' (*ibid.*, 500).

Wittfogel gives Weber credit for at least directing the attention of science to the city (or, in any case, to his focus on this research object)[38]. In fact, this author is much more heavily inspired by Weber's work in his own analyses than his numerous explicit references (in agreement and critique) lead us to suspect.[39] Wittfogel sees the particular superiority of Weber's enquiry (particularly in Kautsky's explanations) in the great emphasis placed on the violent military character of the seizure of power introduced by the *conjurationes* (*ibid.*, 75 ff.). Evidently Wittfogel, who at the time supported a very uncompromising theoretical and politically aggressive materialism, sees in this essay an (unintended) approximation to the opinion that the actual process of history has to be explained as the outcome of real, albeit violent (in Wittfogel's view), class struggles. In complete contrast to the opinions held by Neusychin and Stoklickaja-Tereškovič, in principle he certainly considered the 'method' used in the essay on the city entirely unacceptable. While the above Marxist historians are particularly positive in their reception of Weber's guarded approach to theoretical constructions, Wittfogel thinks that Weber had ultimately achieved no more than a 'phenomenal nihilistic chaos' (*ibid.*, 99) because he had refused any guidance by the materialist 'doctrine of the basic law of development that governs all history' (*ibid.*, 28).[40] Wittfogel in turn designed a schema that was to permit the conceptual and theoretical apprehension of the conditions and stages of development of a city bourgeoisie within the context of universal history (*ibid.*, 111). But even from the perspective of Marxist researchers, such as comments by Neusychin and Stoklickaja-Tereškovič seem to suggest, the schema certainly could not represent a scientifically fruitful application of this 'doctrine'.

It is difficult to explain why this early Marxist critical discussion of Weber's essay on the city, which had to start with been greeted with so much interest and far-reaching agreement, has not been resumed and developed until this day.[41] It cannot be on account of the fact that Weber's enquiries have in the meanwhile had a significant impact on, or even played a dominant role in, the research of primarily non-Marxist historical (particularly medievalist) social science on the city. There is no doubt that this essay by Weber is always present in this particular body of literature. The first section of the essay on conceptual explanation has been included in a new collection of contributions made on the subject matter by non-Marxist researchers.[42] However, this does not imply, as one Marxist author believes (Mägdefrau, 1977, 399), that this 'collection of innovative essays', or even the entire non-Marxist research in the field, is characterised by its 'heavy reference to Max Weber's typology on the city'. In fact, this is quite out of the question. The allegation that, for example, Sombart's judgement[43] inspired a remarkable reception of *The City* within the domain of non-Marxist sociology is even less applicable.[44] Accordingly, we cannot even attach an anti-Marxist label to Weber's essay in terms of its 'objective' function (Mägdefrau, *op. cit.*, 381),[45] let alone in the absence of any substantive argumentation in this direction. Rather, all the signs seem to confirm that a resumption of the substantive and methodological discussion contained in *The City* (and this implies, at the same time, the method of historical sociological research in fact practised by Weber in general) would show these categorisations to be utterly useless.

5.4 Problems of culture (science and art)

A broad section of the Marxist critique considers Max Weber as *the* theorist of the cultural superstructure. This firmly entrenched perception of Weber, which is essentially based on misunderstandings and misinterpretations of *The Protestant Ethic*, has led to scant acknowledgment of not only the materialist aspect of his scientific essays, as noted, but also his contribution to the study of so-called superstructural phenomena (at least those in the non-religious sphere). This may be consistent with the assumption that Weber approached this level of social reality in a systematically inverted way, in that he allegedly saw ideal factors to determine the historical-social course of events 'in the last instance'. The present work has repeatedly shown this *a priori* schema of interpretation to be unproductive, and also how it effectively inhibits the process of knowledge. This is strikingly shown when Marxist authors detach themselves from this schema and engage in a substantive discussion of Weber's cultural-sociological analyses. The insight that these analyses (including *The Protestant Ethic* measured by its own limited claims) cannot be seen as an expression of superstructure-idealism by no means suggests in turn that they do not offer some starting points for a differentiated materialist critique. Undoubtedly Weber's enquiries into the genesis of society and the impact of cultural 'meaningful relationships', with all due consideration for material factors, distinguish themselves, and not by sheer accident, from the comparable analyses of a decidedly materialist perspective.

The most important distinguishing characteristic seems to be that Weber assumed an empirical scientist should, in principle, have to concede to these historical worlds of meaning an autonomous 'determination' and legitimacy, i.e. one that cannot be indefinitely reduced to other forms of experience and interpretation. I have already referred above to this fundamental Weberian assumption in relation to his work on the sociology of religion. But Weber logically thought that this also applied to the remaining major cultural worlds of meaning. However, this neither implies that Weber was unable to analyse serious ruptures and contradictions within and between these different cultural worlds of meaning,[46] nor that he had thus deprived himself of the chance to pursue a critique of ideology characteristic of the Marxist tradition. On the contrary, a much earlier hypothesis proposed that the critique of ideology could indeed increase its rigour if it confronted the claimed 'significance' (one that was not seen to be illegitimate at the outset) of historical systems of meaning and value with their real social contexts of emergence and realisation.

The second specific difference of Weber's cultural sociological research is linked to this fundamental perspective. Evidently Weber predominantly worked on the assumption that special importance should be attached to the (internal) meaningful evidence and consistency of the systems of interpretation and value in an enquiry into specific historical-social processes. Thus he did not advocate a quasi-metaphysical notion of ideas as the subjects of history. Nor did he claim a mysterious 'inner dynamic' of meaningful relationships for the purposes of explanation. Rather, the conception underlying the stated leading assumption is that:

(a) all the more complex overlapping and persisting forms of social action are dependent on the organisational and legitimational achievement of developed patterns of interpretation and values; and that

(b) the tendency towards evidence, systematisation and consistency, which represents a universal characteristic of culturally meaningful relationships, is directly interrelated with this social achievement of organisation and legitimation.[47]

All the research-oriented fundamental assumptions of the Weberian sociology of culture originate in the same 'basic outlook' on social action that was discussed earlier. The fundamental assumption of rationality dealt with explains *firstly*, why in 'interpretative sociology' cultural systems of interpretation and value actually constitute the focus of research interest, and *secondly*, why they are thematised essentially according to their immanent rationality and social achievement of rationalisation.

Even the small number of detailed Marxist contributions on Weber's work on cultural sociology do not deal with this fundamental problem. The question of rationality and rationalisation is certainly acknowledged and discussed as a leading question in these enquiries, but its implications and productiveness are underestimated. The fact that Weber, in his analyses on occidental science and art, concentrates on a very specific form of rationality – namely, rationality in a formal and technical sense – is not explained by the special nature of a specific historical development (and perhaps a specific research interest in this development), but by the logical limitations of Weber's perspective.[48]

This limitation should seem far less crucial with respect to the object of science rather than art, for example. As a matter of fact Marxist authors do not criticise Weber's observation that modern science belongs to the sphere of formal and instrumental rationality or that it represents the highest and most effective expression of this form of rationality.[49] This implies that Marxists simultaneously accept that the process of rationalisation encompassing all spheres of social life, *so far as* it is bound up with the emergence and application of modern science, generally possesses this formal and instrumental character.[50]

At this point Marxist theorists are certainly faced with the serious question of whether the absolutely inevitable process of science regulating and governing social practice remains confined to the limits of instrumental rationality in socialist conditions as well, or whether science and the regulating and governing process of science take on an entirely different (i.e. material) character of rationality within socialism. The Weberian conceptions are seen to result in the problem that they do not permit us to make any qualitative distinctions in this respect. However, these conceptions do lead to the assumption, which is completely opposed to that recently held by Weber's successors (e.g. Aron, Habermas and Schluchter), that the largely identical process of science and technology regulating and governing life would entail a progressive structural convergence between socialist and non-socialist social systems (Kvesko, 1974, 13 f.).

Here resides a *logical* difficulty for Marxist theory since it starts out with the dual basic assumption that the sphere of material production has determinative significance on the whole of social life and that scientific or scientific-technological knowledge would, to an increasing extent (and *a fortiori* in socialism), have to become the 'primary force of production'. This basic assumption coupled with the absolutely fundamental and programmatic establishment of materialist theory on scientific rationality make it impossible to put forward convincing arguments against the conclusion drawn by 'convergence theorists'. The fact that the politics of the socialist states orient themselves to a material value system of a political-ideological nature, while being totally independent from perspectives of scientific (economic or techni-cal) rationality on central issues and frequently in diametrical opposition to them, thus working against the tendency towards convergence, can neither be adequately comprehended and explained nor justified on the basis of these theoretical presuppo-sitions. The degree of independence or dominance of the political-ideological sphere seen to be politically necessary and exercised therefore finds no correspondence at the level of scientific discussion on the structure and consequences of the process of rationalisation.[51]

The overall agreement with Weber's formal-rational apprehen-sion of science, as determined by his historical-social science analyses, accordingly generates fundamental problems for Marxist theorists because of its implications on political and scientific policy. The final chapter will discuss the extent to which a political-ideological critique of this concept of science, or its 'realisation' and application by Weber (see also Kozyr-Kowalski, 1964), appears convincing in approaching these problems.

In any case it seems *a priori* plausible that these difficulties could have been overcome by a critique of Weber's formal and instrumental – and thus far the seemingly politically neutral – notion of rationality. This type of critique is, however, a central element of those contributions that critically discuss Weber's analyses on art. Here we are essentially talking about an essay by A. Lunačarskij (the People's Commissary for Education after the October Revolution), which first appeared in 1925, and about a more recent work by P. Gajdenko (1975).[52] Both essays primarily deal with Weber's paper on the sociology of music, but Gajdenko in particular also engages in more general considerations on the sociology of art.

Lunačarskij in his general appraisal classifies the paper on music as one of those 'half-products' supplied by Max Weber throughout his work. But even this 'half-product' was welcomed by the

'Marxist enterprise' and constituted a 'very valuable element' for the socialist construction (1962, 35). Lunačarskij sees the overall cause of Weber's limited potential in Weber's (conscious) dispensation of a 'unified dominant standpoint, a unified method' (*ibid.*, 34). But he traces the specific limitations of the enquiry into music back to the determinative leading idea of 'rationalisation'. In Lunačarskij's opinion this leading idea had crucially narrowed Weber's research perspective, particularly in three respects.

Its first consequences was that Weber had almost totally 'ignored' the 'physical substratum' and the 'physiological aspect' of music (*ibid.*, 37). This dual natural basis of all music could be detected both in 'primitive music', which is a purely 'instinctive thing',[53] and in that evidently all 'rationalisation of music' generally has to 'move within a range of sounds which physiologically please us' (*ibid.*, 37 f.).[54] According to Lunačarskij it is the neglect of the 'natural substratum' that expresses itself in Weber's 'uncritical rationalisation of primitive social thought' in general (*ibid.*, 43).

Lunačarskij's second criticism is intimately linked with this first negative effect of the Weberian perspective on rationality. He believes that Weber systematically neglected the 'emotional aspect' of music whose fundamental importance could, in turn, be clearly deduced from the 'most primitive song of the savage' (*ibid.*, 39 f.). The third relevant shortcoming of Weber's enquiry, according to Lunačarskij, is that Weber – despite a promising start – had not sufficiently clarified 'to what extent the rationalisation of music reflects specific social conditions' (*ibid.*, 41). Lunačarskij thinks that Weber had evidently apprehended the real historical-social conditions as factors that interfered with a process running its course in accordance with rational psychological laws; in other words, that Weber did not interpret the rationality of the process as a genuine social fact.

It is not possible to subject Lunačarskij's critique to detailed examination here. But it is possible and necessary to add some considerations of a more general nature.

To start with the last point, a serious imbalance does exist in Weber's work concerning, on the one hand, the extent and intensity of his treatment of the immanent rationality of musical development and, on the other, the sociological aspect of the process. There is no doubt that one would like to see Weber's brief references to extra-musical causal relationships much more elaborated. However, the fundamental question arising from the introductory considerations of this section is whether processes of rationalisation within specific cultural spheres can lay claim to sociological interest only to the extent that they can be directly and consistently explained as a function of external social factors (for example, the need for economic and political authority).

To begin with a conception of this kind does not adequately consider[55] that, as a rule, cultural (here, artistic) production also has its own social basis, which is more or less differentiated from the total societal context, and that this social subsystem may contain a specific dynamic that is reflected at the level of cultural production as a process of progressive rationalisation. Social differentiation and specialisation of this kind (with this consequence) is evidently a special characteristic of the development of occidental art (particularly since the Middle Ages).

But beyond that Lunačarskij's critique fails to appreciate that a process of rationalisation in any one sphere of culture, if only specific external and internal marginal conditions and general incentives are given, can essentially derive its dynamic and purpose from the fact that the immanent possibilities of a specific cultural creation or invention (for example, specific systems of sound and harmony) are progressively developed and exhausted. Developments in the domain of science in particular can engender the growth of additional crucial impulses and viewpoints in such a process in the sphere of art (but also religion). Weber in fact works with such an assumption in relation to the history of the rationalisation of European arts, especially music and paintings). This is something that is not emphasised by Lunačarskij, but it is indeed rightly stressed by Gajdenko.

The second major point of Lunačarskij's critique argues that Weber's perspective of rationalisation does not permit him to see the 'emotional aspect' of music. As a matter of fact it is true that Weber's paper almost exclusively deals with the problems of musical production (composition and performance) and here again specifically with the 'technical' prerequisites and their development. This does not imply, however, that logically only this intellectual and technical side can be thematised from the perspective of rationalisation and that the affective conditions of production as well as – above all – the reception of works of art should necessarily be excluded from the enquiry. The observation that there could be processes of rationalisation at the emotional level of artistic production and reception may seem absurd at first. However, it is entirely acceptable even within the context of Weber's broader understanding of rationality. It is not only conceivable, but an empirical fact, that the development of a genre or form of art is in a significant respect presented as a process of clarification, differentiation and refinement (sublimation) of the emotional 'meanings' expressed and perceived in artistic creations. But, from Weber's point of view, such a process should be described with the category of 'rationalisation' because this process progressively enhances the 'communicability' of meaningful contents (of an affective type in this context).

This idea cannot be elaborated further at this stage, but I refer the reader to what has been said elsewhere on the interrelationship between rationality and communicability. It was noted then that rationality interpreted in terms of communicability is an indisputable social fact and that it would therefore be inappropriate to proceed from a logical distinction between rationality and sociability, and to then seek or construct possible (more or less accidental) linkages.

At any rate it is established that there are no arguments of this kind in Weber's paper on music nor in his other comments on the sociology of art. On the contrary, Weber concentrated so exclusively on the issue of artistic 'techniques' and their rationalisation that these latter comments are more likely to refer to an actual shortcoming in Weber's work than, for example, to Lunačarskij's critique. To the extent that it relates to Weber's enquiry into music, Lunačarskij's critique is both understandable and appropriate. On this basis it is impossible to draw any general conclusions with respect to research in cultural sociology oriented to the problems of rationality and rationalisation. The references provided should make it clear that to do justice to this discussion one would need much more far-reaching and fundamental analyses, in which the treatment of the problem of rationality within the framework of Marxist theory on superstructure and ideology would have to be included.[56]

Lunačarskij's third point of criticism, namely the elimination of the 'physical', or 'physiological' substratum in Weber's enquiry, is also related to the last considerations. Even if there were a substratum of the type suggested by Lunačarskij – which is still a controversial issue among specialists today – it would as such still not constitute a social fact. Besides, Lunačarskij's notion that 'primitive' and 'primeval' music represents this physical basis 'in its pure state' prior to all cultural superstructuring and that all 'aesthetic rationalisation' not only starts out from this natural basis, but is also determined in its logical possibilities and limits is, to say the very least, most speculative. It cannot be asserted that it is constitutive and essential for a 'materialist' theory of music (and art in general) to appeal to a primary nature in this way. Rather, what Marx observed concerning the 'conflict between man and nature' in general would have to apply to artistic 'work' too: that the 'raw material' here as ever has to be presented as superstructure and mediated through human and, more specifically, social activity. With reference to musical production this means that its historical origin can be located only where the level of the instinctive generation of sounds, or sequences of sounds, is crossed and an (elementary) form of symbolic communication has been reached. This, however, is undoubtedly the case with the 'most primitive song of the savage' to which Lunačarskij refers.

What is particularly questionable though is that Lunačarskij evidently wants to ascribe to that 'physical substratum' a normative quality in the sense that any 'aesthetic rationalisation' is set a definitive limit beyond which music (and art in general) would have to become unnatural. This is obviously the starting point of all efforts to derive a very specific 'realism' as *ideal* art form from a 'materialist' treatment of art and to make it binding for the production of art. According to this conception the detachment of 'aesthetic rationalisation' from the reference to nature necessarily leads to a 'progressist', 'rationalistic', 'technocratic' and 'formalistic' aberration of artistic creation characteristic of the latest developments in bourgeois art (and its aesthetics). In the 'Preamble' to her essay Gajdenko observes that it is precisely these developments in Weber's rationalistic conception of art (more recently adopted and developed by Adorno in particular) that have undergone decisive grounding and justification (Gajdenko, 1975, 115).[57]

In the face of this argumentation it is necessary to establish that the effort to derive normative orientations from an ahistorical and pre-societal nature utterly contradicts the 'founding ideas' of historical materialism. Each abstract dichotomy of ('primitive') nature and society, or rationality ('culture'), and above all each attempt to declare nature the ultimate norm-orienting authority in cultural issues, simply cannot be compatible with the principle of Marxist thinking that concrete nature too has always been mediated by history and society. The endeavours to counter the rationalism, formalism and subjectivism of modern art and aesthetics with the notion of 'natural', and therefore obligatory, art are by no means based on any genuine Marxist presuppositions, but rather on, for example, actual or supposed political requirements.[58] Besides, historical knowledge of such endeavours clearly shows that they, however grounded, did not in any case exactly encourage the development of art.

It does not seem convincing within the framework of a sociological discussion to confront Weber's perspective of rationality with some factors of primary nature. On the same basis it is very questionable whether this perspective is not utterly inadequate for research into the substantive aspect of the 'intellectual ideal contents' of art (Gajdenko, 1975, 122); in other words, it is worth asking whether Weber's perspective should not be labelled 'formalistic' at least in this sense. This question forms Gajdenko's focus in her critical treatment of Weber.

Gajdenko, prior to her critique of the narrowness of Weber's research perspective, notes that it is precisely this research perspective that facilitated Weber's illumination of a very important aspect of the European history of art. Because the leading concept of 'value relevance' was determined by his interest in the problem of rationalisation,[59] Weber had recognised the interplay between art and science in its fundamental significance and had especially appreciated that the visual artists of that epoch 'were the first experimental scientists who resolved the technical problems of their century' (Gajdenko, 1975, 121). Gajdenko thinks (perhaps with some exaggeration) that Weber had in fact been the initiator in drawing attention to this problem.

The shortcomings of Weber's sociology of art, according to Gajdenko, represent the obverse to this constructive perspective: since Weber's interest focussed on the formal-rational and technical aspect of the development of art, and therefore on the interrelationship between science and art, he ignored the wider historical context. The 'intellectual, ideal aspect' of art and its development could become apparent only if the development of science and art was related to the 'essential changes' in 'social, religious and intellectual life' as a whole (*ibid.*, 122).

It is difficult to dispute the observation that Weber's paper on music is characterised by such one-sided treatment. Moreover, one cannot explain this adequately by saying that one is faced with special difficulties when seeking to interpret (i.e. identify and evaluate the embodied historical-social meaningful relationships) the contents of that most abstract form of art, music. Weber's brief references to the visual arts (to which Gajdenko primarily refers) are similarly characterised by a one-sided perspective. But the question is whether we can conclude that Weber's considerations on the sociology of art are logically limited, merely on the basis of his actual neglect of the 'meaningful aspect' (Gajdenko).

Gajdenko asserts that Weberian sociology is thus logically limited and explains this in terms of its linkage with the principle of ethical neutrality. But it is by no means true that the principle of ethical neutrality prevents research into the 'intellectual, ideal contents' of art. It is absolutely feasible to explore this meaningful aspect from the specific perspective of rationality and rationalisation on the foundations of the thesis of ethical neutrality, as the considerations of Lunačarskij's critique have revealed. Neither the formal and technical character of scientific rationality, nor the thesis of ethical neutrality derived from it, imply that extra-scientific meaningful contents and object-specific forms of rationality and rationalisation cannot be thematised on the *side of the object*. The actual limit to social science research, according to Weber, is set where the meaningful contents of art and its distinctive rationality are not merely analysed, but are also subjected to substantive *evaluation*. A particular instance of this is that in the framework of science it is possible to speak of 'progress' in the arts only in as much as the concern is with the processes of progressive formal rationalisation, or developments, on the level of the artistic means or techniques of production. Even the incorporation of more extensive social and cultural processes of change into the analysis of the sociology of art (demanded by Gajdenko) would not fundamentally extend the potential of social science research in this respect. The enquiries of the critique of ideology exploring the 'intellectual, ideal' aspect of art from the perspective of its emergence and function in socio-economic and political conflicts of interest also can only ever lead to *hypothetical* substantive evaluations, and accordingly to *hypothetical* state-ments on progress in art. Even in this case value orientations ultimately come into play that can no longer be grounded by empirical method alone, as previously discussed (Chapter 3, Section 2).

It is a question of fundamental significance whether it could and ought to be the task of (social) science to give decisive and exhaustive information on the meaning and (relative) value of works of art and their 'ideal contents'. This would involve both considering the meaningful contents attached to art exclusively from the perspective of scientific rationality, however defined, *and* judging it purely by the standard of such rationality. Art would thus represent an incipient form or a fundamentally inferior substitute of science, although useful for specific purposes. It would have to portray, on the level of 'sensory awareness' and via the medium of the 'beautiful illusion', what science comprehends in 'essence' through strict logic. This viewpoint, advocated by Hegel in its classical form, evidently found particular favour among Marxist theorists of art and was adopted by them.[60] However, this conception is dubious not only because of its inherent substitution of the Hegelian concept of science (as absolutist-idealistic philosophy) with the idea of a radical empirical social science, but its expressed claim of dominance, or even monopoly, of scientific rationality that goes far beyond Weber's assumption of rationality that determines his analyses in the sociology of art.

There is no doubt that the above critics of Weber do not themselves advocate this claim of dominance, at least not explicitly. But neither do they make it clear what form a logical alternative to Weber's solution of this fundamental problem in the sociology of art in particular and the sociology of culture in general could take.[61] Weber's solution is characterised by a basic ambivalence. On the one hand, it is based on the assumption that the different cultural systems of interpretation and value can claim a distinctive 'legitimacy' in the face of science. However, on the other hand, his solution is guided by an interest in clarifying the rationality content of these heterogeneous systems of interpretation and value, in general, and their content of formal or technical (i.e. scientific) rationality, in particular. This ambivalence does not harbour any contradiction. Rather, it arises from the need to carry the potential of scientific research into cultural phenomena, and therefore simultaneously to clarify the extent of scientific 'disenchantment', to the furthest possible degree without neglecting the 'distinctive logic of distinctive objects'.

5.5 Rationality, authority, bureaucracy

It is not particularly controversial among interpreters and critics of Weber that the problem of 'rationality and rationalisation' (Weber) dominates the whole of his historical-sociological and conceptual-theoretical work. Not only is this clearly reflected throughout his work,[62] but Weber himself explicitly admitted that this was the main reference point. Weber's far-reaching and highly differentiated scientific research perspective is derived from his initial, entirely concrete, historical and everyday experience of a specific, 'modern occidental', process of rationalisation. This interrelationship between a pronounced extra-scientific concern and a fundamental scientific enquiry, then, constitutes a classical example of what Weber (with Rickert) called 'value relevance', and what is today popularly known as a 'knowledge-directing interest'.

From this perspective, it is both obvious and legitimate for Marxist interpreters of Weber to be particularly concerned with the manifest or even concealed basis of this knowledge-directing interest. Similarly, it is admissible to work on the hypothesis that his interest is, in the 'final analysis', based on class and therefore, essentially, domination. This hypothesis evidently becomes even more plausible if it is possible to attribute an explicit, and above all apparently 'positive', linkage between the conceptions of rationality and domination.

Marxist authors who critically examine Weber's problem of rationality predominantly work on the basis of this hypothesis. Accordingly, the thematic relationship between rationality and domination in Weber's work is approached from two angles.

Firstly, they are concerned with this relationship in terms of logic, by looking at those class or domination interests that express themselves in 'rationality'. Secondly, they concentrate on Weber's treatment of the problem of domination, in general, and bureaucracy, in particular, by mounting a critique of ideology within this framework of reference.

Marcuse (1972a) presented the most fundamental, and obviously most influential, critique of Weber's conception of rationality.[63] His central thesis is that Weber's conception of rationality and rationalisation offers an apparently value-neutral framework of reference for social science research and precisely because of this is of great ideological use to particular interests of domination. These ideological contents are concretely expressed in the guiding thread of the rationality question in Weber's analysis of 'modern occidental capitalism'. Since this analysis operates with the apparently value-neutral category of rationality, and beyond that creates the semblance of necessity, if not even 'reason', by means of this category, it 'objectively' serves the defences of domination by a specific class, namely the bourgeoisie. According to Marcuse, it is difficult to see through this interrelationship because the meaning of domination is, as it were, 'built into' Weber's category of rationality. He continues that Weber's rationality is an 'instrumental', or 'technical' and 'formal' reason, but that it could *per definitionem* function exclusively as an instrument of domination and control over both natural and social processes. This leads Marcuse to suspect that the 'concept of technical reason' is inherently ideological.

> Not only the application of technology but technology itself is domination (of nature and men) – methodological, scientific, calculated, calculating control. Specific purposes and interests of domination are not foisted upon technology 'subsequently' and from the outside; they enter the very construction of the technical apparatus. (*ibid.*, 223 f.)

'What a society and its ruling interests intend to do with men and things' is already installed in the technology as an 'historical-social project' (*ibid.*, 224).[64] The ideological-legitimatory function of technical reason is defined by Marcuse in more detail elsewhere: 'Today, domination perpetuates and extends itself not only through technology but *as* technology, and the latter provides the great legitimation of the expanding political power, which absorbs all spheres of culture' (1972b, 130).

The discussion on this type of fundamental critique of Weber's conception of rationality has to clarify two questions in particular. The first one relates to the assertion that Weber had understood and had to understand 'rationality' as technical, instrumental or formal rationality in the final analysis. The second question is closely linked with the first, but is primarily of an empirical nature. This is whether Weber provided an appraisal of the significance of technical and formal rationality for the development of modern capitalist (and socialist) society that was inadequate in logic and possibly even distorted on ideological grounds, and in the process concealed the function of ideology and domination contained in this type of rationality.

Both questions cannot be exhaustively dealt with here. It is, however, necessary and possible to attempt some fundamental clarification.

Marcuse refers to Weber's 'bourgeois reason' (Marcuse, 1972a, 225), but means that of 'the formal rationality of capitalism' (*ibid.*, 224 f.).[65] This is indisputable in so far as Weber, as an empirical scientist, felt 'tied' to the formal rationality of modern science.[66] Moreover modern science can be assigned to the bourgeoisie and capitalism both in historical and socio-economic terms. However, neither of these facts leads to the inevitable conclusion that rationality could be *thematised* merely as 'formal' or 'technical' in the framework of Weberian social science. A look at Weber's conceptual-theoretical as well as material analyses shows that such a limitation is really out of the question. Besides the distinction between formal and material rationality (to which Marcuse also referred), Weber's analyses indicate such a wide diversity of types and dimensions of 'rationalisation' that their systematisation would not only be difficult, but their subsumption under the chief concept of formal rationality utterly out of the question.[67] If we could specify a fundamental meaning of rationality in Weber at all, it would be most suitably characterised as the already cited category of 'communicability'.[68]

Concerning the second question regarding the role of formal rationality in the development of capitalist (and socialist) society, Marcuse's objections (as those of a Marxist) seem surprising at first sight. Weber refers to the significance of specific material (namely, religious-ethical) value orientations to explain the genesis of modern occidental capitalism. In contrast, as we have already noted, Marxist critiques constantly emphasise economic factors as playing the sole determining role 'in the final analysis'. Besides this, and in connection with corresponding statements by Marx, they establish that it is the development of the productive forces that represents the real motive power of history. No one has equalled Marx's rigour in his conception that the laws of movement within capitalist society are a product of economic and technical rationality. Of course Marx also believed that the capitalist mode of production would eventually be transformed into economic and technical irrationality and therefore (still on technical-rational grounds) this would inevitably lead to the abolition of the capitalist relations of production.

But this expectation is neither shared by Weber, nor indeed by Marcuse (who thus far abandons one central Marxist assumption).[69] Rather, both establish that the advanced process of technical rationalisation by no means necessarily entails a radical change in socio-political or authority relations on the grounds of technical rationality, but instead has the obverse effect both in fact and in legitimation, by leading to the stabilisation, if not 'ossification', of existing relations. Further, Marcuse concedes that the *technical* potential for the rationalisation of the capitalist economic and social system even half a century after Weber's corresponding thesis is clearly greater than that of the socialist system.

The opinion shared by Marcuse and many other Marxist authors (see, for example, Bader *et al.*, 1976, 316; Korf, 1971, *passim*; Kuznecov, 1975, 9; Devjatkova, 1968b, 129; Čalikova, 1970, 22; Vincent, 1973, 169 f.) that, faced with this development, Weber's narrow conception of rationalisation merely permitted resignation (or 'fatalism') or else an escape into irrationalism, particularly by showing faith in the liberating power of a charismatic leader, is inappropriate in this context. Although it is difficult to ignore, it is here of only secondary importance that, as noted, Weber by no means conferred an independent claim of rationality merely to scientific-technical and formal-rational positions. This acknowledgment in logic aside, Weber saw in a concrete historical and social situation both the possibility and necessity for contrasting the processes of 'concretisation' and 'depersonalisation' with a *materially* rational and modern idea of value, namely that of human and civil rights.[70] Whether this idea of value could succeed against the power of technological rationality is of course an empirical and above all practical question. It is also a highly discussable problem of how one can realise this idea of charismatic personalities without seriously damaging its content.[71]

In the view of many Marxists the ideological (and consequently fatalistic) nature of linking the conception of rationality with that of domination is shown most strikingly in Weber's analyses on the problem of bureacracy. The fact that precisely this problem meets with extraordinarily great interest among Marxist authors, and that not only Weber's conception of rationality but also his sociology of domination is approached almost exclusively from this angle,[72] has of course its specific and by all means practical political reason. The reason is that critical analyses on the authority relations in the socialist states are, as a rule, primarily directed at the progressive bureaucratisation evidently characterising those states. A critique oriented in this way was expressed at an early stage against corresponding developments in the Soviet Union, and possibly more resolutely by Marxist theorists than by non-Marxists.[73] Marxist critics justifiably appealed to the conception of Marxist classics (particularly that of Marx) that bureaucracy represents a specific expression of (late) bourgeois domination which would have to be eradicated in the course of the socialist revolution and replaced by radical democratic forms of self-administration.[74] In view of this conception and post-revolutionary reality which corresponded so little to it, Weber's assumption that socialist revolution would not lead to the abolition but rather an extension and acceleration of bureaucracy would appear to have been particularly scandalous and in need of critique.

Weber grounded his assumption by saying that 'rational socialism' in particular could by no means dispense with the specific rationality (i.e. especially the transparency, or 'calculability', and efficiency, meaning 'precision', 'continuity' and 'expediency') of a bureaucratically organised 'administration of the masses'. Weber asserted that indeed 'the need for constant, tight, intensive and *calculable* administration' would have to increase in rational socialism, and saw the 'specific rational fundamental feature' of bureaucratic administration as 'power through knowledge' (*WG*, 165). It is this 'specifically rational' aspect of bureaucracy that is evidently of special importance for the development in socialist states. In an earlier section of this book (p. 12) it has already been established that not only the materialist classics, but also the leading Soviet theorists, saw a crucial characteristic of socialist society in its scientific grounding, organisation and direction to an extent that had not previously been experienced nor considered factually as well as ideologically possible in pre-socialist societies.[75] From this point of view it would be absolutely feasible to characterise the specific socialist claim of its legitimate domination, and particularly also in the revolutionary phase, or during the subsequent phase of a dictatorship by the proletariat or 'its' party, with the formula of 'power through knowledge'. At any rate, materialist theorists were convinced that a claim of power thus grounded was in direct agreement with the goal of comprehensive and substantial, i.e. not merely political and 'formal', democratisation of all authority relations, and beyond that an abolition of all domination by people over people. (Evidently this conviction ensures a strong subjective faith in the legitimacy of its own authority among its followers,

even if 'formal' democratic procedures are suspended for shorter
or longer periods of time.)

Weber's analyses indicate that this type of one-way positive
linkage between the radical scientific rationalisation of social
contexts of action, on the one hand, and democratisation, on the
other, does not exist. There is no doubt that modern mass
democracy is dependent on a transparent, calculable, depersonalised (non-partisan) and efficient administration, not only for
technical-organisational but perhaps also for ethical-political
reasons.[76] But neither this fact as such nor the fact that the
'knowledge' in question is, in principle, both universally valid and
universally accessible (i.e. public)[77] could lead us to infer that in
such a situation there could be no antagonism. The production and
appropriation of the requisite specialist knowledge and (above all)
its social and political application necessitates certain organisational rules (specialisms, institutional differentiation, hierarchical
structures, etc.) that are diametrically opposed to the principles of
radical and comprehensive democratisation.

Weber's fundamental observation in this respect is 'that "democracy" as such, despite and because of its inevitable and
unintentional promotion of bureaucratisation, opposes "domination" by bureaucracy and this being the case possibly makes for
very perceptible contradictions and inhibitions in bureaucratic
organisation' (WG, 729). The Marxist critical treatment of
Weber's conception of bureaucracy largely leaves this fundamental problem undiscussed.[78] This applies particularly to Marxist-Leninist theorists, although it is precisely these theorists who in
general firmly support the idea of the 'scientific guidance and
direction' of all social processes. This entails the central point of
Weber's argument on the interplay between rationality and
domination in socialist bureaucracy also remaining untouched.
Obviously Weber's specific 'reference to value', on the horizon of
which the antagonisms between sweeping social rationalisation
and democracy are demonstrated, is neither noted nor shared by
many of these theorists. Thus Kramer, for example, apodictically
asserts that 'bureaucratism' is 'essentially alien' to socialism, while
simultaneously observing that 'a society which wants to overcome
spontaneity, as is the goal of socialism, and is even in a position to
be able to do so, naturally needs a highly organised managerial
apparatus' (Kramer, 1968, 187). The overcoming of 'spontaneity'
is of course an essential characteristic of the process that Weber
identified and criticised (for ethical-political reasons) as a process
of bureaucratic rationalisation. Kramer thus initially confirms the
Weberian thesis that 'rational socialism' *a fortiori* cannot dispense
with bureaucracy (in the sense of a 'highly organised managerial

apparatus'). In fact this is a conception that is characteristic of all Marxist-Leninist theorists. Neither bureaucracy, in Weber's sense, nor its permeation in all spheres of life are criticised, but only its perverse form of appearance as 'bureaucratism'. Kramer expands on 'bureaucratism' by saying

> that the managerial apparatus becomes autonomous, it begins to assume its own existence and its function is exhausted by purely and simply serving the parasitical section of society, in order to protect and realise its political, economic and ideological goals (Kramer, *ibid.*)

In many respects this conception is problematic and of course particularly in relation to both the traditional Marxist interpretation of bureaucracy and the prevailing conditions in actual contemporary socialist states. Firstly, there is obviously no compelling link between the two elements of 'bureaucratism', i.e. the growing autonomy of the managerial apparatus and its changing function to serve a class other than that of civil servants and functionaries. When, for example, Bukharin and Preobrazhensky find a 'partial *restoration of bureaucratism* within the Soviet order (1966, 183), or when Lenin speaks of 'our genuinely Russian (although Soviet) bureaucratism' (*UBM* 1, 1925, II), these theorists have the 'growing autonomy' of the civil servant apparatus in mind, not its late bourgeois function of ideology and domination. Unless these two factors can make a separate appearance the existence of a socialist bureaucratism would imply that even post-revolutionary societies are still 'antagonistic class societies' (Kramer, *op. cit.*) – something no Marxist-Leninist theorist would care to admit. Finally, the distinction between (good) bureaucracy, meaning a highly organised, comprehensive 'managerial apparatus' staffed by scientifically trained specialists, and (bad) bureaucratism is not in accordance with the radical democratic ideas of self-organisation and self-administration outlined primarily by Marx in his analysis on the Paris Commune and corroborated by leading theorists during the initial years after the Russian Revolution.[79]

Marxist critics see the crucial shortcomings and ideological character of Weber's analysis on bureaucracy in his failure to perceive the 'class base' of bureaucratic domination (thus, e.g. Kvesko, 1974, 16 and Seregin, 1974, 91) and in his thematic treatment of bureaucracy purely as a problem of social rationalisation or organisation (Seregin 1975, 72; Špakova *et al.*, 1973, 79, 83 ff.).[80] But, in fact, the same theorists fail to resume the class-theoretical analysis and critique of bureaucracy inaugurated by

Marx, i.e. that bureaucracy is a specific form of appearance of political domination). On the contrary, the merely alleged class-neutral bourgeois bureaucracy is contrasted with the socialist 'power through knowledge' that embodies a degree of rationality both with a view to its comprehensive and profound basis of knowledge and the organisational efficiency of the planning and managerial apparatus of party and state. The socialist bureaucracy is assumed in logic to surpass the potential of a bureaucracy based on the class interests of a minority. Socialist bureaucracy is obviously even given credit for its material rationality, because it fulfils its function on the basis of scientifically established, and therefore universally binding, substantive goals and norms. Weber (like the bourgeoisie in general), on the other hand, had only been able to demonstrate the bases of legitmacy of bureaucracy in secondary terms, namely in terms of its formal and technical rationality.

But, according to Weber, it is in fact the sheer formal character of bureaucratic rationality which facilitates and necessitates its ethical-political critique (for example, an ethical-political critique oriented to the idea of individual responsibility or to the principles of democracy). Such a critique is obviously ruled out in the case of the scientific planning and managerial apparatus under 'rational socialism', and therefore, by inference, the superior (material) rationality that is embodied, or at least realised, by this apparatus.

This approach, defending the overall tendencies towards bureaucratisation within socialist states, is no longer acceptable to a great many Marxists both within and outside such socialist states. Rather, these tendencies are consistently contrasted with Marx's radical democratic and 'humanist' notions (for example, by 'praxis philosophers', by J. Elleinstein or R. Bahro). At the same time, several Marxist authors fall back on Weber's considerations for an *explanation* of these tendencies (cf., e.g. Tadić, 1973). As a rule though these same authors still hold the opinion that Weber could at best only establish the irrational aspect of bureaucratic rationalisation (Devjatkova 1968, 129) and then resign in the face of it, because of the systematic (and ideological) limitations of his scientific conception. The question is whether existing and even now predominant Marxist theory (and practice) is not determined to such an extent by the idea of scientific rationality that independent, ethical and political considerations are granted even less legitimacy and space than was the case with Weber. The already somewhat dated discussions about the autonomy of ethical principles under the domination of real socialism, and the most recent critical discussions on the issue of 'human rights', not only dealt or are dealing with actual power and interests in maintaining power, but also with a Marxist conception of rationality and legitimacy which

1 accepts ethical and political-ethical considerations only in the context of historical materialism, i.e. including (or so it is claimed) strictly empirically based analyses; and
2 asserts, in the case of doubt, the superior (good) reason of technical rationality and its 'conformity to material laws' (in both the spheres of development of productive forces and socio-political organisation and direction).

5.6 Blank areas: economy, state, law

A review of those fields or dimensions of Weber's work which have been subjected to a more or less thorough discussion in the Marxist critique makes it apparent that above all two large areas have been omitted:

1 Weber's economic sociology in the narrower sense, to which large sections of *Economy and Society* are devoted, goes almost unmentioned. The same applies to Weber's empirical, or methodological research, enquiries into the situation of agricultural and industrial workers.
2 Only small sections of Weber's analyses in the field of political sociology have been covered.

To be sure it is idle speculation at this stage to ask why precisely these, no doubt very important, parts of Weber's work have largely escaped the attention of Marxist research. The crucial reason perhaps is that Marxists assumed that these fields had long formed the centre of interest in the Marxist social sciences, that they were therefore already comprehensively and exhaustively researched and that extra-Marxist endeavours were least in need of consideration. In fact there are hardly any Weberian fields of research whose subject matter more closely approximates the traditional research emphases of the materialist theoretical tradition. But this does not imply that they are therefore uninteresting for the present discussion of Marxism. On the contrary, that the obverse may be true is indicated by several general references.

The significance for materialist theory of the Weberian sociology of economic action and economic orders is that it represents an attempt to apprehend the economic sphere in concept and theory as a sphere of social action of a specific type. From the Marxist perspective a critical treatment of this attempt would in the first place have to clarify to what extent it corresponds with the intention of materialist theory to apprehend and explain 'material' human activity as a historical-social factor. For example, could we employ Weber's conceptual-theoretical analyses to examine the economic process described by Marx in *Capital* from its sociological aspect – or does that 'anatomy of bourgeois society', at least implicitly, contain a sociological perspective of its own? Does the difference reside in that Marx provides an analysis of the 'objective', real structure and laws, whereas Weber limits himself to the subjective or appearance aspect of events – or does this distinction amount to a 'naturalistic' or 'economist' misunderstanding of Marxian theory? Does the decisive characteristic of a materialist theory of economic processes reside in that it considers the constitutive meaning of factors which are not first and foremost 'constituted' through social action (and thus far called 'material') – or does each adherence to a simple extra-social fact contradict the radical social science orientation of the political economy founded by Marx?

These questions are the subject of great controversy in internal Marxist debates, and it is completely out of the question to give adequate attention to them here. The sole aim is to make clear that it is an unresolved problem of the Marxist tradition of thought as to whether material social practice possesses a fundamental dimension that cannot in principle be described by way of genuine social science concepts. Marxist theorists see such a dimension in, for example, concrete nature as such and in concrete productive forces (whose functioning is also subject to natural laws in the narrower sense), or else in that 'second nature' produced by the 'alienation' of human activity. (The differing apprehensions of 'materiality' or 'concreteness' has already been pointed out above.)

It is apparent that detailed clarification of this point is required in order to decide whether a fundamental difference to Weber's sociological perspective is indicated here. This perspective is defined by the assumption 'that all "economic" processes and objects are characterised as such entirely by the *meaning* they have for human action in such roles as ends, means, obstacles, and by-products' (*ES*, 64).[81] In Chapter 4, with references to several Marxian statements on the social importance of 'economic categories', it was surmised that Weber's basic outlook of social action does not constitute a contrast to the knowledge-directing interest of the Marxian political economy. Moreover it was assumed that, despite a logically comparable basic outlook of this kind, it is possible that the directions and levels of conceptual-theoretical abstraction diverge significantly.

This opinion is obviously not shared by Bader *et al.* in the one and only Marxist work devoted to a portrayal of Weber's 'fundamental sociological concepts' of economic action. These authors maintain that Weber, by operating with the background of a 'subjectivist' theory of value could neither adequately apprehend nor explain conceptually the objective (structural) economic realities and determinants particularly of the capitalist mode of production (e.g. value, commodities, money, capital, market etc.) (Bader *et al.*, 1976, 193 ff.).[82] To examine this in more detail should prove a rewarding task in future analyses.[83]

In this context Weber's studies on the situation of agricultural and industrial workers should be of interest in so far as they are marked by their heavy emphasis on 'material' realities and factors in the narrower sense (on the one hand, economic situations, interests and conflicts of interest, and, on the other, material and psychological determinants of working conditions). Even if the different timing and contexts of origination of these works were taken into consideration, it would still be possible to advance and examine the hypothesis that the 'naturalism', or the shortcomings in social science terms, of those works represents merely the obverse of Weber's decidedly sociological perspective on his conceptual-theoretical definitions in *Economy and Society*.

Marxist theorists seem to find Weber's political sociology even less amenable to critical treatment than his economic sociology. The central problem may be that Weber attributed much greater autonomy and independent inner dynamic to political relations and processes than seems possible within the scope of a materialist theory of the political superstructure. According to very widespread opinion it is indeed a constitutive hallmark of materialist theory to apprehend and explain political domination only as an – explicit or implicit – expression and function of powerful economic and class interests. This opinion further suggests that any divorce of the political sphere from the material situations and conflicts of interest is itself an element of that ideology by means of which bourgeois class domination creates the illusion of a 'general will', particularly in advanced and already precarious capitalist conditions.

The theoretical Marxist discussion centring on the materialist theory of the state has been most passionate in recent years and at present constitutes probably the most dominant part-area of internal Marxist argument. The revitalisation of the problem is obviously motivated above all by the dual experience that, on the one hand, the capacity for survival of capitalist bourgeois systems is interrelated with progressive expansion and the intensification of 'state activity' and, on the other hand, the expected 'association of free producers' by no means emerged in the course of the revolutionisation of the relations of production in socialist coun-

endorse this classification see the anxiety as inherent in the social position of the petty bourgeoisie, continually threatened as it is with pauperisation and with demotion to the ranks of the proletariat.

Here we touch upon an important point – what are the social conditions in which thriftiness will thrive? Those who saw the petty bourgeois as exercising thrift in a sense for which the rentier may serve as model, were led to do so just as much because the relevant slogans were to be found in petty bourgeois ideology, as because certain facts (e.g. savings banks statistics) went to show that the petty bourgeoisie was actually putting these slogans into practice. In both senses, thriftiness of the rentier type qualifies as a bourgeois virtue: it is a virtue not only recommended by the bourgeoisie but actually practised by them. Describing Mincel's shop in *Lalka* ('The Doll'), Prus writes: 'Failure to be thrifty, more precisely, failure to lay something by every day, be it only a few pence, was in Mincel's eyes something like theft.' Accordingly, he sacks a couple of assistants for not 'laying something by'. Here fear of pauperisation is not the only relevant factor. As I have already pointed out, what is crucially important here is *stability* of income, which need not necessarily be large. Modesty of income in itself renders saving necessary if larger items of expenditure are to be met, and, by the same token, adequate private insurance cover is desirable, particularly in a society whose social security system does not exactly set one's mind at rest. The *regularity* of the income, however, is an inducement to adoption of the 'penny by penny' principle; it is comforting to know that each month sees one's balance augmented by a constant sum, from which one can put something aside for a rainy day. Even where this form of saving becomes in time an irrational obsession, it still requires and assumes a certain faith in the stability of social relations. It is well known how, after the First World War, devaluation hit the petty bourgeoisie in the countries affected; and everyone knows that the savings banks always do their best to instil a feeling of trust and confidence into their clients. Skilled workers earning better wages and not threatened with unemployment become infected with the petty bourgeois spirit, while the casual worker and the artist who lives on occasional earnings are less attracted to thriftiness. Once they are in receipt of monthly pay, artists cease to lead a *vie de bohème* in the Young Poland sense: they get married and settle down, they have children and a balanced budget – sometimes even a bank account!

Given the insidious way in which it can turn into an irrational obsession, saving did not always recommend itself to the petty bourgeoisie, especially in so far as it did not lead to increased income. But if we go beyond the purely financial aspect of the matter, we may recall what Marx said about the danger of losing in order to live, that which makes life worth living (see p. 22). Literature offers us a whole gallery of hopeless human beings smothered by their passion for saving money or spending it on 'things that will last'. In his *Voyage au bout de la nuit* Céline describes a married couple who for about fifty years have been living with the dream of possessing their own house. For fifty years they grudge every penny they spend. Finally, they have paid off the house – a house built out of themselves like a snail's shell – and Madame Henrouille is as devoutly happy as a nun who has just taken communion: for a short time anyway – and then she looks around for a new reason for saving!

It has become customary to agree that thrift was a useful slogan in the days of primary capitalist accumulation. But let us be precise: what sort of thrift are we talking about? The thrift advocated by Franklin was in no sense a rentier type of thrift – it was rather thrift in aid of the perpetual rotation of money, of putting money to use in the conviction of its generative powers (see above, p. 75). It was not thrift dictated by apprehension and a desire for security: it was thrift imbued with the creative impetus of youthful capitalism.

As for the anxiety allegedly felt *vis-à-vis* parting with objects which are known to have had their day but which may yet come in handy, it is interesting to see how this attitude has varied according to the production relations obtaining in the capitalist countries. As I said in the previous chapter, during the period of over-intensive production in the United States people were encouraged to stop cherishing their belongings unreasonably, and were urged instead to discard lots of things as 'worn-out' which would hardly have seemed so to a European. Pressurised by the fashion industry men threw away their hats and bought the latest model, and women emptied their wardrobes. Over and above the production relations which determine people's attitudes to property, other economic factors appear to be at work here. It seems that someone who is not earning will take less kindly to discarding 'worn-out' property: after all, such a person is more immediately aware of the loss than of the ostensible gain. Hence, it would seem, hanging on to things is primarily a characteristic of housewives who are not earning, and for whom various forms of thriftiness are the only means for 'earning' at their disposal. If this is so, one result of the economic independence of women must be a large-scale jettisoning of junk.

As we have seen, the slogans of thriftiness played no part in the mores of the Polish aristocracy, though a measure of thrift would no doubt have served their interests as much as anyone else's. The nobility were concerned with demonstrating their freedom from economic worries, a freedom which was the badge of their class and their social prestige. When the aristocracy lost its supremacy, delusions of traditional grandeur remained. It is difficult to say how far this retention of atavistic attitudes was accompanied by their realisation in practice. There is no shortage in our literature of noblemen who can count! Rzewuski (to whom we shall return in a later chapter) is an excellent example of the numerate nobleman. The impression of the aristocrat's budget which the townspeople formed, was based on their observation of those gentry who came to town at carnival time, loafed about in expensive taverns and lost ostentatiously at cards. They caught the limelight; but to take them as representative of the nobility in general would be imprudent, especially in the case of Poland, where the nobility were so numerous and financially so heterogeneous that no generalisation is possible. Many of them hardly differed, if at all, from the middle classes in life-style.

We may pause here for a moment to ask ourselves precisely what it is that offends those who dislike thrift.

What forms of thrift are meant? Do essential components of thriftiness offend, or merely *accidentia* bound up with it?

In its small-scale aspects and attitudes thrift has always aroused hostility in certain quarters. When thrift was practised in a small way by the well-to-do who were under no economic pressure to do so, it was castigated as miserliness or avarice. In his *Characters*, Theophrastus comes down particularly heavily on what he calls *mikrologia*, a Greek term for everything implicit in the English word 'meanness': 'The Penurious man is he that will come to a man's house ere the month run out for a farthing's worth of usury; and at the club mess will reckon how many cups each has drunk . . . and if a servant of his break a year-old pot or dish, he will subtract the price of it from his food. Should his wife drop a half-farthing, he is one that will shift pots, pans, cupboards and beds, and rummage the curtains . . .'.

For Theophrastus, meanness comes under the heading of petty avarice and is lower in the scale of values than covetousness for gain or vulgarity – which is his way of saying (without any nuance of class prejudice) that even a rich man may be a bumpkin if he fails to behave with the requisite polish. The bumpkin 'if he has lent his plough, or a basket, or a sickle, or a sack, he will remember it as he lies awake one night and rise and go out to seek it'. The parsimonious man 'when a public contribution is asked in the Assembly, [he will] rise without speaking or depart from the house. At his daughter's wedding he will . . . covenant with the serving-men he hires for the feast that they shall eat at home. When he sits down he will turn aside his frieze-coat when he has nothing under it [or: which is all he wears].' As Theophrastus sees him, 'the mean man's way is, when he entertains his friends to a feast, not to put enough bread before them . . . [he will] measure out his household's corn with his own hand, using a Pheidonian measure with a knocked-in bottom and striking it off very even . . . if his sons go not to school the full month because of the sickness, will reduce their school-money accordingly. . . . Should his club meet at his house, needless to say he will put down to the common account the fuel, lentils, vinegar, salt and lamp-oil which he provides.'[8]

The obsession with economic factors which characterises all of these examples and which is exhibited in circumstances where one might expect other factors to prevail, is something which many of us find repellent. No one will be surprised if a man takes some care at table not to spill soup on his trousers. But if the same man hesitates to go to the help of someone injured in a street accident in case he gets his new suit spoiled, his hesitation will be viewed in quite a different light. Trying to avoid wasteful eating habits seems perfectly natural; but a Sztemler shocks people when he wails over a half-emptied glass – not simply because he can well afford the 'waste' but because of his failure to enter into the spirit of the occasion, to 'take part' in social conviviality. The Sztemlers of this world remain isolated from social claims and social graces, preferring to ruminate gloomily over the waste and destructiveness with which they see themselves surrounded.

Our hypothetical case involving the victim of a street accident pinpoints a third reason why a certain kind of thriftiness appears as meanness, emotional frigidity, an egocentric inability to take the interests of our fellow creatures into account. In the caricatures of the thrifty person which we find in literature, this trait is almost invariably present.

A fourth factor which many people find repellent in the thrifty person is the dash of the irrational which seems to be implied. At bottom, thrift need imply neither meanness nor absorption in the minutiae of house-keeping; but when the moment demands from us something other than egoism or unreasonableness, psychological constraints can be very strong, and nowhere stronger than in the case of the miser who finds it painful to spend his money or part with his property. This is again a common type in literary criticism of thrift.

The maxims of thriftiness are so closely bound up with the bourgeois way of life that even under the changed conditions of a socialist society they have retained their format, however unsuited this may be to the new demands made upon it. For the sociologist, it is intriguing to see the detritus of the past continuing by force of inertia into the present. What I have in mind is the economy campaign run in Poland by the PKO, under whose auspices the textbook *Pracą i oszczędnością* ('By Work and Thrift') was published in 1948.

The title itself invites comment. 'People get rich by work and thrift' is one of the maxims in Franklin's Almanac – maxims which were thoroughly assimilated by subsequent bourgeois thought. Have we then to complete the title of our propaganda pamphlet with the time-honoured slogan 'Enrichissez-vous!'? Nor is the Franklinesque gospel limited to the title: in the text we read:

> That's how it is in human life,
> Each of us wants to know
> Whether he's going to have a full purse,
> Or live in poverty.
>
> We'd all like to be lucky
> And have plenty of what we want,
> But more often than not we've no idea
> How we're going to get it.

And a little further on:

> Let's set out to work hard,
> And add penny to penny;
> Then the contents of our purse
> Will at once start to grow.

These verses printed and published in People's Poland could quite easily have been cribbed from a selection of his best sayings made by Franklin himself. Obviously, the way to making one's pile *à la* Franklin is now barred by nationalis-ation of production and its means, and by taxation, e.g. estate duties: but the spirit would appear to be one and the same, which is not something, it seems to me, that socialist ideology could convincingly endorse.

Our pamphlet not only links happiness with financial resources, not only does it treat human labour as a way of making money by adding one penny to another, but it also recommends an isolationist attitude and preoccupation with one's own personal interests and ambitions, as in the days of private enterprise. The quatrain 'Awkward Conversation', for example, runs as follows:

> Lend you a few zlotys!? – Haven't got them, pal . . .
> That's a conversation you'll often hear;
> Whoever saves in the PKO and depends on himself –
> He'll have a care-free mind, and help when he needs it.

With this, we may well compare the egoistical attitude displayed in the well-known fable of the ant and the cricket, as told by La Fontaine and Krylov. The cricket comes to the ant asking for a loan, whereupon the thrifty and diligent ant replies:

> I never lend anyone anything,
> It's one of my faults,
> Perhaps one of my lesser faults,
> But you're not going to mend my ways.
> Rather, you tell me this –
> What have you been doing all year,
> That now you have to go a-begging?
>   – All day and all night
>   I sang without stopping.
> You sang!? Fine, my good fellow,
> Now you can dance to your own tune.

Is the ant as here portrayed, a model to be copied? If so, do we run the risk of taking over not only its thrifty foresight, but also its social frigidity and its lack of understanding of the artistic impulse?

I am not concerned with taking the author of this pamphlet to task. After all, it is hardly surprising that any attempt to boost the virtue of thriftiness should have to tread well-worn paths, given the amount of propaganda devoted to this theme in bourgeois literature; though the climate of this propaganda should perhaps be recognised as alien in the new conditions, and in conflict (as in the fable of the ant and the cricket) with the ideals of socialism.

Nor is it my purpose to develop an anatomy of thrift which would be in keeping with the new social structure and with the guidelines of life in a socialist society. It is clear that one would first of all have to make a sharp distinction between thrift in the public and thrift in the private sector. The due administration of public money and property cannot be subject to any of the strictures we have made regarding the various forms of thrift, nor is it in any way threatened by the psychological deformations which are so often generated by a private obsession with thrift. No doubt the campaigns run by the savings banks, urging people to be thrifty, should contain a clause warning clients of the risks they run of becoming deformed by over-economising ('thrift may damage your mental health'?) – after all, obsessional economising might in the long run prove more harmful to the state than the temporary loss of revenue which such a clause might entail. As I said, these are questions that go beyond our present brief; but I think that some of the points we have raised in the present chapter may well prove helpful in their adequate formulation.

Chapter 5

The merchant and the 'gentleman' in Daniel Defoe

For fame of families is all a cheat
It's personal virtue only makes us great.
(Defoe, *The True-Born Englishman*)

1 The life of Defoe

Franklin was a practical man who drew primarily on the living world surrounding him for his examples and his moral and ethical precepts. Nevertheless, certain personal contacts with thinkers, and certain books he came across in the course of his self-education, were not without effect on the formation of his personality. It is well known that in his youth he delighted in John Bunyan's *Pilgrim's Progress*, and, as I mentioned above, he copied out whole passages of the *Spectator*, which was published by the two Whigs Addison and Steele. We also know that he was under the influence of Daniel Defoe, who was still alive when Franklin first visited England. Between the model English merchant as presented by Defoe and the sort of problems Franklin was working on, there is an exceptionally close connection, and it is worth our while to examine this model merchant who antedates the first edition of Franklin's Almanac by about seven years.

Defoe lived in a turbulent age and he led an equally turbulent life. Anyone working on the history of England in the late seventeenth and early eighteenth centuries will find Defoe's career extremely instructive, as its restless course enables us to penetrate behind the scenes of many of the most important episodes of the period. For present purposes, all we need from this rich canvas are those facts relating to our theme: in the first place, Defoe's model merchant and

127

his personification in the figure of Robinson Crusoe; secondly, the relation between this model and certain aristocratic models.

The Foe family was probably of Flemish origin.[1] The 'de' was added by Daniel, who made a practice of writing it separately from 'Foe', thus betraying his weakness – a desire to be known as a gentleman, an affectation which showed itself in his manners and his dress throughout his life. In 1706 he finally chose a coat of arms, to which his birth did not really entitle him: his father had been a candlemaker and, later, a butcher. The mother, it is true, had a drop of aristocratic blood in her veins – something about which Daniel was wont to boast. He was born in 1660, the year in which Samuel Pepys, then aged twenty-seven, began writing his diary. Young Daniel was deeply affected by two catastrophes which befell London – the plague in 1665 and the great fire of 1666. Fifty-seven years later, in 1722, he described the plague in words of doubtful reliability in comparison with Pepys's day-by-day account of those dark times. Reared in a Nonconformist and fervently devout milieu (his father was a Baptist), Daniel had to experience something of the persecution meted out to Dissenters. Several well-known incidents in his life bear witness to this – for example, the arduous copying of the Pentateuch by hand, a task undertaken in the fear that rumours that the Papists were about to confiscate printed Bibles might well be true. His parents put Daniel in a clerical seminary where, under the direction of an understanding tutor, he studied in his native language not only theology but also many practical skills. The fact that he never learned the ancient classical languages – something with which his enemies liked to taunt him in later life – put him at a disadvantage in comparison with those of his contemporaries who had had a university education. This inferiority complex comes out in the posthumously published *The Complete English Gentleman* (about which more later), a work in which the author tries, not always successfully, to show some acquaintance with classical studies.[2] Education in a seminary failed to make a cleric of Daniel. He opted for a career in commerce, and after a few years' apprenticeship with a London merchant

and marriage to the daughter of a rich merchant, he opened
a shop which, in spite of the rules he worked out for the
model merchant, he was never able to run properly.

We need not follow all the zigzags of Defoe's career. His
life story, full as it is of puzzles and hoaxes, is by no means
easy to reconstruct, and every fresh bit of research makes
revision necessary. We know that Defoe was not satisfied
with what he made out of the shop, and that his head was
permanently full of ambitious schemes. We know that he
was attracted to politics and that he was ready to intrigue,
spy and inform for anyone able to pay well for such services.
In *The Complete English Gentleman* Defoe has hard words for
the Poles, whose behaviour in the elections, he says, shows
them to be 'false, perfidious, treacherous, mercenary,
unsteady, not to be trusted upon the solemnest oath'.[3] Do
they not eat the bread of one candidate for the throne, only
to desert him and support another? One day they are for the
Saxon, the day after for the Swede, 'as the money could be
got or the party was strongest' Here, amply provided with
awful examples, is a full description of practices which Defoe
permitted himself to pursue throughout his life.

Defoe's moral balancing act did not endear him to writers
of the period. The insults which Addison hurled at him were
perhaps, in part at least, motivated by Defoe's attempts
(unsuccessful as it turned out) to undermine the position of
Steele, Addison's collaborator, by laying information against
him accusing him of high treason. Gay, the author of *The
Beggar's Opera*, and Swift were equally bitter in their
denunciation of Defoe. Later critics of Defoe have quoted
Samuel Johnson: a man who seeks social advancement by
ingratiating himself with the rich and powerful, cannot
afford to take virtue as his guideline.

Beset on all sides by creditors and political enemies who
more than once threatened his life, Defoe lived alone and
had little to do with his family. It is a trait which we find
repeated in the lives of his fictional characters. He was
attached to his youngest daughter, Sophie, and yet could
cause her anguish by haggling with her fiancé for two years
over the dowry. In his lonely life, a dedicated servant seemed
to be enough. He incorporated his dreams of the faithful

servant in his fictional characters, and in his minor writings he twice expresses regret at the demoralisation, laxity and breakdown in the spirit of service.

Any attempt to give a complete list of Defoe's works is fraught with very serious difficulties, as Defoe, always keen to hoodwink the public, often attributed his works to others. In his *Histoire de la littérature anglaise* Taine lists 254 titles. In 1912, Defoe's English biographer W. P. Trent drew up a catalogue of 370 items. A large part of this vast output is ephemeral and has long since lost any interest it may have had. There remain, however, many works of lasting value. Defoe reacted to whatever was happening around him, and English journalism has much to thank him for. Apart from the journal which he published from 1705 to 1713 he wrote political pamphlets, treatises on trade and on 'correct' religious policy. He described England and her customs in great detail. As he regularly seized on anything sensational, the criminal element plays a big part in his writings. He wrote on ghosts and phantoms, on the devil, on a man who was dumb till the age of fifty-eight but who found words just before his death to proclaim his religious convictions and to foretell the fate awaiting Great Britain. He wrote of the deaf mute who could write down the name of anyone he happened to meet. All of this is passed off as authentic, which seems to me to smack not so much of a Puritan dislike of fiction as of a keen eye for the market value of authenticity. As everyone knows, when you are telling an anecdote it helps a great deal if you can say it actually happened. Thinking up stories and trying to hoodwink people enabled him to picture in the most minute detail things he had never witnessed, and made of him a swindler of near unique gifts. As Taine says, his imagination was 'toute remplie et comme bourrée de faits'.[4] In 1924, when Dottin, one of Defoe's most conscientious biographers, wrote his biography, it was still believed that Defoe had travelled at least in Europe. Study of evidence provided by those of his contemporaries who really did venture beyond the confines of the British Isles does not endorse this claim, and it now seems certain that Defoe described his experiences as a globe-trotter without once leaving his native country.[5]

Not surprisingly, his visions of foreign parts are somewhat confused: penguins, seals, tortoises and parrots all live together on Robinson Crusoe's island. The minute detail of these descriptions bears witness to the extraordinarily plastic nature of Defoe's imagination, and underlines the truth of the French saying: The liar is never short of detail.

Of all Defoe's works, *Robinson Crusoe* is incomparably the most popular. The list of editions and translations in the Bibliothèque Nationale takes up two volumes of the catalogue. Another very popular work of his was *The Family Instructor*, in which Defoe expatiates on family life, something to which, as we have seen, he paid singularly little attention in practice. Tribute has also been paid to his inventive flair, as expressed in his *Essay on Projects*, which covers a wide range of inventions and improvements to existing devices; and his tales and recollections of the Great Plague in London have been much admired. But so far as I know, no one has taken any interest in his 'model merchant', the figure which concerns us here.

Himself a merchant, Defoe was less concerned with the fancy goods and haberdashery which formed his official stock in trade, than with the pen. In this respect, his business acumen displayed itself not merely in his readiness to offer his pen to anyone willing and able to pay for it, but also in his keen eye for what the market wanted. His life being what it was, full of ups and downs, it often came about that Defoe could venture forth only on Sundays – the one day in the week when debtors could not be arrested!

Defoe remained a Puritan to the end of his life, though fundamentally and in keeping with the spirit of the age, he was inclined to be tolerant and rather free in his attitude to dogma. Robinson Crusoe introduces freedom of religion into his 'state', comprising as it does a Spanish Catholic, Man Friday who is a Protestant, and Friday's father who is a pagan. Only once did our author feel impelled to treat a question of religion seriously, and that was when he produced a pamphlet urging that inter-denominational marriages should be banned.

He was no republican; he believed in king and protectionism. He was also a nationalist, a point to which we shall return. It would be difficult to find in Defoe any trace of that faith in social harmony which a few decades later imbues the works of Adam Smith, underpinning both his economics and his theory of moral empathy. Had Defoe's view of the world been as optimistic as this, he could never have written *Moll Flanders*. He took society as he found it.

We know very little about his views on aesthetics. According to Taine, the concept of the beautiful was a closed book to him.[6] He seems to have had very little time even for such Puritan authors as Milton; he denounced the contemporary theatre as a hotbed of sin and even opposed a production of *Hamlet*. Both as a person and in his output, Defoe bears striking testimony to the fact that a sense of the beautiful is not a necessary part of the artist's equipment.

2   The model merchant

We come now to our main subject – the model merchant who, in the shape of Robinson Crusoe, turns into the model man in general, and the relationship between this bourgeois model and English aristocratic models. Our discussion will turn very largely on two works by Defoe which have been rather neglected by researchers. Students of Defoe have been for the most part literary historians who are primarily interested in Defoe as the progenitor of a new literary genre – the novel – and who therefore give no more than the bare titles of works which do not interest them. The two works that concern me are *The Complete English Tradesman* and *The Complete English Gentleman*. It was towards the end of his life that Defoe began to round out his conception of the model merchant – that is, round about 1725, when Franklin was in his late teens.

Defoe begins methodically by defining exactly what he has in mind when he uses the word 'tradesman'.[7] The *Homines oeconomici*, he says, can be divided into three categories. The first comprises those who do not themselves make what they sell. This is the category of 'tradesmen' in the exact meaning of the word, and it is with these that Defoe intends to deal in his book. The second category comprises those who make what they sell: that is, they are craftsmen. Finally, there are those who make things but do not sell them: as examples of this class, Defoe mentions manufacturers and artists. Within his first category, Defoe further distinguishes the 'merchants' who import goods from abroad; some of these – the 'merchant adventurers' – are specifically connected with the sea. It should be made clear at the outset that in the course of his book the author does not stick rigorously to the classification set out in its first pages. In his usage, the word 'trade' is an umbrella term covering the activities of the man who sells wool shorn by himself off his own sheep's backs, and of the shopkeeper who sells ready-made clothes made from that same wool. And, in spite of his opening strictures, those who make what they sell come more than once within his purview, as, indeed, do those who only produce (see, e.g., ch. XXVI). However, I do not think we are distorting Defoe's thought if we use the word *kupiec* to render 'tradesman'. Primarily, what Defoe has in mind is the sort of business he himself ran. When he uses the word 'tradesman' he is thinking of the man behind the counter serving a customer, and not of a large enterprise engaged in large-scale and impersonal transactions.

If Defoe sings the praises of the tradesman, this is not simply because of the personal gain deriving from his occupation, but also because of its social importance. Tradesmen are a 'public blessing' for England. The pride and glory of the English are above all their 'mercantile pursuits'. Trade is a far more decisive factor in the power of England than anything she might achieve in the military field. Furthermore, trade has led to the discovery and colonisation of new lands beyond the seas. King Charles II said that the tradesmen of England are the real English nobility: and not without reason, when one considers the role they play in the country's affairs. They carry the greatest burden of taxation, they bear the brunt of war. The tradesman is considerably better off than the minor nobility, whose annual income is smaller and who are up to the ears in debt thanks to their prodigal way of life. See how the tradesmen look after the castles they acquire – and compare this with the way the members of the aristocracy neglect their ancestral homes. Landed property is like a stagnant pond, trade is a gushing fountain.

Moll Flanders is hard put to it to find herself a 'gentleman-tradesman' as husband – that is to say, a tradesman who looks 'like a gentleman', who would 'become a sword' and whose coat does not show 'the mark of the apronstrings'; and it is only after several false starts that she finds this 'amphibious creature, this land-water thing'.[8] In *The Complete English Tradesman*, however, Defoe does not seem to think that the 'amphibious creature' is all that rare. In England, as he sees it, the expression 'gentleman-tradesman' is by no means nonsensical, for there is a continual progression from tradesman status to the aristocracy and vice versa. Tradesmen are continually flocking to the College of Heralds to buy themselves coats of arms which can be painted on their carriages, and embroidered wherever there's room. And if their right to a coat of arms cannot be established, they 'begin a new race' in no way inferior to those who claim a proud ancestry. On the other hand, impoverished gentlemen of good family do not hesitate to protect their line by looking for a spouse in the world of trade and commerce. Defoe devotes a whole chapter (vol. 1, ch. XXIV) to an enumeration of families now famous who owe 'their rise' to some past business deal or other, and who owe their fortune to prudent inter-marriage with merchant families – a theme to which Defoe returns in *The Complete English Gentleman*. His list is both instructive and numerically impressive. The rarest case is that of marriage between an impoverished gentlewoman and a member of the tradesman class. Here, Defoe sees nothing more than female stupidity; forgetting that by general social agreement binding upon all sorts of hierarchic groupings (whether of high and low castes in India, or of 'superior' majority and despised ethnic minority in European society) the man raises the woman to his status, while the woman 'falls' to the level of the man she is marrying. We need not press the point here. But it is for these reasons that 'downward' marriages of women are, as is well known, rather infrequent.

Although Defoe makes no secret of his approval of this fusion of the aristocracy with the tradesman class, he does not advise his model tradesman to 'ape the gentry' or to cultivate social relations with 'society'. Time may indeed be spent very pleasantly in high society – but more profitably in one's own milieu. In forming relationships in general, one must primarily seek those which can be profitable. It is with the average tradesman, that is, with those of medium status, that Defoe feels most sympathy and solidarity. Rich merchants come in for the sharp edge of his tongue. He warns his readers against their tyranny and the role which they are only too keen to play in ruining those less well off than themselves. His recipe for the country's health is a numerous class of medium tradesmen (see ch. XXXVIII). As I said, 'tradesman', as Defoe uses the word, is a rather elastic term. In general, it covers all those who share in the circulation of ready-made goods: that is, retail traders, wholesalers and all sorts of middlemen. Defoe's view is that these latter should be as numerous as possible (ch. XXXVII). The longer the chain, the more people are employed, and the more benefit accrues to the country in general. The more people are employed, the more the consumption of basic necessities is assured, grain prices remain stable, and farmers are thereby enabled to pay the rents on which agriculture depends.

Defoe now passes to a consideration of the main virtues of the tradesman – the model tradesman as he ought to be, if he is to be both rich and morally above reproach. As in Franklin, wealth and morality can hardly be separated. The only difference is that whereas Franklin places more emphasis on the notion that virtue will in itself engender riches, in Defoe's case the stress is rather on the reverse proposition – that riches are bound to make their owner virtuous. Moll Flanders prays to be protected from need so that she will not have to steal, being convinced that crime always enters through the gates of neediness. And in the satirical poem 'The True-Born Englishman' Defoe assures the reader in very similar words that

> Where vice prevails, the great temptation
> Is want of money more than inclination.[9]

The tradesman must be diligent and industrious. He must supervise his shop in person, and never leave it during business hours: no excursions, no dabbling in politics, no involvement with political parties. Defoe makes much of the anecdote (autobiographical, no doubt) of the man who was a good patriot but a bad tradesman, so he went bankrupt and landed in jail.

A business must not be left in the hands of the assistants, who should always be kept on a tight rein. They must report on where they go and with whom they consort. They must be indoors by nine o'clock in the evening. As far as possible they must be deprived of the 'liberty of doing evil'. It would seem that Defoe himself made good use of this august precept by exploiting his workers, for his contemporaries reproach him with operating a 'sweatshop'. There is another good reason why the owner should always be present in the shop: at the psychological moment he can intervene in a sale and convince the customer that even if he, the owner, knows he can't ask for more, he isn't going to knock anything more off.

The tradesman must be thrifty. He cannot allow himself expensive amusements or major outlay on anything frivolous. 'All manner of pleasure should be subservient to business.' He who makes a calling of pleasure will never pursue his calling with pleasure. Amusements rob a man, so how can they be called 'innocent'? They are miscreants who rob the master of his shop and steal his time into the bargain. Gentlemen-landowners can allow themselves the pleasure of breeding horses and hunting, but the tradesman cannot. The pleasures of family life are all he can afford. The tradesman who does not rejoice in family life will not enjoy his business for very long. However, one must be careful about starting a family too soon. The tradesman who marries as a journeyman lives to regret it. Parents who believe that by letting their son marry early they are saving him from profligacy are merely deceiving themselves. It is a poor bargain that offers sobriety in exchange for a lifetime of slavery and short commons. Defoe writes with feeling on this theme, and quotes with approval the custom in Holland and Germany, where a girl's immediate reply to a proposal of marriage is to ask the man if he can support her.

The tradesman must be patient and self-possessed. When he places himself behind the counter, he must forswear passion, anger, resentment. He must watch with composure while women rummage through his wares with no intention of buying anything. This is, as a matter of fact, in his own best interests, as there is always the chance that a woman may take a fancy to something or other – for example, on Saturdays, when she visits the shop not because she wants to buy something but simply because she is keen to get away from the housework. The tradesman must be polite; he must know how to behave to well-to-do customers, he must have 'good language' for the poorer sort. People must find buying from him a pleasure, so that they leave the shop satisfied, regardless of whether they have gained or lost on the deal (ch. XXXVI).

The tradesman must be prudent. He must be careful not to engage in too many ventures, and must guard against over-buying and extending or accepting excessive credit. Credit extended must never exceed one-third of the credit he himself receives. He should never stand surety for anyone. Nothing is so secure as to render caution superfluous. Even when one has reached a certain degree of affluence, one must still remember to go forward slowly and carefully to avoid falling backwards. One should not lose one's head over grandiose projects, which is what 'trade-lunatics' do. Defoe lays great emphasis on that feeling of security which is for him an indispensable component of happiness.

The tradesman must be honest. Honesty wins for him both the credit and the trust on which his very existence depends. Credit in the eyes of others is for the tradesman what virtue is for a maiden, the one irreplaceable jewel. Hence, for Defoe, there is nothing worse than defamation, character assassination. Robbing a tradesman of his 'credit', his trustworthiness, is something worse than stealing his goods: it partakes of murder, and indeed Defoe calls it 'trading murder'. Trustworthiness is gained through 'just, fair and honourable dealings'. Charles II may have been a king but no one was very keen to lend him money!

The tradesman must keep his books with meticulous accuracy. Here Defoe indulges in what is for him unusual moral grandiloquence. A tradesman's books are his rudder. 'A tradesman's books, like a Christian's conscience, should always be kept clean and neat.' Taking stock of the day's dealings is rather like reviewing one's conscience. A tradesman's books should always look as though he had not another minute to live. For Defoe, keeping accounts up to date in every last detail was clearly a matter of inner harmony. People can still be found today who will not lay their heads on the pillow until they have itemised the day's outgoings, however trivial. For them too, the business of correlating the day's dealings with their bank account is a matter of conscience. When they do go to sleep it is with a peaceful mind: duty has been done, nothing has escaped notice, not even the newspaper bought on the way home, or the casual tip.

The tradesman is, however, allowed certain departures from strict honesty. For example, he may ask a customer to pay more than he intends in the long run to take. If this custom has become obligatory, it is largely because of the customers themselves who say they cannot pay more than a certain price and who then agree, penny by penny, to do so. The Quakers oppose this practice but are themselves guilty of inconsistency. If the tradesman says he cannot make a reduction, his words are not to be taken literally. 'Cannot' here means 'cannot reasonably' or 'cannot without lowering the market value of the goods'.

Another area in which the tradesman must be allowed a little latitude is that of failure to meet financial obligations. A promise cannot be other than contingent. When a Christian promises something, this is always with the tacit understanding that he will keep his promise 'if God will' (!). If Christian morality demanded of the tradesman that his 'yea' be unconditionally 'yea' and his 'nay' 'nay', no tradesman could be a Christian. This is a matter of vocational necessity. But if a man makes a conditional promise from the outset – if, that is, he makes the only sort of promise he can in fact hope to keep – no one will labour under the delusion that he is going to stick to the letter.

The tradesman may also 'gild the lily': that is, he may extol his goods in words calculated to con the ignorant into buying them. Technically this is dishonest, but, as far as Defoe is concerned, the dishonesty is a matter of degree. In its extreme form, the practice is tantamount to passing false coins, and Defoe condemns it unreservedly, even in cases where the false money has been acquired in good faith. A bit of sales talk, on the other hand, is treated leniently. Indeed, the customer incites the tradesman to the use of rhetoric by belittling what he is buying, and preening himself when he thinks he is getting a bargain. Here as everywhere else one should try to observe a golden mean.

Defoe reserves his strongest words of obloquy for price-cutting: a public calamity, as he sees it. Here we see traces of the old guild solidarity which free competition was later to oust completely. (It is instructive to compare, for example, the Memoirs of Rockefeller, where we find a very different attitude to price-cutting!) Price-cutting, says Defoe, is practised by

1 Young Tradesmen newly set up; and they do it to get a trade.
2 Rich old Tradesmen, who have over-grown Stocks: and they do it to keep their trade, or perhaps to hurt others of the same business.
3 Poor Tradesmen who are obliged to sell to raise money.

The first two cases can be condemned out of hand. By cutting his prices, the fledgling tradesman is only fooling his customers into thinking that this is the shape of things to come – a piece of folly for which they will one day have to pay dearly. Rich merchants ruin their less well-to-do colleagues, and even if they themselves benefit from cut prices, it is at the cost of the whole nation's welfare. These opinions show Defoe, as I said, ranged wholeheartedly on the side of the medium tradesman.

He is also on the side of individualism in business. The tradesman should unite with no one. The more honest and industrious an associate is, the more dangerous he is. If you are forced to join in business with someone else, it should be with a man younger than yourself, as there is then less chance of his gaining the upper hand. Some tradesmen are even reluctant to initiate their wives into business matters, lest the womenfolk take over and run things. But in this they err. The fact is that by making one's wife act as helpmeet, she becomes easier to manage; and in any case it is advisable that the wife should know something about the business so that she can take over in the event of the husband's death. She should not be reduced to playing the lady – receiving guests and taking trips abroad.

Defoe would not be the eighteenth-century writer he is if he had nothing to say on the classic theme of his time – luxury. His Puritanism could only reinforce his feelings on this score.

Can the tradesman be blamed if he sells luxury objects? The answer is a tolerant negative. Human frailties support trade: trade does not create them. 'The fault is not in the trade, but in the man.' No doubt it is regrettable that luxury goods do so much for the development of trade and commerce, and that the livelihoods of so many people should be founded on moral delinquency. But if luxury goods were abolished, how many people would be out of work? Anyway, if luxury goods were not available in England, people would simply go to France for them – which would hardly be in the best interests of English trade. Perhaps the best solution would be to manufacture luxury goods for export only, relying on judicious control of the home market, and educating the gentry (whose fashions are aped by other classes) to curb their lavish and extravagant tastes and follow the example of the Quakers, who 'deal in finery and ornament but never wear them themselves'.

As we see, Defoe's Christian mentality requires him to preserve only his own people against corruption; if other peoples choose moral ruin, that is their own lookout. Defoe is a nationalist, and in this book he sometimes exhibits a sort of nationalist megalomania. England has the biggest trade turnover, and the best and most vigorous people. It has the most favourable climate. All this serves as background for Defoe's main thesis – and one which is moreover very much in his own interest – that English goods are best. He wants promotion of exports and protection against imports. He is irritated by women who want French silk. For their edification he relates the anecdote of the merchant who sells a customer English silk as French, duly priced to take the perils of smuggling into account, and thus making a nice bit of profit.

If a tradesman is facing bankruptcy he should not give way to despair. He should declare himself bankrupt without further ado. It is a unique peculiarity of the tradesman's calling that he can fail, pick himself up and regain public confidence. Public opinion is more lenient in this domain than anywhere else; and it is in commerce that a man is most accurately and justly assessed. Trade is not a masked ball in which people try to appear better than they really are: it is an open forum where one is what one is, shorn of all pretence.

I have taken from Defoe's book only those details which serve to highlight the nature of his model tradesman. I have ignored the mass of information given on other subjects, such as how to write business letters, how to keep books, details of what men and women belonging to different classes wear (from shirts to overcoats) together with notes on where these articles are produced. As the author of *A General History of Trade* (1713) Defoe knew a great deal about these matters, and his work is of enormous interest to the economic historian and to the historian of dress. The book is well written and reads like a novel. It contains a lot of common sense and a lot of moralising (often in the style of Alfonso da Liguori), some examples of which I have quoted. As I said, in the figure of the model tradesman, Defoe is not offering us a reflection of himself but rather a corrected edition of himself. Defoe's tradesman must be settled, but Defoe himself was not. He must be a family man, whereas Defoe was more inclined to shake off his family as an encumbrance which he could very well do without. Finally, the model tradesman should not get involved in grandiose schemes or keep on building castles in Spain – something Defoe was all too ready to do, throughout his life.

3   The model tradesman in action: Robinson Crusoe

Unlike Franklin, Defoe did not start from nothing. His parents were not badly off; the mother had brought a considerable dowry which went into a small business. The boast that one owes everything to oneself – so prevalent in Franklin's writings – is not to be found in *The Complete English Tradesman*. It appears, however, in *Robinson Crusoe*. Here it was a question of putting a castaway on to an uninhabited island and making him start from absolute zero, so as to achieve the maximum effect as, step by step, he increases his equipment, adds to his security, accumulates property and enhances his bodily comfort. 'So that had my cave been to be seen, it looked like a general magazine of all necessary things, and I had every thing so ready at hand, that it was a great pleasure to me to see all my goods in such good order, and especially to find my stock of all necessaries so great.'[10] And all put together out of nothing by dint of one's own industry and patience, with the help, as one critic aptly remarks, of a sound education in an elementary school.

This anchorite version of the self-made man makes its timely appearance in the dawn of capitalism and in the first flush of colonial expansion. Robinson Crusoe goes forth to amass riches, and the book ends, as critics have sourly remarked, not with a bridal procession to the altar but with dreams of gold come true. In themselves, these dreams make Robinson Crusoe a representative of eighteenth-century bourgeois aspirations; but the book also contains elements that transcend its time. The ideal of self-sufficiency combined with the struggle of man on his own against the forces of nature – here is a theme of perennial interest, which explains why the book still appeals as much to the adult as to the Boy Scout who has to win a badge by spending twenty-four hours alone in the forest, using his wits to survive on whatever comes to hand. In an interesting discussion of Defoe, A. A. Elistratova shows how everyday work can be seen in this non-trivial light.[11]

Defoe's ties with his class are so clear that no special flair for sociological investigation is needed to identify him as a typical representative of the bourgeoisie. As Taine wrote of Defoe: 'His imagination was that of a businessman, not that of an artist.'[12] Yet the identification of Robinson Crusoe as the embodiment of the true tradesman had to await, it would seem, the Marxist classics. In a letter to Kautsky dated 20 September 1884, Engels ascribes this observation to Marx;

and Marx himself in *Capital* draws attention to the fact that Robinson Crusoe 'having rescued a watch, ledger and pen and ink from the wreck, commences, like a true-born Briton, to keep a set of books', using the watch to note the average time spent on the manufacture of each object.[13] More recently, P. Dottin, an authority on Defoe, has made a very thorough job of identifying the tradesman elements in Robinson Crusoe, albeit in somewhat exaggerated fashion, a point to which we shall return. Earlier readers tended to take a rather more sentimental view of Robinson Crusoe. Taine saw in him a very English model of heroic willpower. Rousseau too took a sentimental view of the book and tried to model the figure of Emile on it. But Defoe's book is very far from being a celebration of the simple life; our castaway is only too keen to make full use of whatever tools and equipment he can salvage from the civilised world, in order to ensure a maximum of civilised comfort in the given conditions.[14]

What initially moves Robinson to leave his home is a desire to acquire property: 'a wild and indigested notion of raising my fortune'. This acquisitive motif runs through the whole book, though it is complicated by restlessness and a fatal thirst for adventure, which does not allow Robinson to settle down after the disasters of the first voyage, even though he has more than enough capital to start a business.

In the given conditions on Robinson's island all the bourgeois virtues find their fullest application and justification. Brought up as a gentleman, the castaway has a plain choice before him: acquire the bourgeois virtues and survive – or perish. Here he has to be provident, thrifty, industrious, patient and dogged. Here he has to think in terms of profit and loss, and he has to cope methodically with his difficulties.

Robinson's punctiliousness in book-keeping and business method leaves nothing to be desired. No reader can fail to be struck by the lists, inventories and balance-sheets drawn up and set out, both for the various deals made during Robinson's first voyage and for the articles brought from the wreck to the island and stored in his cave: indeed for all of his property. In some cases, this passion for listing

everything seems strangely out of place. Two episodes in
particular have been singled out by the critics. The first of
these is the balance-sheet set out as any careful merchant
would wish to see it, in two columns, exhibiting the pros
and cons of Robinson's situation. The 'debit' column starts
off by facing facts: he is a castaway on a 'horrible desolate
island'. But, says the 'credit' column, 'I am alive, and not
drown'd as all my ship's company was'. On the 'debit' side:
'I have not clothes to cover me'; on the 'credit' side: 'But I
am in a hot climate', etc., etc. (p. 50). The second case
concerns the fight with the cannibals. On p. 172 we find
the balance-sheet of this encounter meticulously set out as
follows:

>   3 killed at our first shot
>   2 killed at the next shot
>   2 killed by Friday in the boat
>   2 killed by ditto of those at first wounded
>   ___   etc. etc.
>   21 in all

In my opinion, it is a mistake to see in this passion for
classifying, listing and arranging things nothing more than
the mind of a tidy shopkeeper. There is a dash of the scientist
here as well. When Moll Flanders is casting her eye over the
ship-captains in search of a husband, she starts off by
dividing them into two categories – (a) those who own their
own ships, and (b) those who are still trying to do so.
Those in the latter category who are hoping to realise their
ambitions via marriage are further sub-divided into (a) those
who expect to succeed thanks to their wives' money, and
(b) those who expect to succeed because of their wives'
connections. This fondness for collecting and collating information, so characteristic of Defoe, is in fact something no
researcher can afford to dispense with.

As to the business of making money, we note that in
The Complete English Gentleman Defoe advises against any
attempt to speed it up. Robinson is also rebuked for trying
to do too much at once. In Brazil things go very well for
him: but 'I could not be content now but must . . . pursue

a rash and immoderate desire of rising faster than the nature of the thing permitted' (p. 30). This was to lead to a whole series of further misfortunes. In the long run, however, the desire and the determination to get on do bear fruit. Throughout his twenty-nine years of absence Robinson's Brazilian plantations are working for him. 'I cannot describe my emotion at the sight of so much wealth.' And further: at the sight of his riches he 'turned pale, and grew sick and had not the old man run and fetched me a cordial I believe the sudden surprize of joy had overset nature and I had dy'd upon the spot' (p. 206). Thus did Robinson come finally into the promised land.

It is not only a desire to make money that runs through Robinson's account of his doings. There is another theme as well – colonial expansion: the dream of splendid business deals in which savages hand over their gold dust and elephant tusks for strings of beads, rubbishy trinkets and looking-glasses. Such transactions are the more pleasing in that both parties are satisfied and the deal does no harm to anyone: it merely exploits different cultural values. Robinson dreams of having slaves and of lording it over them, a role for which – of this he is certain – an Englishman is most particularly well suited. The ill-starred expedition which ends with ship-wreck and Robinson's arrival on his desert island, is in fact bound to pick up slaves in Guinea where Robinson's companions 'desired to bring the negroes on shoar privately, and divide them among their own plantations' (p. 31). As Dottin wrote in 1924, *Robinson Crusoe* is a textbook of colonial practice, written in the conviction that the white man's mission is to take civilisation to the savages; the notion of the 'white man's burden' lies at the root of Anglo-Saxon imperialism.[15]

The present work is not meant to be a monograph on Defoe, and I cannot go into all the fascinating themes to be found in his great novel. For our present purposes, Defoe serves to illustrate the development of bourgeois morality; and Robinson can be taken as a model for that caricature of bourgeois morality which was to emerge in the course of the nineteenth and twentieth centuries (see Chapter 2). As we saw, critics in these centuries took the bourgeoisie to task for lacking those traits which are associated with aesthetic culture. Like Defoe himself, Robinson is certainly very short on culture. It has often been remarked that Robinson is never moved to contemplate his environment in disinterested fashion. Once only does he remark on the beauty of the peaceful sea – and as he has just been sea-sick in a storm, one feels that his appreciation is not purely aesthetic. [16]

Bourgeois morality is persistently accused of being callous and inhuman, and indeed evidence for this can be found both in its theory and in its practice. Witness the heartlessness of Moll Flanders, who thinks of nothing but her own material interests. Even her own children are of no concern to her. When her accomplice in numerous robberies is arrested, Moll's main worry is lest he give her away. Happily, however, the landlady 'sent me the joyful news that he was hanged, which was the best news to me that I had heard a great while' (p. 209). Nor can Robinson be absolved of cold-blooded self-interest. If Robinson felt any qualms about selling his faithful slave, Xury, they derived neither from moral scruple nor from affection. Again, it has been pointed out that when Robinson does anything to help or benefit someone else, he does so mainly to enjoy the satisfaction of playing the part of gracious master or good angel. What is particularly striking is that in such a realistic account as this, in which every detail is reproduced with photographic precision (especially where economic matters are concerned) Defoe lets Robinson live for twenty-nine years without ever thinking about women; though the book was certainly not designed for children. 'I was remov'd from all the wickedness of the world here. I had neither the lust of the flesh, the lust of the eye, or the pride of life' (p. 95). That is as much as we are ever told about Robinson's sex life. 'The merchant worthy of the name', writes Dottin on the subject of Defoe's heroes, 'has no time for falling in love. Any free time he may have at his disposal is to be used for improving his social position, for becoming a real gentleman.' [17]

The total neglect of the sexual impulse in *Robinson Crusoe* is not the only inherently improbable detail in the book. It is highly improbable that Robinson could live for twenty-nine years on his island without aging and without forgetting his mother tongue. On his first encounter with his countrymen he expresses himself in the English language with the fluency of one just home from the City. When a book is written in a couple of months, a few oversights like this are only to be expected; but Robinson's freedom from 'lusts of the flesh' may not be a simple case of oversight. Such matters seem to have played no great part in Defoe's own life. His biographers have ferreted out a transient affair with an oyster-seller, but even here it seems that Defoe was as usual playing the gentleman and only spent his money on the lady in a moment of relative prosperity.

This delicacy is preserved in all sorts of imitations of *Robinson Crusoe*, and this is perfectly reasonable and understandable in so far as these imitations are read mainly by children. D. Marion says that love and 'Robinsonism' are mutually exclusive (incompatible) in literature of this sort.[18] Of course, it all depends on what is meant by 'Robinsonism'. If, for example, Sienkiewicz's *W pustyni i w puszczy* ('In Desert and Wilderness') is included in this genre of post-Crusoe imitations, then Marion's assumption is incorrect.

The presence of a cautious, bourgeois distrustfulness has also been detected in *Robinson Crusoe*. And in fact, Robinson, treating everything as he does as a business transaction, always starts by getting absolutely clear what he has to spend and what he expects in return. He likes to have contracts in writing. As a particularly interesting example we may take his first meeting with his countrymen after twenty-nine years of solitude. Robinson loses neither his head nor his tongue. When the captain, marooned by his mutinous crew, asks him for help, Robinson is ready: 'Good! . . . my conditions are but two. 1. That while you stay on this island with me, you will not pretend to any authority here, and you will upon all occasions . . . be govern'd by my orders. 2. That if the ship is or may be recover'd, you will carry me and my man to England passage free' (p. 186). Robinson had all the money he had saved from the two wrecks, and his insistence at such a time on free passage to England shows that his business acumen had not deserted him. Happiness at being rescued had not fuddled his wits.

Moll Flanders shows the same sort of calculating distrust of others. She does not let herself be carried away by her feelings, and she has a down-to-earth contempt for those who do. It is her practice to demand written agreements in advance, while she herself is always able to wriggle out of any agreement whether written or witnessed. When she sets out to prove to her husband that he is her brother, she first of all demands a written certificate guaranteeing that, no matter what she tells him, he will do nothing detrimental to her (obviously financial) interests. Later, when her husband-brother sends goods to her from Virginia, and asks her to sign a form relinquishing her right to make any future demands, she is still equal to the occasion: 'I managed so well in this case, that I got my goods away before the release was signed, and then I always found something or other to say to evade the thing, and to put off signing it at all' (p. 123). When one of her children is sent to a boarding school at a cost of £10 a year, she tries to retain the right to visit him, a privilege which costs an additional £5 a year, and she is delighted to find that she has in fact secured that right without binding herself officially to pay the extra amount (p. 170).

As I said above, Moll feels nothing but scorn for people who give in to their feelings: and those who allow themselves to be swayed by love are no exception. When she robs a drunk during a chance sexual encounter in a carriage, she is moved to indignation at the thought that anyone could be so stupid as to take such a risk with an unknown woman. 'There is nothing so absurd, so surfeiting, so ridiculous,' she fulminates in connection with this episode, 'as a man heated by wine in his head and a wicked gust in his inclination together . . . vice tramples upon all that was in him that had any good in it.' She never forgets herself: 'I was not wicked enough to come into the crime, for the mere vice of it' (p. 104).

Some students of Defoe who start with a prejudice against the mercantile way of life, have shown themselves perhaps over-zealous in identifying its features in Robinson Crusoe and ascribing thereto a course of action and behaviour which would, in fact, be that of any sensible person in similar circumstances. Dottin, for example, sees the tradesman in Robinson in the fact that he keeps the money salvaged from the wreck carefully stored away at the back of his cave. But surely that is what anyone would do who had reason to hope that one day he would get out of his predicament. Similarly, his defences by night against an as yet unknown Man Friday are hardly 'une méfiance prudente qui convient en affaires' but simply a wise precaution which is not specific either to our author's class or to his calling.

The personal morality of Defoe and of his heroes, whose views and vicissitudes reflect very explicitly the views and vicissitudes of their creator, is by no means easy to define. According to Taine, Defoe was insensitive in matters of honour, and, while he may have observed the basic precepts of morality, 'les susceptibilités délicates de l'honneur' were alien to him.[19] Later assessment of Defoe, as more evidence accumulates on his way of life, is not so favourable. The fact is that his own life and experience taught him that the dividing line between good and evil is rather elusive. In *The Complete English Tradesman* for example we read: 'It is certainly true that few things in nature are simply unlawful and dishonest, but that all crime is made so by the addition and concurrence of circumstances.'[20] Puzzling words, perhaps, but it is never easy to arrive at an objective evaluation of people's actions. Defoe shows tolerance and forbearance in moral judgments. When Robinson is watching the cannibals landing he says: 'what call, what occasion, much less what necessity I was in to go and dip my hands in blood, to attack people who had neither done, or intended me wrong, who as to me were innocent, and whose barbarous customs were their own disaster, being in them a token of God's having left them to such stupidity and to such inhumane courses; but did not call me to take upon me to be a judge of their actions, much less an executioner of his justice . . .' (p. 169).

We know how deeply Defoe was convinced that a man's morality depends on his material state, on his property: and this in two senses: (a) a man can afford to be virtuous when he has money, and (b) one and the same action will be assessed quite differently depending on whether it is performed by a rich man or a poor one. Much attention has been paid to Defoe's thesis that the environment plays a big part in the formation of a person's morals. We find a good illustration of this in *Moll Flanders* where the criminals deported to Virginia turn into model colonists. But Moll herself, often quoted in this context as a victim of circumstances, is sufficient reminder that matters are not so simple. For Moll is an inveterate recidivist; and indeed in very few cases can it be said that she is forced to act as she does because of circumstances. As a child, she has a promising conversation with her foster-mother, in which she seems to grasp that if she is to become a lady (her highest ambition) she has to earn her keep. But alas, Moll does not want to work. Her idea of becoming a lady is by marrying a 'gentleman'. When she is left a widow for the first time, she has £120, not a bad nest-egg for a new start in life, but that does not prevent her from taking to thieving and prostitution. More than once she takes herself to task for being too greedy. We are indeed shown Moll penitent in old age, Defoe evidently believing that this spectacle was called for, or at least assuming that the reader would expect it. But some critics are of the opinion that in Defoe's eyes Moll is the positive heroine of the book. It is not easy to take sides here. Like all of Defoe's books, *Moll Flanders* is written in a hurried, slapdash manner, and is full of contradictions. The book has no plot to act as a unifying force, hence there is no definite conclusion and no specific moral to be drawn. It is simply a string of, on occasion, rather wearisome adventures, reminiscent in some ways of the knightly romances. The book was aimed at the sort of market which is today catered for by the thriller and the detective novel. To safeguard himself against charges of depravity, the author assures us in the preface that he has avoided lewd descriptions and immodest expressions; and that if he has told such a tale of crime and degradation, it is simply the better to bring out the beauty of repentance (and the better, be it said in passing, to stimulate the reader's appetite, the penitence being shrewdly left to the last pages of the book). The book also purported to serve as a warning to those finding themselves in a situation similar to that of the heroine and exposed to comparable temptations; also to those who don't take care of their property when there's a fire (the occasion for one of Moll's jobs) or who don't keep hold of their watches in crowds.

The preface to *Moll Flanders* is so packed with interest for the sociologist and the historian of morals, that it is worth while looking at it in more detail. It abounds in rationalisations and self-justifications of the sort familiar to us from *The Complete English Tradesman*; and although we are well accustomed to incessant moralising in English Puritan literature, in Defoe's works in general this reaches such a degree of fervour that we may well pause to wonder why. Could it be that he 'doth protest too much'? We can also discern psychological layers laid down during his childhood in a Puritan setting; and his dialogue with his conscience is not conducted solely in the interests of the reader.

When Moll steals a necklace with gold beads from a lone child, she tells herself: 'I had given the parents a just reproof for their negligence in leaving the poor lamb to come home by itself' (p. 186). When a fleeing thief throws away a package which Moll promptly grabs, she vindicates herself: '. . . but as I had only robbed the thief I made no scruple at taking these goods and being very glad of them too' (p. 187). When she robs the randy stranger in the coach she justifies her actions along lines that might be summarised as 'It's better for him that way, you never know who he might get mixed up with.' The victim must always be shown to possess some fault which in a sense legitimises her own actions.

We find the same sort of self-justification and rationalisation in Pepys's diary. When Pepys breaks his pledge not to drink any wine, by taking 'some hypocras', he persuades himself that it is 'to the best of my present judgement only a mixed compound drink and not any wine' (29 October 1663). When he breaks another pledge by going to the theatre, he convinces himself that the pledge did not really apply to court theatres: and besides, by walking home instead of taking a cab, he had not incurred the expenditure which his pledge was designed to avoid: '. . . my conscience knows that it is only the saving of money and the time also that I

intend by my oaths . . .' (13 August 1664). When he pays
less tax than he should, his excuse is ready: '. . . I thought
it not decent for me to do it, nor would it be thought
wisdom to do it unnecessarily, but vain glory' (5 April 1667).
When he reads what he admits to be a 'lewd (French) book'
he rationalises: '. . . but what do no wrong once to read
through for information sake' (9 February 1668). (He is
careful, however, to burn it 'so that it be not found among
my books to my shame'.) Looking for ways out and salving
one's conscience wherever possible is all too human; but
Puritan culture was particularly severe in its moral precepts
and rigorous in their application, and this sort of thing
always breeds an abundance of ways of explaining away
backsliding. The diary of Samuel Pepys is excellent introductory reading to a study of Defoe. Favouritism in the allocation of office, venality, theft of state property – all the
things that turn into abstractions in Defoe are here treated
in a cosy, family sort of way; and the reader is willy-nilly
drawn into identifying himself with this man who is baring
his soul in such intimate fashion.

4   Tradesman and gentleman

As we have seen, Defoe is very much aware of the role of
the bourgeoisie in England, as of the role of the tradesman
(to be discussed in a moment) and the role of money, which
the bourgeois amass and with which anything and everything can be bought. It is true that successful members of
the bourgeoisie lack distinguished ancestors in the landed
gentry class: but they have 'the grand essential', 'the great
fund of families' – money. As a rich merchant replied to
an insolent 'esquire' who had 'upbraided him for being no
gentleman: "No, Sir," sayes the merchant, "But I can buy
a gentleman"'.[21]
  Robinson's father tries to persuade him to give up the idea
of going to sea, and to settle down and make his fortune in
that middle station which is

  the most suited to human happiness, not exposed to the
  miseries and hardships, the labour and sufferings of the

mechanick part of mankind, and not embarrass'd with
the pride, luxury, ambition and envy of the upper part
of mankind. . . . He bid me observe . . . that the
calamities of life were shared among the upper and
lower part of mankind; but that the middle station had
the fewest disasters, and was not so expos'd . . . to so
many distempers and uneasiness, either of body or mind,
as those were who by vicious living, luxury and
extravagancies on one hand, or by hard labour, want of
necessaries, and mean or insufficient diet on the other
hand, bring distempers upon themselves by the natural
consequences of their way of living; that the middle
station of life was calculated for all kinds of vertues, and
all kinds of enjoyments; that peace and plenty were the
handmaids of a middle fortune; that temperance,
moderation, quietness, health, society . . . were the
blessings attending the middle station of life; that this
man went silently and smoothly through the world and
comfortably out of it . . . (p. 6)

But, while praising life in the middle station, Defoe
wanted something better for himself; and his desire for social
advancement can certainly be read between the lines, even
if it is not explicitly expressed. How Defoe's views on the
nobility took shape can best be studied in his last major
work, *The Complete English Gentleman*, written in 1728–9
and not published until after his death. As usual with Defoe,
it had been his intention to publish the work anonymously;
giving the impression in the preface that the book is written
by a gentleman for gentlemen (pp. 20–1).

The book is of enormous interest not only to those
concerned with the changing morals and the cross-fertilisation and superimposition of aristocratic and bourgeois
models, but also for anyone concerned with the history of
education, as the book has much to say on teaching methods
and on educational curricula. Finally, it is a veritable gold-
mine for those studying the morals and the customs of the
English nobility. It was on the basis provided by this book
(among others) that Macaulay was to portray the life of the
English gentry. From a literary point of view the book is

less successful, being disfigured by numerous repetitions, but there is no denying its rich fund of sharp observation, common sense and wit.

Defoe divides the English gentry into two categories which he treats in very different fashion. The first category comprises the first-born of a noble house: that is to say, in keeping with the English law of primogeniture, the heirs to the family estates. The second category comprises the younger siblings. In launching his attack on the first category, Defoe takes the side of the younger brethren who do not give themselves the airs commonly assumed by the first-born. He dismisses without further ado the megalomania surrounding so-called 'purity of blood', whether on family or on national level. Throughout the book, a distinction is maintained between 'gentlemen by birth' and 'gentlemen by breeding or education'. Defoe has little to say in favour of the former and would like to see himself as an example of the latter: they are the real gentlemen (pp. 48–9).

Who is a 'gentleman by birth'? According to the view which Defoe accepts as that current at his time, it is 'a person BORN (for there lies the Essence of Quality) of some known or Ancient Family: whose Ancestors have at least for some time been rais'd above the Class of Mechanicks' (p. 13). Some commentators have taken this 'Class of Mechanicks' or, as Defoe calls it elsewhere, 'the Common Mechanick labouring Class', to be the class of manual labourers, but surely it is rather the class of those in general who have to earn their living. Obviously the tradesman belongs to this class, and so does the teacher; and in one of the dialogues an impetuous scion, regardless of what his younger brother has to say on the subject, proposes to include the clergy and even senior service personnel in this category – after all, they earn money. 'Is not the pulpit your shop and is not this [i.e. the "chaplain's scarf" – Trans.] your apron?' says the noble heir to the parson.

For a certain time at least, our gentleman by birth has been excluded from those who have to earn their daily bread. One should not dig too deep here, however – as Defoe remarks nastily – unless we want to find dirt. After all, the biggest trees have their roots in the dirt and 'the most beautiful Flowers are rais'd out of the grossest Mixture of the Dunghill and the Jakes' (p. 13). Sooner or later we come down to the common herd.

These are not the only reasons why we must look on the notion of 'pure blood' with suspicion. These same ladies who would never under any circumstances consider marriage with an ordinary tradesman, have no scruples about handing their infants over to wet-nurses of proletarian stock, though the nourishment thus provided must undoubtedly affect the child's blood – a theme which Defoe develops with singular pleasure over several pages. It is not only family racism (in which he discerns the class barrier) that arouses Defoe's ire; he also has a go at national racism. When the Tories attacked William of Orange, a monarch beloved of our author, complaining that it was scandalous that a man of foreign extraction should rule over the English, Defoe, who, we may recall, had a drop of Flemish blood in his veins, wrote one of his most out-spoken satires: *The True-born Englishman*. How can anyone speak of a 'pure-blooded Englishman'!? How many peoples has England had to absorb? The local ladies were raped first by the Romans, and then by the Saxons, the Danes and the Normans. The 'pure-blooded Englishman' is the product of a multi-national congeries of robbers and murderers:

> A true-born Englishman's a contradiction,
> In speech an irony, in fact a fiction.

As I said, Defoe presents *The Complete English Gentleman* as though it were written by a 'gentleman of birth', and accordingly he is somewhat restrained in his condemnation of the class; a bird, he may have remembered, does not foul its own nest. He has a few moderate digs at those English heirs who suffer from swelled heads, but works himself into a fury over foreign specimens of the breed. 'Venice and Poland are two particular Countryes, where the notions of nobillity in blood are at this time carryed to the highest and most ridiculous extreme' (p. 21). 'In Poland this vanity of birth is still worse [i.e. than in England, which he has been discussing – M.O.] 'tis there carry'd up to such a monstrous extravagance, that the name of gentleman and the title of a

Starost, a Palatine or a Castollan, gives the man a superiority over all the vassals or common people, infinitely greater than that of King or Emperor, reigning over them with more absolute power, and making them more miserable than the subjects either of the Grand Seignior or the Cham of Tartary, insomuch that they trample on the poorer people as dogs and frequently murder them: and when they do, are accountable to nobody, nor are call'd so much as to giv a reason for it.'

Their behaviour is connected not so much with the Polish Constitution as with Polish pride and conceit. Not only on the basis of what we have learned from personal contact with Poles but from a study of the history of the country as well, we can say – Defoe continues – that the Polish aristocracy are the most overbearing, domineering and provocative in the world. 'A very valuable historian of our times sayes they are proud, insolent, obstinate, passionate, furious' (p. 29).

This onslaught will be of interest to Poles over and above its value as an illustration of Defoe's opinion of aristocratic uppishness. To round off Defoe's view of Poland, however, we must point out that in one respect he comes to a rather favourable conclusion – he finds the Polish nobility, in general, cultured and very well educated. All its members have had a university education gained either in Poland itself or abroad, and although they are not sufficiently fashionable to speak French as their English counterparts do (in fact, they regard French with contempt) they all speak Latin, so that a foreigner with a classical education may travel throughout Poland as easily as though he had been born there.

At least the foreign nobility are educated. Scions of English noble families, however, are not sent to school, as it would be intolerable for nonentities like schoolmasters to be in a position to tell them what to do; to say nothing of the fact that at school they would be forced to meet their social inferiors. So they were educated at home by tutors whose attitude to their pupils was determined by their natural fear of losing a comfortable post. At the conclusion of such an 'education' the heir to the family fortune could not write a letter without making spelling mistakes; he could talk about dogs, horses and hunting and nothing else; he was aggressive and ill-mannered, he talked in a loud voice, swore horribly and drank to excess. If one was found who appeared to be somewhat less ignorant and ill-mannered than usual, it could be assumed that this was a younger son who had been to a decent school and who had become the heir in lieu of his elder brother, who had had to be taken out of circulation for one reason or another. The heir did not administer his property: this would have been beneath his dignity. Nor was he expected to bother his head about enhancing his income. His attitude to money was simple: "tis my proper business to spend it; 'tis my calling' (p. 66). But Defoe's main objection to the elder scions of the English gentry is their ignorance: he presents the heir to a noble family as first and foremost a fool.

The bourgeois attitude to the nobility becomes one of condescension, stemming from an awareness of intellectual superiority. The watchwords of the Enlightenment were of signal value in this context. A little less than two centuries later we find Płoszowski in Sienkiewicz's *Bez Dogmatu* ('Without Dogma') saying with reference to the intellectual superiority which young Dr Chwastowski seems to feel towards him, 'at times he looks at me with real hatred as though he regards it as an unwarranted intrusion that a man whom he regards as an aristocrat should permit himself the pleasure of looking at a book or two and getting to know some authors' (vol. 2, p. 59).

As far as Defoe is concerned, the real gentleman is not the unpolished gentleman 'by birth', but the gentleman 'by breeding'. The gentleman who is short on learning, propriety, morals and manners is forthwith relegated to the 'Throng of the Ploebeii' (p. 18). He is no more than the shadow of a real gentleman. Defoe depicts a young nobleman engaged in a dialogue on these matters with his elder brother (pp. 44 ff.) – a dialogue so heated that at one point both brothers reach for their swords. The younger brother declares that he would never exchange his mental equipment for his brother's stupidity, even if this is embellished with lands and property.

Once the requirement of birth as the hallmark of the gentleman has been annulled, Defoe – who habitually presented himself as a gentleman and who usually attributed his anonymous works to 'a gentleman' – sets about demolishing a second barrier excluding him from membership of the elite. He proposes to remove the ancient classical languages from 'liberal education' on the grounds that they create a class barrier and that they are, in part at least, responsible for the emergence of a closed circle of the elite. Why should people not be taught in their own language? Why should a classical education not be imparted in English? Is it not a fact that we would have no Latin literature at all if the Romans had insisted on studying and writing in the language of some culture older than their own? The whole concept of the 'scholar' must be revised. A man can be educated and be a gentleman without a knowledge of classical languages as long as he knows his own language, the natural sciences, history, geography, mathematics and astronomy, and the modern languages, and if his fund of experience has been adequately broadened by travel. A gentleman may be a scholar without Greek or Latin (pp. 208, 196f.) Here again, Defoe has as usual an eye on his own interests, and like most self-taught men he is reluctant to attach too much importance to the university. One can educate oneself by reading, and it is not absolutely necessary to have completed a course of higher study – towards which, however, Defoe's basic attitude remains one of respect.

By now, the reader is no doubt sufficiently acquainted with the contents of the book to be amply prepared for the proposals which Defoe has to make in his final chapter. In recent years in England – he writes – a surprising number of people have made fortunes in trade, shipping, in the legal profession, in the wars, etc. They cannot as yet be called gentlemen, though they drive about in their own carriages, and carry swords (the use of which, Defoe adds in an aside, should be regulated by law). What these people were is still rather too obvious through the veneer of what they have become. Their speech habits still betray their former milieu. They cannot break the habits of the gold-rush and run after money *per fas et nefas*, just as an old thief cannot keep his hand out of someone's pocket, and an old whore cannot resist doing a bit of procuring. They throw their money and their weight about, and they have no manners: at every step, they give the show away and let people see what they really are (pp. 257–8).

> But where I say I thus give up the founder of the house, I must yet open the door to the politer son, and the next age quite alters the case. Call him what you please on account of his blood, and be the race modern and mean as you will, yet if he was sent early to school, has good parts and has improved them by learning, travel, conversation and reading, and above all with a modest courteous gentleman-like behaviour: despise him as you will, he will be a gentleman in spite of all the distinccions we can make, and that not upon the money onely, and not at all upon his father and family, but upon the best of all foundations of families, I mean a stock of personal merit, a liberal education, a timely and regular discipline and instruccion, and a humble temper early form'd and made the receptible of the best impressions and subjected to the rules and laws of being instructed.
>
> By these things the successors to, and sons of, the over-rich scoundrel, call him as you will, become gentlemen and are without hesitacion receiv'd for such among the best families in Britain: nor do any of the most antient families scruple to form alliances with them by intermarriages, or esteem their blood at all dishonour'd by the conjunccion. (pp. 258–9)

Defoe is arguing that the sons of *nouveaux riches* should be assured of social advancement once they have acquired the polish which money can buy. But he is also asserting that, in fact, this is not unusual in England, and he makes the same point elsewhere:

> Antiquity and birth are needless here,
> 'Tis impudence and money makes a peer.

Lewis and Maude make a similar point: 'In America money makes the man; in England, at least until recently, one had to wait – money made only one's children.'[22]

In Defoe's eyes, 'promoted gentlemen' are superior to gentlemen by birth. He relates the case of a rich merchant who did all the right things to give his first-born a better start in life than was envisaged for subsequent sons (an interesting example of plebeian imitation of the aristocratic institution of primogeniture). The young man was sent to Eton and then to university, while his younger brothers were placed without further ado in the father's various business interests. Property was acquired for the eldest son, who duly administered it in exemplary style. It was well stocked with game and animals, and there were separate stalls for 'the hunters, the running horses and the coach horses'. Everything was done with style and taste. He lacked none of the qualities expected of a noble scion by birth, and he was knowledgeable in matters of sport – but, in addition, he surpassed all his neighbours in education and bearing. He ran his estates well and paid his employees on the nail. He set an example for the whole neighbourhood (p. 270).

The conditions which Defoe sets for 'becoming a gentleman' are not always the same. For promoted gentlemen, a 'remove or two from the first hand' (p. 268) is necessary. Ever more insistent is the demand for education, for polish, personal merit – qualities which can be enhanced by money in so far as this has been come by in irreproachable fashion, and by the lands which can be bought with such money. At times, Defoe drops this last requirement, and the book ends with a poor young man being recognised as a gentleman purely and simply on the grounds of his personal merit. He had been educated before his father went bankrupt; and now he exhibits such polish and is so personable and engaging that upper-class ladies are only too keen to make his acquaintance – indeed, a certain rich lady with landed property has her eye on him. We close the book with a feeling of confidence: another happy and successful marriage of convenience is in sight (p. 278).

'Manners make the man', writes Defoe (p. 242), repeating his own words from a passage in *The True-Born Englishman*. Here we may recall J. Chałasiński's remark in his *Społeczna genealogia inteligencji polskiej* ('Social Genealogy of the Polish Intelligentsia') that the fact that the Polish intelligentsia was largely recruited from the ranks of the impoverished nobility explains why they placed so much store on manners as the only factor distinguishing them from the lower classes. To quote Chałasiński: 'The shakier their material situation became and the less social weight membership of the upper classes carried, the greater the significance which their own way of life – breeding, education and good manners – assumed for them.'

There is nothing surprising in this. As Montesquieu pointed out, politeness derives from a desire to distinguish oneself. 'It is pride that renders us polite: we are flattered with being taken notice of for behaviour that shows we are not of a mean condition, and that we have not been bred with those who in all ages are considered the scum of the people.'[23] But this is a card that can also be played against the alleged *inborn* superiority of the nobleman – as, indeed, Defoe himself does. As Chałasiński sees it, a member of the Polish intelligentsia used his good manners as a defence against demotion in the social scale; i.e. as something that could not be assimilated overnight. Defoe's argument is that way of life should rate as a fundamental value which can be taught and assimilated, if not by one generation then certainly by its successor. He quotes with approval the words of King Charles II, who is supposed to have said; 'I can dub someone a knight but I cannot make anyone a gentleman'; meaning that the personal values that go to make a gentleman cannot be acquired forthwith by investiture or accolade. Thus, manners serve both as a defence against loss of caste and as a means of gaining social advancement. The cult of aristocratic values in the bourgeois ethos may therefore reflect either fear of social demotion or pressure upwards.[24]

In both England and Poland, however, there were good reasons why the nobility itself should attach considerable importance to correct behaviour and good manners. In England, there was a significant degree of fluidity between the nobility and the bourgeoisie, generated *inter alia* by the right of primogeniture, which ensured that younger sons 'came down in the world'. In Poland, as Boy-Żeleński points out in the preface to his translation of Molière's *Le Bourgeois*

Gentilhomme, the nobility formed such a fluid mass that life-style alone distinguished the gentleman.

'Defoe abominates the aristocracy', says Jan Kott without further ado in his preface to *Robinson Crusoe* (p. 9). I find this something of an oversimplification. What Defoe abominates is the airs that aristocrats give themselves, and he would have nothing to say against a revised aristocracy in which he himself could figure. In no way does he reject the aristocratic paradigm: he would simply like to see it realised in an amended and enhanced format. We find a similar distortion of Defoe's thinking in J. Chałasiński's article 'Gentleman i zagadnienie kultury narodowej' ('The gentleman and the question of national culture').[25] I quote: 'As a contrast to his portrayal of the "True-born Eng-lishman", Defoe wrote his book on *The Complete English Tradesman*.' And again: 'The optimistic world of Defoe's novels, imbued with faith in the rational and providential nature of its characters, is a pointed satire directed at the gentleman of a bygone age; it is a new world of struggle and ambition and adventure in which the new, acquisitive tradesman takes on the helpless and ridiculous gentleman.'[26] In my opinion, this does not do justice either to the climate of Defoe's novels or to the problems and uncertainties with which the world he describes is beset. Defoe's world is very far from being as optimistic as Chałasiński makes out (see above, p. 132). Making fun of the 'gentleman' is by no means one of his main themes. In any case, as we have seen, his satire is aimed, not at the gentry in general, but at the inborn arrogance of the eldest born; and even here it is their lack of education and good manners that arouses his wrath, not their 'helplessness' or their ineptitude as relics of a vanished age. *The Complete English Tradesman* is in no sense designed as a contrast to *The True-born Englishman*; the latter pamphlet is a satire in defence of William of Orange *vis-à-vis* the 'pure-blooded Englishman' (see above, p. 155) and has nothing whatever to do with well-born Englishmen. If *The Complete English Tradesman* was meant to form a contrast with anything, it would have to be with *The Complete English Gentleman*; but there is no trace of any such contrast, either in these two works or in any other of Defoe's works known to me. There is of course no doubt but that in Defoe's works we find a new personal model promoted, one made very much in the image of the tradesman. As a general model designed to be imitated, this image is reflected in *Robinson Crusoe* rather than in *The Complete English Tradesman*, which is very largely a professional handbook. But this new model is not designed to oust that of the gentleman. Certainly in *The Complete English Tradesman* those traits and characteristics are described which a tradesman should possess and cultivate if he is to make money: but the *reason why* he should want to make money at all is so that he and, subsequently, his children should acquire the polish that will make gentlemen of them. To the model of the man born with a silver spoon in his mouth, the bourgeoisie now adds a new model of great import – the man who is bent on making money by his own efforts. The harmonious (on the whole) coexistence of nobility and bourgeoisie in England was to promote a gradual and very successful fusion of these two models. The product is admirably illustrated for us in Galsworthy's *Forsyte Saga*.

5   Defoe's tradesman and the merchants of Savary and Franklin

Chronologically, Defoe's model tradesman was the link between the model merchant depicted by Jacques Savary in *Le Parfait Négociant* and the model merchant whose lineaments are discernible in the precepts of Benjamin Franklin. Savary's book, written in 1675 – that is, fifty years before Defoe's book on the same theme – is a vast work of some fifteen hundred quarto pages thickly covered with small print.[27] Translating the word *négociant* by *kupiec*, 'merchant', 'tradesman', 'shopkeeper', we are restricting its semantic field, which appears to be very extensive. In his book on the French Revolution, G. Lefebvre says that in the eighteenth century the term *négociant* had not yet become specifically associated with any one calling: the *négociant* was at one and the same time shipping agent, middleman, carrier, insurance agent, banker and industrialist.[28]

Savary's portrayal of the model merchant was produced

at the behest of Colbert, who had commissioned the writer to provide him with a rationale of trading practice. This explains the nature of the book, a learned work which is clearly not intended for a wide circle of readers but for a select circle of highly placed officials who direct the national economy in an age of protectionism. If Defoe felt solidarity with the tradesman running an average-sized business, Savary is more concerned with the big wholesaler. For him, the highest class of *négociant* is the wholesaler with extensive overseas interests. The retail merchant is dependent on many people of varying degrees of power, while the wholesaler is concerned only with the producers ('*les manufacturiers*', to use Savary's term) who take his orders, and the retailers whom he supplies. This being so, in certain countries even noblemen engage in wholesale commerce. They would never deign to have anything to do with retail trade, as there is something 'servile' about it. In wholesale trade 'il n'y a rien que d'honnête et de noble'.[29]

Savary's book offers primarily a detailed exposition of mercantile law and an extremely interesting section on economic geography, and goes on to cover various commodities, book-keeping, weights and measures, and similar professional matters. Here and there asides are scattered from which emerges a picture of the good *négociant*, along with due consideration of the factors which hinder or promote his career, the education of his children, the rules by which relations between master and journeymen, between tradesman and apprentices should be governed. Much of this material is similar to what we find in Defoe, but its proportion to the rest of the work is different.

Savary was descended from an impoverished noble family which had begun to take a hand in trade as far back as the middle of the sixteenth century. From childhood he was designed for a career in commerce, and he married into a merchant family. In 1658, at the age of thirty-six, and having amassed considerable property, Savary broke with commerce and began to seek ways of rising in the social scale. For some time he administered the fur trade and was supplier to the royal household, an appointment which he lost when the royal superintendent fell into disfavour. This undermined his own position and fortune. In 1667 the king decreed that fathers with twelve living children should be entitled to pensions and other privileges. Savary, who had managed to get himself fifteen children in seventeen years, was, understandably, one of the first to present himself at the royal dispensary. In this he was lucky, for so many applicants turned up that at a certain point the court had to withdraw the offer. So, after his temporary setbacks, Savary landed on his feet, and he spent the rest of his life in security, regarded by his contemporaries as an oracle in matters of mercantile law.[30]

Trade, according to Savary, was created by God in order that concord and love should reign among men. Since God has divided earthly goods in a very uneven fashion, men are forced to make continual exchange in fulfilment of each other's needs. This in turn leads to continual contact among peoples and the growth of amicable relations. We have to thank trade for 'toute la douceur de la vie' because, thanks to trade, everything is everywhere in abundance. With goods so plentiful, it is true, people might well become indolent and lazy, but this is prevented by the desire to make profit and 'le désire de s'élever'. These factors impel people to engage in trade, and indeed most people live by means of trade of one kind or another. We are used to the spectacle of merchants growing richer and richer and securing higher and higher posts for their sons (Savary has the typical French bourgeois respect for high office). Trade makes the country rich, swells the royal coffers, finances great enterprises, covers the cost of wars, and enables the state to run an intelligence service in foreign parts, whose expenses can be settled by cheque.[31] But while lauding trade in general, Savary retains a prejudice against manual labour, allocating a lowlier position to those tradesmen who work with their hands (e.g. confectioners) than to those who only sell or, at most, decorate the finished article and who 'ne font aucun ouvrage de la main'. Those who are forbidden by statute to do manual labour – 'de ne faire ni manufacturer rien de la main' – form a *corps de la mercerie* and enjoy superior social position.[32]

If he is to be successful, a merchant must know his business thoroughly and have wide experience; he must keep his books properly (a theme on which Savary expatiates at great length) and he must be cautious and far-sighted if he is to avoid overstocking and unwise credits. He must be punctilious in the settlement of his debts; he must be thrifty and orderly; he must have the reputation of being a man 'de bonne foi', a man of his word, even if he incurs a loss thereby. Reverses will come his way which he must bear with fortitude. Good health is important if he is to stand up to the rigours of travel. Finally, he should be of good appearance, and should have the imagination to equip himself for several crafts and for the invention of new methods of production.

The merchant thus equipped can reasonably look forward to success, though here Savary lacks Franklin's confidence. In Savary's opinion, such factors as luck play a big part in ensuring success or failure. The wise merchant will steer clear of extravagant living, gambling and women; the time wasted on such things is a more serious loss than the money. Nor should he ever lend money in a frivolous moment to an aristocrat who will pay up only when he feels like it.[33] If virtue does not ensure wealth, it nevertheless fosters the process of gaining it. As for Defoe and Franklin, for Savary too money is a conditioning factor of virtue: 'When poverty comes in through the door, honesty (*probité*) flies out through the window.'

A merchant should approach marriage with the utmost caution, mindful that 'by marrying the daughter you are marrying the commercial fortune or misfortune of her house; this is something that must be deliberated very carefully indeed'. No attempt should be made to force children to take up commerce; people only do well at something for which they have a natural inclination. Children may, of course, be judiciously urged in that direction by example – that is, by pointing to those who started from nothing and made their fortunes, and whose children occupy the highest offices in the land. Children must not be allowed to get it into their heads that their family is already rich, because then 'ils méprisent la marchandise et n'en veulent jamais entendre parler'. Only such instruction is to be given to one's children as will be of use to them in their calling – modern languages, arithmetic, history, geography. Other areas of instruction are not merely unnecessary but positively harmful. Being sent to a 'college' where boys are taught Latin, grammar, rhetoric and philosophy until they are seventeen or eighteen years of age, is not conducive to a career in commerce. Out of thirty young men in such a college four at most will opt for trade. One reason for this is that, at college, they come into contact with the sons of noblemen and are infected by the scorn which these scions of aristocratic families feel for the world of commerce. Even those who do go in for trade don't do particularly well at it, as they don't think very highly of their calling. They treat their masters and their colleagues alike with contempt, and their behaviour is abominable. If apprentices have been in contact while at school with boys who are going into the army, they are even less suited to a career in commerce. They turn out to be libertines who run up debts and probably embezzle money, in the firm conviction that an expedient marriage will save their skins.[34] Why does the French aristocracy, Savary grumbles, not follow the example of those aristocrats in Genoa, Venice and Florence who are not ashamed to engage in trade in the Mediterranean; after all, the younger sons of the English nobility do not deem it a disgrace to take up commerce as a career. But while castigating the closed minds of the French aristocracy, Savary treats them for the most part with servile respect. If we compare his work with that of Defoe, we can see at once that we have to do with two different phases in the evolution of the bourgeoisie. Savary is writing *before* it came to power; Defoe is very well aware of the power wielded by the victorious class to which he belongs.

In their masters' houses, apprentices are required to be God-fearing. Once a day, attendance at Mass is obligatory, and, if necessary, the apprentice must get up half an hour earlier for this purpose. Failure to attend Mass is punished by dismissal. Alas, the good custom whereby master merchants went to Mass on Sundays together with their apprentices and journeymen is dying out, for most employers are as indifferent to the faith as their subordinates. To their master, subordinates must be completely docile and loyal. They must protect his interests against his competitors, and never say anything about his business affairs to outsiders. They are to obey him blindly, never seeking to know why he wishes this and not that. However, if the master orders his apprentices to do something manifestly unreasonable, they are not called upon to obey at once, but should let a little time elapse. If he orders something that is manifestly at odds with his own best interests, they should act as though they had not heard the command. Apprentices and journeymen must live modestly and dress soberly, seeing to it that a proper distinction is maintained between their garb and that of their superior.

I need go no further into Savary's book. As I said, it is of interest to the economic historian rather than to the student of moral behaviour and the evolution of personal moral paradigms. For our present purposes, what matters is that Savary's book and Defoe's *Complete English Tradesman* have one thing in common – their professional approach: they are commercial textbooks. As I pointed out above, Defoe outstripped this purely professional approach in *Robinson Crusoe*, where the hero displays all the resourcefulness of a successful tradesman, which in fact by calling he was not. The influence of the model tradesman on wider circles is already evident in Franklin, whose precepts – addressed officially to a young merchant – make a far wider appeal to all the bourgeois of the New World and beyond. Franklin's thesis that virtue can be measured by its use value, by its utility, is binding not only upon the merchant. It is binding upon everyone, and in Franklin's hands the professional ethics of the merchant become the ethics of mankind in general.

I end this chapter with a glance at a few further points of comparison between Defoe and Franklin. In spite of the completely different social climates they inhabited, there are not a few similarities between the two. The models they created share certain common characteristics: self-dependence, industriousness, perseverance, thrift, patience, meticulous accountancy, methodicalness. In Franklin's case, however, the model is presented with candour and humour, while one detects a slightly false note in Defoe's moralistic poses. Both share a faith in the role of science and of rational thought. 'Under any government, democratic or mixed,' wrote Franklin in his Almanac for 1749, 'knowledge, whether theoretical or practical, is the natural source of wealth and honour.' Defoe was a fervent advocate of education, and in *Robinson Crusoe* he voices his belief that by thinking rationally every man can, given time, master any 'mechanic art'. Neither of our authors has a good word to say for the clergy, Defoe going so far as to say that of all tyrannies 'ecclesiastical tyranny is the worst'.[35] Both are in favour of religious tolerance, and Defoe expresses his pleasure that the large number of sects in England allows people to choose their own ways of going to heaven (a remark repeated by Voltaire in *Les Lettres anglaises*). Of course, Puritan culture is much more deeply rooted in Defoe than in Franklin, who is a long way from the Old Testament. There can be little doubt that Max Weber (the subject of our next chapter) over-rated Franklin's Puritanism; over the years, the freemason certainly gained the upper hand over the Puritan in Franklin.

It is worth pointing out that in Franklin there is no trace of a desire for that social advancement which Defoe dreamed of. Defoe's model tradesman represents the best available *modus vivendi* until one makes one's pile and becomes a 'gentleman'. For Franklin on the other hand, social advance boils down to wealth and respectability. The riches he amassed were used largely for public works, and it never entered his head to spend his money, as Voltaire did, on buying a great country estate and settling down on it. It is true that the Pennsylvanians, whom Franklin was primarily addressing, had no native aristocracy who might have corrupted people by setting a bad example. But there is more to it than that; the petty bourgeois colonists retained memories of aristocratic ways in their folk traditions, and Franklin himself met plenty of aristocrats during his long sojourns in Europe. What is beyond doubt is that for Franklin and in Franklinism it is up to each man to enrich himself *within the framework of his own station in life*; and as the Polish translation of Franklin's *Ways to Wealth* has it: 'Whoever raises his head over the heap should have it pushed down again.'

Chapter 6

The Puritan sects and bourgeois morality in the development of modern capitalism

1 Typological investigation of the modern bourgeoisie

(a) Werner Sombart

So far, we have been considering classical paradigms of bourgeois man. We proceed now to analyse a variety of theories, prominent in the literature of the capitalist countries, concerning certain factors which, it is held, play an important part in fashioning these paradigms. But before we discuss the role played by certain religious sects, both as nurseries of these exemplars and as factors in the evolution of capitalism itself, let us glance for a moment at the views of those who associate the formation of bourgeois models with a certain specific type of man. I do not agree with the sociological attitudes of these authors, and their approach to the problem seems to me to be fundamentally wrong. But one cannot simply ignore theories which were in their day confidently applied to the problems we are discussing, and widely acclaimed.

In his book *Der Bourgeois*, Werner Sombart applied the typological method very thoroughly indeed to these questions. As he puts it: 'Today, when we say that someone is a bourgeois (*Bürger*) we do not mean that he belongs to a certain class (*Stand*) but that he is of a certain type.'[1] It is a type, according to Sombart, which was first successfully nurtured in certain Italian cities, particularly Florence, in the fourteenth century. The urge to make money is as old as the hills; but it was not until Italian capitalism of the Renaissance that a specific type of man appeared who applied himself to

171

the *business* of making money in methodical fashion. In early times, human beings had to concentrate on survival and subsistence and nothing more. Medieval lords and princes showed little interest in book-keeping, preferring to replenish their revenues where necessary by way of contributions in kind, tithes and rents. Their wealth lay in the possession of fine weapons, goblets, dinner services, harness, fur garments, and so on. Town dwellers in the Middle Ages, ignoring economic pros and cons, simply spent whatever they had when they felt like it. It was a novel discovery that one could actually get rich by dint of certain personal virtues such as industriousness, reliability and thrift, the latter construed as a voluntary and praiseworthy exercise, not dictated by force of circumstances. The classic formulation of this way of life dates from the fifteenth-century polymath Leone Battista Alberti, whose influence, according to Sombart, is very considerable.

In the course of history, the bourgeois attitude, as Sombart sees it, undergoes various transformations. Until the eighteenth century, the scene is dominated by the old-style bourgeoisie, but with the growth of capitalism a new type appears. In the early eighteenth century, money is still regarded as a means to an end and nothing more. Life is static, advertising as a means of attracting customers is frowned upon, and attention to quality is the proper way to attract and retain a clientele. Price-cutting as a means of stealing a march on one's competitors is castigated, and there is a certain aversion to technological novelty.

With the growth of capitalism, economic activity increasingly sheds its man-to-man character. The businessman appears, obsessed with his own enterprise and with the profits which he personally can make from it. The classic bourgeois virtues (see Chapter 4, above) are objectified: that is to say, they are transferred from the man to his business. Thrift is no longer a necessary component in the bourgeois way of life and the big operators lead lives of sybaritic luxury. A firm is reliable, not necessarily its owner. The latter demands and gets complete freedom of action, *Ellbogenfreiheit* – elbow room – to shove his way through the world.

Quality ceases to be a primary consideration, and industriousness ceases to be a personal virtue. Sombart's latter-day
bourgeois is drawn into a maelstrom which compels him to
be ceaselessly active in a way that has nothing to do with
the voluntary application of a previous age. Obviously, of
course, it is the big entrepreneur who is being described
here, not the smaller men who surround him. In Sombart's
opinion, however, it is the very existence of these big operators that gives mature capitalism its lineaments. And in an
explicit reference to capitalist attitudes in America, Sombart
describes the infantilism of the entrepreneurs who scramble
for anything that is 'big', anything that gives a feeling of
power, their frenetic search for novelty and their appetite
for change.

It will be clear from his account of the changes in the
meaning of the word that when Sombart speaks of the 'bourgeois' he is not thinking of one single type of being. In the
basic psychological type he distinguishes two variants: the
entrepreneurial type (*Unternehmernaturen*) and the bourgeois
type *stricto sensu* (*Bürgernaturen*). *Bourgeoisnaturen* in general
are those psychological types which are disposed towards or
have an inclination for capitalism: Sombart calls them
'Naturen mit kapitalistischer Veranlagung'. But in this basic
type the two variants are intertwined, and it is their fusion
that generates the spirit of capitalism. The two factors are
not evenly distributed, however, and this imbalance makes
for the emergence of one type or the other. Whether a man
will turn out to be a big entrepreneur or merely a modest
bourgeois depends according to Sombart, on heredity (p.
254). Sombart, as we shall see in more detail later, comes
down heavily on the side of the biological factor in opposition to Lamarckism and all theories which depend on the
notion of 'milieu'. These he associates with liberal and democratic viewpoints (pp. 500–1). Rockefeller, the oil king, must
have had book-keeping in his blood from birth. Nothing of
the sort would ever have entered young Byron's head!

The entrepreneur must be armed with the acquisitive
spirit: he must be '*ein Eroberer*'. He must be able to think
through his long-term plans and put them into practice. He
must be a good organiser, able to get his way whatever

the opposition, a tough and determined negotiator. Here, Sombart uses the word *Händler*, specifically, he says, in a very wide sense. Before the advent of unrestrained capitalism, this sort of nature found its outlet in various shapes and forms – pirates, for example, and those who went in search of new lands hoping to find the Golden Fleece. The great feudal lords were moved by the entrepreneurial spirit when they opened mines on their lands and built foundries and smelting works. To this same category belong such men as Colbert, big speculators in the shares of English companies, the great Florentine merchants who started off with tiny shops which they built up into vast businesses.

The man who wants to combine in his person the qualities of an *Eroberer*, an organiser, and an astute negotiator, must have quick wits and the ability to go straight to what is essential in any situation. He must know people in themselves and in their environment; he must be energetic, bold, quick to take decisions, and while endowed with a rich store of vitality he must not be emotional, lest his feelings should cloud his judgment and frustrate his plans.

Bourgeois natures *par excellence* are not at bottom opposed to the *Eroberer* type, with whom they normally feel themselves to be on an equal footing. In sharp contrast to the happy-go-lucky *seigneurale* natures, they are careful and anxious (*sorgsam*), the people who arrange things and who feel responsible for things, in contrast to people who simply use things. They calculate instead of dreaming. The bourgeois nature is also opposed to the erotic nature – where Eros is defined so widely as to include St Augustine and St Francis of Assisi. For to love is to give out, to distribute; to economise is to store up and lay by. This is what the bourgeois does with everything, time, money, raw materials, methodically recording his profit margins over his expenditure, and bestowing on his business activity a halo of sanctity.

Neither the development of the bourgeois as thus outlined, nor its breakdown into two variants, can be accepted without considerable reservations. There is no justification for regarding post-Renaissance Italian capitalism as the first manifestation of the 'spirit of capitalism' if by 'capitalism' we mean no more than the unfettered pursuit of profit. In the opinion of Ludwig Brentano,[2] trade linked with capitalism as thus understood had been going on in Italian towns, particularly those on the seaboard, from time immemorial. We shall come back to this point in due course. In the Middle Ages too, men of power sought riches, and in this respect capitalism brought nothing new beyond a shift in the object of cupidity – money instead of lands.

Not a few authors have seen fit to borrow Sombart's typology, but even its initial assumptions seem to me to be highly questionable. Who is this man 'mit kapitalistischer Veranlagung', a predisposition towards capitalism, which can manifest itself in either of two ways? Since its precise criteria remain obscure, one does not know what to do with Sombart's classification. The notion that the types described are biologically conferred is not likely to appeal to anyone nowadays, and Sombart himself made the whole thing ridiculous by lumping Rockefeller together with the 'bourgeois natures' given to an allegedly hereditary liking for book-keeping. It can hardly be doubted that Rockefeller, as the oil magnate he was to become, was always a representative *par excellence* of the great entrepreneurs. Did heredity predetermine the change from bourgeois nature to that of *Eroberer*? And does the very possibility of such a switch-over not invalidate the dichotomy itself? Questions like these never enter Sombart's head. He believes in 'race' and is accordingly very well treated in German encyclopaedias of Hitler's time as a leading critic of socialism and as a historian of capitalism. 'We who believe in blood (*Blutsgläubige*)', he says of himself (p. 281) when criticising those who, as he sees it, overemphasise the role played by the environment. He finds that all the European nations show a certain aptitude for capitalism but in different degrees, both quantitatively and qualitatively. The Celts and the Goths, for example, had and have an underdeveloped aptitude for capitalism (*kapitalistische Unterveranlagung*). Among the Celts, the upper classes like to cut a dash, while the middle classes show no sign of economic initiative. This can be observed in Scotland and in Ireland, and in those parts of France where there is a strong admixture of Celtic blood. In Spain likewise, economic matters were primarily in the hands of the Moors, the descendants of the Celts having little inclination for such things. Those nations which show genuinely capitalistic propensities are divided by Sombart into two groups: those who undertake their economic enterprises in heroic fashion (*Heldenvölker*) and those who show a preference and an aptitude for peaceful negotiation (*Händlervölker*). The first group includes the Romans, the Normans, the Lombards and the Franks. The second group comprises the Etruscans, the Frisians and the Jews. The business men of Florence owe much of their success to the drop of Etruscan blood that runs in their veins. The Dutch are indebted in the same way to the Frisians.

Sombart admits that the biological blueprint is modified in every generation by the elimination of less propitious elements and by cross-fertilisation of types. In Florence, for example, we see the aristocratic element gradually disappearing because it had no real aptitude for trade. In the ranks of the bourgeoisie, the shopkeeper is forced to give way to the big entrepreneurs. Before Leone Battista Alberti could make his voice heard, writes Sombart in connection with the significance of cross-fertilisation, a good drop of huckster blood had to find its way into the blue blood of the Albertis. Failing this, one can hardly imagine Alberti producing anything like the *Libri della Famiglia*. Here, Sombart recalls that Alberti was probably illegitimate. God alone knows who his mother was; at all events, no biographer has been able to give her a name (!).

These racist arguments hardly require serious refutation. We shall have more to say about Sombart, all of whose work bespeaks the extraordinary blindness of this 'sociologist' to social factors and their influence. In any case, no one today doubts the extent to which an aptitude for trade and commerce is a function of social position; there is a rather regular correlation between these callings and the socially underprivileged who cannot hope to rise in the Establishment. We shall return to this point. Here, in passing, we may glance at Sombart's ideas on the Celts. He sees Celts present wherever a Celtic language is spoken – in Scotland, Ireland and Brittany – but fails to reckon with their genetic presence in places where they once lived though their languages have been ousted. This is a crude confusion of race and language of which no sociologist worthy of the name should be guilty.

(b) Max Scheler

Sombart's work on the characteristic typology of the bourgeoisie caught the popular fancy and triggered off a whole series of similar books. 1919 produced Max Scheler's 'Der Bourgeois und die religiösen Mächte', which appeared as part of his *Vom Umsturz der Werte*.[3]

Scheler was a pupil of Husserl, and was the main theoretician of the phenomenological school in the field of ethics. As an adult he was converted from Judaism to Catholicism and promptly became its most fervent apologist. Certain sections of Polish Catholicism were very much under his influence. Scheler combined a faith in an absolute world of values, apprehended through direct intuition, with a dislike of everything democratic; he extolled what was noble and aristocratic, viewed movements coming from below with deep suspicion, and believed firmly in the part played by heredity and 'nobility of soul' in isolation from environmental influences. All of this was expressed in a very bombastic and high-flown style. Scheler's work, often very intelligent where it is intelligible, can perhaps best be called intellectually perverse.

For Scheler, as for Sombart, the bourgeois is a 'biopsychical type' (*ein biopsychischer Typus*) to whom Scheler imputes all the qualities which he (Scheler) personally finds objectionable, basing this verdict on nothing more concrete than the 'intuitive insight' characteristic of the phenomenological method. Scheler's intuitive insight, however, expresses itself in the same language used for the general condemnation of the bourgeoisie in the late nineteenth and early twentieth centuries.

There is nothing new about the distinction between men who are bold and venturesome and men who are anxious and timid: 'hommes ouverts et hommes clos', to use Bergson's terminology, outgoing, generous natures and buttoned-up natures – in a word, noble natures and bourgeois natures. The first type, to which Scheler intuitively believes himself to belong, likes to take risks: danger is its habitat. Its sovereign confidence in its own value puts it beyond feelings of envy. People belonging to this type are not obsessed with looking after themselves and their interests; supremely confident of and in life, they can take life easily. This confidence releases them from the insurance mentality, and makes for generosity and openness; they take people as they are instead of assessing them in terms of utility.

The second type – to which our stock bourgeois belongs – is deficient in vitality. He is therefore anxious, continually seeking reassurance and safeguards. Since he does not trust even himself, he looks for confirmation that he is of *some* value, in what he is able to achieve. Permanently worried and suspicious, he has an uneasy relationship with his environment. He compares himself enviously with others; he never does anything generous and never forgets himself. He is always drawing up balance sheets. Because he cannot trust himself, he equips himself with a catalogue of restraints – things he must not do. He never asks: 'Is this the right thing to do?' His attitude is 'What's in it for me?' Since his sexual life is not integrated with his life as a whole, it is accompanied by a feeling of guilt. Scheler is one of the most eloquent critics of the *ressentiment* factor in bourgeois mentality. In his monograph on this theme, he derives the slogans of the French Revolution from envy[4] – especially the slogan of 'equality', which, he asserts, is based on bourgeois *ressentiment* of the privileged classes.

(c) Eduard Spranger

Spranger's name figured fairly prominently in the German weeklies during the years of Nazism. In his *Lebensformen*[5] this pupil of Dilthey's distinguished six basic human types which attracted considerable attention in pre-war intellectual circles. These types are alleged to be 'ideale Grundtypen der Individualität', consciously selected in a social vacuum by means of *reflection*, which Spranger describes as 'isolating' and 'idealising'. The six types thus selected are: (1) the theoretician; (2) economic man; (3) aesthetic man; (4) social man; (5) the man of power (*der Machtmensch*); (6) religious man. Of the six, it is economic man that interests us here. The specific character of economic man does not depend (as Spranger himself points out) on whether we are dealing with a peasant, a craftsman or a worker in industry. Economic man is the man governed by economic motives, which are treated as stable and enduring, regardless of who is governed by them or what ends they serve. Variables such as these are left out of account.

Spranger's economic man always considers the use-value of things, and allows that use-value to take precedence over all other values ('der ökonomische Mensch im allgemeinsten Sinne ist also derjenige, der in allen Lebensbeziehungen den Nützlichkeitswert voranstellt', p. 148). *Nützlichkeitswert* is further defined as that which satisfies our need for survival (*Lebenserhaltung*) or our biological needs (*physische Lebensförderungen*).

With use-value and its associated economic motivation thus defined, it should logically follow that the peasant cultivating a couple of acres to keep himself and his family alive typifies *Homo oeconomicus*, while Rockefeller in his later years when, with his biological needs secure, he was buying up his rivals in the American oil industry, does not. But Spranger comes to a different conclusion. The small peasant daily and permanently bound up with satisfying his biological needs, is ignored when 'economic man' is being discussed, while Rockefeller emerges very clearly as exemplifying the genre. This comes about because Spranger allows his concept of 'economic motive' to expand to a point where he completely forgets his own premises, and the concept itself is totally transformed. This becomes clear when we find him asserting that economic needs are 'insatiable', and that the economic motive can easily turn into a demonic obsession. Here, Spranger seems to have forgotten all about the 'biological survival' he originally posited.

To return to 'economic man'. As we have seen, this type measures the value of anything in terms of its usefulness or lack thereof. Economic man looks upon people either as consumers or as producers – as links, that is, in the economic chain which is his main concern, as labour, as buying and selling potential of varying degree. Economic man values those virtues which are economically effective: industriousness, thrift, reliability, orderliness. He is egoistic, since altruism and business are mutually exclusive. His relations with his fellow men are described by Spranger as 'mutualism'. This seems to mean a fair exchange of services, and due observance of the principle of *do, ut des*.

Economic man needs plenty of elbow-room so that he can push his way through the world. He needs a legal system which protects private property. For him, the most important area of law is that which regulates economic relations; the state is often simply a supra-individual economic institution. God is understood as a sort of general dispenser of goods. He gives man his daily bread, causes his flocks to multiply, guides the vessel bearing merchandise, and sends the sun to shine or the rain to fall on the crops. In applying the category of usefulness, Spranger's economic man is thinking rationally, for usefulness may only be identifiable in the long term; it is not necessarily something that can be appreciated forthwith. Here, rationality is explicitly identified with cold-blooded calculation, the opposite of action as dictated by some whim or other. In Chapter 2 we saw that economic man is often said to be insensitive to beauty, and, in full agreement with this, Spranger announces that 'what is useful is normally the enemy of what is beautiful' (p. 154). At most, economic man may use what is beautiful to enhance his economic success. Patronage of the arts as practised by rich entrepreneurs is generally designed to enhance their standing in the credit stakes.

Such, in broad outline, is the very abstract, not to say artificial, figure of 'economic man' as we find him in Spranger's work: a description which really fits only a type bred in and by certain forms of European urban capitalism, but which Spranger presents as though it were an invariant, found in all economic systems. Spranger's imagination does not reach beyond those economic forms to which it is accustomed, and he fails to recognise the purely contingent character of certain traits in his allegedly general model of economic man.

It is true that Spranger admits a certain differentiation into sub-types within the framework of his general model. Within the corpus of those governed by economic motives there is, for example, a distinction between those who mainly produce (*Erzeuger*) and those who mainly consume (*Verbraucher*). Further, those who work with goods are to be distinguished from those who operate with money, who deal in abstractions, like the banker or the speculator in stocks and shares. Spranger has particularly hard words for the money-grubber, whose life of Spartan austerity is both negative and unproductive. This is usually the role of women in bourgeois families: not the only telling observation Spranger has to make in his criticism of different types of economic man. But these moments of insight are not enough to rescue the work as a whole. The book suffers from the inadequacy of its starting point – the assumption that all those governed by the economic motive share this 'motive' as a common homogeneous factor; and many of Spranger's subsequent reflections do nothing to redeem this faulty point of departure.

Even if we were to limit Spranger's 'economic man' exclusively to the ranks of the tradesman/merchant – the category which theoreticians have usually taken as a basis for their generalisations – we are then faced with a gallery of characters who can hardly be brought within the confines of any one schema. How can we compare the settled urban merchant of late nineteenth-century Western Europe with the traders who sailed the seas in earlier times, risking their lives at the hands of pirates; men who discovered new lands, like Marco Polo, or English traders like Thomas Betson, the medieval wool-merchant, whose life has been reconstructed for us in such fascinating detail by Eileen Power[6] on the basis of his correspondence. How do we fit in the Polish merchants who slipped past the baronial keeps of Niedzica and Czorsztyn, in constant peril of being robbed?

And yet, theoreticians keep on trying to identify constant traits in this most elusive of characters. Thus, Kautsky in his *Foundations of Christianity*[7] considers in general terms the influence which trade exercises on the human mind, and which differs, as he sees it, from that exercised by agriculture or by a handicraft. The merchant is less conservative than the farmer or the artisan, since his calling demands a certain degree of initiative and receptiveness to new ideas. Accordingly, he should not be tied to one place, he needs to be mobile (a requirement with which, as we have seen, Defoe would not agree). While the arts and handicrafts present man with an array of concrete problems, thinking in terms of bank balances and percentages generates and develops abstract powers of reasoning. The merchant must not shut himself up in one branch of production. What he actually buys and sells is a matter of indifference as long as he buys cheaply and sells advantageously – in other words, as long as he makes a profit. The work involved in making goods can interest him, according to Kautsky, only in so far as it has a bearing on the price. The farmer and the artisan can look forward to no more than a limited degree of comfort and resources, but the merchant has literally infinite prospects; all he needs is an insatiable thirst for profit, a thirst which will not shrink from cruelty to others in the attainment of its ends (as happened for example, in colonies).

Kautsky writes: 'It is not the "productive" activities like agriculture and handicrafts, but "unproductive" trade that forms those mental capacities that constitute the basis of scientific research.' At the same time 'disinterested thought, the quest for truth rather than for personal advantage, is the last thing to characterize a merchant'. 'Trade develops the requisite mental traits, but not their application in science. On the contrary, where it influences science, its effect is to falsify it and twist it to its own ends. . . .'[8] Thus, Kautsky admits the possibility of disinterested thought in science, indeed he asserts that this is a necessary condition for its existence. '. . . the merchant is, down to the nineteenth century, at once the most international and the most national member of society'. We have seen an example of this in the case of Defoe. He was a confirmed nationalist when it was a question of barring foreign imports, but his own trade interests made him concurrently an operator who recognised no international barriers.

(d) The psychoanalysts

The proposition that a certain type of man is particularly attracted to and interested in goods and money is one that appeals to psychoanalysts, and they have duly come up with various theories as to how this particular type is engendered.

Interest in money and property, some of them claim, is a surrogate for interest in one's own excrement.[9] The child's first produce is its first possession; and its subsequent attitude to property is determined by its attitude to this first act of production. All reactions to having, owning and spending have an irrational element in them, conditioned by the infant's anal training. Thus, the 'anal-erotic' type, comprising those who are fascinated by their excrement, produces financiers! This type parts more readily with paper money than with coins: a trait which we are asked to see as a relic of nursery practices. The financial expansion of the middle classes could not really take off until the introduction of paper money as a readily manageable currency – one reason for this being that there was less incentive to hoard it. From this initial interest in possessing things there derives, according to the psychoanalytic school, a whole series of other traits – orderliness, methodicalness, pertinacity, cleanliness, a propensity for collecting things, a tendency to dictate to others and a tendency to promulgate and propagate ideas. It can then be said, according to the psychoanalysts, that the social conditions in which the bourgeois came to power favoured the 'anal-erotic' type whose representatives thereupon assumed the leading role in bourgeois society.

Pecunia non olet: very telling words for the psychoanalysts. Here speaks the true 'anal-erotic' type whose interest in and attachment to money often takes on manic dimensions. Just as an obsessive hatred of religion is often the result of disappointment in and continuing need of religion ('religion-deficiency'), so do the psychoanalysts construe attacks on money as evidence that money is not something that we can be indifferent to.

My own attitude to these essays in typology may be briefly summarised. There is no difficulty about accepting the fact that there are many different ways of approaching and participating in economic life; and, consequently, attempts to classify these different attitudes are not *a priori* unacceptable. Again, it can hardly be doubted that the merchant's calling will affect his character in one way or another, a theme explored by Kautsky. If, however, I continue to have certain reservations on this score, it is for several good reasons. For one thing, far too much stress tends to be laid on the biological component; for another, it is not always clear exactly what domain we are supposed to be dealing with: is it biology, history, linguistics, philosophy or what? This is a particularly disturbing factor in the work of Sombart and Spranger, in connection with their vague and dubious figure of 'economic man'. Then again, we find a typology which may very well fit people living in certain specific economic conditions being applied wholesale to people in general (Spranger, Scheler). Finally, the alleged connection between certain characteristics as specified and their putative source or basis is, if not always as preposterous as the theories of the psycho-analytic school, unconvincing to say the least.

2   The religious factor in the formation of the modern bourgeois ethos

(a) Max Weber

The popularisation of bourgeois morality of the Franklin type in those countries where the advance of capitalism was most rapid, was accompanied by the emergence of certain religious sects. Not surprisingly, the part played by these sects both in the formation and in the spread of bourgeois morality has been the object of study by specialists in this field.

The religious factor in the formation of the modern Western European bourgeoisie was the theme of a particularly stimulating study by Max Weber entitled *Die protestant-ische Ethik und der Geist des Kapitalismus*. This made its first appearance in 1904–5 in Numbers XX and XXI of the *Archiv für Sozialwissenschaft und Sozialpolitik*. Its subsequent appear-ance in book form and its translation into several languages brought the author widespread fame, though Weber is not exactly the easiest of authors to read.

The order in which I propose to take up Weber's main points is purely one of convenience; it is not meant to reflect the order in which they arose in his creative output. I am not suggesting that Weber used these ideas as points of departure, or that he arrived at them in support of an already formulated hypothesis. I am guided by a need for clarity; analysis and criticism of the logical interconnections between these ideas will follow this summary account of them.

Observation of social life, Weber writes,[10] shows us certain convergences which invite explanation. Research undertaken (under Weber's direction) in Baden showed that the Catholic population paid less tax on capital than the Protestants. The same fact was also observed elsewhere in Germany. It was also easily established that fewer Catholics than Protestants took part in the great capitalist enterprises. Breakdown of the school population by religion showed that whereas Protestants went to the polytechnics and the *Realgymnasien*, Catholics tended to go to the *Gymnasien* and the universities. Similar patterns of convergence were detected in the economic structures of other countries. Thus, Catholic countries like Spain and Italy were industrially backward, while Protestant countries like England and Holland were advanced. The English historian R. H. Tawney, who popularised Weber's ideas in England, quotes an anonymous English pamphleteer who wrote in 1671: 'In the Popish religion there is a kind of natural unaptness . . . to business, whereas, on the contrary, among the Reformed the greater their zeal, the greater their inclination for trade and industry . . .'[11]

Was there then something in Protestantism that was particularly conducive to the development of a capitalist economy? An analysis of Luther's teachings led Weber to discount him as a source of the new capitalist upsurge. It is true that some of the component factors are to be found in Luther – opposition to the monastic way of life, the drive to take up a calling in the temporal world. And Luther had nothing but praise for work. But his teachings were still hedged about with what Weber calls economic traditionalism. The pre-capitalist worker did not ask how much more he could earn in a day if he worked harder; what concerned him was how much work he had to do in order to earn the minimum he needed to survive. He preferred a reduced existence and less work to an enhanced existence and more work. Unsuccessful attempts were made to overcome this pre-capitalist attitude by introducing contract work and also by reducing rates of pay – this latter course of action in the belief that men will only work when forced by want to do so (pp. 44–5). But the biggest successes in the gradual education of people towards working for the sake of work were chalked up by the ethico-religious component in the Puritan make-up.

Weber uses the word 'Puritan' in the sense in which it was applied in the sixteenth century to that brand of ascetic Protestantism which was then on the increase in England and Holland. The four main types were: (1) Calvinism, widespread in Western Europe; (2) Pietism, which, in its later phases, was found mainly in Germany; (3) Methodism, originating in England whence it spread to and achieved great popularity in the United States; and (4) the Baptist movement. The Quakers and the Mennonites should also be mentioned here. These sects differed on various doctrinal points, but all shared a common ethos, a general way of life which finds its classic expression perhaps in Calvinism.

What was it in Calvinism that fostered the mental attitudes favourable to economic activity? Calvin taught that human beings are predestined by God for salvation or for damnation. Calvinist man is on his own. He cannot look to the sacraments for help as the Catholic can, nor to any other magical rite or ceremony. In worldly success the Calvinist sees a sign of grace, following in this respect the Hebrew prophets; not for nothing was Calvinism called by its English adherents 'the English Judaism'. The Calvinist can assure himself of success in this world by vigilant and methodical self-control, and by nothing else. Work must be his obsession from morning till night. The Calvinist ideologist Richard Baxter allots very little time indeed to sleep. All pleasures are sinful, including those derived from the arts and the pleasures connected with the senses. Man's sexual life should be strictly limited to what is necessary for procreation and for health. The whole Calvinist way of life centres round what Weber calls *innerweltliche Askese*, an asceticism *within* the social framework, in opposition to the *ausserweltliche Askese* practised by the anchorites and hermits who fled from society and the world. Riches are seen as a reward for an exemplary life. Thus, the acquisition of wealth becomes an ethico-religious mission, a vocation; and the marriage between religion and economics takes on the dimensions of a mass movement. The Puritan gets rich 'involuntarily'. His work adds incessantly to what he already has. Since he is not permitted to enjoy life, he invests. Neither Baxter nor Wesley, the spokesman for the Methodists, is under any illusion on this score. They know that what they are enjoining upon the faithful must lead to wealth, to something, that is, which is fraught with peril for the human soul. 'We must advise all Christians', writes Wesley, 'to work as much as possible and to save as much as possible so that in the end they may be rich.'[12]

While severely limiting consumption, the Puritans sanctioned the desire for possessions. This new attitude to life spread upwards from the rank and file. It was a characteristic not so much of big entrepreneurs as of small artisans and shopkeepers who had grown up in a hard school: sober, hard-headed, solid men. Heavenly bliss did not recommend itself to these men of action. Nor did they, once they had made their fortune, run to the College of Heralds in search of a coat of arms, or seek to disguise their sons' origins by getting them commissions in the army. Franklin, whom Weber takes as the classic example of the type, got nothing out of his wealth, according to Weber, beyond an irrational pleasure in the feeling that he had 'fulfilled his calling' (*irrationale Empfindung guter Berufserfüllung*). During the great upsurge of the Italian cities, large sums were paid into church coffers as conscience money (*Gewissensgelder*). In other words, those who were busy making their fortunes had bad consciences – connected no doubt, *inter alia*, with the fact that they felt themselves guilty of the sin of usury. What the Florentine capitalists of the fourteenth and fifteenth centuries were doing was either outside the sphere of morality or in contradiction to it (*aussersittlich*, or, rather, *widersittlich*) (p.

60). All this had changed. A way of life which was repugnant to the man of the pre-capitalist age now received full ethical endorsement. In the Italian towns, Franklin's way of going about things would have been, in Weber's opinion, simply unthinkable. In the interim, however, Puritanism had endowed the profiteer with a clear conscience. Calvin had said that the worker is submissive to God only when he is poor – which did much to justify the payment of low wages. The attitude to beggars underwent a radical change. To beg when you could work was now seen as a sin. If a man was poor it was his own fault, and there was no need to waste any sympathy on him.

The Puritan way of making money differed fundamentally from the Jewish way. The Jews used their native wits to practise a sort of cowboy capitalism. Puritanism systematised capitalism by means of the rational, long-term organisation of work (p. 18). With time, the religious motivation faded, but the way of life it had helped to mould survived, for the simple reason that it worked. Guild organisation and fellow feeling ceased to cramp the style of those who wanted to make money. The role of the guilds was taken over, at least in part, by the sects. But the guilds had united people in the same calling: too much success on the part of any one member could adversely affect the interests of other members and be a disruptive influence within the guild. (As we saw, Defoe considered price-cutting the worst crime anyone could perpetrate against his colleagues.) The sects, however, united people belonging to different callings. Success achieved by any one member of the sect could only redound to the credit of the sect as a whole and enhance its reputation. It may be that the guilds were a necessary step on the road to capitalism; but it was the ascetic sects which justified and legitimised the individualist approach to economic enterprise that brought about its great upsurge (p. 236). The conviction that one should hearken to God rather than to man was also one of the most influential factors in the formation of modern individualism (p. 235).

The propitious effect of Puritanism on the acquisition of property by its adherents can be traced in the history of Puritan families in England and the USA. In the Autobiography, Franklin mentions the Quakers as a particularly important element in the industry and trade of the United States. Frederick William I regarded the Mennonites as essential to Prussia's commerce, and did not persecute them although they were adamant in their refusal to do military service (Weber, p. 28). The positive usefulness of ethics of the Puritan type is underlined by the fact that wherever the type appears in other parts of the world, it is invariably attended by the same economic spin-off. Weber mentions the Moravian Brethren (to whom we shall return) and in subsequent volumes of his *Religionssoziologie* he takes up this theme anew in connection with the Jain sect in India.[13]

With origins going back to the sixth or seventh century BC, the Jains form one of the oldest and most exclusive sects in India. Monastic members of the sect were required to be homeless and itinerant lest they become attached to things. The wide mass of Jain adherents, however, were advised to settle down in one place and stay there so as to avoid exposure to temptation in alien surroundings.

The Jains were forbidden to take life: a prohibition which extended particularly to weak, defenceless beings. A Jain could, however – and this was even recommended – take his own life, preferably by starving himself to death, when he had achieved sainthood, or if he could no longer control his passions. The principle that no other life should be taken in any circumstances is carried by them to extreme lengths. Orthodox Jains will not light a lamp lest insects be attracted to the light and perish therein. Water is strained before being boiled. They cover their noses and mouths lest the exhalation of their breath cost some tiny creature its life. Ground is swept before they set foot on it. They do not cut their hair but pull it out by the roots to avoid harming their own parasites. They will not walk through water. Clearly, there are very few factories or workshops in which Jains can work; nor can they be farmers as the plough would endanger small creatures living in the soil. They cannot practise any craft which requires sharp instruments, nor any that involves a naked flame. Trade is about the only occupation left open to them.

Jains are forbidden to covet or become attached to riches,

though not specifically forbidden to *be* rich. Similarly, in Europe, Protestants were permitted to be rich, as long as they did not commit the cardinal sin of enjoying their riches. Like the Quakers, the Jains are bound to absolute truthfulness; even exaggeration is forbidden. Any Jain who departs from absolute honesty and dependability in commercial deals runs the risk of being reborn after death in the shape of a woman. The practical effect of these precepts has been 'honesty is the best policy', as recommended in the West. Jain honesty is proverbial, as is their wealth. Only in trade can total observance of the rules for *ahiṁsā* be ensured, and so we find the sect playing a very large part indeed in this field, and one hardly warranted by the relatively small numbers of the sect. Those Jains who are forbidden to travel settle down as bankers. Merchants and bankers alike are bound by an áustere asceticism which (again as in Puritanism) has led to their further enrichment. But their wealth did not go into industrialisation. This was impeded by the traditionalism of India's economic structure, on the one hand, and by the isolation in which the sect found itself, on the other. Its ritual practices are another factor making for this isolation.

Jains are forbidden to overindulge in eating, and they may not eat meat or use any sort of narcotics or indulge in ostentatious display. Cleanliness, conjugal fidelity, inner discipline and control of their passions and affections are binding upon them. They have to feed the hungry, give water to the thirsty and take care of animals. The fifth vow, which bound the Jain monk to *aparigraha*, excluded love for anyone or anything: for love leads to desire and passions. There is no scope here for love of one's neighbour – not even for love of God. There is an empty space in the heart of the Jain monk. God, even if he exists, is not concerned with this world. So the Jain does not pray and expects no forgiveness for his sins by way of repentance.

In spite of this officially imposed frigidity, solidarity among members of the sect was very strong, and, as in the case of the American sects, this has played no small part in their economic success. Every adherent felt he could count on his fellow believers, and if he had to move from home he would be at once taken in as a member of the family; though we can hardly speak of a 'brotherhood' in the early Christian sense of the word.

Jains are mainly town dwellers, though Weber does not recognise Jainism as a bourgeois phenomenon. The founder of the sect, who belonged to the Kṣatriya caste, died about 600 BC. Membership of the sect was drawn largely from intellectuals, and its saints were always of royal blood. The princely families took an active part in it, and this was tied up with Jain efforts to rid themselves of Brahmin pressure. The high point of Jainism does not coincide with the growth of bourgeois influence; rather, it is concurrent with a fall in bourgeois prestige and in the power of the guilds. The geographical dispersal of the sect favoured its independence from the growth of the bourgeoisie. Nor can we say that Jainism, separate from the bourgeoisie as it was, may yet have served bourgeois interests; for the burden it placed on its members was such that they could never have undertaken it had they been guided by economic interests alone.

So much for Weber's account of the Jains and their beliefs. It can be checked and amplified by a reading of J. F. Muehl's interesting book *Interview with India*, published in 1950 (see especially pp. 34–58). Muehl is an American writer who travelled widely in parts of India, turning a keen eye on the glaring economic exploitation and identifying the Jains in their role as bankers, as described by Weber. In the villages of Kathiawar, Muehl found plenty of evidence (to be corroborated elsewhere in India) to show that the blood-suckers of the Indian villagers are the *baniyāṁ* – the merchants and particularly the money-lenders who are for the most part Jains. According to the local people, the money-lenders own everything that is worth having in any given area, and they have everyone in their pocket by charging 40 per cent on loans. Those who cannot pay up forfeit their property. Whatever a villager in this grim position can make from his fields and his crops goes to pay the interest on his loan. When this fails, the victim is compelled to work for his minimal keep – i.e. without pay – in the quarries belonging to the money-lender. The same money-lenders also own the jewellery shops into which innocents are enticed and encouraged to live beyond their means; they are particularly cajoled into vying with each other in laying on marriage feasts they simply cannot afford. Jain concern for the life of the meanest insect is allied with singular indifference to the fate of their fellow men. They hire low-caste men to sweep the streets in front of them. In this process, many a small creature comes no doubt to an untimely end, but this hardly matters: the point is that the Jains do not have their demise on their consciences. They wear white garments, as many colouring dyes are of animal origin. They spread sugar and grain before their houses to feed the ants, and keep watch to make sure that none of this is stolen by starving children. The Brahmins, say the natives, are negligible in comparison with the *baniyāṁ*, who allow the Brahmins to go on existing for the simple reason that they find it easier to buy them than to do away with them.

Thus, Weber links a certain ethos, a certain way of life, with economic efficiency, though he does not claim that this efficiency was consciously or unconsciously *intended* by the founders of this way of life. Weber denies that the Reformation in Europe can be explained in terms of its economic factors alone as a 'necessary stage in historical development' (vol. 1, p. 83).[14] An infinite number of factors played a part in shaping the Reformation. He also categorically denies the suggestion that he favours the simplicist and doctrinaire thesis that capitalism was a product of the Reformation. Certain forms of capitalism antedate the Reformation. All Weber wants to do is to establish 'whether and in what degree religious factors were involved alongside other factors (*mitbeteiligt gewesen sind*) in the formation of the spirit of capitalism and in its quantitative spread to other parts of the world; and which cultural traits in a capitalist setting can be traced back to religion' (p. 83). It is a fact that capitalism did not develop in the Southern states of America, although people settled there precisely for business interests; while it did develop in the Northern states where people had originally settled so as to be able to practise their religion in freedom. Franklin's activities antedate the development of capitalism in the United States. When Franklin arrived in Pennsylvania trade was still in the barter stage, and there was no trace of anything that might be called a large-scale business venture. Here, Weber takes a stance opposed to historical materialism, while elsewhere he recognises its validity. One cannot lay down hard and fast rules; an infinite number of seminal factors underlie historical phenomena, and one must be very cautious. In general, Weber is averse to historical materialism as an all-purpose thesis. As he sees it, Franklin's bourgeois morality was not *designed* for economic reasons and purposes; but it *survived* because it was eminently suited to promote these purposes.

(b)

We shall now try to analyse and criticise Weber's arguments; and we shall take the opportunity to look at other factors which may have contributed to the development of that 'capitalist spirit' which Weber associates specifically with Puritanism.

Let us consider, first of all, how to formulate Weber's most basic assertion in the work under review. The title itself suggests a first thesis which can be formulated at one level as the modest claim that certain phenomena are *concurrent* in historical situations; and at another level as the more substantial claim that certain phenomena are the *causative* agents behind other phenomena. At the first level, Weber's thesis can be formulated as follows: the development of the Puritan ethic *coincided with* the growth of *the capitalist spirit* (1a). At the second level, it reads: the Puritan ethic *was conducive to* the growth of the capitalist spirit (1b). In both versions, psychological relationships are invoked, and indeed any discussion of this first thesis must take place at least partly in the realm of psychology. More important than this first thesis, however, is the second thesis which links that set of beliefs which went to form the Puritan ethic, not with other psychological factors, but with the development of *capitalism* itself. Like the previous one, this thesis too can be formulated at different levels, but Weber comes down explicitly on the side of the more substantial claim: namely, that the Puritan ethic was conducive to the growth of capitalism (2). Finally, one of Weber's most significant claims is the following: the business of making money is transferred in Puritanism into an ethico-religious mission *on a mass scale*; and this is something for which there is no historical precedent (3). We shall now consider each of these arguments, the first two of which are not sufficiently differentiated either in Weber's own treatment of them or by his admirers and his critics.

(1) As we saw, Weber recorded a tendency for Protestants to go to the *Realgymnasien* and the *Technische Hochschulen*, while Catholics showed a preference for the *Gymnasien* and the universities. Assuming that the figures are accurate, and accepting Weber's interpretation – that these figures show Protestants to be practical, sober and matter-of-fact in comparison with Catholics – we may admit this observation as an argument in favour of a real connection between religion and a certain way of life.

But it is not so easy to put this into more precise language. Exactly what factors on each side are thus connected? Accepting for the present that we have a fair idea of what 'the Puritan ethic' is (though, as we shall see, there are difficulties here too), we come to a halt at its correlative – the 'spirit of capitalism'. Weber avoids defining this formally, in either positive or negative terms. What this 'spirit of capitalism' is will only emerge in the course of further considerations (p. 30). For the moment, we have to make do with an example which serves as a sort of *Veranschaulichung* of the concept. For his example, Weber goes to some of Franklin's sayings, of the kind known to us from Chapter 3 above. From his commentary on Franklin's words we gather that in Weber's opinion someone can be said to be inspired with the spirit of capitalism if he devotes every minute of his life to making money, if he regards making money as a vocation, and denies himself the enjoyment of life he could so well afford. But Franklin does not only urge us to make money; he also recommends patience, industry, thrift and reliability. If the general content of Franklin's teachings is supposed to be a *Veranschaulichung* of the 'spirit of capitalism', then it is hardly surprising to find a connection between this spirit and the Puritan ethic: for we are defining the one in terms of the other. In such circumstances, the connection between the two is *ex definitione* established.[15]

Some critics[16] have taken Weber to task for misrepresenting Franklin's thought by making an arbitrary selection from his writings and ignoring those passages in which Franklin, harking back to the wisdom of the ancients, explicitly denounces lust for gold and over-attachment to and enjoyment of this world's goods. I think this criticism is misplaced. Franklin's statements, made over a long life, are by no means homogeneous, and there can be little doubt that in his personal life he did not always live up to the example he enjoined upon his youthful readers. In any case, Weber was not concerned with reconstructing Franklin's ideological lineaments, but with illustrating and exemplifying what he called the 'spirit of capitalism', and to this end he made use of a selection of Franklin's utterances culled from the Almanacs: justifiably, we may think, as it was precisely the Almanacs that reached the widest reading public and had most to do with turning the 'spirit of capitalism' into a mass phenomenon.

A more serious objection to taking Franklin as a model lies in the realisation that the advice which Franklin gives the young tradesman is neither new nor in any way particularly related to the epoch, but is, as Brentano points out, quite simply the sort of advice that any merchant would give his apprentices anywhere on earth. According to Brentano, what we have here is nothing more than the traditional ethic of the petty bourgeois, as practised by them from the late Middle Ages onwards. Advice very similar to Franklin's was given by Johann Gottlieb Nathusius, the German industrial pioneer whose life – again like Franklin's – is a rags-to-riches story. As Brentano says: 'The allegation that Puritanism gave birth to the spirit of capitalism as a mass movement is simply unacceptable' (p. 154). However, even Brentano has to admit that Puritanism *favoured* the growth of capitalism by getting rid of such human resistance as stood in its way.

I agree that the virtues which Franklin recommends in his Almanac, and which we discussed in Chapter 3 of the present work, can be regarded as the professional ethic of the small merchant or artisan in general, and that this ethic is both temporally and spatially far more widely distributed than Weber allows. It is not irrelevant here to remind ourselves that a 'puritan' ethic is ascribed to the merchants of the Hanseatic League, long before the appearance of the Calvinist Puritanism with which Weber links Franklin. But even granted that the saying 'Time is money' does not date from Franklin, it is still true, I think, that the great expansion of this sort of life-style, and the fervour with which it was preached, represent something new. Of course, Franklin was not the first to stress the value of time. And also before Franklin there must have been people who calculated their day-to-day activity in terms of profit and their idle moments in terms of loss. But it would be difficult to find anyone else who was enough of a moral evangelist to convert an age to this way of thinking.

Even if we agree that what Weber calls the 'spirit of capitalism' finds its expression in the slogan 'time is money', we are still left with a problem: exactly how can Franklin's Almanac morality serve as an example of Puritanism? The point is important for Weber's thesis which postulates a concurrence between the spirit of capitalism and Calvinist ethics – that is to say, with the Puritan ethic *par excellence*. Franklin himself, as we know from the Autobiography, broke with religion at an early age, retaining for his personal use a rather vague sort of deism. As for the Almanac, we have to remember that it must be treated as a record of his views on what people *ought* to do, not as a statement of his own personal belief. It is a very earthy production, easy-going and jovial, free of religious overtones, whether general or particular, and in no way burdened by the doctrine of predestination – the doctrine to which Weber ascribes such an important role in the launching of the 'spirit of capitalism'.

Now there is in Polish literature a figure who illustrates that particular mixture of economics and religion which Weber detects in Puritanism, better than any of Franklin's sayings: a figure who is not only a nobleman but very probably a Catholic into the bargain. This figure is to be found in Henryk Rzewuski's essay 'Mammon' which forms part of his *Mieszaniny Obyczajowe* ('Medley of Customs'). In this essay, Rzewuski provides an extraordinarily interesting and subtle typological study of the worshippers of Mammon. His description of one of them – Kleon – follows, in somewhat abbreviated form:

> Kleon is in every respect a virtuous man. He is a good father and a pleasant neighbour, full of kindness and consideration for servants and subordinates. Although like all of his fellow worshippers [i.e. of Mammon – M.O.] his heart is set above all things on getting money, yet he would not commit the smallest act of dishonesty for all the treasures of Attila. He is not entirely devoid of the spirit of sacrifice, and sometimes he has even managed to do something magnanimous; and, considering that he is a collector of property, he is on the whole helpful and obliging. But with all this he pushes the worship of gold to heights of idolatry unattained even by these [i.e. other worshippers of Mammon – M.O.] and although all his actions are righteous, his ideas are all the more distorted. For he clings to a stubborn, immovable and unswerving faith that God has laid upon every man, particularly those who have children, the obligation to make money and to amass property honestly, on pain of risking salvation. The profitable direction of his business interests is in his opinion not merely something appropriate, suitable and useful, something no one could object to, but a duty which can never be neglected . . .
>
> Any setback, however small, arising from his own oversight distresses him, not so much because of the material loss involved as because his conscience tells him that he has not done his duty. Amidst all his wealth, and even when he feels himself to be innocent, this thought gnaws at him. Convinced as he is that property is a bequest from God, which the owner is entitled to keep as long as he can justify possession by his work . . . if at the end of the year he can say that he has not increased his property as much as he might have, and as much as he has on previous occasions, his recalcitrant conscience upbraids him, as though someone were damaging his property. The good Kleon is, as you see,

neither the poet nor the philosopher of Mammon, but
its theologian . . .

When he is merriest, let his ear catch the clink of coins,
if only a few, let his eye glimpse the presence of money
– and at once the smile leaves his lips and his countenance
assumes a grave and ascetic look. In a rapture like that
induced by the sight of the most holy mysteries in a
mind not yet deformed by sin, he seems to perform a
mental act of ardent prayer. If an acquaintance of his
loses his fortune, and even if this acquaintance cannot
be faulted on any grounds more serious than careless
book-keeping, Kleon will hold him in contempt as a
criminal whose company decent men should shun as they
would a leper. And if someone should decide to stop
hoarding his wealth and to start using it to satisfy his
needs and wants, Kleon will regard him as Dante
regarded those neutral souls rejected by both heaven and
hell.

To be wasteful is, for him, to be sacrilegious, and I
am convinced that in spite of his boundless thirst for
gain, if it were suggested to him that by throwing a gold
coin into a swamp he could instantly double his wealth,
he would indignantly repudiate such a scandalous
suggestion. . . . The worship of money is so deeply
ingrained in him and so unadulterated that he would
gladly see it distributed among all the peoples of the
world, even if this meant a palpable diminution in his
own coffers. Hence he loses no opportunity of
evangelising his fellow creatures, of explaining to them
honourable ways of making money. He will not refuse
to go to someone's estate to introduce a better system of
management for the owner, and he will devote himself
to this with unflagging dedication; and not only a mile
or two miles but a hundred miles will he travel without
any further reward beyond the inner conviction that he
is thereby spreading the gospel and worship of money.
This is a true apostle of Mammon . . .

The quotation merits the space given to it. It is not only
a good illustration of the attitude described by Weber, but

also provides an example, albeit a complicated one, of what is loosely called 'economic motivation'. If we had any data on the relative incidence of this attitude among the aristocracy of Rzewuski's period, we could use this material to counter Weber's thesis of a specific connection between worship of money and bourgeois Puritanism. But we have no such data; and in so far as we can produce no more than one individual case, Weber would no doubt promptly reply that while he must admit the possibility of Puritan attitudes even in such an unlikely ambience, it was Puritanism and Puritanism alone that transformed these attitudes into a *mass* movement.

There is no mention of predestination in Franklin's Almanacs; indeed, as far as I am aware, the concept plays no part at all in his theoretical system. Yet Weber stresses the role of this doctrine in the development of the 'spirit of capitalism'. So this may be the proper place for us to consider the effect of such a doctrine on the human psyche. Here we enter the field of experimental psychology; that is, we have to try to imagine what effect this doctrine would have on us if we believed in it. What we are talking about is not a belief in what might be called the inevitability of historical processes and the effects of this inevitability, but rather the belief that our lives are determined, preordained in advance.

In ancient Greece, fatalism was regarded as a doctrine which lamed initiative and led to what was called *lógos argòs*, 'indolent reason', encouraging supine submission to the wave bearing us. But Muslim fatalism did not disarm its adherents: on the contrary, it spurred them on to deeds of military valour. Thus, not only may variants of the same basic concept be distinguished, but, significantly, the effects of that concept may vary in different social conditions. In the case that concerns us here – the effect of the Calvinist doctrine of predestination on human behaviour – it was not only Weber who took this doctrine to be an activating factor; Engels did so before him, though the two thinkers interpreted the doctrine in rather different terms. 'Calvin's creed', wrote Engels,

was one fit for the boldest of the bourgeoisie of his time. His predestination doctrine was the religious expression of the fact that in the commercial world of competition, success or failure does not depend upon a man's activity or cleverness but upon circumstances uncontrollable by him. It is not of him that willeth or of him that runneth, but of the mercy of unknown, superior economic powers; and this was especially true at a period of economic revolution, when all old commercial routes and centres were replaced by new ones, when India and America were opened to the world, and when even the most sacred economic articles of faith – the value of gold and silver – began to flutter and to break down.[17]

And in Engels's work on Feuerbach we read:

The Calvinist Reformation served as a banner for the republicans in Geneva, in Holland and in Scotland, freed Holland from Spain and from the German Empire and provided the ideological costume for the second act of the bourgeois revolution which took place in England. Here Calvinism justified itself as the true religious disguise of the interests of the bourgeoisie of that time.[18]

How are we to understand the conformity which Engels describes, between Calvinism and contemporary bourgeois enterprise? At first sight, the belief that economic sense does not depend on us or on our own efforts hardly fits in with the picture of the self-made man as lauded by Franklin, the man who takes pride in the knowledge that everything he has he owes to himself alone. What Engels probably means is that the activating role of the belief in predestination lay in the fact that it incited people to take risks: just as the realisation that the hour of death was predestined for every man incited the Muslim to warlike bravado.

Weber, however, saw the activating power of the belief in predestination in a different light. As he saw it, the belief induced people to start guessing whether they belonged to the elect or the damned. Success on earth might rate as a signal that one was in fact among the elect: so success was something worth pursuing. But the choice of business success as a criterion whereby a man might know whether he was damned or not is far from convincing. As Westermarck very aptly says, why should it occur to anyone that high profits are a sign that God has blessed him? We may accept that the Old Testament spirit plays a part here, 'but I maintain that the chief solution of the problem lies in the influence of the capitalist spirit over theological dogma'.[19] So for people to accept such a criterion, conditions must have been favourable.

To continue along Westermarck's line of thought: other criteria, no worse if no better, can be envisaged to fit the situation. For example, it would be very natural for people reared in the Christian tradition and accustomed to regard themselves as predestined for either heaven or hell, to hit upon the idea that the best way of finding out once and for all whether one belongs to the elect or not, would be to do absolutely nothing at all: for God does not desert those whom he has blessed, even if 'they sow not, neither do they reap'. Anyone who survived in such conditions, having taken no thought or care for his economic existence, might well imagine himself to be among those on whom God's grace has fallen.

If the doctrine of predestination seems to have lent itself very well to the justification of personal privilege *vis-à-vis* the exploited, and to pacification of one's own conscience, it still seems to me that Weber has not succeeded in making a good case for the alleged connection between a belief in predestination and the 'spirit of capitalism'. I simply do not see *why* Puritanism in its Calvinist edition should provide an impetus towards self-enrichment; although it is abundantly clear that, in the event, it was indeed attended by such a process. To put it another way: in so far as the role of a belief in predestination is concerned, Weber's psychological thesis seems very questionable; but this does not necessarily detract from his non-psychological tenet, to which we shall return in a moment. The urge to make money was also a characteristic of those Puritan sects which did *not* accept the doctrine of predestination. The virtues enjoined by the Puritan ethic, even if they were not generated by this urge, served it very well, in that they were indeed factually useful in the process of making money. The connection set up between the ethic in question and certain historical processes is, in spite of the title of Weber's paper, the most original and important part of his thesis. We proceed now to consider it.

(2) While the fact that the Protestants chose to follow the more practical walks of life bespeaks a congruence between religion and vocation, the fact that Protestantism spread mainly among the bourgeoisie, that the larger enterprises were in Puritan hands, that they paid more tax on capital and that industrial development was largely confined to the Protestant countries – all this ties up with Weber's second thesis. It is this second thesis which Tawney underwrites, pointing out that in England Puritanism spread first and foremost among the middle classes, while the aristocracy viewed it with disfavour; and that data for the first decade of the seventeenth century show that most of the Calvinist clergy and most of their flocks were to be found precisely in the most highly industrialised districts of England.

The thesis that in England, the United States and Holland, the Puritan ethic favoured and fostered the development of capitalism in the seventeenth and eighteenth centuries is not disputed, though the relative importance of this factor has been variously assessed. More on this in a moment. But Weber seems at times to go beyond this historical setting and to state his case in *general* terms: claiming that *wherever* a Puritanical ethic makes its appearance, similar results ensue. In support of this general thesis he brings in the Jains and the Moravian Brethren. We recall that Weber flatly rejected the idea that Jainism was a bourgeois ideology in either sense of the word (i.e. generated in a bourgeois setting or serving bourgeois interests). Now industriousness plus honesty and abstemiousness certainly lead, if not to capitalism, at least to making money. In connection with the Moravian Brethren adduced by Weber in support of his thesis, it is perhaps worthwhile here drawing attention to the interesting opinions expressed by S. Kot in his book entitled *Ideologia polityczna i społeczna braci polskich zwanych arianami* ('The Political and Social Ideology of the Polish Brethren or Arians').

In the second half of the sixteenth century the Polish Arians went to Moravia to visit the Moravian Brethren, the founders of a primitive Christian community of a Communist nature. They returned disillusioned and disappointed, having found the members of the community coarse in thought and remote from their original ideals. An anonymous member of the delegation wrote:

> Apart from what is contributed, a hundred or several
> hundred or several thousand in currency units, since all
> work in this society and no one is allowed to be idle, the
> likelihood is that a great deal of property must be theirs,
> for what they do they do for their own upkeep, and they
> give nothing to any outsider whether rich or poor . . .
> and since each makes more than he can eat and drink and
> no one wears flashy clothes or squanders his resources,
> it is certain that they must have no small amount tucked
> away in sacks or in coffers . . .[20]

But even if the Moravian Brethren and the Jains seem to corroborate the thesis of a connection between an ascetic industriousness and making money (not the same thing as capitalism!), the abstract formulation of the general case must still arouse our suspicions. Brentano has pointed out that when and where the aristocracy accepted the Reformation, the attendant results were different. In his work on economic individualism Robertson has shown that the South African farmers are Calvinists, which does not seem to have made businessmen of them, and in present-day Holland farmers and fishermen are Calvinists while Catholicism is spreading in the industrial areas.[21] These observations do not refute Weber's thesis, but they must make us rather more sceptical as to its general validity. We may say then that the Puritan virtues are conducive to the process of making money, provided certain specific social conditions are satisfied. The questions (a) Who exactly is it who is adopting these virtues? and (b) In what conditions? are very pertinent.

As I said above, there is a relatively large consensus of agreement on Weber's thesis as *historically* valid; and Weber's development of it has been widely acclaimed. Some students of the subject have voiced doubts, however, regarding what they see as an exaggeration of the role of Puritanism. These sceptics point to other factors in the development of capitalism, which Weber has either played down or simply ignored.

(a) Brentano has particularly drawn attention to Weber's failure to appreciate the role played by Catholics in the development of capitalism in Holland. He names certain Catholic families from the south of the country who made large fortunes and who allayed any moral scruples they may have had by making donations and establishing trusts.

(b) According to Weber, Calvinism contributed to the growth of capitalism by fostering the drive to make money, and by discounting the scruples traditionally associated with worldly riches. As regards this latter point, Brentano holds that the political writers of the Renaissance – especially Machiavelli – had just as much to do with making wealth respectable as the Calvinists; while the writers on economics of the same period, in their writings on money, prices and exchange, recommend concentration on making a profit. Here, Tawney agrees with Brentano.

(c) Weber may also be held to have ignored the role played by the discovery of the New World and India in the development of capitalism, and the economic changes that followed these discoveries. Likewise, he failed to take into account the great increase in the population of Western Europe.

(d) Other writers have stressed what they see as a most important factor in the predominantly Puritan climate surrounding the growth of capitalism, namely the fact that the Puritans were excluded from any participation in public affairs – a ban which lasted in England till 1828. Consequently they were forced to seek an outlet for their abilities in trade and industry, the traditional outlet for marginal communities in any given social setting.

On his return from England in 1729, Voltaire wrote in the *Lettres Anglaises*: 'No one who does not belong to the Anglican Church can hold public office in England or Ireland' (from the 'Letter on Religion'). And in the fourth letter – on the Quakers – we read: 'Quakers cannot be members of Parliament, nor may they hold public office, since in each of these cases they would have to take an oath, which is something they are not willing to do. Consequently they are forced to engage in commerce.' Weber's riposte

here would be to say that where it is Catholics who form
a persecuted minority they do not show the same intense
economic activity as do Protestants: an answer which will
not satisfy all of his readers.

If the capitalist activity of the Puritan sects were no more
than what is normally to be expected from a group excluded
from public life, it would have to be recognised as an
example of what Weber calls 'pariah capitalism' – which is
to be distinguished from 'Jewish capitalism' by virtue of its
business *methods*, as suggested above. But then it is not the
development of capitalism that is bound up with religion so
much as its specific *character*.

There is another factor connected with Weber's historical
thesis which I think is helpful in determining the temporal
limits within which this thesis is of significance for England,
the United States or Holland. I mean the heterogeneity of
the Puritan doctrine, a factor which Weber fails to take
into account. Brentano has drawn particular attention to this
factor, and is followed here by Tawney, who has used original sources to corroborate Brentano's findings.

Even when we limit ourselves to Calvin's direct doctrinal
successors, we cannot fail to be struck by this lack of
homogeneity. According to the authors I have just quoted,
it is simply not true to say that Puritanism in its Calvinist
form made a clean break with tradition, and that by putting
the businessman's scruples to rest it removed – for a certain
time at least – a main obstacle to free capitalist expansion.
Richard Baxter, the theoretician of early English Calvinism,
taught that in selecting a calling one must be guided
primarily by its ethical status, secondly by its usefulness
to society, and only then by consideration of its probable
remunerative return. In *The Life and Death of Mr. Badman*,
John Bunyan, a writer to whom Franklin owed not a little,
shows himself to be by no means in favour of the 'Buy
cheap, sell dear' code of practice; for this involves taking
advantage of the customer's gullibility, the urgency of his
need, or his particular attachment to the object being sold.
All of which runs counter to Pauline doctrine and to natural
law which requires us to do unto others as we would have
them do unto us. The buyer–seller relationship must be

governed by charity. Over and above this, one can hardly sell at an exorbitant price without being guilty of falsehood and fraud and without making ill use of our God-given knowledge by denying it in others. Is it possible, asks Brentano, to imagine a more outspokenly anti-capitalist directive than this?[22] Weber seems to regard Bunyan as a typical representative of the capitalist spirit, basing this verdict on Bunyan's favourite parallel between the relationship of the sinner to God, on the one hand, and the relationship of client to seller, on the other. But as Brentano sees it, here Bunyan is simply making use of comparisons which would be readily understandable to his petty bourgeois readers.

This assessment of early Calvinism is, as I said, corroborated by Tawney, who points out that Baxter requires the merchant who foresees a drop in prices to warn others. If a rise seems likely, he is permitted to stockpile goods, but only in so far as this will not lead to further inflation with the undesirable social consequences that this entails. He is not at liberty to conceal defects in goods; indeed, he is called upon to point them out. If he makes a bad business deal he is not permitted to recoup his losses by taking advantage of a third party, which would be equivalent to claiming the right to rob others because someone has robbed you. It is sin that is to be avoided rather than financial loss. And the lust for gain is bad for the soul, if not as lethal as idleness.[23]

Nor is it true to say that Puritanism was in itself enough to equip the businessman with a clear conscience. The 'business is business' principle which sets the moral keynote for economic affairs, did not make headway without some difficulty; as Tawney, true to the spirit of historical materialism suggests, it could not do so until those economic conditions favourable to it had been established.

The fact that bourgeois morality changes gradually in the direction of liquidating moral scruples which impede the free expansion of capitalism will come as a surprise to no one. Certain factors tend to speed up this process: e.g., according to some authorities, the process of colonisation, which knew no scruples in its economic dealings with native populations. St Paul's dictum that lust for money is the root of all evil is then consigned to oblivion. So too is the medieval doctrine according to which a man who trades can only please God with difficulty, if at all ('homo mercator vix aut nunquam potest Deo placere'). A basic change takes place in the attitude to charity. From being a sin, severity towards the poor becomes a virtue. As early as 1649 Parliament voted to give beggars the choice between work and a beating. Later, Berkeley recommended that beggars be seized and made to work for the general good for part of the year. High prices and low wages are justified on the grounds that the proletariat is thus prevented from indulging in extravagant behaviour when they get their weekly pay. Economic exploitation becomes a social duty.[24]

And yet moral scruples could not be entirely laid to rest. Had it not been so, it would not have been necessary to whitewash business interests and economic selfishness by propagating the idea that he who serves his own best interests thereby serves the general interest; or to come up with a new definition of personal interest which, properly understood, harmonises conscience with business, and egoism turns out in the long run to be indistinguishable from altruism. The law of supply and demand had also an ethical function in that, *inter alia*, it justified a rise in prices.[25] In an article entitled 'Ethical Aspects of Mercantile Relations' printed clandestinely in 1943 during the German occupation and dealing with the pathological maltreatment of the Polish economy by the occupying power, I tried to show how very real is the dichotomy within the man who has been taught to believe in altruism and mutual help and who tries to square that belief with the salesman's principle 'Give as little as possible, take as much as you can get.' We know to what lengths people will go to disguise the salesman attitude in cultures to which it is alien. When an Eskimo exchanged his fox skins for European goods, a transaction for which the European had crossed half the globe and the Eskimo had risked his life went almost unnoticed in a couple of days of feasting and palaver. There is a good description of this sort of thing in Peter Freuchen's book *Arctic Adventure* (1935). Commercial deals between Polish peasants, unused to urban life, and town dwellers took a lot of time – and not only because the peasant was slow to make up his mind and usually had to ask his wife's advice. From the peasant's point of view, a commercial deal, crude and unadorned, had something offensively meretricious about it, and, accordingly, it had to be approached only after a lengthy pow-wow on other matters: and even then hesitantly, unwillingly, as it were. In some quarters it is held that one of the functions of the middleman was to depersonalise the object for sale, to dissociate it from its previous owner whose conscience would not allow him to make a profit from somebody with whom he was in direct contact. Some researchers also point out that the Jews who were brought into towns to enliven trade, undertook this role partly at least because they formed a separate group alien to the rest of the environment – thus removing the scruples of both parties to a commercial transaction. Qualms connected with trading are therefore rather generally distributed, beyond our own cultural milieu; nor is it strange that Puritanism should also have failed to allay these ethical scruples.

(3) We turn now to Weber's claim that the process, whereby the business of making money took on the dimensions of a mass ethico-religious movement, was something novel and unprecedented, a new phenomenon for which we have to thank Puritanism. The literature on this subject is very extensive, and all we can do here is mention some of the most hotly contested issues.

Brentano stresses the pre-Christian origins of the initial breakaway from what Weber calls traditionalism. In the cities of the Italian seaboard, trade had been on the increase through classical times and thereafter; and the principle that it was legitimate practice to get as much as one could from a client was endorsed by the supreme authority – Roman law. Here Roman law profited from the Stoic doctrine that wealth is one of the things which are to be preferred to poverty. Stoic teaching on the unity of the universe and the identity of human nature with the nature of things was also used by Roman law to prove that what is useful for one must be useful for all. In the light of this doctrine – a godsend in the eighteenth century – everyone has the right to use something of lesser value to buy something of greater value; for, by serving one's own interests, one is best serving the community. The carte blanche thus handed to the businessman was in fact contrary to the teachings of the Church; but the Church retreated, withdrawing more and more from its erstwhile uncompromising stance and contenting itself with entrusting the poor to the rich, whose consciences could after all be eased by the giving of alms.

Several writers see St Thomas Aquinas as playing a part in the formation of an attitude which Weber associates exclusively with Puritanism. As Sombart, for example, shows in some detail, St Thomas did not oppose social advancement via the acquisition of riches: he merely deplored and condemned the abuse of money. *Liberalitas*, a virtue praised by St Thomas, and representing the golden mean between *avaritia* (avarice) and *prodigalitas* (prodigality), is described by him as a disposition which organises the feelings connected with the possession and the use of money. St Thomas held time to be *pretiosissimum*, of exceptional value, and idleness (*otiositas*) to be the root of all sin. According to Sombart, St Thomas's views on the desirability of suppressing the erotic impulse by means of a general subordination of the affections to reason were to provide fodder at a later date for the custodians of bourgeois morality. The scholastic ethic knows nothing of an ideal of poverty; and the concept of capital in its modern sense is found, together with the term, in Christian writers of the pre-Reformation age, for example, in St Bernard of Siena. At that time, the levying of interest on loaned capital was in principle still condemned, but not the investment of money in enterprises. In other words, profit was condoned where financial risks were incurred. Thus, by making investment attractive, the prohibition of levied interest actually *fostered* the capitalist spirit. This argument is in flat contradiction of the generally held belief that the prohibition of interest *hampered* the development of capitalism, and that economic activity could not take off until this prohibition was lifted; and Sombart regards it as his main contribution to the subject.

As far back as the Middle Ages it was held that money acquired through merit and enterprise in mundane affairs was pleasing to God, who looks with favour neither on the rich spendthrift nor on the idle usurer. According to

Sombart, we see the emergent outlines of bourgeois morality in the guilds. Members of a guild were supposed to be industrious, thrifty and provident; and these pressures turned them into respectable citizens not so very different from the later bourgeois image of the respectable man. Weber's point that there was, in the Middle Ages, no *mass* process of self-enrichment construed as an ethico-religious mission, draws from Brentano the riposte that medieval people were well acquainted with the idea that hard work was one way of serving God: witness the writings of various Church Fathers and the Rule of St Benedict on work in the monasteries.

The inclusion of St Thomas among those who are alleged to have shaped bourgeois morality was particularly strenuously resisted by Scheler, who, as an ardent Catholic detesting everything bourgeois, sought to lay the whole responsibility for the growth of bourgeois morality on Protestantism, and to absolve Catholicism from any complicity in this respect. In his book *Der Bourgeois und die religiösen Mächte*, Scheler reminds us that St Thomas places greater value on the virtues connected with study and learning than on the practical virtues; and if he advocates work, this is simply because idleness is an invitation to sin. Suppression of the sexual impulses is important, not because these are detrimental to economic activity but because they hinder absorption of the self in God. The rationalisation of life that we find in St Thomas is, according to Scheler, totally different from that ascribed to the Puritans by Weber. Thomist rationalisation is that of Aristotle. St Thomas's belief in a static, steady-state order of things also runs counter to the capitalist way of thought. And Scheler concludes: even if traces of incipient capitalistic spirit could be found in St Thomas, his influence in this respect would still be minimal, for Thomism was designed for the educated priesthood, not for the masses.

The part played by the Renaissance in the formation of bourgeois morality has already been mentioned. One author after another has emphasised this point, and Sombart treats Leone Battista Alberti as a forerunner of Franklin, a judgment hotly disputed by Weber. As Chapter 8 below is devoted to this thorny question, I shall not pursue it here.

Those who draw our attention to the presence of the 'spirit of capitalism' in fifteenth-century Florence and Venice, and in southern Germany and Flanders at the same time, are undermining not only Weber's thesis that the spirit of capitalism, as bound up with Puritanism, is something new, but also – if we bear in mind that these are all Catholic areas – his claim that Catholics are economically non-starters.

When we move on to the Reformation, we find Weber's theories again being challenged. Let us recall that, with regard to their relative fertility as sources of economic impulse, Luther and Calvin are seen by Weber in a very different light. Weber regards Luther as still embedded in what he calls 'traditionalism', and Calvin's interpretation of 'calling' would have been entirely alien to Luther. This is a point attacked by Brentano, who sees no such hard-and-fast boundary between the two reformers. Nor does Brentano accept Weber's thesis of the shift in the interpretation of 'calling' (*Beruf*), alleged to have taken place in the transition period between them.

(c) Conclusions

I have gone into some detail concerning the anti-Weber school, not only because the question whether his theses are valid or invalid closely affects my own argument, but also in order to show some of the difficulties that beset any attempt to arrive at a synoptic standpoint in this complex arena. I may summarise my own conclusions as follows:

(1) I attach little significance to Weber's first psychological thesis on the alleged connection between the 'spirit of capitalism' and the Puritan ethic. Neither outright acceptance nor outright rejection is possible, as the thesis is not clearly formulated, and in particular it is not clear whether two sets of phenomena are here alleged to be *concurrent with* or *dependent upon* each other.

(2) The second thesis may be formulated as follows: the doctrines promulgated by the Puritan sects were found to be of use in the process of making money. As long as we restrict this to certain periods and certain places, the thesis can hardly be doubted. In a note in *Capital* Marx says that

Protestantism fostered the growth of capitalism if only because it did away with an overabundance of feast-days and holidays!

(3) But can a thesis which is acceptable when put in contingent terms such as these remain acceptable when it is expanded into a general law capable of application to all times and places? In spite of the opposition it has had to face, Weber's claim that a new ethic, a new way of life, was generated in conjunction with Puritanism and became a mass movement seems to me to be justified; and we shall return to this point in Chapter 8 when we are discussing the controversial figure of Leone Battista Alberti. Several of Weber's observations are very apt – particularly his emphasis on the part played by the sects in breaking up guild closed shops and opening up paths to economic individualism with its creed of ruthless competition. Much had changed in England since the days when Defoe could regard price-cutting as virtually a crime, and the sects, it seems, may very well have had much to do with this change.

(4) We recall that, according to Weber, relations between the base and the ideological superstructure – i.e. in this case, between capitalism and the Puritan ethic – took shape in more than one way. In Pennsylvania, Franklin's teaching outstripped the actual growth of capitalism; while in Italy the capitalist base existed without a corresponding ideology, and can indeed be found coexisting with an ideology that ran counter to its own interests. In fourteenth- and fifteenth-century Florence, Franklin's pro-capitalist attitude would have been condemned out of hand – which hardly supports, as Weber sees it, the claim that the Puritan ethic was born of capitalism.

As to the first of these points, the historical materialist can reply that Franklin was in a position to import his ideology from England, where, in the early eighteenth century, the tide of capitalism was in full swell. The possibility of a delay in the base in relation to an imported ideology was pointed out by Marx, who wrote in his *Contribution to a Critique of Hegel's Philosophy of Law* that while the Germans were philosophically the contemporaries of their present (*Gegenwart*), historically they were not. As to Catholic Florentine capitalism, the view accepted during its efflorescence that, after making his fortune, a man could ease his conscience by giving alms, this is indeed an ideology (which Weber does not take into account), but one differing from that which Puritanism was later to offer to the economically active bourgeoisie. Admittedly, this is not a complete answer; for example, it does not tell us why Italian capitalism provided itself with precisely this superstructure, while English capitalists a few centuries later accepted views and attitudes which the Florentines could never have stomached.

(5) Within the complex of ideas characteristic of Puritanism, Weber traced the drive towards money-making to the belief in predestination; while the drive itself demarcated the bourgeois virtues as that complex of virtues likely to favour its advancement. Weber saw this as a case of ideology preceding and anticipating the economic base. But the first link in this chain is not very strong. As I have already said, there is absolutely no reason why a belief in predestination should encourage a man to evaluate his chances of being among the elect on the basis of his success in business. But if this link is severed, the urge to make money becomes a phenomenon whose mass character must be explained in terms of the economic conditions of the period. And if a belief in predestination is not enough to explain why people should seek economic success (after all, there are other ways of finding out whether one belongs to the elect or not), neither is it a necessary component in the generation of the urge to make money. Franklin himself is a case in point here, since there is no trace of any such belief either in the Autobiography or in his homilies. If a belief in predestination is essential to Calvinism, one may well wonder why Franklin was ever chosen as an example of Calvinist doctrine at work.

(6) If Weber overestimated the role of the religious sects to the detriment of other factors, especially the economic factor, this was due in part at least to his insufficient investigation of the way in which the teachings of these sects was received by other classes and in conditions other than those that were to be found in England and the United States during the seventeenth and eighteenth centuries. If Calvinism as received by other classes and in other conditions produced

different results, the claim that religion played a special part is seriously undermined.

(7) Another strong argument against Weber's theses is provided by the lack of any uniformity in Puritanism in the course of its historical development. If Puritanism initially resisted capitalism, gradually yielded to it and finally gave it its full blessing, it would appear that these changes of heart could only take place when the requisite stage of historical development had been reached.

The arguments pro and con will continue; but like all 'Which came first – the chicken or the egg?' problems, this one too is likely to remain unsolved. Perhaps we should just admit that where there are eggs there are chickens – and where there are chickens there are eggs, and leave it at that.[26] It is a concurrence that is much easier to verify.

Chapter 7

Resentment as a petty bourgeois trait

In the preceding chapter we considered the extent to which the Puritan sects may have influenced the genesis and the successful propagation of the moral precepts which imposed themselves so rapidly on eighteenth-century England and America, and which were on the defensive only 150 years later. We shall now look at the putative origin of one trait which is persistently mentioned as typical of bourgeois morality, and which is always linked with Puritanism. We have already come across this trait in company with other features of the bourgeoisie (see Chapter 2): it is the tendency towards keeping a malicious eye on what other people are doing, a tendency to be shocked and scandalised by their behaviour, even when this in no way impinges on the interests of those who resent it. This propensity is known as *ressentiment*, a word so difficult to translate into other languages that German writers like Nietzsche and Scheler use it without attempting to provide a German equivalent; though Scheler explains that it denotes a sort of vindictive rancour which he detects in the morality of Western Europe, dating from the time when the bourgeoisie first makes its voice heard, up to its triumph in the French Revolution. So far, we have been analysing general rules of bourgeois behaviour; here we shall consider moral practice: a practice, however, which was not without its own influence on precept – for example, in the criminal law. The field we now enter has attracted a wide spectrum of commentary which invites critical assessment.

1   Moral indignation and petty bourgeois psychology through the ages

Here I have in mind mainly the work of the Danish sociologist S. Ranulf, particularly his book entitled *Moral Indignation and Middle Class Psychology*.[1] Moral indignation, according to Ranulf, is an atavism which expresses itself in a specific disposition: 'a disinterested tendency to inflict punishment'. 'Disinterested' because it applies to situations where one's own interests are in no way threatened or eroded. This disposition is unevenly distributed in different social groups, which, according to Ranulf, goes to show that what we have here is not simply a question of mutual guardianship, an interested exchange: for if this were the underlying reason the tendency would be universal and evenly distributed.

Ranulf sets out to show that this tendency is particularly characteristic of the petty bourgeoisie, or the 'lower middle class' as he calls it. Weber had pointed to a connection of this sort, and he suggested that the austerity of Puritanism attracted adherents precisely from this class. In Ranulf's hands, however, the field becomes wider; his thesis is that wherever the petty bourgeoisie is sufficiently influential to put its stamp on the literature, the journalism and the legislation of a society, a typically Puritan tone of disapproval and severity becomes prevalent. In other words, Puritanism appears here, not as a specific historical occasion, but as a certain type of morality: a morality in which a sort of sadism, alleged to be characteristic of the petty bourgeoisie in general, is a key element. It is evidence for this type of morality that Ranulf seeks to track down in various societies ranging from Homer to the present day.

Ranulf is very critical both of theories which seek to explain social phenomena in terms of cultural influences, and of the 'guesswork' frequently used in sociological practice to establish interconnections between phenomena. Although such guesses may be what Ranulf calls 'plausible guesses' – i.e. they may contain a high degree of probability – they remain, none the less, guesses. The task which Ranulf sets himself is to verify his own hypothesis by means of empirical methods. And while in the case of Weber the formal side of the exposition leaves much to be desired (the author himself often does not seem to know which thesis he is defending,. and which argument is related to which thesis) both of Ranulf's works, the present one and his earlier book on a related subject, are fine examples of the methodical and conscientious application of inductive reasoning to the social sciences.

In illustration of Ranulf's thesis we may take some of his 'positive' and 'negative' cases. The positive cases comprise social groups in which the tendency to inflict disinterested punishment is strongly marked, and in which, at the same time, the petty bourgeoisie is demonstrably in the ascendant. Negative cases include situations where the petty bourgeoisie is either not present as a separate and distinct class, or, if present, is devoid of influence; and where at the same time we can find no trace of excessively punitive measures coupled with an exaggerated tendency to find fault with others: or, if such measures *are* present in the society, they are demonstrably designed to protect certain interests – i.e. they are not *disinterested*, which is the point at issue in this context.

It goes without saying that Ranulf was not able to verify in person all of his original sources, and that he had to accept much of his material at second hand. Nor was he able to draw on all of the available data. Exhaustive treatment was ruled out, not only because of the sheer numbers of social groupings, but also because many of these groupings have either not yet been adequately researched, or have been studied by researchers who were, in general, not working from Ranulf's angle, so that he could hardly draw upon their conclusions for his own purposes. A more exhaustive investigation of the subject would require collective studies on a major scale. Ranulf himself saw his work as a modest contribution, to be continued, he hoped, by others.

Following the author himself we start with the positive cases. Under the influence, no doubt, of contemporary events in Germany (the book was published in 1938), Ranulf begins by considering the National Socialist movement. The petty bourgeois character of this movement was clearly discernible in the elections held in 1930 and 1932. A sig-

nificant memorandum was issued by the Prussian Minister
of Justice in 1933. This condemned the laxity said to have
characterised the administration of the law under the Weimar
Republic, called for more severe sentences, introduced
punishment for a whole series of newly defined offences and
abolished the practice whereby 'extenuating circumstances'
could attract a more lenient sentence or even a verdict of not
guilty. In his treatment of Nazi Germany, Ranulf made good
use of a book published three years earlier – *The Nazi
Dictatorship* by F. L. Schuman (published in 1935). Ranulf
took strong exception to Schuman's excessively psychological, often psychoanalytical inferences, but agreed with
him by and large that the terror reigning in Germany was
not entirely generated by German 'defence' requirements (or
rather 'aggressive requirements' in the light of later developments), but was in some measure an outlet for the frus-
trations of the petty bourgeoisie, who had been until then
both economically underprivileged and sadly lacking in
prestige.

Ranulf next turns his attention to the proverbial Puritans
of seventeenth-century England. Here, however, he does not
depend on second-hand results, but reproduces the results of
long and detailed study of source material – Puritan publications for the years 1640–63, held in the British Library.
Ranulf's considered judgment is that one can hardly doubt
the sado-masochistic character of this material. Here pride
is rebuked, just as the theatre-goer in fifth-century Athens
expected a tragic performance to show retribution for hubris,
the sin of lording it over others. The writers studied by
Ranulf are scandalised (again as in fifth-century Athens, a
point to which we shall return) by blatant success, by enjoyment of life, by care-free happiness. Sin must not be tolerated. Relapse into greater sin is seen as the inevitable consequence of and punishment for sins already committed. Maso-
chistic tendencies join forces with sadism, and both find their
expression in the image of a pitiless God. We find the same
sort of thing, as Ranulf reminds us, in the Jansenists: morbid
rehearsal of one's own torments in hell, contrition for original sin, contemplation of predestination in the certain
knowledge of one's own vileness.

The reader may well wonder, of course, whether this is anything more than the chosen armament of the bourgeoisie in their fight with the privileged classes. It was, after all, this uncompromising single-mindedness that gave Cromwell's Roundheads the edge over the Cavaliers on the field of battle. The same sort of inflexibility can be found in the ranks of the ascendant Italian bourgeoisie. And if military strategy dictated adoption of this attitude, it would, of course, cease to be *disinterested*. But as far as the Puritans and their French blood-brothers, the Jansenists, are concerned, Ranulf would probably continue to claim that their fanaticism cannot be entirely explained away on grounds of military strategy.[2]

Rigour is characteristic of bourgeois morality as long as the bourgeoisie is engaged in the process of gaining and consolidating power, and before it starts to make money. Once firmly installed in power, the bourgeoisie feels it can afford some relaxation in moral rigour. So it was with the Dutch bourgeoisie once they began to rake in the interest on monies advanced all over Europe. If people who have made fortunes retain anything in the way of moral rigour, this is usually expressed *vis-à-vis* the poorer of their fellows, whose poverty is attributed to idleness and lack of foresight. But personal interest in maintaining this sort of moralising attitude is not so difficult to explain: the reprehensible morals of the French aristocracy provided a very useful Aunt Sally for the French bourgeois as they reached out for power.

Ignorance of Danish prevents me from making due use of the work by the Danish sociologist V. Vedel on the Middle Ages, in which the author underlines the sadistic elements in the ethos of the medieval craftsman.[3] But Ranulf uses this material as one of his positive cases (p. 18). He also claims that the growth and development of the United States go to prove his case. The planters of the South and the colonists of the North were recruited from the same social classes. Calvinism made no headway in the South, because there the process of making money got off to an early start (p. 35). The Southern planters were guided by a feudal and patriarchal morality which was incomparably laxer than that of the North. They supported the arts, and even allowed themselves a degree of free-thinking (e.g. Thomas Jefferson); as a general rule, they were more inclined to extol virtue than to punish wrong-doing.

In the North, moral rigour slackened as wealth grew. Even the lineaments of God were transformed. The pitiless Jehovah turned gradually into the benevolent Creator who is not primarily bent on restricting men's lives. In the eighteenth century, a clergyman who wanted to make a public example of his parishioners' sins was himself ousted from office. A new type of cleric made his appearance, one able to adapt to the demands of a new society, and far removed from the ferocious theocrats of the seventeenth century. The place of virtue in the raw was taken by respectability, the cement of a social order founded on money.

All these changes are tied up, not only with a higher standard of living, but also with a growth in the prestige of the petty bourgeoisie. This is what gives the United States its peculiar stamp and style; while in Europe on the other hand (according to Calverton, whose monograph on America provided Ranulf with a lot of material)[4] the tone for the middle classes was set by the *grande bourgeoisie*, which was under the influence of aristocratic culture. It is this difference, according to Calverton, which accounts for American insensitivity to the arts. As regards the United States, Ranulf could have used Dreiser's *American Tragedy* as grist for his mill; here the opposition between petty bourgeois and grand bourgeois morality runs precisely along the lines he indicated. It is hard to say how Ranulf would have reacted to certain traits described by the Lynds in *Middletown* (cf. Chapter 3) – e.g. to the 'we're all buddies' atmosphere on which they lay so much stress. He would probably have answered that this was something which the standard of living in Middletown apparently permitted; and the fact that one seemed to have fewer buddies in times of economic depression would appear to bear out his thesis.

So much for Ranulf's 'positive cases', or at least the most important of them. We shall now look at some of his negative cases, which, given his definition (see above), go to support his argument.

The ideologies of various aristocratic groups (medieval barons, knightly orders, etc.) favoured a cult of individual virtues which could be practised by persons aware of their own superiority – such virtues as magnanimity, protective-ness towards the weak, and so on; but moral rigour was lacking, and such concepts as sinfulness and humility (i.e. concepts which could not be squared with the self-esteem and dignity of the upper classes) could not take root. After a cursory review of these ideologies, Ranulf embarks on a lengthy study of Catholicism.

The indulgence which the Catholic clergy of the late Middle Ages showed to their flocks is well known, and equally well known is the vast apparatus of ways and means of guaranteeing forgiveness of sins. The cult of the Virgin Mary became ever more popular, and this in itself bespeaks the need felt to have in heaven an intercessor of infinite tenderness, one who required only a devout litany from the sinner for her to grant him absolution (pp. 116–19). The imposition of celibacy on the clergy cannot be seen as an example of disinterested effort to control the lives of others; for the celibacy requirement was very much in the interests of the Church. Nor can Catholic treatment of non-Catholics, or the savage persecution of heretics, be taken as examples of 'disinterested interference'; the Inquisition was a defence mechanism of the Church, not of morality. 'Heretics who were admitted to be patterns of virtue were ruthlessly exter-minated in the name of Christ while in the same holy name the orthodox could purchase absolution for the vilest crimes for a few coins' (p. 135). Ranulf links this trait of Catholicism with the fact that it was primarily powerful ecclesiastical dignitaries who had most to do with its shaping and development.

In the early thirties, there appeared in Copenhagen a book by Grønbech on Teutonic culture[5] on which Ranulf drew for another of his 'negative cases'. Teutonic society provides no counterpart to the petty bourgeoisie, nor was there any pressure in it to ensure that the perpetrator of a crime (by their standards) should suffer. There was, however, pressure to ensure that the honour of an injured party was salvaged. The family took action on behalf of the injured party, just as the kin of a wrong-doer were supposed to take up arms on his behalf, even if they could not sanction what he had done. Broadly speaking, this is the ethos of the Icelandic sagas.

Ranulf's book is largely taken up with data relating to Europe. The Far East and exotic peoples are considered if at all, in very summary fashion, and the selection of material is unavoidably very haphazard. Nowhere does the author find anything that might seem to contradict his hypothesis; though it might equally be said that he finds nothing to support it either. This goes particularly for primitive societies. In none of the works he studied in this field could Ranulf apparently find any evidence of an inclination to indulge in the disinterested persecution and punishment of others. And in so far as law is developed among primitive peoples, it seems to be along lines rather similar to those of our own civil law. Ranulf was unable to come to any hard-and-fast conclusions in this field, as evidence both for and against his thesis could be found (cf. the ethos of the Israelites).

So much for Ranulf's subject matter and his method. Let us now look at his results.

Ranulf makes no claim of originality, either for his hypothesis that the petty bourgeoisie is characterised by moral strictness, or for his second thesis – that resentment plays a part in the shaping of certain moral attitudes. The latter thesis has a long tradition behind it, stretching back to the Sophists, which was well known to Ranulf. The task he set himself was to verify a hypothesis which proposes certain concurrences: though he did not shirk the attempt to provide these with some degree of motivation. Sociologists, it seems, are more agreed on identifying a disinterested inclination towards inflicting punishment in the petty bourgeoisie than on offering any explanation as to why this should be found in this milieu more than in others. Vedel says that the tendency to 'oversee' the lives of others is, in general, characteristic of congested urban situations. In his monograph on the bourgeoisie, Sombart expresses the view that the virtues of the bourgeoisie are dictated by something more than mere economic necessity. It is true that the bourgeois must be industrious and thrifty if he is to survive. But he is also moved by the desire to be different from the upper classes, whom in his heart he envies, and whose customs he therefore castigates as 'scandalous' and 'shocking'. In the light of this argument, resentment would then be a reason for parading customs and habits differing from those which one cannot allow oneself: that is to say, it would be a causal factor in the formation of petty bourgeois morality. Ranulf does not go along with this. As he sees it, the petty bourgeoisie had no option but to adopt certain virtues, a process in which resentment did not play a causal part but was rather the consequence of an imposed discipline combined with an awareness of one's underprivileged status. 'Until the contrary has been proved, it will be better to assume that the bourgeois virtues have been practised in the main only by those upon whom they were forced either by the material conditions of their lives or by the moral rigorists among whom they were living, and that resentment against all who were more fortunate has been the regular outcome of this forced self-control. The disinterested tendency to inflict punishment may be identified with this resentment' (pp. 42–3).

Let us return, however, to Ranulf's central thesis, to the concurrences whose existence he wishes to prove, and let us see whether the evidence as adduced tends to bear out Ranulf's thesis or not. We have first of all to cope with certain conceptual difficulties. Two of these are of fundamental importance in Ranulf's work, and concern (a) the exact nature of the petty bourgeoisie, and (b) the exact nature of the disinterested inclination to inflict punishment.

The concept of the petty bourgeoisie is taken over by Ranulf without any sort of gloss or commentary, just as though it were something clearly understood by everyone. The distinction between 'upper middle class' and 'lower middle class', or between 'upper bourgeoisie' and 'petty bourgeoisie', is explicitly based and sustained on certain criteria of property: unstable criteria, that is, which do not always make it unequivocally clear which bracket is being discussed. If income alone is to decide to which class an individual belongs, intellectuals and representatives of the artistic *vie de bohème* would forthwith have to be included in the petty bourgeoisie; and this could not but affect Ranulf's thesis, since the types corresponding to his image of the petty bourgeois are shopkeepers and artisans. In the light of his conception of the petty bourgeoisie, Ranulf's attempt to use Goblot's book *La Barrière et le niveau* in support of his thesis is a complete *non sequitur*. The group described by Goblot belongs (as I said in Chapter 1) to what was called '*la bonne société*' in France during the years just before the First World War. It consisted mainly of the big industrialists and those drawing good salaries in the learned professions: people, that is, who regarded advanced education for their children, particularly their sons, as something self-evident and beyond question. It was a group belonging to the highest stratum of the middle class both in terms of income bracket and of life-style. If this group is really to be transferred to the lower middle class, we are in a sort of limbo where we lose all possibility of checking the author's assertions, since we no longer know precisely to whom they are supposed to apply. If, on the other hand, this group is included here by an oversight, identification of bourgeois obduracy within it renders questionable Ranulf's assertion that this obduracy is the result of financial restriction and vanishes with a rise in the standard of living.

As for the concept of an inclination to indulge in the disinterested persecution or punishment of others, we note that whenever the author finds a case of severe punishment being inflicted in a *non-bourgeois* milieu, he has to demonstrate, if his thesis is to survive, that this punishment is meted out *in the interests* of those inflicting it; and conversely, whenever he finds punishment being inflicted in a *bourgeois* set-up, he has to convince himself and us, if he is to use this as evidence in his book, that *no sort of self-interest* is served by the punishment. It cannot be said of Ranulf that he alters facts to suit his case; on the contrary, intellectual honesty is one of his main assets. Nevertheless, the reader is bound to wonder here and there whether either a punishment or its severity, adduced as evidence concerning a given society, has been correctly identified as 'disinterested' or not. How are we to decide, for example, to what extent the severity of the criminal code in Nazi Germany is to be explained by aggressive policies which required the installation and maintenance of an internal terror apparatus, or by the need of the petty bourgeoisie to let off steam? The social psychology we apply here is a good example of that 'guesswork' which Ranulf explicitly rejects throughout his book.

As I said, Ranulf's weakness lies in his acceptance of 'the petty bourgeoisie' as something isolated and static. He makes insufficient allowance for the interplay of various class interests. We lack information on the way the petty bourgeoisie fits into the stratification pattern in this or that country: who is above it, who below? We lack information on the distribution of forces: who holds the reins of power, who would like to get their hands on them? Moral rigidity, as I said above, has often been recognised as characteristic of groups which are in opposition – of those who are fighting the privileged classes in order to take over their privileges. If all these factors were to be taken into account, the situation as depicted by Ranulf would become a great deal more complicated, and his results would not be unaffected. A standard of living which Ranulf treats as though it were in isolation, would then be seen in its true association with other factors. And we have to remember that 'standard of living' is so central to Ranulf's thesis concerning the disinterested persecution of others that he expects to find this persecution attested even in a milieu which is not petty bourgeois in the strict sense but merely 'lower-middle-class-like conditions of life'.

Since standard of living plays so crucial a part in generating the desire to find fault with and persecute others gratuitously, the question obviously arises – why do the financial restrictions experienced by the proletariat not have the same consequences? At all events, no theoretician, as far as I know, has detected any such tendency among the proletariat. Scheler's answer would be that the proletariat is too remote from the seat of power to harbour resentment, which, again according to Scheler, is a typical reaction in those who are not too far from the privileged classes. As Mandeville pointed out in the eighteenth century, the pauper does not envy the magnate his carriage: the gap between them is too wide. But the owner of a carriage and pair will sleep badly when his neighbour gets himself a four-in-hand. And again according to Scheler, wherever legal and political equality is combined with economic and social inequality, there is a fertile hotbed for *ressentiment*. Ranulf was well acquainted with Scheler's views, which he criticised vehemently; but he was not able to disguise the cracks in his own argument.

If I have devoted a lot of space to Ranulf's views, it is because his work, though it is limited to the study of one factor only in the petty bourgeois ethos, is a very painstaking and conscientious investigation into admittedly rather fortuitous data. I have pointed out what I believe to be faults in it, and I cannot pretend that I find the book convincing; but it is a most interesting methodological experiment and one carried out with great honesty. Wherever the facts do not support his case, Ranulf is the first to draw the reader's attention to this: a rare virtue indeed among researchers! It is, moreover, one that we find even more in evidence in Ranulf's other major work, to which we now turn our attention.

2   Resentment in the tragedy and the legislation of ancient Athens

The groundwork for the thesis which Ranulf advanced in the book we have just been discussing was laid by him in his two-volume work on Athens in the fifth and early fourth centuries BC. Extracts from this work appeared in Danish in 1930; the complete work appeared in English in 1933 (vol. 1) and 1934 (vol. 2). The full title is *The Jealousy of the Gods and Criminal Law in Athens: Contribution to the Sociology of Moral Indignation*. In this work, Ranulf set out to show that 'disinterested indignation' and 'disinterested pleasure' in seeing others punished are not only closely linked with resentment but are in fact its social contours. And, secondly, he was concerned to show that the living conditions of the petty bourgeoisie generate resentment, which tends to decrease as and when economic conditions improve.

No trace of disinterested pleasure in seeing others punished is to be found in the *Iliad*, an epic addressed to the aristocracy. In it, gods and humans alike are indifferent to wrongs inflicted on others than themselves: punitive action is attendant upon *personal* injury. The gods are personally offended when oaths are broken, guests are betrayed, a call for help is ignored. During the fifth century, however, a change takes place in Greek literature. The gods begin to show themselves ready to take punitive action even in the case of crimes which they themselves have instigated. And it is not only the perpetrator of such a crime that is punished: the guilt of the fathers is visited on the sons as well, as in the case of the House of Atreus. This form of divine justice is guided by no rational principle. The lives and the property of the Athenians would have been a great deal safer had the gods not taken a hand in the administration of justice; for their contribution, far from preventing the spread of crime, actually fostered it. The gods are envious. They punish people who are distinguished by wealth, power, fame or happiness. The bravado which Achilles displays in the *Iliad* would not have gone unpunished in later literature. In Aeschylus, Agamemnon, returning home, hesitates to step on the crimson carpet spread before him as for a conqueror, lest this provoke the rancorous envy of the gods – which was precisely Clytemnestra's reason for having the carpet laid in the first place.

It is this moral evolution as reflected in the Greek vision of the gods that Ranulf traces through Greek literature, in the historians from Herodotus to Thucydides, and in Greek legislation. As regards the literature, Ranulf has gone to enormous trouble to provide a careful analysis of virtually every play of Aeschylus and Sophocles, which he then contrasts with the very different moral climate pervading the works of Euripides and Aristophanes. Ranulf's primary aim in investigating this body of material was to establish the relative incidence of the following three factors: (1) punishment meted out by the gods to the guilty; (2) punishment inflicted out of caprice or for reasons of expedience; (3) punishment inflicted as a result of divine jealousy or resentment. This third factor increases in amplitude over the period between Homer and Aeschylus; while neither Aeschylus nor Sophocles makes any ethical distinction between these three different types of motivation. Only in Aeschylus' last work – *The Eumenides* – does he show a hint of change of direction.

Orestes is not punished for the murder of Agamemnon: Aeschylus explicitly rejects the concept of inherited culpability in the House of Atreus. Here is the first hint of preventive punishment, the need to deter people from committing crimes: a need which, according to Ranulf, plays absolutely no part in the genesis of punishment. Like Aeschylus, Sophocles sees nothing untoward in the continual harassment of men by the gods. In Sophocles, the chorus has a certain sadistic severity about it. Only in his last four dramas does Sophocles show any departure from his previous views.

The moral climate of the Greek theatre shifted further in the same direction when Euripides came on the scene. Euripides is fond of depicting extreme tension which is favourably discharged by the intervention of the gods. In his dramas, the gods often retain the properties they were invested with in the earlier drama. They are still envious, as we see from Euripides' frequent allusions to the perils inherent in great happiness; and Agamemnon envies his retainers their modest lot, for it is not good, as he sees it, to be distinguished in any way whatever from one's fellows. But if the character of the gods has not changed, the attitude of the author to their behaviour has changed markedly. Euripides censures the gods for their harassment of the innocent, for their harassment of those who have committed crimes to which they were driven by the gods themselves, and he censures them for their harassment of the innocent relatives or even the countrymen of a reprobate. In general, Euripides adopts a humanitarian attitude. He defends women (Medea) and stands up for second-class citizens such as illegitimate children, slaves and barbarians. It is more difficult to classify Aristophanes' views on moral issues: for Aristophanes was an opportunist and his moral indignation could be turned on or off at will to accommodate a political interest.

These developments in the Greek theatre are paralleled, according to Ranulf, in Greek historiography from Herodotus to Thucydides. Herodotus sees the Greeks as resentful and the gods as inclined to persecute people for no very good reason; and he fails, as do Aeschylus and Sophocles, to distinguish between punishment for wrong-doing, on the one hand, and punishment inflicted for reasons of caprice or envy on the other. In Thucydides, it is already permissible to praise Pericles, and Pericles himself makes a distinction between arrogant boastfulness and rational evaluation of power. As Ranulf sees it, it is not only because he wants to interpret history as causal connection – i.e. without *deus ex machina* intervention – that Thucydides rejects the older concept of the gods. Had he wished to let the gods keep the features with which his predecessors had invested them, he could still have amalgamated these traditional features with a causal explanation of events (Ranulf does not say how Thucydides was to achieve this feat). In so far as he did not attempt such an amalgamation, it is clear that preservation of the traditional divine features was not something that mattered to him.

Ranulf next turns his attention to Athenian legislation, in particular to Solon's *grafè*, which he finds highly instructive. It is only from minor fragments that Solon's legislation can be reconstructed, but from these fragments it is clear enough that any citizen had the right to bring a charge in a matter in which he himself was not personally or directly interested. It is true that in the case of murder only a blood relation had the right to bring charges; but if no blood relation did so, a third party could indict the blood relations for their failure. In the same way, a man who failed to divorce his wife once she had been found guilty of adultery, could be indicted by a third party. Attempts at explaining these laws away on grounds of their expediency – e.g. by claiming that Solon's *grafè*, by authorising strangers to intercede on behalf of the defenceless, aimed at preventing creditors from selling debtors into slavery, parents from selling children and brothers from selling a sister – fail to satisfy Ranulf, who still sees here a tendency towards disinterested control of and interference in other people's lives. No such tendency, he asserts, is to be found in the Draconic Laws. The severity of the Draconic Laws has, it seems, been exaggerated over the centuries, and even where their severity is beyond doubt this was for a specific purpose. They recognised a distinction between intentional and unintentional homicide, the latter being punished less severely. Later, this distinction became obliterated in the Greek dramatists (at least in so far as the spectator was concerned); the perpetrator of a crime knew that where there was no premeditation he had a right to expect sympathy.

Ostracism – the right to have any citizen banished without trial for ten years on the strength of a vote alone – also fits in very well with Greek mentality in the first half of the fifth century BC, as Ranulf sees it. Ostracism was admirably suited to serve as a blow-hole for resentment felt against anyone who was outstanding by reason of birth, fame, property, nobility (cf. the case of Arystides). There have been many different interpretations of ostracism, which is usually taken to be a form of insurance against tyranny. Ranulf sees it as providing evidence for his thesis.

Let us here remind ourselves of what he is trying to do. His task is twofold: (1) he wants to show a connection between resentment and moral indignation, associated with a 'disinterested tendency to inflict punishment'; and (2) he uses the example of ancient Athens to show that his tendency depends on certain social conditions.

In Greek, as Ranulf points out (vol. 1, pp. 106–11), analogous words may serve to designate both the property of arousing envy and the property of provoking moral rebuke: or, one and the same word may cover both concepts. Outrage at a misdeed has an element of envy in it. The term *anepíphthonon* means at one and the same time 'not provoking envy' and 'not arousing moral objections'. The Greeks first imagined the gods as envious beings, and only subsequently did they conceive of them as beings who dispensed justice. A trespass punished in this second phase still bears the odium off ts first-phase status as an act which provoked divine envy.

We cannot spend too much time on this point; nor can we take up the question of just how far we can ascribe sadism to the Greek tragedians and the Greek legislation which Ranulf adduces as evidence, or whether this sadism (assuming it to be present) can be equated with Puritan sadism. The attempt to link moral indignation with envy is very interesting for anyone who is researching the history and methods of moral evaluation; but we are concerned with bourgeois morality, with which only the second of Ranulf's theses is in any way connected.

As for the social background to this disinterested tendency to inflict punishment on others, Ranulf looks for this, not in the origins of the authors concerned, but rather in the social position of the audiences on whom these authors could count. He sees Aeschylus and Sophocles as appealing to a petty bourgeois clientele, or to a public which, while not actually belonging to the petty bourgeoisie, lived in 'a complex of middle class conditions of life' (p. 283). It was a hard and primitive way of life, and one hostile to technical advance. The moral conflicts depicted by these tragedians and the image of the gods which they presented, must have fallen on very receptive ears in such an audience. In the Periclean period, Athens flourished at the cost of her 'allies' and there was a considerable and general rise in the standard of living. If the writers and teachers of this period show less severity and rigour than the older writers, this is due to either of two reasons: either, like the Sophists, whose recruits were drawn very largely from the privileged classes, they were addressing themselves to the upper classes, or they were addressing a petty bourgeoisie for whom things were now going very much better, and whose change in taste points to 'a certain causal interdependence between poverty, envy and the zeal for justice' (p. 146).

Talk about morality is usually so lacking in precise observation and, alas, so rich in platitudes meant to edify the reader rather than to deepen our knowledge of the subject, that Ranulf's conclusions, though they may not satisfy everyone, should certainly give us food for thought. By now, the reader should have formed some idea of Ranulf's work – though trying to condense the contents of two large volumes into a few lines is a somewhat hopeless task. Here, as in his later work, Ranulf is very well aware of the factors that go to complicate his task. He is his own sternest critic. Often in view of the complexity and inconsistency of the textual material he is grappling with, he has to suspend judgment – which hardly helps the reader who is expecting some sort of codified conclusion. Precisely in the case of the alleged connection between the 'disinterested tendency to inflict punishment' and the social background of this tendency, the author's results are swallowed up in a morass of provisos, stipulations and retractions. A few of his results are, however, relatively firm, and my concluding remarks on Ranulf's work concern these.

Such problems as the mechanism of moral indignation and moral rebuke, and the irrational nature of punishment, which are of concern to Ranulf, are really side issues as far as we are concerned. But it is worth remarking that Ranulf has not taken into sufficient account the fact that resentment or envy can explain the origins of only *one* type of moral condemnation. It is difficult, for example, to see resentment at work in cases where we react with indignation to a betrayal of confidence, or where we react angrily to the humiliation, the exploitation and persecution of the helpless. The motive singled out by Ranulf is doubtless *one* of the motives which have to be taken into account; but the sub-title of his book suggests, rather ambitiously, that it is going to be a contribution to the sociology of moral indignation *in general*. Is 'moral indignation' to be understood in a restricted sense, perhaps, as nothing more than shopkeeper's gall? But then there would be *ex definitione* no point in setting out to demonstrate the connection between moral indignation and the related disinterested tendency to inflict punishment on others, on the one hand, and rancorous envy on the other. As for the irrational elements which Ranulf claims to have detected in condemnation and punishment, his arguments do little to counter the claim that both legislation and morality are instruments serving the completely rational interests of the ruling classes. In the wide field of moral judgments in general, and of those which achieve codification in the shape of legislation in particular, one can always find some for which there appears to be no immediate rational explanation, and others which serve very pertinent ends. An enterprise aimed at analysing the whole field of negative moral reactions cannot afford to make do with either the former or the latter in isolation.

So much for the first 'dependence' which Ranulf sets out to demonstrate. As for the second – the alleged link between a disinterested tendency to inflict punishment and a specific social background and the role of the petty bourgeoisie in that background – this seems even more open to doubt.

We are accustomed to regard the age of the Greek Renaissance as the period in which the middle classes gradually came to power. This is how Socrates saw it. Euripides, fortifying himself with arguments similar to those used by Aristotle, sings the praises of the 'middle class citizens' (*mézoi polítai*).[6] When the political status of the bourgeoisie is enhanced – so runs the thesis which Ranulf outlines in this book and amplifies in *Moral Indignation and Middle Class Psychology* – a disinterested tendency to inflict punishment on others should figure more and more markedly in the literature of the period. In point of fact, it seems to decrease. According to Ranulf, this is due not only to increased prosperity but also to the fact that the petty bourgeoisie submits voluntarily to the influence of the aristocratic models which set the tone in the time of Pericles. In addition, Ranulf attributes the mitigation in moral stringency to the influence of these aristocratic circles, which conform to older ways of thinking only in so far as their popularity is thereby enhanced. So it is not true that the petty bourgeoisie is invariably given to moral rigidity: its fanaticism is mitigated when its standard of living rises, and when its principles are mollified by the influence of aristocratic models. Why this second factor should have been operative in Athens in the time of Pericles, but not in the years immediately preceding Pericles, is not sufficiently explained by Ranulf. Nor are we informed why the upper-class Aeschylus had to adapt to public taste at a time when the petty bourgeoisie was politically at its weakest, while the writers of Periclean Athens – who were derived, if not from the aristocracy, at least from the privileged classes – could force their preferences on the public at a time when the petty bourgeoisie was at its political zenith. The individualism of Euripides and his rejection of the doctrine of hereditary sin may well be seen as bourgeois traits, as examples of typically bourgeois rationalisation, and not as a victory for the anti-bourgeois ethos, one associated with growing wealth. In any case, as regards Ranulf's process of development from moral inflexibility to greater lenience, and from gods who punish men out of caprice or envy to gods who dispense justice, we have to point out that Hesiod (whom Ranulf ignores) certainly complicates the picture, if only because at a time when the Greek gods were still acting enviously and capriciously, his Zeus was already the custodian of justice. It is true that by virtue of the class to which he belonged, Hesiod stands somewhat apart from the line of development which interests Ranulf, but none the less, the nonconformity of his pantheon must be taken into account in any final evaluation of Ranulf's arguments.

It is, by the way, curious that, at a time when the Greek gods were taking a particular delight in tormenting people for fun, sexual licence was the order of the day. This is noteworthy because moral rigidity is primarily characteristic of that life-style whose classical expression is English Puritanism. Anyway, as Ranulf points out, sexual abstinence was not regarded as, in itself, a virtue in classical Athens (vol. 2, ch. VII) – at least, as far as men were concerned. Solon understood the needs of the flesh very well indeed, and, as is well known, provided brothels staffed by slaves. True to his time, he also accepted homosexuality: 'Happy is he,' he said, 'who loves boys, horses, hunting dogs and guests.'[7] The Athenian cult of nudity was found shocking in eastern Greece, and even in Ionia.[8]

The tendency to keep an inquisitive and spiteful eye on what others are doing and to indulge in malicious comment thereon, is linked by Ranulf with a low standard of living or at least with what he calls, rather vaguely, 'the conditions of middle-class life'. Other writers, however, have seen in this nothing more than a natural consequence of urban congestion, especially in small towns. It is a truism that in small towns people are always poking their noses into other people's business.

But is it true? Is the mere fact of living in such a huddle that we can all keep an eye on each other, enough in itself to generate this attitude of disinterested malice? If so, we might expect to find it widespread among peasants whose daily life is spent almost entirely under each other's eyes. But as far as I am aware, no student of peasant *mores* has ever identified this trait among them, and my own conversations with peasants, aimed at eliciting this kind of information, have never yielded any trace of a readiness to indulge in disinterested malice. On the contrary, what emerged from such conversations was evidence of great tolerance among peasants; and I was left with the impression that for those who live 'in public', as it were, a degree of mutual tolerance is obligatory – for the very simple reason that otherwise life would be impossible.

It would seem then that mutual supervision facilitated by close physical contact is not enough to generate the malicious inquisitiveness that interests Ranulf. It is not only environmental factors that play a part. In big cities too, any group forming an island in the community – *émigré* populations, for example – suffers from this sort of ill-natured prying into other people's affairs, no matter how far apart the individuals concerned actually live. In Paris between the wars, for example, every Pole knew what a fellow-countryman was having for dinner on the other side of the city.

Many more questions remain to be answered in connection with Ranulf's thesis. For example, assuming that the tendency he claims to have identified exists, is it evenly distributed between the sexes? If, as Ranulf alleges, it has expressed itself primarily in literature, journalism and legislation, then men must have been mainly responsible for propagating it, as it was mostly men who were active in these professions. But if enjoyably scandalous and scandalised comment on what the neighbours are up to reduces to gossip over the garden fence, then women must take pride of place. And if this is so, we may plausibly look for the causes in the manner in which women have to live in petty bourgeois families. The narrow circle of depersonalised activities available to someone who is tied to the kitchen and her children, the lack of outlet in such confines, a type of work whose product is hardly even noticed, it is swallowed so quickly – all of this generates bitterness and a feeling that such work is not sufficiently valued, a feeling compounded by the self-denial imposed on the economically dependent woman in a family with a restricted budget (see above, p. 31).

This sort of life is not, however, exclusive to the petty bourgeois woman. It is also the life-style of most proletarian women, which leads us back again to a central problem for Ranulf's case: how does the petty bourgeois compare with the proletariat in this respect? The suggestion that mutual tolerance is a function of the standard of living seems to be convincing; but then the tendency to indulge in disinterested fault-finding should be detectable among the proletariat as well. If it is not, some additional and so far unidentified factor must be responsible for its appearance among the petty bourgeoisie.

Chapter 8

Bourgeois morality in the early Italian Renaissance: Leone Battista Alberti

As we saw in Chapter 6, the theories which have been advanced to account for the origin and spread of moral precepts of the Franklin type are at odds with each other on many points. For Weber, such precepts represented a new phenomenon closely linked to Puritanism, while other writers claimed to detect similar phenomena much earlier – for example, in the Italian capitalism of the fifteenth century: a claim which, if substantiated, would refute both Weber's thesis of a special link between Franklinism and Puritanism and his thesis that what we have here is an historical innovation whose protagonist was Franklin. Both parties in this dispute appeal to what is claimed to be a particularly representative figure of the fifteenth-century Florentine bourgeoisie – Leone Battista Alberti; one party underlining the similarities, the other pointing out the differences. Sombart treats Alberti as a precursor of Franklin, while Weber dismisses this as nonsense. Since a solution one way or another of this moot point is of some importance for my own argument, I devote the present chapter to Alberti, in particular to his treatise on the family and how it should be regulated. It is this treatise which lies at the centre of the dispute. Time spent on it is very far from being time wasted, either for those interested in the treatise itself and the questions it raises, or for those concerned with the general history of morality. Alberti's work provides us with a fascinating picture of life in the Italian Quattrocento, and no one concerned with the study of the Renaissance can afford to ignore it.

1   Some biographical notes on Alberti

Alberti's distant ancestors were feudal lords whose family seat was a castle in Valdarno.[1] At the beginning of the thirteenth century they moved to Florence and proceeded to blend gradually into the ranks of the bourgeoisie, then in its ascendancy. To facilitate this process they dropped the family name during the fourteenth century and adopted the name of the Alberti family:[2] a family which occupied no mean position among Italian middle-class families, having produced some of the outstanding jurists and bankers of the period. For reasons which are not clearly understood, Leone Battista Alberti's grandfather was expelled from Florence, and Leone Battista was born in exile in 1404. As his father's married state is documented from 1408 onwards only, his biographers have taken Leone Battista to be illegitimate. This is not certain, however, and in my opinion rather too much stress has been laid on this detail.

After the early death of his father, Alberti went through a difficult time during which he devoted himself to studies of which his family did not approve. He was later to grumble about the unfavourable conditions besetting him in his youth; in such an atmosphere, he remarked, only hunchbacks, cripples and those with no sex appeal could study. He seems to have taken a doctorate in canon law. At the same time, he indulged an interest in an extraordinarily varied range of subjects covering not only the humanities but also physics and mathematics (Vasari describes him as 'bonissimo aritmetico e geometrico') and he also wrote a celebrated treatise on architecture. He was active in almost all branches of literature. His comedy written in Latin was long taken to be a genuine classical piece. This is one of many such apocryphal pieces written at the time as a sort of test of the extent to which one had absorbed classical culture. He wrote many treatises – on the splendours and miseries of the intellectual life, on love, on inner peace, and on the family, the one which interests us here. His earlier works are written in Latin; later, he used the Tuscan dialect. Alberti was not only a writer but a painter, sculptor, composer and an architect to whom Vasari ascribes an imposing list of achievements. In intellectual range and power he may well stand beside Leonardo da Vinci, who was born when Alberti was forty-eight years of age.

Alberti anticipated Leonardo in his ability to combine theory and practice in the solution of problems. His investigations in the field of mechanics may be naive and amateurish but, as M. A. Gukowski points out in his monograph on Leonardo's mechanics, they represent a major advance on the mechanics of classical times and of the Middle Ages. The crucial difference is that Alberti's investigations were not of an abstract philosophical nature but arose from the rational handling of certain technological requirements.[3] W. N. Lazariev also stresses the importance of Alberti's atelier in the development of the practical applications of science.[4]

His biographers portray Alberti as a man bent on developing not only his mental powers but also his physical prowess, and there are many anecdotes concerning his ability to jump higher than others, break in wild horses and throw coins right over church steeples. We are told also of his exercises in asceticism, designed to develop that spiritual fortitude which he called *virtù* – a term here used in its classical sense, which is by the way not the only sense in which Alberti customarily used it.

Everything we know about him shows Alberti as a very successful man. He was handsome, good company, he enjoyed adulation and recognition from all and sundry. His opinions were valued, he was consulted about the future, he was called a 'second Socrates' and the pride of Florence. Vasari writes: 'Leone Battista was a man of the most courteous and prepossessing manners, the friend of great men, accessible to all; with all he spoke politely, he spent his whole life in a dignified manner as became the true gentleman he was ('visse onoramente e da gentiluomo, com'era'); until at last having reached ripeness of age, he went contentedly and quietly to a better life, leaving behind him a name that was renowned indeed.'[5] Leone Battista returned to Florence, benefiting from the circumstance that the Albertis had been given permission to return to their birthplace on condition that they did not meddle in public affairs. When Alberti used the word *patria* he was thinking of Florence. He remained there till his death.

For present purposes, Alberti interests us mainly because of his treatise on the family. His was far from being the only treatise produced on this subject at this time. Some students of the period see the reason for the proliferation of similar treatises in the weakening of the family bond during the Renaissance. People no longer wanted to have children, families broke up. One of the best examples is provided by the Alberti family, whose members were scattered all over Europe. Alberti's treatise is in four books. The first three were written in 1434 when Alberti was thirty; the fourth – on friendship – was written in 1441. The free but, on the whole, faithful adaptation of Book III, erroneously attributed to Pandolfini, which was in circulation from the fifteenth century onwards under the title *Trattato del Governo della Famiglia*, enjoyed particular success and fame. It was not until 1886 that Alberti himself was finally identified as the author of this adaptation. In what follows, I shall make use of the 1802 edition, the text of which is in a very personal mixture of Latin and Tuscan. There are two modernisations of the text (Mancini, 1908, and Pellegrini, 1911) but neither of these has been available to me. In quotations I retain unchanged the author's peculiarities of spelling, etc.

2   The household as portrayed in Alberti's treatise

The treatise on the family is written in the form of a conversation between a father and his five sons. In the 1802 edition, the father's name is given as Agnolo; in other editions he is usually called Gianozzo. He is an elderly man who talks to his sons, most of whom are already married, in a way which shows respect for experience of life rather than for learning. Some scholars believe that what we have here is in fact a portrait of Alberti's grandfather, to whom the author is said to have been deeply attached. Although the preference for worldly knowledge over book learning hardly fits our picture of Alberti, we may fairly take it that the views put in Agnolo's mouth are by and large those of Alberti himself.

Semantically, the word *famiglia* is not adequately rendered in English by its etymological counterpart, 'family'. *Famiglia* is rather equivalent to 'stock', 'kindred', and is used in this sense when we speak of the Pizzi family, the Strozzi family or the Medici family. As here used by Alberti in the extended sense, it refers not only to the family nucleus – i.e. the parents and their children – but also to nieces and nephews, the household staff and serfs in the common dwelling they all share. Not only sentiment but prestige also requires that all the members of the extended family should live under one roof, in that the size of the 'family' is not without influence on its public standing ('la copia degli uomini fa la famiglia pregiata', p. 101). Reasons of security and of economics also play their part here. At a common fire people warm themselves more cost-effectively than at separate fires. Separate meals need more servants: two tables need two tablecloths. 'I could never agree to your living under other roofs,' says Agnolo to his sons, making it explicitly clear that he is speaking as a man of experience rather than as a man of learning ('come uomo piuttosto pratico che litterato', p. 102).

The family should live in a villa on the outskirts of a town. Not a rented house: the family must have its own house, preferably built by its own members (here speaks the architect in Alberti). And if the house is to adorn its surroundings, it must be built with care and taste. An attractive site should be chosen in a good (in the class sense) neighbourhood; due attention should be paid to the aesthetic quality of the view, and the hygienic properties of the site. This latter requirement is probably due to Alberti's recollections of a terrible plague which he survived but which left an indelible impression on him. The villa should be surrounded by its own arable land, of sufficient size to guarantee economic self-sufficiency. In addition to the villa and its surrounding lands ('casa e possessione') the family should have a *bottega*. This does not mean quite the same thing as 'shop', its modern equivalent. In Alberti's usage, it is rather a sort of enterprise producing foods – in this case, wool or silk. Agnolo recommends these two products ('lavorare lane o seta'). They are secure investments, the work is not heavy, they give employment to many, and they are therefore both beneficial and useful. The family described by Alberti is engaged in weaving wool, in keeping with Florentine custom of Alberti's day; it was not until later that Florence became a centre of the silk industry.[6] The wealth of Florence in its wool-weaving period is well known. According to historians of the economic life of the period, the raw wool was distributed among the householders of the city to be woven and dyed by them in their own homes. Alberti often mentions the role of the middle-men – the so-called *fattori* – in this production process. These were probably engaged in the purchase of the raw material which came (as we know from various sources) from as far away as Britain, its distribution to the domestic workers and doubtless in the sale of the finished product.

The household is run on patriarchal lines. Age carries authority. The father is the ultimate authority, and to him the sons address themselves with deep respect and devout obedience. He himself often appeals to the authority invested in the dead, thus accentuating the link with his ancestors ('nostri vechi, nostri antiqui, nostri maggiori'). He is not heavy-handed in his treatment of his wife and children, his servants and serfs. In particular, love rather than fear is the keynote of the husband–wife relationship. Personal authority rather than coercion should be used in dealings with one's children ('usare autorità piuttosto che imperio'). Servants must be supervised, for 'the master's eye fattens the horse'.[7] But at the same time they must be well treated and praised where praise is due, for 'good grows when praised'.

The household should be peaceful and congenial. All of its occupants must be busy with their various tasks from morning to night; not a moment is to be wasted. The household should remind one of the beehive or the anthill, with all the members of the colony actively and permanently engaged in augmenting and safeguarding their supplies. 'Man is not born to spend his life asleep, but to be active' (p. 92). No one can afford to be idle; everyone must be continuously engaged on his or her allotted task ('non oziosi ma continuamente operosi'). Good husbandry ('masserizia') manages body, soul and time. These things are at our disposal, and we must use them appropriately. The body should be strong, healthy and comely ('sano, robusto e bello') – a far cry from the medieval outlook! We must learn to rule our passions. Envy must not be allowed to upset an even tenor: one should bide one's time, cheerfully and patiently. This pleasant domestic atmosphere is stressed by Alberti over and over again. His attitude to sorrow or sadness recalls Cicero's struggle with this illness of the soul, as known from the *Tusculanae disputationes*, a struggle to be taken up later by Montaigne. A man must get up early and plan his working day methodically: organised time is time effectively lengthened. Time is lost not only by the idler but also by him who does not know how to use it efficiently. 'He who can manage time effectively, will master everything else' (p. 128). But while everyone must work, this is not to say that intensive toil and drudgery must be the order of the day. One should not overdo things. There is no trace of the ascetic or the fanatic about Alberti. The working life must be punctuated by moments of happy and well-earned inactivity. Luxury is frowned upon, but the house should be comfortable; and articles, though simple, should be genuine and of the best quality, because then they last longer and give more pleasure to the eye. Silver ware is not necessary for everyday use, nor is fancy food. Fancy dishes are for guests and invalids. For the members of the household 'cittadinesca in modo' cooking is all that is needed: that is to say, a good standard of plain, unpretentious food, something similar to the 'good home cooking' or *cuisine bourgeoise* of our own time. The family should lack for nothing; but possession for the sake of possession is not an attitude that finds any favour with Alberti. Over and over again he repeats that the man who does not know how to make use of his property might as well not have it. It is good to know how to make a fortune – but one must also know how to utilise it. Life is there to be lived. Alberti quotes the awful warning of the rooster which was being fattened up for the cooking-pot: when he realised this, he stopped eating altogether and that was the end of him.[8]

Everyone wants to get richer; Alberti is explicit about this. Every pauper wants money ('ogni povero cerca d'arrichire'). But to augment what one has, one needs not only productive capacity but also thriftiness. Alberti divides expenditure into two categories: necessary and unnecessary expenditure. This second category is further subdivided into permissible and frivolous (*pazzia*). Necessary expenses are those incurred in the upkeep of the family, the estate lands and business interests. Expenditure on ensuring the family's comfort and safeguarding its due social position also comes under this heading. Such expenses must be undertaken without procrastination, making sure, of course, that you are getting full value for your money. Where family honour and the *patria* are threatened, something spectacular is called for: then, we must be 'splendidi, magnifici, potentissimi'. Under the heading of expenditure which is unnecessary but permissible, Alberti puts such things as painting the loggia, buying silverware and fine carpets, expensive clothes, fine books and the best horses. In contrast with the first category, these expenses can be deferred. Perhaps the whim will pass, and even if this is not the case, at least one has had time to think things over. In this way, one spends less and one experiences pleasurable anticipation – one looks forward to buying things in the future.

Finally there is frivolous expenditure. Here, Alberti's normal tone of moderation and restraint deserts him. Anyone who supports a lot of idle parasites who bestir themselves only to lick their patron's boots, must be crazy; such rogues and villains ('scellerati e viziosi uomini') are worse than wild beasts or poisonous snakes. Affecting friendship, they insult it. They breed idleness in those whom they flatter, so that one ne'er-do-well can ruin a whole family. They are to be shunned like the plague and so are those who support them. These hard words are aimed at practices among the nobility, and the same tone of censure will be heard when the *signori* next come under attack.

The subject of the well-balanced budget – in which expenditure never exceeds income – is a favourite one with Alberti. Among the concluding moral precepts with which the third book ends, precepts urging justice, equity, peaceableness, self-possession and modesty, the reader is again reminded: 'Let your expenses be equal to or less than your income.'

Alberti was greatly taken with book-keeping, then a

novelty, and advises us always to have our pens at the ready ('sempre avere la penna in mano'), so that we can take careful notes as we go along. It is becoming for a merchant to have his hands permanently ink-stained.

Thrift secures a man's independence. Alberti reminds us of the proverb which says that he who finds not a penny in his own purse stands even less chance of finding one in someone else's (p. 60). Thrift enables you to come to the aid of your blood relation, your friend or your country in the hour of their need. On the other hand, one must never behave like a skinflint. There is a golden mean between miserliness and frivolous expenditure. This golden mean is *liberalità*. In particular, however, one must not begrudge any expenditure which redounds to the honour of the family and enhances its good name and reputation. 'Fama, gloria, onore' are the prizes won by means of wealth and personal merit: this is an oft-recurring theme in Alberti's treatise.

As I said, the household property, the cultivated lands and the wool enterprise provide the economic basis of Agnolo's family. At least, this is how Agnolo/Alberti sees the situation; and this is what he recommends in conversation with his sons who, quite exceptionally, reject his advice and assert that what really matters is money. Money, as the sons see it, is the nerve-centre of everything. If you have money, you can satisfy all your needs and indulge all your fancies: if you have no money, you are unlikely to have anything else. Money can do something to help the man who is forced into exile or who falls on evil days in other ways. Money will provide you instantly with lands, agents, implements, cattle. Everything can, in a sense, be contained in one small purse. The father criticises these views from the standpoint of security: nothing is 'meno stabile', more unstable and less enduring than money. Hoarding money is a risky business, which generates an atmosphere of suspicion. If money is stored under lock and key, it is of no use to anyone; for nothing is of value unless it is put to valuable use (p. 172). The man known to possess money is exposed to all sorts of temptations; some people will give him bad advice, others will bear him ill-will. Agnolo agrees with his sons that in the case of war, for example, buildings may go up in flames:

but possession is not surrendered. Land is a sure investment. If it is infertile one year, it brings forth tenfold the next. Practice and experience help us to find the happy compromise. Since money is the most useful standby in time of war and landed property comes into its own in time of peace, the wise man will see to it that he has both. 'Not all in money and not all in landed property, but part in one and part in the other.' And again: 'The good husbandman should not restrict his resources to money alone, nor to property alone, but he should divide what he has and allocate it to both' (p. 173).

All financial transactions should be conducted in a clear and honest manner ('chiaro e netto'). Alberti has a low opinion of people who borrow money; his advice is to keep out of their way, though here some care is necessary lest others think you a miser. Be particularly careful not to lend money to the rich. It is better to give a rich man ten dinars and write them off, than to lend him a hundred. From *signori* you cannot even expect thanks, let alone repayment of a debt. They are pleasant to you in so far as you are of use to them. They spend their lives in idleness, eating other people's food and avoiding work. You may have good points but that is not what interests them. Around them, they collect a bunch of rogues and villains to whom restraint, sobriety and probity are alien concepts. As far as possible, avoid the rich. If you give them what they want, they will ask for more. They become insatiable. If you give to one of them, it is assumed that you cannot refuse another. Promises turn into obligations, loans are interpreted as gifts, and gifts are money thrown away. The *signori* will seize upon any little slip you may make, any lack of concentration, to hang on to the money you have lent them. They will do you harm and slander you in order to postpone the day of repayment. The people whom Alberti holds up to us as model exemplars of the sound life, get their good name through their virtue and not because of their flamboyant life-style; through merit, and not by acting to the detriment of others.

1 At the exhibition, by Daumier

2 Art and the Philistine, by Norwid

3 Benjamin Franklin, after Carmontelle

4 The idle and the industrious journeyman, engraving from Hogarth's 'The Fellow 'Prentices at Their Looms', from *Industry and Idleness*

5 The banker and his wife, by Matsys (Louvre)

6 The model merchant, 1675 frontispiece from Savary, *Le Parfait Négociant*

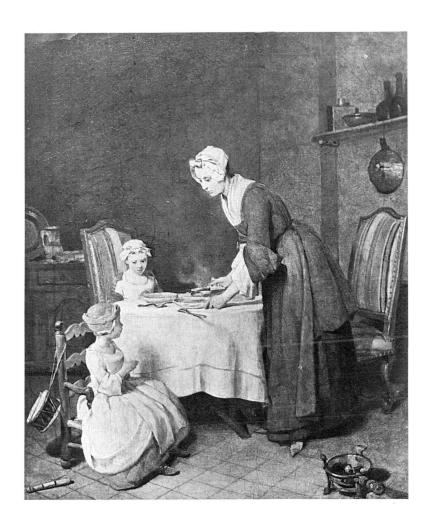

7 Saying grace, by Chardin

8 Name-day present, by Daumier

9 'They didn't dance like that in Empire days!' by Daumier

10 The concierge shapes public opinion, by
Daumier, from *Actualités*

11 'I'm nobody, I'm no good, I'm a layabout
right enough – but I'm not a grocer!' by
Gavarni, from *Masques et Visages*

12 'Bourgeois! Now there's a right old bunch of creeps!' by Gavarni, from *Masques et Visages*

3   Male and female exemplars in Alberti's treatise

Certain figures stand out in Alberti's description of family
life. Some of their characteristics have already been
mentioned. In what follows, we shall round off our picture
of these paragons.

The least medieval trait in Alberti is his faith in man
and in man's extraordinary possibilities. In man there is
something of a god – a mortal god, perhaps, but still a god.
Man is born into a nexus of endless possibilities. If he is to
realise any of these possibilities in practice, he must know
how to master his environment and turn everything to his
own use. This is where good organisation and good administration come in. This wider meaning of 'good husbandry' is
what Alberti understands by '*masserizia*', rather than the
restricted sense given to the word by Sombart; and it is in
this wider sense that Alberti calls it a 'sacred thing' ('sancta
cosa'). Control one's own body; control the passions; control
one's property; control time! Learn to use friendship for
your own ends; learn how to draw some profit even from
intercourse with villains. Sexual desire is a special case in the
control of the passions in general: never let love take such a
hold on you that you cannot shake it off when the time has
come to do so. Should a situation arise in which we can no
longer control our own fate, we must submit, and in Stoic
fashion seek no more than is within the compass of our
possibilities. The precept of self-control is intimately bound
up with Alberti's conviction that man can control his
environment.

Alberti has that same faith in science which is a little later
displayed by Leonardo; and again like Leonardo and, much
later, Franklin, he is always trying to apply science to the
business, however trivial, of everyday life. As an architect,
Alberti's inventive powers have been much admired. He
himself tells us how much satisfaction he derived from
inventing hitherto unimagined mechanisms, or solving
mathematical problems. In contradistinction to the ancients,
he also valued handicrafts and admired a well-finished
product. For Alberti, knowledge had moral value; as in
Leonardo's case, *verità* and *bontà* are closely linked. He

revered men of genius, speaking of them in language which reminds us of the Romantics.[9]

In man and in his surroundings alike, order must reign – not so much the orderliness cultivated by Franklin as the moderation advocated by the ancients. The happy medium between 'too much' and 'too little' ('il mezzo fra il poco e il troppo') – this is what we must seek. Order subsumes peace and beauty. We are reminded of Xenophon enthusing (in the *Oikonomikos*) over neat rows of footwear, orderly sets of tableware, stacked coverlets.[10] Alberti too stresses the aesthetic beauty of orderliness. It is pleasing and restful to cast one's eye over a grove of trees planted in orderly rows or a well-laid-out garden.

This orderliness which lies so close to Alberti's heart is to be found in all his own utterances, even in the choice of words. His language is never vehement or extravagant. In discussion, things must be viewed quietly and soberly from all sides. It is thus that Alberti discusses the question whether money should be given to young people. On the one hand, money in the hands of the young is no less dangerous than an open razor. But, on the other hand, shortage of money has led many a young man into crime. Should young people be brought up in the town or in the country? There is something to be said for each alternative. In town, a young man has a better chance of distinguishing himself in some way, and also he can make first-hand acquaintance with the wicked ways of the world – which is all to the good, as one should be able to recognise what one has to avoid. At the same time, country life has its strong points which are not to be despised. On three issues only in the whole treatise does Alberti express outright condemnation – the rich man's support of hangers-on, the parasitic existence of the *signori* and their reluctance to pay up, and, thirdly, the question of high urban office, a point which we now take up.

Alberti also wrote a treatise on tranquillity. That he should extol the quiet life is very understandable when we consider the turbulent age into which he was born. In point of fact, he survived both plague and exile, and the family was able to cope with political favour and disfavour alike. But his attitude to high urban office is negative, and not only because such posts were closed to him. Of course, a sheltered life at home is not exactly the best way to win the renown which Alberti sets such store by, but Alberti tries to convince us that an adverse fate dogs the steps of outstanding men. One should not line one's pockets in high office at the expense of others; and those who have refused to do so have not been properly recognised and esteemed. An adverse fate dogged Aristydes, who was expelled by his fellow citizens simply because he was the most just of men. In a well-structured state, the reins of government should indeed be in the hands of the best citizens ('migliori cittadini') but, failing this ideal arrangement, it is better to avoid high office. In any case, what one must never do is neglect one's home for reasons of public office: of all things, the family is the most precious ('più cara la famiglia che alcuna altra cosa').

But everyone desires fame and fortune, and if this may not be attained via public office there remains (at least according to the '*Treatise on the Family*') only one way to do so: with the help of the domestic virtues and one's own wealth. Alberti lists the qualities his sons should acquire: industriousness, restraint (*sobrietà*), caution, good manners in relations with others (*facilità*), civility (*civiltà*), fairness, modesty and honesty (*onestà*). This last term occurs with varying meanings in different contexts.[11] Elsewhere, this list of virtues includes *umanità*. If we take this word to indicate – as the context seems to suggest – an attitude of kindly forbearance and understanding towards our fellow men, we find ourselves with an expression which adumbrates the *humanité* of Helvétius, which the historians of the French Enlightenment sometimes treat as an eighteenth-century addition to the virtues.[12] A man's behaviour must be characterised by *dignità*. In all his gestures he must show his dignity and his maturity. Here we have something very close to that bourgeois 'respectability' which appears in the portrait of the nineteenth-century English gentleman at the same time as the bourgeoisie took this exemplar to its heart; and close also to the *dignité* which Goblot describes as characteristic of the French bourgeoisie.[13] It is to this quest for respectability that Goblot attributes the changes in men's fashions which took place in the nineteenth century, changes which indicated 'respectability' as much by colour as by cut. This respectability was the bourgeoisie's way of making up for its lack of noble birth. Semblance of virtue is not enough; nothing but genuine virtue will do for Alberti. 'Ingegnatevi esse quali voi volete parare': 'try to be what you want to seem to be' (p. 97).

Idleness, greed, profligacy and truculence are to be avoided. We must strive consciously to avoid wrong-doing, and to use our talents to gain ourselves a good name, and the goodwill and love of our fellow citizens. It is not enough for Alberti to be respected: he wants to be loved as well.

Following the great classical authors, Alberti wrote a treatise on friendship, a theme which also comes up for discussion in the text that concerns us here. Agnolo explains to his wife: no one who detracts from my good name is my friend. My friend is someone to whom I can show respect when he is present and whom I can praise when he is absent. It is easy for the rich to find friends. Friends are *utilissimi*, 'highly useful', a statement which suggests that for Alberti a friend was a sort of ally or partner. Since friendship is, in a way, insurance, Alberti advises us to test our friends very carefully, as we would test a bow or a horse in peacetime so as to be sure of their quality in the hour of need (p. 187). They should also be tested in small matters; in this way, we can form some idea of how they will behave in matters of moment. In principle, however, one should appeal to friends as little as possible. A man should be self-sufficient, and it is better to have others under obligation to you than vice versa. It is right to be generous to our friends – but always bearing in mind that a loan often leads to a quarrel in which a friend may well be lost. In the case of a conflict of interests, 'why should I consider his interests rather than my own?' ('perche debbo io avere piu caro l'utile suo, che il mio?') (p. 177). No secret is made of the self-interest displayed by Agnolo and his family. From this angle, the family appears holding staunchly together in a posture of cautious distrust *vis-à-vis* strangers ('gli strani'). The father's advice to his sons – plant your trees at the edge of your property so that their shade falls not on your ground but on that of your neighbours – has become famous (p. 108).

As regards relations with an enemy, it is not right to react to hatred with hatred, but one must answer trick with trick and violence with violence. Here is the voice of Machiavelli rather than Christian counsel to turn the other cheek. Of course, it is for a man to behave thus; a woman will do better if she takes evasive action.

As I have mentioned Alberti's unchristian attitude to his enemies, this may be as good a place as any to stress that his whole manner of thinking is worldly and secular. It is true that he tried his hand at writing psalms, but this was a literary experiment on the part of a man who could not bear to leave any literary form untried, rather than an expression of deep religious conviction. God plays very little part in Alberti's life; religious motivation is alien to him, and if he expects any reward for a good life it is here on earth in the shape of wealth, affection and respect.

At the beginning of this rather detailed account of Alberti's treatise on the family, I said that the father teaches the sons how to go about the business of living. The absence of daughters from these tutorial sessions is understandable. In Alberti's conception of the family, women played a distinctly secondary role. Men are the better creatures ('animi grandi ed clletti'), endowed so by nature: and in the conventional prayer intoned as he leads his bride into the new house they are to share, Agnolo asks God to give him sons.

The husband trains and schools his wife. In this field he has very wide possibilities. As a rule, he takes her in all her youth and inexperience from the hands of her mother, whose task it was to keep her pure for marriage and to teach her the domestic arts of spinning and cooking ('filare e cucire'). While Alberti's male exemplar is derived from patriarchal tradition, his model woman is reminiscent of Ischomach's wife in Xenophon's *Oikonomikos*. As in the class war, in relations between the sexes the rules are made by the stronger side in their own interests: and these interests have not changed much since Xenophon. One chooses a wife in the light of certain criteria: her virtues, her family and her dowry. Alberti lays particular stress on virtue. Once she is married, a woman must look after the household. In the prayer I mentioned above, the couple pray for wealth, friends and reputation for the man; for the woman, purity, conjugal fidelity and the qualities that go to make a good housekeeper. Conjugal fidelity on the woman's part adorns the family as nothing else can: it is a jewel which will be handed on to the daughters as part of their dowry. Only the virtuous woman can be truly beautiful. God has specially severe punishments in store for those who break their marriage vows: they are stigmatised by public opinion ('infame') and always unhappy. A wife should be attractive only to her husband. Thus, make-up is not only reprehensible but point-less, as the husband knows what his wife looks like anyway, and has no need of artificial aids. Agnolo tells his sons how his wife – their mother – applied rouge to her face at their wedding, in the belief that she was making herself look more attractive. Gently (this is how to rebuke a woman) he had told her to go and wipe it off. It does not pay to treat women harshly; a little affection will work wonders. The rouge episode is developed at some length. It is all very reminiscent of the passage in Xenophon where Ischomach forbids his wife to paint her face, and criticises her use of built-up soles to increase her height. Good-naturedly, both authors suggest that if married women want red cheeks they should get them the natural way – by hard work. As Alberti puts it: no idling, no looking out of the window, just keep on bustling about the house getting on with your work – that will bring the colour to your cheeks and give you a healthy appetite into the bargain. Both the aristocratic and the bourgeois ideol-ogists of classical antiquity are agreed on the need for women to be active. We may recall that the king of the Phaeacians – who describes for Odysseus the way of life at his court as follows: 'the things in which we take a perennial delight are the feast, the lyre, the dance, clean linen in plenty, a hot bath, and our beds'[14] – has a wife who is well known for her excellent housekeeping, and a daughter who lends a hand at washing the clothes with the servants. Students of human attitudes to labour and industriousness have perhaps tended to forget that things have not always been equally well ordered for men and women. In the wealthiest bourgeois families in late nineteenth- and early twentieth-century Europe, women were allowed no more than a decorative and purely inactive role, and it was up to men to defend this role as tenaciously as they defended their class position itself. In the case of Alberti, we have to do with a partitioning of labour. This is bound up with the conviction that it would be not only unseemly but actually degrading for men if women were to undertake employment (p. 132).

In Alberti's treatise, the husband conducts his bride to a well-stocked house which is ready and prepared for her, and their life together begins with him showing her where everything is kept. No witnesses are present when the husband shows his wife where the jewellery is hidden (the bedroom is the best place). It is not for her to look at his family records or his correspondence ('scritture'). For the husband, these things are sacred ('quasi come cosa religiosa') and it would be dangerous to expose them to female curiosity and tittle-tattle. It is always safer to make sure that a woman *cannot* cause trouble, rather than simply relying on her not wanting to!

To her husband, a woman owes obedience and respect. Purity and modesty, respect and humility ('onestà e modestia, riverenzia e umiltà') – these are the womanly virtues. The woman should listen rather than speak (p. 148). She must be discreet, refrain from discussing her own affairs or asking questions about other people's. She must learn how to control the servants, she should not gossip with them or listen to them when they tell tales. When a member of the household staff has to be admonished this should be done gently and with understanding. Outwardly she is to preserve her dignity (p. 166), which should be combined with cheerfulness. 'A happy woman is always the most beautiful' (p. 164). If she looked downcast, one might think she had been up to something. In her hierarchy of values she must put 'l'onore' before possessions, and 'l'onestà' before expediency (p. 166).

4 Alberti's position: pioneer of bourgeois morality?

Having acquainted ourselves in some detail with Alberti's views as set out in the *Libri della Famiglia*, it is now time to try to assess the author's position in the general history of bourgeois morality. It is not a subject on which there has been any general measure of agreement.

In his well-known work on the civilisation of the Italian Renaissance, Jakob Burckhardt saw Alberti in the light of the typological approach characteristic of late nineteenth-century historians, as a typical man of his age. Alberti is the typical polymath: his economic insights are combined with a mastery of philosophy, literature, architecture, sculpture and painting. He is a man of exceptional aesthetic culture. Burckhardt credits him with the discovery of the beauties of nature, of forests and cultivated fields, the beauty of old wrinkled faces.[15] There is no need to go into further detail here; but this is certainly not the petty bourgeois book-keeper with inky fingers, anxiously scrutinising his rows of figures, as Sombart sees him.

For Sombart, Renaissance Florence is the 'Bethlehem of the capitalist spirit' and Alberti is its prophet, playing the same representative role as Franklin was to play three centuries later. A straight line leads from the one to the other[16] via such writers as Savary and Defoe. Alberti was anticipated by the classical authors who wrote on economics, especially by the Roman writers *de re rustica*, and he makes use, often in somewhat garbled form, of themes current in late antiquity; but for Sombart he is in many ways an innovator. For example, Sombart thinks it was an innovation for a rich man to talk about economic matters without being ashamed ('Das war etwas unerhört Neues', p. 138). Then again, the very concept of the sound economy as one in which income is never less than expenditure, is seen as a bourgeois-capitalist attitude completely at variance with the aristocratic life-style ('eine grundsätzliche Verwertung aller Maximen seigneuraler Lebensgestaltung'). With Alberti, the idea of thrift makes its appearance ('Die Idee des Sparens trat in die Welt!'). This has nothing to do with the pinching and scraping to which the poor man is forced by his circumstances; it is a new situation in which the 'good husbandman' becomes an ideal for even the rich man to aim at (p. 139). This bourgeois ethic, in which we can already discern the Franklinesque adage 'Time is money', is, according to Sombart, saturated with *ressentiment vis-à-vis* the high and mighty – a trait which completes the classical lineaments of the bourgeoisie.

For Weber, Alberti is the great Renaissance polymath and genius whose treatise on the family is concerned not with making money (*Erwerb*) but with good housekeeping (*Haushaltung*). From the Puritan point of view, Alberti's solicitude for the family's reputation and the classical–pagan orientation of his life-style would both have to rate as faults, being excluded from Puritanism by its asceticism which Weber called 'asceticism within the world' in contradistinction to the otherworldly asceticism of the saints. The world of literature and the arts, to which Alberti allotted a cardinal place, is entirely missing from this world of Puritan asceticism. Puritanism on the one hand, with its religious motivation and its doctrine of wealth as a reward or bonus, and Alberti on the other – these are indeed two different worlds.[17]

Yet another view of Alberti should be mentioned here. Those works of Alberti's in which he castigates the indifference of his contemporaries to the arts and sciences, and in which he praises artistic achievement and the man of genius above all things, are probably uppermost in the mind of Miriam Beard when she links Alberti with Boccaccio as one of that band of Renaissance writers who led the revolt against capitalism. As we have seen, Alberti pursued his studies against the wishes of his family, who would evidently have preferred to see him in banking or commerce. Boccaccio (the son of an agent in the Bardi firm of bankers) was also loath to follow in his father's footsteps, so he satirised bankers in the *Decameron*, and regretted every moment of his life which he had wasted on business matters. Beard sees both Alberti and Boccaccio as renegades in the setting of Renaissance capitalism, and as figures to be compared perhaps with Ruskin and Morris.[18]

An enigmatic figure, then, whom critics see in very different ways. Can we arrive at a fair picture of the man on the basis of a study of his works as we know them?

In Book I of Aristotle's *Politics* we find an interesting differentiation made between the art of satisfying one's own needs and those of one's family (which Aristotle calls *oikon-*

omia) and the art of making money for oneself (*he ktetikè tekhnè* or *he khrematistikè tekhnè*). *Oikonomia* may utilise the means amassed with the help of the second 'art' but is something quite different from it.[19]

For all creatures, Aristotle writes, Nature has provided ways and means of survival and livelihood: for example, mother's milk for the newborn. Some peoples live by hunting, others by fishing, others again by pillaging their neighbours. Most, however, live by agriculture. These ways of earning a living are all natural ways. War too is natural when it is directed against peoples who are born to serve others but who are recalcitrant. These natural ways of satisfying natural needs belong to *oikonomia*, which is a bounded field.

But there is another art of conquest – the art of enriching oneself – and this field has no limits. One can make use of anything and everything in two distinct ways, just as a man can use a pair of boots: he can wear them or he can trade them. In itself, exchange does not belong to the art of self-enrichment, as in the beginning people exchanged only those things which they required to satisfy their mutual needs. But it was from this type of exchange that the art of making money arose. As exchange was extended to wider and wider territories, money became necessary, as the articles exchanged were not always easily transportable. Thus was developed a new art – the art of making money which knows no quantitative frontiers.

Aristotle's differentiation is not entirely clear, and he himself does not seem to be entirely satisfied with it, but it provides a useful peg for our further analysis of Alberti's work. Clearly, Alberti's economic interests were nothing new; and long before the bourgeoisie there were those who dealt in such matters without being ashamed to do so. Marcus Terentius Varro (116–27 BC) mentions more than fifty writers on rural economy; and Seneca's contemporary Columella (1st century AD) in the first book of his *De re rustica* (the most extensive Roman work on agriculture) gives an impressive list of previous writers on this theme, beginning with Hesiod and Democritus. The list is joined fourteen hundred years later by Alberti, who knew Columella's work well, and who, according to many researchers, was to include in his treatise on the family not a few reflections on economics culled from Xenophon. Not all of the works mentioned in Columella's list have survived, but we can use Aristotle's distinction to divide those that have survived into two categories: those taken up primarily with the organisation and good running of a domestic economy, and those which are mainly concerned with making money. Thus there is a clear difference between the *Oikonomikos* of Xenophon, which can certainly be put in Aristotle's first category, and the reflections of the elder Cato in *De re rustica*, where much stress is laid on making money and where the presence of Aristotle's *ktetikè tekhnè* is very marked. We find the latter art in its purest form in Franklin's *The Way to Wealth*. In between are many transitional forms, all of which – once we have made due allowance for period, local conditions and the author's origins – will show a tendency to fall into one or other of these two categories, a tendency dictated by the very nature of the problem.

Xenophon, a landed aristocrat who is not unlike an old Polish country squire, returned from his military expeditions laden with booty which enabled him to buy an estate and devote himself to agriculture. In the *Oikonomikos* he has Socrates (whom Plato presents in the *Phaedrus* as believing that nothing can be learned from nature) intoning a hymn of praise to farm-work and taking a keen interest in what sort of soil is best for ploughing, sowing, weeding and fertilising (!). Xenophon recognises only two kinds of occupation – that of the warrior (*polemikè tekhnè*) and that of the farmer (*geōrgía*), and he despises handicrafts as 'fireside occupations' (Sinko's translation of *banausikái*).[20] Handicrafts involve too much sitting about at home and insufficient time for meeting friends, and as a result, both body and mind suffer. Men who go in for such occupations make poor defenders of the fatherland. Ischomach, whom Xenophon presents as an exemplary character and model husbandman, certainly cares about money, as long as it is fairly come by (*kalōs*); he is said to honour the gods, he is hospitable to his friends and helps them in their hour of need, and he contributes to enhancing the environment. All of these motives, if we leave out the gods, crop up again in Alberti. In his treatise as a whole, however, we are concerned with the efficient management of resources, well-organised husbandry, rather than with making a lot of money.

The money motive is much more to the fore in the work of the elder Cato. He too speaks up for agriculture, but not for class reasons; as is well known, he was of plebeian origin and a sworn enemy of *nobilitas*. For him, agriculture is a safe occupation. True, it is easier to make money by trading or by lending money, but the former is a risky business and the latter is shameful. Running his farm as he does, Cato behaves much more like a merchant than like a country squire. Plutarch says that he was so intent on getting as much out of his estate as possible that he resented having some of it laid out as gardens. It is also known that he rejected out of hand any idea of following the aristocratic example and making money out of military adventures. Cato's plantations near Rome were a profitable enterprise into which he put a lot of thought, keeping an amazingly accurate check on prices, and making sure that the estate he would leave behind would be bigger than the one he inherited. It is perfectly natural for economic problems to be formulated in terms of profit and loss, and this is a recurrent and inherent theme in treatises of this kind.

Columella's mind runs along similar lines: for example, when he advises against squeezing tenants too hard for ready cash. It is better to get them to work, as this is both less troublesome and in the long run more lucrative. Again, he advises that slaves should be consulted when a new job is being started, as slaves work better when they have a say in things. As for profits, his recommendation is that the work efficiency of slaves should be raised *certamine*, that is, by encouraging competition among them and making sure that they are not short of tools, for loss of a slave's time is more expensive than tools.[21] But nowhere in Columella does thought in terms of profit and loss bulk as large as it does in Cato's text, where it is unmistakable even in cases where we might expect to find a rather different attitude. His purely business attitude to slaves is well known: old or sick slaves should be sold off, a suggestion which Plutarch found shocking. One should be pleasant to neighbours, he advises, as it is then easier to sell one's wares to them ('opera facilius locabis'), and get help with tools and equipment.[22]

To return to Alberti: as I said above, there was an upper-class element in Alberti's family background. Vasari writes: 'He was born in Florence of the renowned Alberti family' ('della nobilissima famiglia degli Alberti'). The family's move to the town at a time when the bourgeoisie was coming to power was by no means an isolated case. Many a feudal lord went into banking or commerce and proved that he could earn his living in this way. In Alberti's treatise, Agnolo is indeed proud of his family tree, but he makes no bones about accusing the *signori*, in good bourgeois fashion, of idleness, bad faith and welshing on debts – in fact, of being altogether a pretty hopeless bunch. In Alberti's eyes, a property near a town is not so much a lucrative enterprise as the perfect place to spend one's life. Of course, if you want to do something big in politics, the town is the right place for you, though the less said about town habits the better (they are 'orribili a dirle', p. 111). Avoid official posts in the town like the plague – and it was no doubt recollections of the plague he had survived in his youth that induced Alberti to prefer residence not too near centres of population. Columella, whose writings Alberti knew well and often quoted, regarded agriculture as the only upright way to increase family resources ('rei familiaris augendae') and as an occupation with nothing underhand about it: war is inseparable from harm done to others and trade by sea is unnatural, for man is a land animal. Making one's fortune by hard work, by usury or by toadying to the rich, are all equally contemptible. But while accepting agriculture as the only worthwhile occupation, Alberti has a new way of looking at it: landed property is not only a good investment for money earned mainly by trade – it is also very attractive as somewhere to live! This is new: Cato and Columella might sing the praises of life down on the farm, but they were careful to live in town, keeping an eye on their property from afar, and only dropping in on it from time to time, unexpectedly, as they explain, so as to keep their agents on their toes. Columella shrewdly adds that he promises his agents more visits than he actually makes. For his part, Alberti drinks in the beauty of the countryside and never wants to leave it. He looks upon efforts to amplify resources by means of trade as unseemly both for himself and for members of his family (p. 104).[23] But, unlike Xenophon, he has a high regard for handicrafts.

Sombart and Weber are poles apart in their attitudes to Alberti. Can we say that either of them has hit the mark in their assessment of this great Renaissance figure? And if not, why not?

Sombart is wrong in believing that Alberti is the first representative of the upper class to discuss economic matters in general, and agricultural matters in particular, without being ashamed of doing so. Many aristocratic writers preceded him in this. Again, it is difficult to go along with Sombart when he sáys that the very concept of good husbandry as husbandry in which income and expenditure are equally balanced, is specifically a bourgeois-capitalist concept. No treatise on the economics of management, whatever its setting, is going to recommend living above one's means! It may be true that no aristocrat *could* write this sort of treatise, but if one did it is fairly certain that he too would be chiefly concerned with balancing the books.

Industriousness is also one of the stock recommendations in all books on good housekeeping. Already in Xenophon we find the well-run household compared to a beehive. According to Plutarch, Cato felt he had to reproach himself if he allowed any of three situations to arise: (1) if he betrayed a secret to a woman; (2) if he travelled by sea when he could go by land; and (3) if he wasted a day in idleness. Nevertheless, isolated instances apart, it is true that industriousness was not uppermost in the minds of the well-to-do, nor was it very much in evidence during the Middle Ages. In Alberti's time, there was a notable shortage of labour in the Italian wool industry, so much so that foreign labour had to be attracted by the offer of advantageous conditions. Some years before Alberti, St Bernard of Siena had urged people to be more industrious, saying that if idleness is to be the distinguishing characteristic of the aristocrat, then the pig is the most aristocratic of them all.[24] For Alberti, the exhortation to work was not simply a useful slogan for employers keen to get more out of their workers: it was something that applied to everyone, master, mistress, servants, alike – the whole *famiglia*. And what he meant by it was not an ascetic, Franklinesque type of industriousness, but activity in tolerable and unforced stretches ('senza noja e fatica') and hence not detracting too much from the comforts of life.

It is with Alberti, according to Sombart, that the concept of thrift comes on the scene. But *masserizia*, the word which Sombart renders as *Sparsamkeit*, really refers to the art of running a household (or a business) without incurring a loss: that is, by making sure that the books are balanced. This is very remote indeed from the thrift preached by Franklin. It is true that Alberti advises us to hesitate before spending money on unnecessary luxuries, thereby allowing time for the whim – if whim it is – to pass. But at the same time he says that money spent on the comfort and outward appearances of the family is money well spent which should never be regretted.

'If you are behindhand with one thing, you are behindhand with everything,' said Cato; and Columella, too, bewails the ineluctable passage of time. The time factor could hardly fail to bulk large in the minds of these writers as they planned their economic enterprises. But Sombart was not alone in considering that time began to play a special role in Alberti's Florence. Acute awareness of the importance of time is widely held to be characteristic of a social class in the ascendant, as the bourgeoisie was in those days. As A. von Martin writes,[25] from the fourteenth century onwards clocks were striking the hours in all the larger Italian cities. Self-regulation by clock-time is something the Middle Ages hardly knew.

I think the observation that time hardly matters to a static society is well made, and there can be little doubt that Alberti set particular store by time. But equally I think that it is going too far to link him with the Franklinesque adage 'Time is money'. Counting the minutes to the accompanying clink of silver is alien to Alberti. For him, time is just one of the things we should learn to use in planned fashion. That a man who wanted to find room in his life for so many things, a man who farmed, built churches, sculpted, painted, wrote and took an interest in technological novelties and in solving mathematical problems – that such a man should want to make the most of his time need surprise no one. But this is still not the attitude to time recommended by Franklin – the attitude of the man who is 'making money', the man for whom every moment of relaxation or recreation is converted into currency and duly noted in the debit column.

Alberti too wanted to be wealthy. It is a desire not limited to Protestants. For a short space of time, the Catholic Church tried to observe the gospel teaching that one cannot serve God and Mammon; but soon poverty of spirit was enlisted to do duty for real poverty, a convenient transfer based on the postulate that the spirit was not dependent on worldly goods. An eloquent exposition of this belief is given by St Francis de Sales (1567–1622), whose treatise on the devout life has an introductory chapter entitled 'On poverty of spirit preserved in the midst of riches'. Here, St Francis writes: 'Poor in spirit is he whose spirit is not taken up with riches.'[26]

The rich man, according to St Francis, must behave like the apothecary who stocks poison but does not poison himself with it. A man may possess riches as long as they occupy his house or his purse but not his heart. 'To be in fact rich and at the same time poor as regards his emotional attachment to these riches – this is a great happiness for the Christian, for thereby he enjoys the privileges of wealth in this world and the merit of poverty for the world to come ("il a par ce moyen les commodités des richesses pour ce monde et le mérite de la pauvreté pour l'autre").'[27]

Addressing Philothée, St Francis urges her to combine wealth with poverty as thus understood. She is to be mindful of temporal things and, at the same time, despise them. Chapter XV is entitled 'How we are to practise true poverty, being none the less rich'. It is God's wish that for love of him we should seize every opportunity of adding to our worldly resources. We can check whether we are in fact doing this for the love of God by giving alms to the needy from time to time: treating wealth as a garment which can be removed at will, and not like a skin which is part of ourselves. But those who are really poor should make a virtue of necessity ('de la nécessité vertu') and comply meekly with God's will, remembering that they are in the goodly company of Christ, the Virgin Mary and the Apostles.

These quotations go to show that the desire for wealth can always be justified in one way or another, and that Catholicism lends itself to rationalisation in this respect just as readily as any other ideology. While there can be no doubt that Catholicism knew very well how to serve both God and Mammon, we have to agree with Weber that Puritanism was an efficient factor in the 'democratisation' of the thirst for gain, its spread to the ranks of the ordinary people. It was for these ordinary people that Franklin's Almanacs were specifically designed. Alberti's treatise on the family was aimed rather higher, at those who had landed property and some sort of industrial interest. There is no trace in Alberti of the role which money plays in Franklin's homilies. For Alberti, economic activity is in no way coupled with religion; the process of making money is not treated as some sort of moral and religious calling, nor is virtue made dependent on wealth and position.

Indeed, any comparison of Alberti with Franklin shows us that Sombart's attempt to treat the former as the precursor of the latter is quite untenable. Everything about Alberti's life-style, including his morality, fixes him firmly in the ranks of the *grande bourgeoisie* which was the end product of the fusion between aristocratic and bourgeois elements. Alberti reminds us in some ways of the rich French bourgeois families of the nineteenth century, or of the Buddenbrooks (for example, Thomas Buddenbrook combines high-flown ambitions with dislike of the aristocracy); with the difference that the atmosphere in Alberti's villa is altogether brighter and happier than is the case in the Puritan austerity of the Hanseatic towns. It is unlikely that Alberti read from Boccaccio rather than from the Bible at family soirées (the Bible was read on Thursdays in the Buddenbrook household) but he certainly preferred Petrarch to the Gospels.

Obviously, the fusion of bourgeois and aristocratic elements which went to produce an Alberti, proceeded along different lines from the fusion of comparable elements that was to take place in England and France at the end of the nineteenth century. We know that several feudal lords figured in Alberti's family tree. These gentlemen had come to terms with the decline in their fortunes and had entered the ranks of the bourgeoisie, combining their own proud traditions with its economic efficiency. This particular fusion of aristocrat and bourgeois is very characteristic of the Italian Renaissance, and it has its own unmistakable indices. The cities were usually locked in mortal combat, and the merchant had to know how to leap into the saddle. Alberti himself was known for his horsemanship, and in the treatise on the family he exhorts men to defend their wives, their households and their fatherland with 'blood and sweat' ('con sudore e con sangue') (p. 132).

Another non-bourgeois trait in Alberti is his thirst for fame and personal distinction. This is generally regarded as typical of the ebullient individualism of the Italian Renaissance – a natural outburst of creative energy after liberation from the shackles which had curbed human enterprise during the Middle Ages. Giordano Bruno regarded the appetite for fame ('l'appetito de la gloria') as the only effective spur ('solo et effecacissimo sprone') goading man on to heroic deeds.[28] There is a striking proliferation in Alberti's pages of terms like *buona fama, buono nome, gloria, onore, riputazione*; and of such phrases as 'to be the object of recognition is of all things the most beautiful' ('l'onore . . . cosa bellissima'), 'fame is something sacred' ('divina cosa la gloria'). One is reminded of how one warrior seeks to outdo the other in acts of personal distinction in book after book of the *Iliad*. Of course, Alberti's values are not those of Homer's heroes. In the *Iliad* it is birth, personal service and personal estate that make the grand heroic gesture possible. In Alberti, the last two factors predominate, with the difference, however, that personal service is only exceptionally understood as military service; and if the grand gesture is possible, this is thanks not to the spoils of war, but to resources amassed by daily work and careful husbandry based on a balanced budget.

The bourgeoisie is always being taken to task for its lack of any appreciation of the fine arts – a shortcoming which, in its turn, is supposed to give a distinctive tinge to 'bourgeois morality'. Alberti on the other hand always takes the aesthetic point of view. As he sees it, the artist should occupy a leading place in society. Bad temper, gluttony, debauchery are above all *ugly*. The human body is beautiful and should be shown nude in art: a viewpoint opposed not only by the clergy for whom nudity was scandalous, but also by the feudal lords for whom it was altogether too democratic.[29]

In contradistinction to the morality associated with the Puritans, virtue for Alberti was something joyous and full of charm ('la virtù è tutta lietà e graziosa'). Everyday life should also be a joyous affair. Sombart sees in Alberti the man of *ressentiment*, taking a swipe at the feudal lords. It is true that no love was lost between Alberti and the aristocrats, but, as we read his works, we are not aware of stoked-up hates and bitterness; there is no trace of his 'getting his own back'. It is in vain that Sombart tries to present Alberti as the stock figure of the illegitimate child with all its complexes. There is no venom in Alberti. He is a man without sharp corners, urging gentleness with young people and subordinates, and recommending correction rather than punishment: which seems only natural in a man so successful, so gifted in mind and body, a man who was able to live the life he wanted and to achieve the fame he had dreamed of.

Franklin was brought up on the Old Testament. Mancini (who edited Alberti's works for publication) lists thirty-one Greek and fifty Latin authors to whom Alberti refers in two of his works alone! In almost every line he wrote we come across some trace of late antiquity. From antiquity Alberti took over various themes which do not always go happily together with what he himself had to say. Thus, his advocacy of careful husbandry is intertwined with the melancholy Stoic reflection that wealth and power do not depend on our own efforts (p. 81): a somewhat false note in a work that is shot through and through with optimism. It would be difficult, of course, for a man so deeply embedded in his age and, at the same time, drawing so heavily on the past, to be entirely consistent in his views. We must be on our guard against the common practice of cultural historians who, when they come across a trait which is seemingly at variance with the rest of an author's work or with the general tone of a culture, either try to distort the trait till it fits in, or treat it as an alien admixture. At the root of such practices lies the conviction that, properly researched and presented, a culture will be seen to be homogeneous and man consistent: a patently erroneous tenet which disfigures many a historical work.

In my discussion of Alberti's morality and his historical position, I have tried to avoid the sort of language used for this purpose by Sombart and Weber. I have not tried to determine whether or not he displays the 'capitalist spirit', because the concept is simply too vague to serve as a criterion in comparative studies. Since the dispute arises primarily from a comparison of Alberti with Franklin, a writer who is alleged to exhibit the 'capitalist spirit' in its classic form, I have tried, using an admittedly imperfect but still, I hope, rather clearer terminology, to compare the *ethos* of these two writers. In conclusion, we may recall the words used by Engels in his preface to the *Dialectics of Nature* to describe the Italian Renaissance. Even if in some respects the real Alberti falls short of Renaissance man as portrayed by Engels, we can say of him in Engels's words: 'The men who founded the modern rule of the bourgeoisie had anything but bourgeois limitations.'[30]

Chapter 9

Bourgeois moral catechisms at the time of the French Revolution

The morality which Defoe and Franklin enjoined upon the petty and middle bourgeoisie had become an object of derision and contempt by the second half of the nineteenth century; and we have to remind ourselves that both men were writing at a time when the bourgeois were very much in the ascendant, both in England and in America. Both came from a Puritan background which, it is alleged, was to favour their capitalist attitudes. Our attention now turns to a country where a Catholic bourgeoisie was preparing to seize power. I have already mentioned the views of the Catholic Savary, which were committed to print by order of Colbert. In some respects, Savary's views coincide with those of Defoe and Franklin; but, unlike them, Savary was exclusively concerned with professional and occupational problems, and saw no need to present the model merchant as a paradigm for men in general, one differing in essentials from the aristocratic model then in vogue. On the eve of the Revolution, the French bourgeoisie had already formed a clear image of their 'new man': one quite unlike the *honnête homme*, the smooth and pampered courtier. It was hoped to launch this new man on the world with the help of a moral code, unconnected with religion, which was to be inculcated in children while still at school. In the last decades of the eighteenth century citizens' catechisms proliferated in France. Allegedly based on the 'principles of human nature', these were supposed to be applicable to men of any time in any place. These catechisms were rejected by the post-Revolutionary reaction, but they caught on again when the Ligue Française de l'Enseignement Laïque was formed in 1866. This league, directed by Ferdinand Buisson and represented in the Assembly by Jules Ferry, was finally successful in 1877 when the schools were completely laicised. The *Catéchismes pour l'instruction morale et civique* which then appeared, harked back in many respects to their eighteenth-century prede-cessors. The evolution of these manuals would form a very rewarding field of study. For the moment, however, we are concerned with only one of them – that produced by Constantin-François de Volney. In April 1792 the Educational Committee of the National Assembly considered a memorandum proposing lay moral education for the schools, based on reason and the natural emotions. A year later, Volney's catechism appeared. Some critics regard this catechism as no more than a commentary on the Declaration of Rights, which Volney helped to draw up. From a multitude of similar catechisms (some of which we shall look at later) I choose this one for detailed study, not because its author is in any way outstanding but because his catechism most faithfully reflects the moral precepts of the French bourgeoisie of his day.

1   Volney's life and character

Volney was the son of an advocate named Chassebeuf; the name Volney is a pseudonym. Professional fees plus the income from a small estate had enabled his father to reach a financially better than average position, which encouraged him to seek social advancement for himself and his children. With this in mind, he changed his name, taking that of his estate – de Boisgiret (in some versions, de Boisgiray) which has an aristocratic ring to it, and so was itself a step in the right direction. His son, however, accepted neither the name nor the chance of a rise in society. When he was a little over twenty he took the name of Volney, and in 1789 he was elected to the States General as Constantin François Chasse-beuf Volney – *bourgeois*.[1]

He had been born in Craon in 1757. His mother died when he was two. He was sent to school and grew up outside the protection of the family circle. On leaving school, financially independent thanks to his father, he went to Paris where he studied various branches of the humanities and medicine. He frequented the circle of the Encyclopédistes and the salon of Madame Helvétius, where he made the acquaintance of Cabanis, Holbach and possibly Franklin. When he inherited his father's considerable fortune, Volney used it to visit Syria and Egypt. The book which he wrote on these countries (1787) brought him fame; it was to be of use to Napoleon in the campaign in Egypt. Volney devoted much time thereafter to erudite works on the linguistics of the Near East (mainly on Arabic and Hebrew), to various activities in the fields of politics and morals, and to attempts to put into practice certain ideas he had concerning agriculture. Immediately upon his return to France, Volney set about preparing for elections in Rennes to the Estates General by issuing a leaflet advocating electoral discrimination against the privileged classes. If these are to be done away with, it must be via a quantitative preponderance of the third estate on the 'one man, one vote' principle, and this is what Volney calls for. But it is precisely from the third estate that many potential voters must be excluded, since they have been too long in the service of the privileged classes to vote for anyone else. Volney justifies this drastic measure in graphic terms: 'There are slaves in Algeria whom we wish to set free: but we must also shoot them in order to keep down the number of pirates.'[2]

As a politician Volney was not very successful, and he had more than one reason to feel embittered. If he reached the Constituent Assembly it was mainly thanks to his gifts as a writer. His attempts to influence events were frustrated *inter alia* by the fact that he was a poor speaker. Also, people seem to have been put off by his too obvious ambition, his sharp temper and his invariably abstract and radical attitude as a legislator. He never reached the front rank, and after 1790 he lost whatever popularity he had. He was accused of having connections with Mirabeau, though we know from the work of Mathiez that he and Mirabeau quarrelled over the question whether the king should be permitted to declare war and conclude treaties. In these matters, Volney sided with Robespierre in taking an extreme radical position, categorically denying the king any such rights. And it was from his lips that the famous warning to Mirabeau was uttered: 'Have a care, Mirabeau! Yesterday the Capitol, today the Tarpeian Rock!'³ In 1791, Volney published his book *Les Ruines, ou Méditations sur les révolutions des empires.* (A Polish translation of part 1 of this work appeared in 1802.) We shall return in due course to this exercise in the romantic philosophy of history, in which Volney reflects bitterly on his afflictions and disappointments. After the dissolution of the Legislative Assembly, Volney went to Corsica, where he ran an agricultural experimental station, in an attempt to find out whether tropical plants could be grown in the Mediterranean basin and Southern France. The idea for these experiments had occurred to him during his travels in Syria, and he now used his own money to cultivate sugar cane, cotton and coffee. After a year of failure, however, he was forced to auction off his venture and return to France, doubly resentful and having made more enemies. But he retained from his year in Corsica a friendship with Bonaparte, whom he met there. In April 1793 his moral catechism appeared: *La Loi naturelle, ou catéchisme du citoyen français.* This was the year of the Terror: Volney too landed in jail, whence he was later released by the Thermidoreans. The catechism was well received by the Montagnards as a handbook of civil behaviour. Volney's fortunes were once again on the upswing, and when the Ecole Normale was established and given the job of providing a new cadre of teachers, he was one of the first to be offered a lectureship. He lectured on history, by which he understood rather the methodology and the philosophy of history. When the Ecole was closed, he went to the United States in search – in his own words – of peace and freedom. In the States, he at once set about making enemies, partly because of his uncompromising and negative attitude in religious matters, partly because of his overeagerness to play a political role in the USA.

Accused of espionage and once again disappointed, Volney returned to France, where he was befriended and entrusted with various missions by Napoleon Bonaparte. And now Volney, who in *Les Ruines* had inveighed against imperialism in general and against the exploitation of Africa and India in the name of trade – this same Volney published in 1798 a panegyric on Napoleon, whom he hailed as the great conqueror and pacifier of Europe. As Napoleon's true intentions became clear, however, a break in the friendship was not long delayed. Volney was an outspoken opponent of the expedition to San Domingo and of the Concordat with the Holy See. When the motion to have Napoleon proclaimed Emperor came up in the Senate in 1804, Volney was one of the four senators who had the courage to vote against it. The day after the motion was carried, Volney, disappointed yet again, tendered his resignation to the Emperor and retired to a country property he had acquired. There he lived as a recluse, occupying himself with scientific and agricultural experiments. Under Louis XVIII Volney was made a peer of France, which did not prevent him from expressing Republican sympathies in his last publications. On his deathbed he refused the last rites: remaining to his last breath a republican, a liberal, and an opponent of religion. In the social sphere, his ideas for reform did not go very far. He feared an excess of power in the hands of the common people, and he had found the bloody progress of the Revolution a terrifying experience. The secret genie through whose lips the author speaks in *Les Ruines* cries: 'Downtrodden people! Awake to recognition of your rights. All authority proceeds from you, all power is in your hands. In vain do kings adjure you in the name of God and their sword. Soldiers! Do not obey these commands! Since God supports the Sultan, your succour is useless; since the sword of Heaven suffices him, he has no need of yours. Be assured, see what he alone can do. . . . Soldiers laid down their arms, and lo, the rulers of the world became as helpless as the least among their subjects. People! Know that those who govern you are only your managers, not your masters; they are set above you but they do not own you; it is thanks to you and your goodwill that they hold power over you . . . for God made all equal and no mortal has a right to oppress any other.'[4] In Volney's estimation, it was precisely this state of affairs that the bourgeois republic had brought about.

2 Volney's Catechism in the light of *Les Ruines*

In *Les Ruines* Volney's intention was to draw lessons from the past for the edification of the present. To the traveller

wandering among the ruins in Asia Minor and meditating
on the fall of so many once-mighty empires, there appears
a mysterious apparition, the genie of the ruins. From this
spirit our traveller seeks to know 'what factors raise empires
up and bring about their downfall; what are the causes that
make some nations develop successfully and others fail; on
what principles may we build our hopes for social peace and
human happiness' (R, p. 19).

In answer, the tutelary spirit expounds a philosophy of
history which takes up the first part of the book. Once upon
a time, people banded together for mutual protection. As
long as they could satisfy their needs by the rational application of joint effort they were able to lead a contented
existence. Unfortunately, those same considerations of self-
interest ('l'amour de soi') which, when applied judiciously,
led to happiness and human progress, began to take an
extreme form and ceased to be rational: and this is the source
of all the troubles that beset man's life on earth. Greed on
the one hand, ignorance on the other, led to the division
of mankind into oppressors and oppressed. The oppressors
destroyed equality among men, and did away with freedom
and with security of life and property. The minority used
all sorts of means to subjugate the majority, including
religion and the clergy, who are the hangers-on of the privileged classes. In all religious systems, the priests have known
very well how to secure certain privileges for themselves
and escape the burdens borne by others. They did not work
in the fields, they did not serve as soldiers, nor did they have
to undergo the hardships suffered by the trader. Instead,
they received the fruit of the labour of others in the shape
of offerings to the Church; and while urging others to work,
they themselves led idle and dissolute lives. They had no
families, thus escaping another source of tribulation. In order
to maintain their authority unimpaired, they invented rites
and ceremonies in which they played a leading part, and in
the course of which they spoke in the name of the gods –
whose utterances were of course always in their own interests. They resisted education for the people, so that they
could retain their monopoly on information and power (R,
p. 193). Volney sums up: 'Faith and hope are the virtues of

dupes from which rogues benefit' ('la foi et l'espérance les vertus des dupes au profit des fripons', C, p. 193).

The rest of *Les Ruines* is devoted to a consideration of various forms of religion. If we are to build ourselves a decent life on earth, we have to reject religion which divides people, and take our stance on that which binds people together – natural law. There is, according to Volney (and here he is in tune with the deism of the French Enlightenment) a God who is a natural product of the human mind ('une production naturelle de l'entendement'); but this is a kind of abstract being, a general mover ('moteur général') whose likeness men naively visualise in their own image. Following Xenophanes and anticipating Feuerbach, Volney declares: 'It is not God who creates man in his image, but man who creates God in his own image' (R, p. 55); and this image changes *pari passu* as man evolves.

This gloomy picture of man's past must not be allowed to rob us of faith in the future. Progress is real. When men finally come to an understanding of natural law and choose to be ruled by it, they will realise that individual well-being is indissolubly bound up with social well-being; the weak will understand that they must stand together; the rich will understand that man's physical nature, of itself, sets a limit to pleasure, and that satiety is followed by boredom; the poor will understand that happiness lies in making good use of their time and in peace of mind (!).

The inculcation of natural law in human society and the erection on this basis of a new morality liberated from the shackles of religion, a morality which will transform the world: this is the end Volney had in mind when he wrote his Catechism. It might be more accurately described as an anti-catechism, being formally very close to the orthodox one though in content it is the diametric opposite. It is written in the same terse question and answer format. In conscious imitation of the Ten Commandments, Volney sets out ten properties of natural law. He sees himself as legislator for the whole of mankind, the 'interpretor of nature herself'. The book is designed to be a school textbook which the author expects to be used in schools all over Europe. Every statement in it is held to be logically derived from fact; and the morality it sets out to inculcate is 'physical and geometrical science, and as such, susceptible like the rest, of calculation and mathematical demonstration'.[5] 'Morality', wrote Volney in *Les Ruines*, 'is a physical science dealing in elements which combine with each other in a rather complicated manner, but which are themselves simple and immutable, since it is from these same elements that man himself is organised' (R, p. 70). Clearly, when he formulated his 'physique des moeurs', Durkheim had his predecessors; but Durkheim's physics of custom was supposed to be a sociology of customs on which ethical norms could be based, whereas Volney founded his norms on the *biological* constitution of man.

3 Natural law

As used by the philosophers of the Enlightenment, the term 'natural law' means four different things, and all four meanings are found in Volney.

(1) In the first chapter of the Catechism, Volney gives as examples of natural law such propositions as: water flows downward seeking a level, it is heavier than air, bodies are subject to the laws of gravity, certain creatures cannot live without air, fire tends to rise upwards, it burns, etc. That is to say, by 'natural law' Volney here understands certain empirical generalisations.

(2) In the second sense, natural laws are understood as imperatives. Failure to adapt to these laws as understood in the first sense – e.g. failure to adapt to the fact that fire burns or that we cannot breathe without air – can have fatal consequences for man. In this second sense, the laws of nature are practical directives by means of which man utilises his knowledge of the world in order to get what he wants or to avoid what he does not want. In non-elliptical form, these directives would appear as teleological norms of the form: 'If you don't want to get your fingers burned, don't put them in the fire.'

(3) In the third and very well-known sense, the elementary human rights are seen as natural laws. In this sense, Volney speaks of freedom and security as 'natural laws' as did the

Declaration of Rights. It was because of its usage of 'rights' in this sense that Bentham attacked the Declaration. It was very clear to Bentham that any 'right' is a right only with reference to certain established patterns, and that any attempt to use 'rights' as a basis for legislation is doomed to failure.

(4) In the fourth sense, natural laws are seen as regularities established with reference to laws in the first sense. Volney's standard definition of natural law is 'l'ordre régulier des faits'. In other words, it is not the proposition that is the natural law but that which the proposition asserts.

Independently of these four meanings, we find in Volney a kind of deified natural law which is referred to in the singular. This natural law has ten attributes. (1) It is primary in relation to all other laws, which are modelled on it; (2) it comes directly from God and is therefore infallible; (3) it is common to all times and all places; (4) it is uniform and unchanging; (5) it is self-evident, being a datum in facts which are invariably accessible to reason and verifiable; (6) it is rational, for it is in accord with reason, while all other laws are contrary to reason; (7) it is just, for it makes the penalty proportionate to the offence; (8) it is pacifist and tolerant, asserting that all men are brothers and have equal rights; (9) it is beneficial to all, since it offers us the means of improving our lot and making our lives happier; (10) it is in and by itself sufficient means to attain this end, since it embodies everything that is good and positive in other laws, their whole moral content. From this list of attributes it is clear that the 'natural law' which they constitute is, rather, a set of laws (mainly in the second and third senses of 'law' as defined above) with a specific moral content from which can be constructed a catechism for the regulation of human behaviour.

As its starting point, the Catechism states that all men seek self-preservation, and endorses this fact in the form of the relevant imperative.[6] 'Seek to preserve yourselves' is a directive arising, according to Volney, *immediately* from the fact that people tend to preserve themselves. But this is to ignore two things: first, that imperatives *cannot* arise from indicative (descriptive) propositions, and, secondly, that even if they could, a crucial link is omitted in what is alleged to be a direct process – the *approbation* given to the statement of fact. In pursuit of his self-preservation, man is governed by personal interest. In this belief, Volney is at one with most of the theoreticians of the period. 'L'amour de soi', 'le désir du bien-être' and 'l'aversion de la douleur' are detailed in *Les Ruines* as the three bases of 'natural law'. 'All our notions of good and evil, of virtue and vice, justice and injustice, truth and falsehood, what is allowed and what is forbidden – concepts which lie at the root of man's morality as an individual and as a member of society – all are derived from this simple and fertile principle [i.e. of self-preservation – M.O.], all are related to it and are measured by it' (C, p. 113).

Though Volney says in *Les Ruines* that it is as natural for people to seek their own happiness as it is for stones to be affected by gravity, in the Catechism we find pleasure presented, not as an object of desire but rather – like pain – as a signal indicating whether the course we are on is favourable or unfavourable to our self-preservation. Pleasure is in no way reprehensible (as religion suggests): underlying this notion is the fact that we tend to give the gods we worship our own human characteristics. And in remarkably close anticipation of Spencer, Volney asserts that men have created their gods in the likeness of wicked and envious human despots. 'In order to placate the gods, man sacrificed to them whatever he held dear, and flouted natural law by going to the extremes of self-denial. Wrongly supposing his pleasures to be crimes and his sufferings expiation, he was forced to love suffering and abjure pleasure' (R, p. 48). Like Hume and Helvétius, Volney will have nothing to do with the idea that virtue is based on abstention: ascetic virtue is rejected out of hand. Virtue is the practice of those actions which are useful to the individual and to society and in the last analysis ('en dernière analyse') this utility value reduces to preservation of oneself ('conserver le corps'); and whatever promotes this process of self-preservation is pleasurable. Since man's first duty is to stay alive, the worst of crimes is to take his life away. Virtues are to be graded according to their efficacy in saving lives. Telling words, coming as they do from a man who conceived his Catechism in the days of the Great Terror. Volney's medical studies and the material-istic outlook characteristic of the so-called Ideologists, the group to which he belonged,[7] meant that the role of biological values was strongly emphasised and dietetics were given a share in morality. What and how we eat affects our nature. Easily digested foods make us cheerful and ready to feel affection for our fellow creatures and help them. Eating vegetables – which are not very nutritious – makes a man soft, lazy and work-shy, etc. 'Long experience taught the ancients that dietetics is an important part of morality' (C, p. 126).

The first commandment – 'Conserve-toi'! – is accompanied by three others. These are: 'Improve your mind!' 'Control yourself!' and 'Live for your fellow creatures so that they may live for you!' These three directives are mentioned in the same breath with the first and cardinal commandment, to which, however, they play a rather subsidiary role. The second touches on education. In order to know natural law, education is necessary; for the concepts which are expressed in these laws are not inborn, and we cannot hope to attain them by blind instinct alone. Self-control is necessary, because passion is dangerous to health, indeed to life. The principle of reciprocity which provides the third directive governs the whole of social life and serves self-interest properly understood. We shall return to this point a little later.

4 Volney's model citizen

Volney's list of virtues – which he divides along traditional lines into personal, family and social virtues – allows us to put some flesh on the abstract and terse formulation in Volney's text, and form some sort of a picture of the French citizen as moulded by the Revolution.

He is, first of all, enlightened. Knowledge illuminates his surroundings, teaches him the relations between cause and effect which obtain therein, and thus ensures his survival. Without this enlightenment, man works in the darkness, as though he were blind. The argument and the metaphor remind us that we are in the age of the Enlightenment.

Volney is diametrically opposed to Rousseau's thesis – that man in his natural state is and does good. As he sees it, only eccentricity or misanthropy could possibly countenance condemnation of knowledge on the grounds that it has been abused. This is tantamount to ordering people's tongues to be cut out on the grounds that they have misused words. Man in his natural state is 'an animal, as vicious and predatory as a bear or an orang-utang' (C, pp. 110, 42).

The knowledge acquired by man enables him to be far-sighted and provident. When he acts, it is with his eyes fixed firmly on the future. The '*honnête homme* will almost always forgo immediate and impromptu gain so as not to jeopardise the future, while the rascal will do the exact opposite and throw away a great return in the future for the sake of a small but immediate gain', (C, p. 154). This passage, like many another in the Catechism, shows a key change in the meaning of the words *honnête homme*. In the courtly pages of a Chevalier de Méré, as in the majority of eighteenth-century writers, we should have to understand by this expression 'a polished man' or 'a well-bred man'. Now, the *honnête homme* is a decent, upright, respectable man – a definition for which financial solidarity gives the key-note.

The moderation recommended in Volney's third postulate will be observed by the *honnête homme* in eating and drinking and in his sexual life. Graphically, Volney describes the calamitous effects of dyspepsia. As regards wine, he is not foolhardy enough to forbid wine to the French; but he does advise moderation. He has particularly lurid descriptions of the awful results of sexual over-indulgence, though, at the same time, he condemns celibacy and monastic abstinence. Natural law prescribes a well-regulated sex life, with women being called upon to make more concessions to purity than men. The author adduces rational grounds for his dictum that women should observe greater sexual restraint than men, and should avoid any sort of extramarital liaison. For one thing, women run the risk of pregnancy. Where this happens in an extramarital relationship, they become 'the object of shame and public contempt' and they have to 'eke out the rest of their lives in bitterness and misery, to say nothing of the cost of bringing up a child, or children, without a father. The expense leads to pauperisation, and they are ruined both physically and morally. They lose their health along with the looks that were their original downfall. Doubly disadvantaged by debts and bastards, they are no longer attractive to men, which means that they can no longer hope for financial support, and can only lapse into poverty, degradation and penury, and thus eke out their last miserable days' (C, p. 129). Conjugal infidelity is fraught with greater risks for women than for men because it often involves theft – in the interests of illegitimate issue – of an inheritance which is by rights the sole property of legitimate issue. Evidently, the voice of natural law spoke in thoroughly traditional vein to the co-author of the Declaration of Rights; and Volney saw no reason why he should seek to influence popular disapproval of extramarital pregnancy. It should be remembered that the Declaration was exclusively a declaration of *male* rights.

For self-preservation and health, it is not enough to have an adequate stock of knowledge and be capable of restraining one's potentially harmful passions; one must also be courageous and industrious. Courage helps us to protect our lives and property and to fight against oppression in defence of our freedom and independence. It also helps us to face up to setbacks. Courage is doubtless a function of certain organic properties, for we see it exhibited in greater or lesser degree in wild animals. If only we knew which properties are involved here, we could try to cultivate them. Clearly, Volney's biological tenets are no impediment to his typically eighteenth-century view that man can be transformed. 'An understanding of education can . . . depending on how it is employed, perfect or degrade individuals and races to such a degree that they are completely changed in nature and aptitude' (C, p. 135). In Volney's thought, this conviction is tied up with a faith in those stable and enduring properties common to all men which allow us to formulate certain eternal and immutable laws of nature.

In the context of natural law, activity is a virtue. We can worship the Supreme Being only by acting in accordance with his immutable laws, and work is the only valid form of prayer ('travailler c'est prier'). Work develops various virtues in man, protects him against improper desires and gives him health and strength. Of all shortcomings, sloth is one of the worst: it makes a man 'intemperate, greedy, spendthrift, ill-tempered, ignoble, squalid and contemptible' (C, p. 137). Work enables a man to support himself, and if he is abstemious and prudent, it will make him rich as well. Poverty is not a sin; still less is it a virtue. Usually it is both result and cause of our own shortcomings, for, if a man is painfully aware of basic deficiencies in his livelihood, he may well use illicit means in an effort to fill the gaps. Here once again we have the connection between wealth and virtue which we found in Franklin, and Volney could well repeat after Franklin 'an empty sack will not stand upright'. In contradistinction to Defoe, Volney would agree with Franklin that virtue is a sufficient condition of wealth rather than that wealth is a necessary condition of virtue. But the fact that virtue is a sufficient condition of wealth means that the pauper has only himself to blame for his poverty, since this must be due to his shortcomings: so the privileged classes can have a clear conscience. Volney adds a warning: wealth is not in itself a virtue, but still less is it a shortcoming. It is a tool, and a tool is good or bad depending on how it is used.

The model citizen, as Volney sees him, will run his family household wisely and benignly. *Economie* will rule, in the sense given to the word in classical antiquity (see p. 107 above). The word will also, however, be used in its narrower meaning – limitation of expenditure to the satisfaction of basic necessities. The man who saves money is safeguarding his future, and protecting himself from worry and privation. Applied on a mass scale, the practice of *économie* will lead to national prosperity. 'Rich in all that he has not consumed, a man gains vast resources for exchange and trade; he works, he produces, he sells more cheaply than others, prosperity and success smile on him, in his relations with others as in his own affairs' (C, p. 157). Only when he consumes less than he produces, or less than he owns, can he afford to be liberal: 'if he consumes more than results from his labour, he necessarily encroaches upon his fellow citizens'.

Up to a point, a man's virtue may be gauged by his success

in balancing his budget. 'A sure way of knowing the extent of a man's virtues or vices is to be found out if his expenses are proportionate to his fortune, and calculate from his want of money, his probity, his integrity in fulfilling his engagements, his devotion to the public weal, and his false or sincere love of his country' (C, p. 159). The *honnête homme* is known by his budget; and a man's attitude to money is symptomatic of his moral level.

In the eighteenth century, moralists and writers on economics were virtually obliged to make some sort of pronouncement on the subject of luxury; and here Volney is hard put to it to find words adequate to express his abomination. The man who gets a taste for luxury is always in need of money: 'and every method of procuring it becomes good and even necessary to him; at first he borrows, afterwards steals, robs, plunders, turns bankrupt, is at war with everyone, ruins and is ruined' (C, p. 158). No less devastation is caused by luxury on a mass scale. A nation wallowing in luxurious living is consuming its own national product, and is left with nothing for export. Its international situation is weakened, and domestic affairs get completely out of hand. 'From luxury arises the iniquity of judges, the venality of the witness, the improbity of the husband, the prostitution of the wife, the obduracy of parents, the ingratitude of children, the avarice of the master, the dishonesty or theft of the servant, the dilapidation of the administrator, the perversity of the legislator, lying, perfidy, perjury, assassination and all the disorders of the social state' (C, p. 159).

These unusually strong words in condemnation of luxury may be contrasted with the eulogy of luxury contained in Bernard Mandeville's *Fable of the Bees*: two very different treatments of the same theme, both from the pens of bourgeois authors. The difference between the two can be explained by their belonging to very different phases in the rise of the bourgeoisie. Volney is launching his attack on court and aristocracy, while Mandeville's is the voice of a bourgeoisie resting on its laurels and well satisfied with what it has achieved. But even if this explanation fits the present case, it does not suffice to explain the divergencies of opinion on this subject among other bourgeois authors, nor can these divergencies be explained in terms of petty bourgeois hostility to luxury and its defence by representatives of big capital. There is no clear distinction between Helvétius and Holbach in terms of historical situation or personal position: yet the former tolerates luxury and quotes Mandeville in its defence, while the second rejects it utterly.

Examination of what writers on this theme actually have to say suggests that these different attitudes were generated, if not by different notions of what constitutes luxury, then at least by a different selection of facts within the general context. Thus, in Volney, any trace of living above one's means is described as 'luxury' and naturally attracts condemnation from anyone as keen on balancing the books as Volney. But by the same token, Volney's quarrel with luxury loses its class character. In his *Système sociale* Holbach is mainly concerned with luxury at royal courts. As he puts it: 'At court, luxury is at home.' By virtue of their pomp, courts induce citizens to engage in morbid and incessant rivalry, an exhibitionism which awakens great bitterness among the poor. In republics there are no such glaring differences between people's budgets.[8] In the second chapter of his *De l'esprit* Helvétius refers to such luxury articles as velvet and lace. He writes: 'Sensible women contribute less to the state coffers than do fashionable women. By giving alms, the former support loafers, while the latter provide employment for the working masses. . . . They feed useful citizens, while the former nourish superfluous elements, even enemies of the nation.'[9] However, returning to the same theme in *De l'homme*, Helvétius declares himself against luxury on the grounds that it intensifies the polarisation into the very rich and the very poor, a division which he deplores.[10]

Helvétius and Holbach have different things in mind when they expatiate on 'luxury'. But that is not to say that these thematic variants go all the way to explaining the differences that divide them. If luxury was a burning issue in the seventeenth and eighteenth centuries, it was not for the first time; there was already a considerable literature on the subject, which ought to be taken into account. We should also bear in mind that luxury was officially condemned by the Church, and that some at least of the voices raised apparently in its defence were really making themselves heard in the struggle against asceticism – a struggle which runs through the whole of Enlightenment thought.

5   Volney's model citizen in society

Natural law makes man a social being, if for no other reason than because of his own organic properties. The sexual urge drives men and women to unite to produce and rear offspring. Natural law makes us sensitive to the sensations and emotions of our fellows in a mutual sympathetic reson-ance which Volney calls 'co-sentiments' (an exact parallel to Adam Smith's 'fellow-feelings'). If man is to survive, a human environment is necessary. Only 'minds led astray by their own eccentricity, offended pride or their disgust over the crimes of society, could have come up with such a fiction as "the noble savage", a fiction entirely at variance with their own vision of perfected man' (C, p. 112). Here, Volney is taking issue not only with Rousseau but with the whole eighteenth-century myth of the noble savage. Man in his savage state (Volney always represents him as isolated and alone) is in every respect a slave: he cannot eat when he wants to, rest when he is tired, or warm himself when he is cold, for his whole life is beset with dangers.

In tune with his time, Volney sees society as an assemblage of people with common needs living together. This assem-blage is governed by the cardinal law of equity: do unto others as you would have them do unto you. From this single precept all others are derived, recommending compassion, integrity, sincerity, generosity. The cardinal directive is based on three properties which are inherent in man's physical organism: Volney was always on the look-out for biological confirmation of his theories. All of us have eyes, mouths, ears and hands: all of us have an equal right to live: and all of us have the right to own what we need to keep ourselves alive. The three properties reappear in abstract form in the Declaration of Rights: equality, freedom and right of property. 'Equality' here is equality before God, but not yet on the social plane, because these congenital proper-

ties are unevenly distributed, both qualitatively and quantitatively. This none too clear argument from 'man's physical
organisation' becomes even more suspect when it is applied
to freedom and property. Volney goes on: everyone is
naturally endowed with the sense organs which are adequate
for self-preservation. No one needs other people's eyes and
ears; we are all independent by birth (this is in flat contradiction of the previous claim that sexually and biologically we
depend on finding partners). From the postulate that all are
independent by birth, we are then to infer that consequently
no one is subject to anyone else, and that no one has the
right to subjugate others. But this proposition is not derivable from the previous one, not only because postulates
cannot be derived from statements of fact, but also because
an entirely new theme is here introduced. By continually
confusing postulates and statements of fact, Volney finally
arrives at the conclusion that human rights are among the
properties based on man's physical organism, and asserts
that all men have their own bodies at their own free disposition and the products of their work likewise – an assertion
which is less a statement of fact than a *pium desiderium*.

Since nothing belongs by nature to anyone, it follows that
a man can give something to another man only on a basis
of reciprocity. As we saw, the fourth of the Catechism's
basic precepts is 'Live for your fellow men so that they may
live for you.' What we give and what we receive must always
be evenly balanced. The *loi de réciprocité* means that all the
social virtues are profitable for him who is endowed with
them. Everyone stands to gain from being virtuous, and
there can be no doubt that men will become good and
reasonable as soon as they realise that this is in their own
interests. Volney leaves disinterestedness out of account. His
view of mankind, like that of Helvétius, is very reminiscent
of La Rochefoucauld: which rather shakes the customary
view of the latter as the portrayer of nothing more than an
effete and decadent aristocracy. Volney sees the advancing
bourgeoisie in the same way as La Rochefoucauld. Man
always acts in accordance with his own interests, but if a
good catechism is put into his hands he soon learns that
virtue pays dividends. Scoundrels (*les fripons*) are those who

miscalculate and who imagine that they are being smart (*fins*). Such commandments as 'do not steal' and 'do not kill' are simply a question of sound calculation: so is mercy. 'Le crime est toujours un faux jugement.'[11] From the principle of reciprocity it follows that a wrong can be indemnified only by way of restitution. All forms of expiatory self-mortification are, according to Volney, perversions which degrade and corrupt man and merely encourage him to commit more crimes – another swipe at the Church and its vision of not only an earthly measure of justice but also of justice in the world to come.

Volney's model citizen is cool and reserved. The Catechism itself is reserved and stiff in language, and eschews emotion even where we might have reason to expect it, for example, in sections dealing with family life. In their children, parents are rearing guardians for their last days, and the affection which children feel for their parents is 'a practice which is useful both for them and for their parents'. Children are in debt to their parents for the work and expense involved in their upbringing and education. Self-interest requires affection to be shown to father and mother, for if your children are set a bad example in the treatment of parents, they will behave in the same way towards you yourself. Self-interest again dictates that husbands and wives should show each other affection; for 'married couples who do not display mutual affection breed quarrel and dissension in the home, they are the cause of strife among the children and the servants, and they allow bad habits to take root among both; all the occupants of the house are wasteful, light-fingered and good at lining their own pickets; income falls with nothing to show for it, debts are run up, the disgruntled spouses avoid each other or take each other to law, and the family breaks up and lands in ruin, degradation and penury' (C, pp. 143–4). Some critics have seen the reason for the cold reserve of the Catechism in Volney's own character, traditionally linked with his refusal to be guided by his family in his early days. But we have to remember that Volney's coldness and reserve are deliberate, part of a planned approach. He was concerned to show that it is possible to lead a harmonious social and conjugal life based on nothing more than the built-in tendency common to all human beings to safeguard their own interests, which, sooner or later, always turn out to be the essential conditions for their survival. It was in this sense that Volney described his system as *rational*. In this sense it was 'physics and geometry'.

In the preface to the 1826 edition of the Catechism (probably written by Volney himself) we read that hitherto moralists have treated man as a child, ordering him to be good, otherwise spirits and ghosts will come to punish him. 'Now the stature of man's mind is more advanced in growth, it is time that it should hear the language of reason . . . when men should be taught . . . that the radical source of their melioration and moral improvement is to be looked for in their organisation . . . and in the very constituent elements of their existence' ('les mobiles de leur perfectionnement se tirent de leur organisation même').

6 Volney's Catechism compared with others of the period

I have chosen Volney here for detailed analysis on two counts: as one of those responsible for the ethical content of the Declaration of Rights, and as a representative of the French moralists on the eve of the Revolution. How far other thinkers more or less closely connected with the *Encyclopédie* had any influence on the slogans of the Declaration of Rights may well be gauged from a study of the Catechism. Common to the pre-Revolutionary moralists and Volney is the ambition to 'construct a morality as one constructs an experimental physics' ('faire une morale comme une physique expérimentale'), as Helvétius puts it. Both in its content, the problems it tackles, and in the manner in which it justifies its conclusions, the ethic endorsing this form of morality is anti-religious. Volney did not hesitate to express this openly, while Helvétius was more cautious, preferring to put his attacks on religion into the mouths of others. As regards the content, this was concerned less with spiritual salvation than with the organisation of a corporate life on earth which would provide a measure of happiness for everyone. Ethical precepts had to be properly and rationally based instead of being blindly accepted as revelations from above, and there was to be no place in moral catechisms for articles based on nothing more than tradition. Common to all of these eighteenth-century systems was their starting point in a specific view of man and his nature: that is to say, a psychological starting point. Where the traditional Christian ethic had sought to curb human nature, which it saw as corrupted by sin, the eighteenth century demanded that this voice be heard. And when this voice made itself heard, it proclaimed that all men are governed mainly if not exclusively by self-interest, and that this fact had to be accepted since attempts to hide it were doomed to failure. But at once we are confronted with the problem of harmonising man's obligations with his interests. In a letter to Frederick II, dated 21 January 1770, d'Alembert wrote: 'The source of morality and happiness is the close union between our true interests and the discharge of our obligations.' At the same time, d'Alembert underlines the difficulty of convincing those who are dying of starvation that it is in their true interest to be virtuous (and die) when they see a chance of stealing a loaf and getting away with it. D'Alembert goes on: 'Had I been able to find a satisfactory answer to this problem, I would long ago have produced a catechism of morals.'[12]

It was a problem in which Volney saw no particular difficulty, since he saw no conflict of interests either here or in the subsequent stage – between one's own interests and one's own obligations. It is our obligation to help others, thereby and at the same time acting in our own interests. The disobliging man cannot count on help from others, nor can the man who has his eye on other people's property expect others to respect his. This state of mutual balance is preserved by sanctions which may be called 'natural' by analogy with Rousseau's natural retribution. If Emile broke the window-pane it was natural retribution that he should die of cold. For Helvétius, the harmony of interests was neither 'naturally' nor automatically assured in this way. Rather, it required a competent legislator to introduce an appropriate system of rewards and punishments which would ensure that virtue was seen to pay off, while crime was always exposed as the outcome of faulty calculation. This Utopia of 'perfected legislation', which Plekhanov saw as the characteristic eighteenth-century bourgeois Utopia,[13] was later to blind Bentham to the exclusion of all other solutions. In Helvétius, the concordance of interests is an artificial construct: in Volney it is a natural datum. The difference between the two is largely due to Volney's propensity for thinking in biological terms. True, both in legislation and in morality, Helvétius tried to retain certain basic and general human tendencies as his starting point – e.g. the tendency to avoid pain and to seek pleasure. But this did not prevent him from stressing over and over again that man's mental world depends entirely upon the circumstances in which he lives and develops: i.e. upon the form of government and legislation, and upon the habits acquired in his given habitat.

As I said, in Volney's ethics, as in the ethics of most of his contemporaries, there is explicit acceptance of human nature as it is. No attempt is made to change or suppress it as in religious ethics. 'Suppression of the passions', writes Diderot, 'humiliates exceptional men. Constraint destroys the greatness and energy of nature.'[14] Christian ethics taught that man's sinful nature must be curbed; not so the new ethics. 'Rien n'est moins dans le goût de jour':[15] nothing is less to the taste of the time than the idea of constraint applied to the natural self, as a contemporary writer put it. Vauvenargues remarked, not without irony: 'Some authors treat morals as they treat modern architecture – as a matter of convenience.'[16] Volney's morality is devoid of heroic abstinences and heroic conflicts. The happiness he holds out is a quiet happiness in an atmosphere of security and serenity (*douce aisance*). This *douce aisance* is, for Volney, the crucial factor: which is why he does not forget, when praising certain forms of behaviour, to remind the reader of the financial basis which permits them. Decline into indigence is the threat Volney constantly uses when he is intent on dissuading us from a given course of action.

Contrary once again to religious ethics, Volney, along with the rest of the eighteenth-century French moralists, is less concerned with the intention or motive behind an action than with the results. Again, this is in keeping with the mood of the times, as we see from the enormously interesting book by Charles Duclos (whose real name was Charles Pineau) entitled *Considérations sur les moeurs de ce siècle*. The book appeared in 1751, seven years before Helvétius's *De l'esprit*, and provides a fascinating guide to the mental climate of the period. A plant is known by its fruits, writes Duclos in his analysis of human conduct.[17] Everyone follows his own self-interest, and the actions arising from this basic and common motivation are identifiable as 'good' or 'evil' only in the light of their consequences. Duclos sums up the attitude of the time as – be useful to your fellow creatures and try to please them. Another argument which Helvétius uses to discredit the search for motive turns on the difficulty of identifying any such motive: even the person concerned may not know *why* he is acting in this way. Volney states flatly that intention in and for itself cannot be either a merit or a crime. A virtue can be identified by its public utility. It can be simply defined as 'la pratique des actions utiles à l'individu et à la société' (C, p. 117). Virtues which are not verified by public utility are described by Helvétius as 'vertus de préjugé' or presumed virtues. In both writers 'utility' means utility for the human body or person. For Helvétius, pleasantness and unpleasantness of whatever nature is in the last resort physical; every good, as Volney emphasises even more strongly, is in the last resort organic good.

Of all the ethical systems which the French Enlightenment bequeathed to us, the system which Volney develops in his Catechism is the most 'bourgeois' in tone, if by this we mean the typological definition we reached in Chapter 1. Duclos's book, which preceded the Catechism by some forty years, still contains traces of the aristocratic ethic and the domination of the upper classes. The 'man of honour' still lives in its pages, reminding us of Aristotle's *kalokagathos*. 'The man of honour', writes Duclos, 'thinks and feels *avec noblesse*. He does not act in obedience to laws; he is not guided by reflection, still less by imitation. He thinks, speaks and acts with a kind of superiority, and he seems to be his own legislator.' And further: 'Honour is the instinct of [for] virtue and [acts as] its courage. It does not stay to deliberate, it acts without pretence . . .'[18] A far cry from Volney, whose model citizen deliberates and calculates – indeed, this is the trait which colours his entire relationship with his fellow men. He is governed by the principle of *do, ut des*, a principle totally alien to the munificence and magnanimity of the aristocratic ethic. Volney defines this as the principle of reciprocity. We may usefully call it so, with the proviso, however, that it should not be confused with the principle of 'an eye for an eye, a tooth for a tooth', which is also, in a sense, a reciprocal principle but one entirely different in nature, one underlying all forms of vengeance and retribution prescribed by the aristocratic ethos. In European literature, we first find the *do, ut des* principle, as we now understand it, in the *Fables* of Aesop – which were enormously popular in the eighteenth century – and in Hesiod's *Works and Days*, where we find a current of ethical thought differing widely from that informing the courtly epic. In Hesiod, the principle of reciprocity regulates man's relations not only with his fellow men but with the gods as well. We cannot expect the gods to smile upon us unless we make due sacrifice to them. Since opportunities for reciprocity are more frequent among neighbours, and since a neighbour can be more readily helped in his hour of need, Hesiod is mainly concerned with establishing neighbourly relations on a basis of reciprocity. 'Take fair measure from your neighbour and pay him back fairly with the same measure, or better, if you can; so that if you are in need afterwards, you may find him sure.'[19]

On the face of it, the principle of *do, ut des* seems to offer a degree of motivation for our behaviour. Volney's directive 'Live for others, so that they may live for you' offers first a recommendation and, secondly, a sound reason why this recommendation should be followed. We could perhaps put it in the form of a teleological rule: 'If you want people to live for you, live for them.' Volney's directive has a positive and a negative side. The negative aspect is: 'Do not do to others what we would not like done to ourselves, for fear of retaliation.' The positive aspect is: 'Do to others what we would welcome for ourselves, in the hope of recompense.' It is clear that Christian humility and turning the other cheek are incompatible with this attitude; as the Catechism itself points out (p. 152), these Christian precepts merely encourage bloodshed and oppression. Only when there is equilibrium between what we give and what we receive ('la balance du donné au rendu est en équilibre') – only then can we say 'This is well done.' This equilibrium is the very basis of social existence ('base fondamentale de toute société').

The same two recommendations which I have treated as two variants of the principle of reciprocity are also taken up by Duclos. Compliance with the negative encoding – 'Do not do to others what you do not want done to yourself' is called by both Duclos and Volney *probité*: it reduces to just behaviour and it can be made obligatory in a legal sense. Not so in the case of the positive encoding, which Volney treats as the expression of *charité*, and compliance with which Duclos is the first to construe as a virtue. He writes: 'A righteous prohibition must be obeyed; virtue enjoins, but consequent action is voluntary.'[20] The distinction is repeated in the ethics of the French Enlightenment and provides a groundwork for the related distinction later to be made by the Utilitarians, and which in Poland led to the differentiation between law and morality proposed by Petrażycki. It is not possible to require or oblige someone to do good: this is the field of morality. It is possible to require people not to harm others, and this is the proper field of legislation and the dispensation of justice: which eighteenth-century writers in both England and France associated very closely with compliance with the law of property in the broad sense, according to which, 'our person, our thoughts, our personal freedom and our possessions all constitute our 'property'.

As I said, Volney's Catechism was one of many. Towards the end of *De l'homme* Helvétius too draws up such a catechism which begins as follows:

Question   What is man?
Answer   An animal, said to be rational, but certainly
           sentient; it is weak, and able to reproduce
           itself.
Q   As a sentient being, what must man do?
A   Avoid suffering and seek pleasure. The search

	for pleasure is a constant in man's nature which is called *amour de soi*.
Q	What else must man, weak creature that he is, do?
A	Join forces with other men for common defence against wild animals which are stronger than men, or to compete with these animals for the means of subsistence: or to attack and take those animals which provide man with food. etc.[21]

The catechisms drawn up in these days were not only for adults but also for children. In 1775, one of the Encyclopédistes, Grimm, wrote a *Draft Catechism for Children*. Similarly, Saint-Lambert, the author of a fervently enthusiastic biography of Helvétius, produced a general catechism for children in the twelve–thirteen age group. This opens in very similar vein to that of Helvétius:

Q	What is man?
A	A being possessed of feeling and understanding.
Q	That being so, what should he do?
A	Pursue pleasure and eschew pain.
Q	This desire to obtain pleasure and avoid pain, is this not, in man, what we call self-love?
A	It is the necessary effect thereof.
Q	Does self-love exist in all men alike?
A	It does, because all men aim at self-preservation and at attaining happiness.
Q	What do you understand by happiness?
A	A continuous state in which we experience more pleasure than pain.
Q	What must we do to attain this state?
A	Cultivate our reason and act in accordance therewith.
Q	What is reason?
A	The knowledge of the truths that conduce to our well-being. etc.[22]

The same sort of worldly-wise programme is to be found

in the Masonic precepts which are so frequent in the eighteenth century. Hazard quotes the following verse:

> The freemason leads his life
> Along a path strewn with flowers.
> In pursuit of pleasure,
> And avoiding suffering,
> Guided always by the sweet precepts
> Of Epicurean morality.[23]

From these quotations it should be clear that what the ideologists of the pre-Revolutionary French bourgeoisie were promoting was not the asceticism which we might have expected of an ascendant class, but the pursuit of pleasure and the avoidance of suffering which Locke and Hume, spokesmen for a bourgeoisie already firmly ensconced in the seat of power, had preached before them. We all know that the leaders of the French Revolution were fond of appealing to Roman exemplars and Spartan virtues, but this was the ammunition of the activist rather than of the theoretician. It is true that Helvétius drew a contrast between the Roman Republic and the French monarchy; but, given the fact that one could not attack the latter openly, one had perforce either to praise the classical republics or castigate surrogate villains in the shape of Oriental tyrants. Neither Helvétius's educational and moral precepts, nor Volney's, would have produced a *civis romanus*. After the English Revolution, Locke replaced Habakkuk; in the French Revolution, Locke, in the guise of his French disciples, anticipated the appeal to Roman models; his tones were discernible in the speeches of toga-draped orators in the National Assembly, and he had not outlived his usefulness even when the French bourgeoisie had successfully stabilised its rule. Volney's works were reissued in 1826 along with a glowing introduction by A. Bossange, and further editions were promised. In fact, as Volney's biographer, Gaston-Martin, points out, if Volney was read in the 1820s it was for the critical insights of *Les Ruines* and the issue of freedom, as raised in the Catechism, rather than that of equality; but none the less he still had his admirers. In Gaston-Martin's opinion, the Catechism had its positive uses in 1830, when those who could remember the bloody days of the Terror had some reason to feel alarmed and threatened, and perhaps found comfort in its reiteration of the basic ideas of obligation and of respect for an acknowledged system of law.

Like all forms of utilitarianism which assesses actions by the criterion of their usefulness, Volney's utilitarianism could be variously exploited, depending on what was understood by the term 'useful'. When 'useful' means no more than 'promoting realisation of a desired aim', what is useful varies with aim. When the term is not applied to means serving an end, it can mean whatever seems good or fitting to the agent using it.

Apart from this purely formal and utilitarian aspect, however, Volney's precepts had a rich and substantial content which lost little of its immediacy in the aftermath of the Revolution. It was a content that went well with Guizot's hints on making money, and with the maxims of a Dunoyer. Often, it is no more than its lack of humour and warmth and its abstract dogmatism that distinguish Volney's Catechism from Franklin's Almanacs. We recall that Franklin's model man was the man who is worthy of credit. For Volney too, financial solidarity takes pride of place, backed up – again as in Franklin – by föresight, which transcends mere living in and for the present, by industriousness, thrift and by moderation in all things.

To return to the hedonism of Volney and his predecessors. How are we to explain the fact that bourgeois writers on the eve of the Revolution, and during it, were so united in urging the pursuit of pleasure and the avoidance of suffering? In my opinion, this hedonism was a tactical move in the fight against the religious ethic which was hopelessly compromised by its long association with the absolute monarchy and the feudal tradition. Evaluation of behaviour and actions purely in terms of whether they brought you pleasure or pain, opened the door to a thorough revision of the received body of ethical precepts, deprived ethics of the authority claimed by virtue of revelation and handed ethical judgments over to the criterion of reason.

Some students of the period see this hedonism as nothing more than a function of the environment in which most of these writers actually lived. They were in fact very well off and well placed in society. Voltaire owned a very large estate and was able to live in every comfort in his château of Ferney. It is not difficult to see why he should be the spokesman of the *grande bourgeoisie*. Helvétius quickly made a fortune on one of the boards administering the royal estates. Neither Baron Holbach nor Baron Grimm had to worry about their daily bread. Others lived not at all badly by their pens – a new way of earning a living which caught on during the Enlightenment. The enemies of the Encyclopédistes not infrequently sneered at their cosy way of life. Thus, for example, in the work entitled *Autrefois, ou le bon vieux temps* (undated, but very probably pre-1817) we find an acrimonious description of the life-style of the Encyclopédistes penned by the aristocratic A. Privat d'Anglemont. According to this writer, they did very well for themselves. 'The kings and the great men of the world both admired and feared them; people believed in them, hoping that they would bring about a better future.' The group met every day at sumptuous dinners given by Madame Helvétius, by Madame Geoffrin (who subsidised the *Encyclopédie*), by Madame Holbach, etc., etc. On Fridays, according to Privat d'Anglemont, they dined at the Neckers', who were Protestants and whose table was therefore not limited by religious scruples.[24] My purpose in quoting these spiteful comments is not to detract in any way from the importance – especially the practical importance – of the work done by these pre-Revolution bourgeois writers, but simply to underline the intriguing position of these people who criticised their contemporary political order while at the same time enjoying more than a few of its comforts. Duclos saw the literary circles (*gens de lettres*) which were springing up all around him, as groups standing apart from the rest of society. He writes: 'Strictly speaking, the pen (*les lettres*) does not confer a post upon one, but it offers a substitute to those who have no post, and carries with it privileges which are not always available to those who are actually placed higher in the social scale.' And again: 'When one has already secured a place which is indisputably higher on the social ladder, one likes to greet people of refined wit and intelligence.' It is flattering.

In the nature of *esprit*, as in play and in love, there is a levelling factor: these are arenas where all men are equal.[25] Thus did the bourgeois writers of the period rub shoulders with higher social circles, and in the salons the elite were pleasantly titillated by that very spirit of rebellion which was to bring about social change on a scale they could not foresee.

In a speech delivered in May 1794 and printed next day in the *Gazette National ou Moniteur Universel*, Robespierre described the Encyclopédistes as follows:

> The most important and distinguished party was the one that went by the name of the Encyclopédistes. It included several worthy men, but a much greater number of ambitious and pretentious charlatans. Not a few of its leading men became important figures in the Government. Not to know something of its influence and its policy would argue a very imperfect notion of the prelude to our Revolution. As far as politics were concerned this party always drew the line at the Rights of the People; as regards the question of morals they were far in advance of the blind prejudices of religious people. Its leaders sometimes held forth against despotism, though they were in the pay of despots; sometimes they wrote attacks on kings, sometimes dedications in their honour. They penned speeches for courtiers and madrigals for courtesans. This party most zealously propagated those materialistic ideas which proved too much for the great and the witty. To the party in question we are in large measure indebted for that kind of practical philosophy which, reducing selfishness to a system, looks on human society as the battle-ground of cunning, which measures right and wrong by the yard-stick of success, which regards probity as a matter of taste or decorum, and the world as the heritage of the astute egoist'.[26]

It would be rather one-sided to view the hedonism of the eighteenth-century bourgeois writers through the amused eyes of La Mettrie as he surveys the world in the 1751 portrait, or through his *L'art de jouir* of the same date. Hedonism has two faces, and it counsels not only the pursuit of pleasure but also war on suffering. We know how strongly Voltaire stresses the latter aspect. When Diderot instructs the Princess de Nassau-Saarbrück (in the introduction to his *Le père de famille*, which he dedicated to her with due humility) on how to bring up her children, he suggests that they should pay more attention to the naked urchins playing in the rubbish of the street than to fine façades and imposing public squares. Only thus will they learn that one bad man can make the tears of hundreds of thousands flow, and that any moral system that divides man from man is a bad system. Goodwill towards men (*bienveillance*) and humanity (*humanité*) are two virtues very highly prized by the Enlightenment.

Summing up: we must first of all bring our study of Volney into line with the Franklin theme which is our main concern. We have noted many analogies between the two men. Disapproval of asceticism, evaluation of virtue by the criterion of utility, praise of industriousness, thrift, moderation, farsightedness, tidiness, the conviction that a man's attitude to money is symptomatic of his moral standards, and that a balanced budget is a pointer to virtue – all of these traits are common to both writers. Franklin gave his advice on the good housekeeping plane, and addressed it primarily to the petty bourgeoisie. Volney addresses himself rather to the middle echelons of the bourgeoisie, as is clear from the attention he pays to family life. Volney's presentation is polished and theoretical, no doubt with an eye to readers on a higher level. Franklin could afford to adopt a tone of good-natured joviality: nothing he said was going to fan polemical fires. No last-ditch feudalists were holding out in Pennsylvania, and the petty bourgeoisie felt very much at home. Volney was in quite a different situation. He was acting as the spokesman of a new class and the codifier of a new morality embodied in a catechism which countered both the feudal paradigm and the religious ethic which had supported it. It is instructive to compare the titles which the two men selected for their works. Franklin offered friendly *Advice* . . .; Volney drew up a dogmatic and peremptory catechism. But the different formats cannot conceal the similarities in content, which go to show that morality of the Franklin type was not exclusively linked with Protestantism; we have just seen it recapitulated in a Catholic setting by a man reared in the Catholic faith and tradition.

Comparison of Volney's Catechism with the work of other eighteenth-century French moralists is instructive on other grounds as well. Donning the Roman toga was just one of the moral poses adopted by the bourgeoisie before and during the Revolution. As it turned out, some of these attitudes survived the Revolution, which points to a certain continuity of thought in spite of the attendant upheavals. The attitude towards pleasure which Volney's Catechism shares with other works of its kind written by his countrymen, may serve as evidence that the asceticism and moral inflexibility which were so characteristic of the Italian bourgeoisie in the days of its upsurge, and of Cromwell's Roundheads, were by no means constant factors in the morality of classes in the ascendant and on the attack.

To sum up: if the anti-clericalism of the French bourgeois moralists is seen as one of the factors informing their hedonism, it remains to be explained why the French bourgeoisie chose this as a key element in their progress towards emancipation, while the English bourgeoisie, on the contrary, took the yoke of a particular form of religion upon themselves and made a fetish of it. Answers to these questions must await further investigation.

Chapter 10

The superimposition of bourgeois and aristocratic models in the nineteenth century

The rabble is so blindly predisposed to honour the
powerful, and its attention to their gestures, features,
tone of voice and manner of behaviour so general, that
if the powerful took it into their heads to show kindness
as well, idolatry would be the result.
(La Bruyère, *Les Caractères*, chap. IX, 'Les Grands')

1 The problem

As we saw at the end of the last chapter, when the French
bourgeoisie launched its revolution it had more than one
ideal of personal behaviour before it. One such ideal was
symbolised in the Roman toga and the Spartan virtues;
another was the life of pleasure to be had from the unfettered
and boundless pursuit of one's own personal interests.
Within this hedonistic category – which links Volney and
Helvétius – further distinctions are possible. Helvétius's
vision of the man of pleasure, as developed in his *De l'esprit*,
is purely romantic. For Helvétius, it is the great passions
that matter, and he is the sworn enemy of the mediocre on
all fronts. The man who is capable of ecstasy and elation
may have great faults as well, but he is preferable to the
mediocrity, however exemplary. Not so with Volney,
whose cult of self-interest points to control of the passions,
and to cold rational calculation as the best way of serving
this end. For Helvétius, the desire for fame is the most noble
of human motivations, and he bewails the fact that it has
been supplanted in commercially minded communities by
the pursuit of wealth. Here again we find the opposite point
of view in Volney, whose ideal it is to enjoy 'the sweets of

299

wealth' in an atmosphere of peace and security. As we saw, Volney disapproved of those who tend to dwell in the present and give no thought to the future (see p. 277 above); while Helvétius, on the contrary, delivers a stirring tirade against 'prudence' in words which betray a knowledge of Mandeville. In Helvétius's opinion, the prudent man is one who imagines future disasters so vividly that he renounces any immediately available pleasure that might lead to them. We read in *De l'esprit*: 'Of all the gifts which heaven can bestow on a nation, unquestionably the most calamitous would be caution if it were to be generally distributed among its citizens.'[1] Where then would we find the soldier willing to put up with the dangers and discomforts of war for a miserable pittance? What woman would indulge in sexual pleasure, with its attendant threat of pregnancy and motherhood? Helvétius's precepts can be identified as 'bourgeois' with regard to the source they emanate from and the milieu in which they circulated; and again we can identify them as 'bourgeois' in that they express the mood of the contemporary bourgeoisie, and promoted, in some respects at least, its contemporary interests. But are they bourgeois in the meaning of the word as used by critics of bourgeois morality in the late nineteenth or early twentieth century? It is not a morality generically close to that recommended by Franklin or by Volney. Only thirty-five years separate *De l'esprit* from Volney's Catechism – thirty-five years which admittedly saw the vast convulsion of the French Revolution. But even this does not entirely explain why Volney should be ideologically much closer to Urbanowska's *Księżniczka* ('The Princess'), which appeared a hundred years later, or to Berkan's *Pamiętniki* ('Recollections'), than to his fellow countryman Helvétius, in whose immediate circle he grew up.

In Chapter 9 we looked at some of the paradigms put forward and adopted in France both before and during the Revolution. In the present chapter we shall see what happened to these after the final take-over by the bourgeoisie, and what relationship they retained, if any, to the exemplars of the vanquished class. We shall limit our investigation to nineteenth-century France and England, two countries whose history runs on different lines but which share many common features in the field which concerns us. The same traits are also to be found in nineteenth-century Germany, and these will be taken into consideration where necessary. Throughout our inquiry, which cannot of course be exhaustive, we shall keep our eyes fixed firmly on two main issues. The first of these is the thesis that a victorious class always imposes its own models on the vanquished class; the second is the thesis that the models favoured by two antagonistic classes are most sharply opposed to each other immediately before and during the final trial of strength: and that, upon taking power, the triumphant class rejects its own models in favour of those belonging to the hitherto privileged class. It is along some such lines that F. Antal sees the development of the Italian cities in the thirteenth and fourteenth centuries. Antal points out that in its heroic age the Italian bourgeoisie adopted a Puritan tone in its attacks on the rich and powerful (*i signori*). The year 1293 – the year of the constitution known as the Ordinamenti di Giustizia – is generally recognised as the year in which the upper middle classes, as organised in the guilds, finally took power. At that time, the burghers still proudly called themselves 'plebeians' and austerity reigned for a certain period after the takeover. Until 1330 those in high office had to sleep on straw and live in Spartan and ascetic isolation. But having entrenched their position, the bourgeoisie began to acquire property and to ape the aristocracy. A new figure steps on to the scene – the *cavaliere del popolo*, the people's nobleman. For a time, the war hitherto waged against the aristocracy turns against the people. An edict of 1388 forbids servants to dress in a way that might make them indistinguishable from the *nouveaux riches*.[2]

As with other classes, the bourgeoisie may be held to have attained to self-awareness when it is not only contented with its position but considers itself better than other classes: that is, when it has attained to a certain class pride which expresses itself *inter alia* in the creation of its own specific models.[3] Let us now take up these points.

2   Praise of the middle class

As far as I am aware, the earliest praise of the middle class
is to be found in Aristotle and Euripides. As I said earlier, T.
Sinko holds that in this they were influenced by an unknown
author who can also be traced in Herodotus.[4] According to
Aristotle, the only well-run state is one in which the middle
class plays the dominant role. It is among the representatives
of the middle class that we should look for the model citizen.
Membership of this class brings maximum happiness.
Middle-class citizens are most amenable to reason; those of
superior birth, wealth, power and appearance are less so, as
are the handicapped. The former often prefer to use force,
the latter are intriguers and trouble-makers. Due in part to
the laxness of their upbringing, the privileged and powerful
are both unwilling and unable to submit to the rule of law.
The upper classes know only how to be despotic and despise
their fellow citizens, while the lowly simply give in and
envy those more powerful than themselves. Neither of these
classes shows any sign of the social conscience and goodwill
with which the model citizen should be imbued. Middle-
class citizens do not covet other people's property as do the
needy, nor are they, unlike the rich, the object of envy.
They are in no danger, since they threaten no one, and no
one wishes to do them any harm. The poet Phoclydes was
right to summon mediety to adorn his life. Middle-class
values may be gauged by the fact that from this class have
come the greatest of the legislators, such as Solon, Lykurgos
and Charendas. The middle class must be numerous and
more powerful than the other two classes together; or at
least more powerful than either one of them so as to make
certain of victory for the party which the middle class decides
to support. In this way, the middle class can prevent either
of the other two classes from gaining the upper hand. Where
the middle class is predominant, there is no dissension and
no rebellion, and for this reason such upheavals are rarely
found in great and truly well-run states.[5] Euripides in the
Suppliant Women has similar words of praise for the 'middle
citizens' (*mésoi polítai*).[6]

But these passages cannot be used to present Aristotle as

a spokesman for the middle class in the later sense of the word. Aristotle is not thinking in terms of *class*; his 'middle citizen' is primarily a man of medium means, even of medium appearance, and the concept has to do with Aristotle's doctrine of the golden mean, rather than with his socio-political views. His contempt for manual labour is well known. This contempt extends to the artisan, who was later to form part of the middle class, and to the abuse of science for any sort of practical gain. The Aristotelian model of the *kalokagathos* is exclusively an elitist one.

So, Aristotle's eulogy of the 'middle estate' hardly fits in with our present theme. For more cogent praise we turn to eighteenth-century France.

When discussing Savary's *Model Merchant* (Chapter 5 above) I mentioned his views on the importance of the role played by trade as a pacifying agent on the international scale. Many writers of the eighteenth and nineteenth centuries were to dwell at length on the subject of trade as the propagator of worldwide amity. Kant was a staunch supporter of this belief. Not for nothing was the Antwerp Exchange dedicated to 'the merchants of all nations and languages'.[7]

In Duclos's book on the customs of eighteenth-century France, the trader or merchant (*le commerçant*) is highly praised for his enterprise. The financier (*le financier*) comes in for rather less adulation. When merchants do well, the whole community benefits along with them: it is, first and foremost, merchants who contribute to national wealth; the financiers are no more than the channel through which the money flows.[8] A similar attitude to merchants and financiers is to be found in Lesage, whose comedies portray merchants in a much more attractive light than financiers. During the Revolution, twenty-eight financiers went to the guillotine in 1794, among them Lavoisier. This category included administrators of the royal estates, who were notorious for their ruthless treatment of tenants.

Particularly fulsome praise for the businessman comes from a writer whom Diderot thought highly of – M. J. Sédaine,[9] author of various plays including *Le Philosophe sans le savoir*, which was first staged in 1765. In this play, we find the father, who combines in his person nobleman and merchant, seeking to counter his son's dislike of the 'humiliating' nature of his father's calling, as follows: 'What can compare, my son, with the condition of him who with one stroke of the pen can command attention and obedience from one end of the earth to the other? His name, his seal require no guarantee, such as is required by the money issued by a monarch as currency – money for which the value of the metal stands surety for the features imprinted on it. The person of the merchant suffices: he signed his name – that is enough.' And again: 'He serves no one people, no one nation. He serves all nations, and all nations serve him: he is universal man ("c'est l'homme de l'univers").' It is a condition of life which has its own integrity, its own honour and its own honesty. 'Suppose adventurers arm kings, war breaks out and the world is in flames. Europe is divided into hostile camps. But the merchant (*le négociant*), whether he be English, Dutch, Russian or Chinese does not cease to be dear to my heart. On this earth it is we who bind nations together and restore peace to them, a peace dictated by the prerogatives of commerce. Such, my son, is the honest merchant.' Only two callings in society are higher than that of the merchant – the magistrate ('le magistrat qui fait parler les lois'), and the soldier who defends the fatherland.

In other words, the aristocracy and the clergy are dropped from the list of those who matter in and to a country. Their place is taken in the eighteenth-century list of acceptable occupations by the artisan, for whom the Encyclopédistes cleared the way by dispelling the contempt previously felt for manual labour.

Those engaged in trade could thus claim an honourable place in society. An interesting eulogy, not of any one calling within the framework of the middle class, but of the class as a whole, is to be found in a work published in 1802 by the French scientist and philosopher Jean-Claude de la Métherie, who also edited the *Journal de Physique*. In this two-volume work, entitled *De l'homme considéré moralement, de ses moeurs et de celles des animaux*,[10] we read:

This class combines the merits of the other two [i.e. the upper and lower classes – M.O.] and is untainted by their vices. The middle-class man who has always lived in middle-class surroundings is not brought up to be haughty and domineering as are those belonging to the upper class. His heart is sensitive to the privations suffered by the poor, his spirit is not coarsened by adversity and has lost nothing of its human goodness; his personal merits permit him to behave with nobility and pride; his work assures him independence; the distinguished functions which he discharges in society ensure that even those members of the privileged class who look down on him, incur, as it were, a permanent debt of gratitude to him. He is of good and gentle manners ('ses moeurs sont douces') and everyone who comes into contact with him is pleasantly taken by his refinement (*urbanité*) and his graciousness (*aménité*). In books he finds ever new sources of pleasure. Thanks to his knowledge of various natural phenomena, he has a wide outlook and a precise grasp of reality. He has rejected the foolishness into which their conceit leads the nobility, and the superstitions of common people as well. His mental horizons may be limited, the higher reaches of thought closed to him; but in this way he escapes the envy, the ambition and the competition which make men unhappy.

And a few lines further on:

The middle-class man is able to secure for himself the greatest felicities but he never over-indulges in these as do the rich. Since his permanent absorption in work leaves him very little time for pleasure, he can never become satiated. Thus it is precisely in the middle class that we find both the most complete virtue and the most complete happiness. The man who belongs to this class has that noble caste of thought proper to the upper classes, but he lacks the prejudices bred in them by their idle vanity. He has the sound common sense of the lower classes, but is untainted by their baseness ('sans en avoir la bassesse'). . . . He is always occupied; he is never bored, nor is he ever enslaved by passion. His body is not emaciated by overworking nor is it worn out by over-indulgence in pleasure. He benefits from regular good health. Peace rules in his soul, and holds out the promise of permanent happiness.[11]

When de la Métherie was writing these words, the aristocracy was already a defeated foe; yet here we find no lack of ceremonial bows in its direction and respect for its models, bound up moreover with a feeling of superiority *vis-à-vis* the common herd. The author compares the middle class to an ill-favoured woman who has perforce to attract attention by exhibiting more substantial and more durable assets. The whole passage makes a case for according the middle class its due position, for awarding it that *considération spéciale* mentioned by N. Assorodobraj in her interesting work on the French bourgeoisie in the period 1815–30.[12] Class self-esteem evidently antedates the formation of individual paradigms. In his work on the French Revolution, Georges Lefebvre says that the bourgeoisie of the period continued to be attracted towards the aristocracy.[13] Assorodobraj makes the same point in her study of that mimicry of the aristocracy fashionable among the industrialists of a later period.

3   Superimposition of bourgeois and aristocratic models in nineteenth-century France

First of all, a glance at the antecedents, the matrix from which this superimposition of models was generated.

In the seventeenth century, the fashionable model was provided by the *honnête homme* of the Chevalier de Méré (1610–85), a courtly model deriving ultimately from Castiglione's *cortegiano*. The Chevalier de Méré devoted his whole life to polishing this exemplar, whose details he discussed in a prolific exchange of letters with personages high and low. Its main traits are set out in the treatise *De la vraie honnêteté*, published after his death.

After eulogising the French court as the greatest and most splendid of all courts, the author points out that whereas in other courts there are people who seek to perfect themselves in one calling or another, the French court is distinguished by the presence of 'idlers who have no occupation but who are not entirely devoid of merit, and who think of nothing but how to live well and look good ("se produire de bon air"). Very possibly it is to this sort of person that we owe this most indispensable word [i.e. *honnête* – M.O.] They are customarily delicate (*doux*) of spirit and tender of heart, proud and courteous, courageous and unassuming; they are neither parsimonious nor ambitious, nor do they aspire to government . . . Their sole aim is to spread pleasure everywhere, and if they ever exert themselves it is with an eye to meriting respect and winning affection.' And further: 'Hence, being an *honnête homme* is not a calling, and if I were asked on what *honnêteté* is based, I should answer that it is no more than a desire to be distinguished in everything that makes life pleasant and enjoyable.'[14]

It was a model that appealed above all to the French bourgeois who were making their fortunes under Louis XIV. Louis did on occasion raise men of bourgeois origin to high office, though, as Montesquieu relates, Richelieu, in his political testament, advised against 'employing people of mean extraction: they are too rigid and morose'.[15] As a classical seventeenth-century case we may take the Colbert family. Colbert himself (born in 1619) came from merchant stock; he made a fortune through protectionism, and became the Marquis de Seignelay. Wishing to acquire some ancestors as well, he seems to have crept into a church in Rheims one night and replaced the modest tablet commemorating the merchant who was his grandfather with a more aristocratic one. In spite of the largesse with which he sold certificates of nobility to bourgeois, and although he made use of bourgeois talent, Louis did not allow them to reside at court – a privilege reserved for those who could produce evidence of nobility dating back at least to 1400. It was only with considerable difficulty that the wives of bourgeois gained the right of being addressed as 'Madame'; for a long time, they were addressed as 'Mademoiselle' so that due distinction might be preserved between them and the wives of the aristocrats.[16] The gulf set between the court and the bourgeoisie was incomparably wider and deeper than it was in England. Samuel Pepys's wife could frequent court, even although her status was so questionable that after her marriage she was ashamed to tell her husband where her parents lived. She also thought nothing of sending to court a basket of exotic fruits which she had herself received from Spain – an act of familiarity hardly conceivable in France.

The gap between the court and the bourgeoisie in France, as compared with England, was paralleled by the gap between the bourgeois and the nobleman. There were several reasons for this. In England, the younger sons of the nobility, having no claim on the family lands and estate which by the law of primogeniture passed to the first-born, tended to go to town and enter on careers in trade. As has often been pointed out, the production of wool by the English nobility formed a link between town and country, while in France the nobleman as a producer of grain was in perpetual conflict with the towns. M. Beard sees an additional reason for the relatively stronger position of the bourgeoisie *vis-à-vis* the nobility in the fact that England's strength lay not in her army but in her navy. In all countries the army was a terrain in which the nobility ruled the roost (though by democratising the use of arms, the invention of gunpowder had done something to change this) while shipbuilding and navigation were the business of the bourgeoisie whom England had to thank for her rule of the seas. As Beard writes, gentlemen were too poor to buy ships, too ignorant to build them and too proud to learn how to do so. In the main, it was the middle classes who carried out England's earliest colonial expansion, and – again according to Beard – if many of them behaved like feudal barons this was because the conditions of life in the colonies were very similar to those in which the nobility had once flourished.[17]

The greater exclusivity of the aristocracy in France did nothing to lessen the attractive power of its models; indeed, it may well have enhanced them. Molière, almost Colbert's contemporary, found plenty of material in his surroundings for his ridicule of bourgeois snobbery. Thomas Corneille, the brother of the great tragedian, added 'de l'Isle' to his plebeian surname.

He surrounded his lordly estate with a muddy ditch,

And haughtily ordered people to address him as
'M. de l'Isle'

as Molière jibes in *L'École des femmes*. As Boy-Żeleński wrote
in his preface to *Le Bourgeois Gentilhomme*: 'Susceptibility to
social glamour, especially to the spell cast by the ancestral
nobility, is surely among the most deeply rooted of all
human feelings. . . . It is worship, as it were, of something
that cannot be bought or acquired or learned: a worship of
breeding, of the virtues and the vices alike which make
certain individuals or even their whole class into a mysterious
and useless "luxury".'

Those traits of the aristocratic model which the *nouveau-
riche* (the word seems to date from about 1670 in France) of
Molière's day wanted to imitate, are portrayed for us in *Le
Bourgeois Gentilhomme*. Monsieur Jourdain wants to be *à la
mode*, he wants to have lots of servants (a nobleman's prestige
depended very much on the number of those dependent on
him); he would like to be able to fence and dance; and he
wants to know enough about music to arrange concerts in
his house and enough about philosophy to take part in polite
conversation. A romance with a titled lady would not come
amiss either.

In the course of the eighteenth century, the courtly paradigm comes in for more and more criticism. In *De l'esprit
des lois* Montesquieu writes: 'Ambition in idleness; meanness
mixed with pride; a desire of riches without industry; aversion to truth, flattery, perfidy, violation of engagements,
contempt of civil duties, fear of the prince's virtue, hope
from his weakness, but, above all, a perpetual ridicule cast
upon virtue are, I think, the characteristics by which most
courtiers in all ages and countries have been constantly
distinguished.'[18] It would be difficult to find a more damning
indictment of the polished loafers lauded by the Chevalier
de Méré. 'The virtues we are here taught', wrote Montesquieu, with aristocrats in mind, 'are less what we owe to
others than to ourselves; they are not so much what draws
us towards society, as what distinguishes us from our fellow
citizens.'[19] More than anyone before him, Montesquieu could

see how much of aristocratic morality served not to distinguish the aristocrat *within* the framework of his own class, but to mark that class off from those inferior to it.

But this critical attitude to upper-class morality did not mean that membership of the privileged classes became any less attractive in the eighteenth century. Citizen Arouet calls himself de Voltaire, buckles on a sword, acquires a considerable estate and takes up residence in a château thereon. Caron the watchmaker, author of *Le Mariage de Figaro*, has himself addressed as 'Monsieur de Beaumarchais'. Derobespierre divides his name into de Robespierre, while Danton adds the apostrophe – d'Anton: two ways of upgrading surnames which might hardly have been expected from leaders of the bourgeois revolution![20]

In his sentimental and highly artificial piece *Le Père de Famille* Diderot stands up for the right of a nobleman's son to marry for love, regardless of his beloved's name and fortune. For inscrutable reasons, the name of the impoverished young lady with whom the scion of the d'Orbesson family is in love is not disclosed: a rather artificial subterfuge which is supposed to keep the reader in suspense. Only when the marriage question is satisfactorily settled does the beautiful maiden reveal that impoverished she may be but is in fact of noble birth, and she reveals her surname to prove it. The reader sighs with relief: that delicacy of feeling which the heroine has displayed from the outset is after all properly sited. We are reminded of Thomas Hardy's celebrated novel *Tess of the d'Urbervilles* (published in 1891), which is a sort of Greek tragedy in an English setting. The peasant heroine who captivates the reader with the subtle refinement of her feelings turns out, of course, to be of noble birth, with a fine aristocratic surname which has been merely been distorted in rural surroundings to the point of being unrecognisable. Similarly, in *Nad Niemnem* ('On the Niemen') Orzeszkowa praises Justyna for choosing a husband from a social sphere other than her own, but shirks depriving him of the noble origins which the reader expects. It was not easy for 'nobleness' to become detached from the 'nobility'.

I have already mentioned the play *Le Philosophe sans le savoir* by M. J. Sédaine. In it, the author – himself once a stonemason and master builder – provides us with a very interesting example of the bourgeois ethic as superimposed on the aristocratic. The hero is a merchant of aristocratic origin. He is highly respected and honoured, and he sings the praises of his calling in the manner I have described. His aristocratic origins are, however, concealed so that he can bring to his business deals not only the talents which are duly his by birth, but also the acquired merits characteristic of the third estate. He values the enlightened age he lives in and sees the duel as a savage superstition to which he himself had to submit as a youth: it was as a result of this experience that he had had to flee the country and take a different, bourgeois name. At that very moment, his son is on the eve of a duel, and the father can see no way of protecting him from it. He can see that his sister is being ridiculous when she despises his life in commerce and asserts that the only place for a gentleman is in the army; but at the same time he cannot rid himself of his aristocratic bent and his chivalrous belief in fair play, both of which colour his business deals.

If the play has a moral it is that the upper classes should take to commerce and business, and that a very useful marriage could be arranged between businesslike reliability and chivalrous honour. In this, the play reminds us of *Lalka* by Bolesław Prus, written almost a hundred years later. In this play, Prus, too, urges the nobility to go in for commerce, and Wokulski is to combine the talents he had from birth with the advantages accruing from the calling he has chosen. Dependability and punctuality may grace kings, writes Prus, but they are obligatory upon merchants, and Wokulski combines these virtues with the style of the gentleman born. Wokulski buys the Łęcki tenement house, it may be remembered, at about 30,000 rubles more than it is worth. True, he is in love, but not every lover with money in his pocket could bring himself to do this. He buys Łęcki's promissory notes and tears them up in the presence of Madame Meliton: 'Is that what a merchant would do?' Our hero is well pleased with the count's opinion of him, when he says: 'Even when clothed in the skin of an industrialist, a nobleman will out, given the right occasion.'

But let us return to France. The passages I have quoted

go to show that the bourgeois writers of the eighteenth century placed considerable value on aristocratic models and noble origins; and that in the best case they supported and endorsed a combination of the chivalrous values with those of the honest man running a shop or an office. Of all the French moralists of the eighteenth century, it is probably Volney, whose Catechism appeared in 1793 at the height of the Revolution, who is furthest removed from aristocratic attitudes. True, Volney did not refuse the title of Count which Napoleon offered him, and under Louis XVIII he became a peer of France; but this does not alter the fact that in his public utterances he remained till his death faithful to the views he had expressed in 1793.

From N. Assorodobraj's work on the French bourgeoisie between 1815 to 1830 we learn that the French industrialist Ternaux did not follow Volney's example. On the contrary, in 1821 he ostentatiously rejected the title of baron offered him by the king, on the grounds that he saw no possibility of reconciling the image he lived by – that of the working man – with a title which would compel him to relinquish his interests in trade and commerce. This roused the industrialists to enthusiasm, and Ternaux, on Saint-Simon's initiative, was hymned by them: but this enthusiasm, to judge by the life and work of Ternaux's contemporary, Balzac, did little to eradicate bourgeois snobbery. Balzac was the grandson of a villager called Balss, but he cooked up a fictitious genealogy for himself, and had a coat of arms painted on his carriage doors. His heroes are obsessed not only with the pursuit of gold, but also with a burning desire to gain admittance to the salons of the aristocracy. In *Le Père Goriot*, the action of which begins in 1819, Delfina de Nucingen, the wife of a rich banker, 'would have lapped up every puddle between the Rue St Lazare and the Rue de Grenelle' to get inside the salon of the Vicomtesse de Beauséant.

Balzac died in 1850, just after the revolutions of 1848. Not surprisingly, the tastes of the bourgeoisie under Napoleon III show little change *vis-à-vis* the situation in Balzac's heyday. For illustrative purposes, we can turn to the most popular plays of the period and the novels read by the mass of the bourgeoisie. It was in 1854 that the well-known comedy writer Emile Augier scored a huge success with *Le Gendre de Monsieur Poirier*, which has held the stage ever since with numerous successful revivals. The action of the comedy takes place in 1846, and the lively dialogue reflects the clash between the bourgeois morality of old Poirier, who has made a fortune out of trading in haberdashery, and the morality of his son-in-law, Gaston, Marquis de Presles, who has acquired along with Poirier's daughter several million francs as her dowry.

With his daughter thus advantageously married off, old Poirier begins to see himself as a baron and a peer of France. Initially, dreams of advancement make him compliant in the hands of his son-in-law, who married only for the money, and who treats the wife who adores him with cynical infidelity. However, the Marquis does nothing to get old Poirier a court appointment of some sort; and the father-in-law begins to tire of paying his mounting debts. Compliance gives way to irritation and refusal. In the ensuing altercations, the author's sympathies are on the side of the upper classes. The old merchant simply does not understand the aristocratic way of doing things – honour and fidelity to one's given word; he has no discretion and he is very short on good taste. When a friend of Gaston's, an impoverished Viscount, offers Poirier's daughter his purse for the poor, old Poirier reacts to this 'munificence' with scorn.

The money-lenders with whom Gaston has run up his debts are charging interest at 50 per cent. But when old Poirier settles the debts he pays only the legally recognised 6 per cent interest, knowing that the money-lenders would never dare to take the case to court; it is a settlement which he feels to be in accordance with 'la plus scrupuleuse probité'. In fact, old Poirier has simply failed to grasp that when a nobleman gives his word he cannot go back on it – and the daughter has to make up the short-fall in the amount due to the money-lenders. 'It's true that I received only half of the money I signed for,' Gaston admits, 'but I am in honour bound to pay the whole sum. My obligation is not towards these crooks, but towards my signature . . .' His titled friend supports him in this: 'We have been divested of our rights, but not of our obligations.' These obligations can be summed up in two words: *noblesse oblige.* 'Whatever happens, we always conform to a code which is stricter and more demanding than the law of the land – the secret code which we call honour . . . Not many people allow themselves to be robbed,' says the Viscount, who is throughout presented in a rather favourable light; 'it's something gentlemen are good at.'

Another bitter altercation arises when Poirier opens a letter written by a woman to his son-in-law, which affords ample proof of Gaston's infidelity. Gaston doesn't mince his words: 'By stealing the secret of my mistakes, you have forfeited the right to judge me. There is something that is more sacred and inviolable than the lock on a strong-box – it is the seal on a letter, because it cannot defend itself.' But once again the magnanimous Antoinette, Poirier's daughter and Gaston's wife, sets things right by burning the letter which had delivered her erring husband into her father's hands. She can understand that it would be shameful to make use of information gained in such a fashion.

The old merchant is devoid of aesthetic culture, while the titled rakes are born with unerring good taste. Gaston buys pictures and views them with the eye of a connoisseur. Once, when the Viscount is in raptures over a landscape by a poor but talented artist, Poirier is more concerned with the fact that the picture is, in his opinion, grossly overpriced: *he* could have got it for far less, considering the artist's needy circumstances. And anyway he doesn't think much of the picture. 'I've got a drawing at home,' he announces, 'showing a dog on the beach, barking at a sailor's cap . . . well, at least you know what it's about. It's a good idea, it's simple and it moves you.' As for artists, one should not encourage them, loafers and libertines the lot of them. 'You hear things about them that make your skin crawl – I couldn't even repeat such things with my daughter present.'

The daughter, for her part, is as unlike old Poirier as could be imagined. The author loses no opportunity of stressing the delicacy of feeling, the magnanimity of this bourgeois girl. Thanks to these qualities she wins over her husband's heart, and the Marquis is moved to exclaim, 'You bear my name better than I do!' The young pair, now very much in love, settle in the country in the family residence of the de Presles family, redeemed thanks to the Poirier moneybags. The way the comedy ends suggests that under his wife's influence the Marquis has renounced his evil ways and his frivolity, and that in future he will be a model husband and father.

The moral seems to be that it is unseemly to rest on the laurels of your ancestors if you yourself have added nothing by your own efforts. Augier castigates the idleness and cynicism of the rich but admires their courage (Gaston is incomparable in the duel, the upstart Pontgrimaud is scared stiff at the very idea of one), their code of honour, their style and their personal charm. This cult of the aristocratic codes and models is accompanied by the conviction that the bourgeois may be in a position to apply these virtues more effectively than the aristocracy themselves; while at the same time the bourgeoisie is not cursed with the nobleman's weaknesses. In a word, you can behave like a gentleman without being a gentleman born.

The same respect for, not to say cult of the nobility can be traced in many of the novelists of the period who kept the French bourgeois supplied with their favourite reading. Let us take a peculiarly instructive example: *Le Roman d'un jeune homme pauvre* by Octave Feuillet (1821–90). The hero, Maxime, comes from high aristocratic stock. His father had lost everything; his mother, driven to desperation by her husband's lack of responsibility, had died prematurely. Maxime and his sister are left destitute. But Maxime is not the man to be dismayed by the prospect of poverty. He faces up to his creditors, and refuses to sell his name in marriage to the first available daughter of some rich upstart. He assumes a bourgeois name and starts work as estate manager to a millionaire family. At every turn, young Maxime shows that there is more to him than meets the eye, and soon he attracts the attention of a rich heiress with whom he falls in love. His rival for her hand tries to put an end to Maxime's chances by getting him to ride a particularly vicious mare; needless to say, Maxime proves himself a born horseman and has no difficulty in handling the animal. (One is reminded here of the passage in the *Odyssey* where, on arrival at the court of the Phaeacians, Odysseus is provoked by Euryalus who calls him 'profit-snatcher' and says that anyone can see he is no sportsman. Whereupon Odysseus at once betrays his noble birth with a tremendous throw of the discus and brilliant swordsmanship.) Not only the gentry but the servants as well detect 'something special' about their manager, but this is not enough to save him from various humiliations. For example, he has to put up with the way in which his beloved brazenly flaunts her social superiority – something which the author seems to take for granted.

Heroic deeds come naturally to Maxime. At the risk of his life, he saves the lady's dog from a swollen stream. 'Honour' is his favourite word, and he is always ready to take up the sword in its defence. While paying a visit to a neighbouring château, he and his beloved are accidentally locked in the tower; she suspects him of having bribed the watchman to arrange this, with a view to so compromising her that they would have to get married – whereupon he leaps from the window at considerable risk to his neck. One day he is working in the family archives in the course of his duties, when he comes across a document which proves that his beloved's father had made his wealth in very questionable fashion, and at the cost of his, Maxime's, own family. His reaction is to burn the document which, incidentally, would have delivered the girl into his hands. It is simply not in his nature to profit from a chance discovery which would humiliate her. His troubles mount, but all is resolved by a windfall: a rich female relative, in the royal line, dies and leaves him an immense fortune. Now he can freely acknowledge his true identity, and when he proposes, his beloved will have no cause to suspect him of being merely interested in her money.

The novel is remarkable for its romantic adulation of aristocratic models and aristocratic titles. The exalted personage who leaves our hero her fortune entertains boundless contempt for English 'gentlemen', and stresses the great gulf set between them and the French *gentilhomme*. This bears out Tocqueville's observation that while in England the word 'gentleman' tended to be applied to an increasingly wide circle, in France the word *gentilhomme* continued to refer to a closed caste which was immune to democratisation.[21]

Feuillet's cult of the aristocracy is combined with a very sympathetic portrayal of Laubépin, the advocate who had in his day served the interests of the hero's family, and who now represents the rich family for which Maxime works: interestingly enough, as Laubépin accepts the Revolution, there is every reason to think that he is of lowly origin, and his views could well be pure Jacobin. But this latter-day Jacobin is remarkably servile and obsequious to the titled persons he serves. Feuillet is a Romantic; and the curious thing is that although Romanticism is a bourgeois movement, it developed under the banner of an adulation of knightly and chivalric tradition and of contempt for bourgeois prosaicness.

We pass now to a somewhat later example of this genre which was so avidly devoured by the bourgeois clientele – *Maître de Forges* by G. Ohnet (1848–1918), the tale of a young industrialist who owns iron and steel works. It is difficult to be precise about editions of French books, as they vary as regards numbers of copies from one country to another; but the fact that the copy I am using belongs to the 396th edition of this novel speaks for itself. The moral of the story can be summed up as follows: industrialists may have no titles, but, provided they are efficient and successful, they can still live the kind of life which was once reserved for the aristocracy. They can furnish palatial homes in good taste, they can acquire *savoir-faire*; they can be magnanimous, selfless, courageous in battle, delicate of sensibility, and ready to defend their own honour and that of their family in a duel if necessary.

The action takes place immediately after the Paris Commune, which the author depicts in a few introductory words. Again we have to do with impoverished aristocracy whose estate is adjacent to a property owned by a *nouveau riche* by the name of Derblay. This Derblay is busy developing a high-quality industrial enterprise in his grounds, which is bringing in a great deal of money. By making his industrialist a foundry-master, the author is deliberately choosing the least compromising branch of industry, for it would be quite permissible even for a nobleman to have his own foundry, brick fields or mills on his estate without losing social face. Derblay asks for the hand of Clara, the daughter of his aristocratic neighbours, in marriage. Clara is not aware (though Derblay is) that her family is financially ruined. She is actually in love with a prince who was brought up by her parents but who has forgotten her very existence, and who, after losing his all at cards, has got himself engaged to the daughter of a wealthy parvenu. When she learns of this projected marriage, Clara, hurt and humiliated, loses no time in accepting the hand of the 'blacksmith' next door, though she does not love him and in fact, after the marriage, refuses him access to her. The noble-minded ironmaster is not put off by the role he has to play; and the young aristocrat has to retain the reader's sympathy, though she takes it upon herself to humiliate her husband to a degree that few would stand for. Yet, thanks to his exceptional character, the husband gradually gets the upper hand. However badly she treats him, he never reminds his wife that she was penniless when he married her; and after the marriage he pays her an annuity on the dowry he has never received. Comparing the prince, her daughter's previous fiancé, with this commoner (*roturier*), Clara's mother has to admit that she cannot tell which is the *gentil-homme*. By breaking his word, the prince has forfeited the one and only asset which in these latter days distinguishes the aristocrat from other classes – fidelity to his given word. Clara falls in love with her husband, and when he fights a duel on her behalf she throws herself passionately between the contestants in his defence.

So everything comes to a happy end. The marriage of the ironmaster's sister to Clara's brother reinforces the union between industry and aristocracy. Casting a benevolent eye on the amity now binding his relative, the baron, with Derblay, Clara's brother says to the baron's wife: 'Your husband, who is a scion of the paladins (*descendant des preux*), embodies ten centuries of military glory. Monsieur Derblay, the son of manufacturers, represents only one century, but it is the century which has given us steam, gas and electricity. And, speaking for myself, I must say that the fraternisation of these two men gives me cause for great rejoicing; in a friendliness born of mutual respect they are welding into a whole two things in which some countries excel – a glorious past and a progressive present.'

We see, then, that after the Paris Commune, the French bourgeois reader continued to be supplied with the same fodder as before from bourgeois writers. It is a literature taken up with the claim of merchants and industrialists to lead a life on the aristocratic pattern; and we must remember that 'society' admitted financiers to its ranks long before it was prepared to consider merchants and industrialists as candidates. Moulinet, the activist chocolate-merchant who appears in Feuillet's novel, reminds us over and over again of old Poirier in Augier's comedy. Aristocrats are unfailingly identified by their pride, their magnanimity, their fine hands and feet and the elegant simplicity of their dress. In so far as the sons of impoverished noble houses think of working, instead of looking for a profitable marriage with a bourgeois heiress, they turn naturally to two callings – the law and the diplomatic service. And for men on the make, the final baptism is still the duel (we may recall Wokulski's duel in *Lalka*).

Books for children were on similar lines. For several decades, French children were supplied with the 'Bibliothèque Rose' series, the most prolific author for this imprint being the Comtesse de Ségur (1799–1874), by origin a Russian. Roger Garaudy writes: 'Such books as *Les Petites Filles modèles* and *Les Malheurs de Sophie* by the Comtesse de Ségur are good examples of the emasculation of the personality which was necessary if a political balance was to be maintained in the adolescent bourgeoisie under Louis-Philippe.'[22]

The heroines of *Les Petites Filles modèles* are both of aristocratic stock. Their mother is a widow, the father having been killed in a campaign against the Arabs. To the family seat in the country in which they live comes another widow of noble birth along with her little daughter; her husband is supposed to have died on a sea voyage (later it transpires that he is still alive). The two ladies dwell under the one roof, providing along with their children an exemplary existence graced by all the virtues. They are gentle, modest, kind to the servants and charitable to the poor. But of course this is what we expect of people who can put 'de' before their surname. Things are very different with the lady who lives near by and who has no 'de' before her surname. She is the stepmother of Sophie, whose adventures are described in the second book. This stepmother is a parvenue pure and simple: she dresses atrociously, ill-treats the servants, beats her children and lets her stepdaughter marry Count Błagowski, one of her own kind.

The success enjoyed by the Comtesse de Ségur was not limited to the reign of Louis-Philippe. The appetite for her works was so voracious that even the flood of successive editions could hardly satisfy it, up to the early years of the twentieth century (the edition I am using is dated 1909). Anyone who knows France will be well aware that the aristocratic model was still very much alive in the inter-war years. Proust's Swann yearns for the aristocratic reservation, when a loveless and unwanted marriage to a woman with no access to it closes the door to the Quartier St-Germain for him too.

In his book *La Barrière et le niveau* (published in 1924) E. Goblot gives an expert and first-hand account of the way in which the French bourgeois aped the aristocratic model and vied with each other in leading parasitic lives. I have dealt with this book elsewhere[23] and there is no need to repeat here what I say there. Anyway, I hope I have produced enough evidence to show how fondly bourgeois France clung to its aristocratic models.

4 Bourgeois and nobleman in nineteenth-century England

We pass now to the scene in England. Some historians date the onset of the English Enlightenment and the concomitant upsurge of bourgeois culture from 1690, the year of John Locke's *Essay on Human Understanding*. It is very interesting to compare the ethical theories propounded by Locke in the *Essay* with his personal and widely differing views as expressed in his *Some Thoughts on Education* published three years later. To judge from the *Essay*, it would be for the teacher to persuade a pupil not to lie by demonstrating to him that *if* he lied, the consequences for himself would be unpleasant. This is suggested by Locke in the *Essay* when he asserts that everyone wants pleasure and seeks to avoid suffering; and that things and actions can be graded in value depending on whether they induce pleasure or suffering. In the later book, however, Locke appeals primarily to modesty, to good reputation and to avoidance of shame and disgrace. The pronouncement 'Esteem and Disgrace are, of all others, the most powerful Incentives to the Mind . . .'[24] could very well figure in any handbook of aristocratic education. Locke was, of course, employed to tutor young aristocrats. Some passages in the later book are addressed to the aristocracy alone, and instruction is even differentiated according to whether it applies to the first-born or to those younger sons who will have to look for a career in the city. However, the educational climate – at times very reminiscent of Castiglione – is not determined purely and simply by the social position of the pupil; often, Locke seems to be addressing his recommendations to all educators and all pupils. While he stresses, as Castiglione did, the importance of dancing and good manners, Locke also introduces several new features into his paradigm of the educated man. He is not enthusiastic about fencing and horsemanship, and in fact admits the latter for health reasons only; he disapproves of playing cards, recommending instead handicrafts as a source of recreation and rest. He also tries to persuade the aristocracy that the study of commercial book-keeping will stand them in good stead. The composite figure that emerges from all of this is a curious blend of compliance with the aristocratic model (in which some students of Locke have seen the influence of Montaigne) and admiration for the 'bourgeois' climate of Aesop's *Fables*, which Locke very warmly recommended to his pupils and which he himself translated for pedagogical use.

We recall that Defoe ridiculed certain aspects of the nobility and poked fun at the nobleman's ignorance, superciliousness, boorishness and financial unreliability. At the same time, however, seeking preferment as he did, and adopting the garb and the behaviour of the aristocratic model, Defoe was trying to cross barriers which blocked his way, whether those of birth or of knowledge of the classical languages – a factor whose role as a class differentiator is explicit both in Defoe's case and in that of Locke. A little later, Henry Fielding ridiculed the same aspects of the nobility in his novel *The Adventures of Joseph Andrews* (1742). Here we meet another ignorant nobleman (whose ignorance the family tutor dare not seek to rectify, as he is under instructions not to correct the young master in anything). This scion is supposed to know Greek and Latin, when in fact he cannot tell Latin from Welsh; he never pays the servants their wages, and he is both impudent and licentious. Yet this same story of Fielding's affords evidence that in eighteenth-century England the aristocracy were everywhere received with obsequious servility. The magistrate obeys the squire's wishes, and even the honest parson Adams, the hero of the book, receives his titled visitors with many a bow and scrape, and likes to throw in a bit of Latin to show that he is not just anybody.

For a particularly interesting example of this consciously promoted fusion of aristocratic and bourgeois models – something which fitted in very well with the good working relationship between the two classes in eighteenth-century England – we turn to the well-known moralising weeklies edited by the two Whigs Addison and Steele. These formed a new genre when they first appeared in the years between 1709 and 1715, and they were imitated in several European countries and in America. In one of these – the *Spectator* – we find the aristocracy represented by the figure of Sir Roger de Coverley, the classic Tory as immutable in his political views as in his love life. For forty years he has lived faithfully with a wife who does not even like him; and throughout this long period he seems to have seen no reason why he should change either his political or his social views. Addison and Steele present their country squire in a very sympathetic light, even if he is not noted for his intellect. We listen indulgently to his comments on first seeing Westminster Abbey and on going to the theatre. In such arenas as these the bourgeoisie feels it has the upper hand. In the pages of the *Spectator* it is not only the modest intellectual level of the aristocracy that is pilloried by bourgeois writers but also its sheer uselessness. The example of the baronet Wimble's family is used to point up the wretched life led by younger brothers in such families, who have to 'reside' in homes they cannot inherit, instead of being allowed to go to town to earn their living. Praise of their own situation echoes through the lines in which Addison and Steele depict this sort of thing. It is seen as quite proper for rich men to take possession of mortgaged family estates, for he who comes to an estate through hard work is more entitled to it than he who lost it through his own negligence. In conversation with a merchant, Sir Roger contrasts 'book-keeping mentality' unfavourably with his own sort of generosity, whereupon the merchant points out that while Sir Roger has to distribute money to his people, he, the merchant, creates conditions for his employees such that they have no need to look to his generosity. While chalking up their own merits, however, Addison and Steele do not neglect to pay homage to the aristocracy. What they would like to see is a fusion of the two sets of values, as embodied in one of Sir Roger's ancestors, who in the prosecution of his affairs was 'as punctual as a tradesman and as generous as a gentleman'. They regard themselves as above party and deplore the practice, widespread in England, of taking party affiliation into account when filling a vacant post or even when criticising a book. The effect of this policy is that unworthy individuals are given high office simply because they have served a party well; while good men are dismissed if they are unable to bring themselves to do what their party requires of them. And if books are to be assessed on the basis of what camp the author belongs to, then decent people will cease to take into consideration due praise or blame for what they do.[25]

The English gentleman is an 'odd, specifically English hybrid of feudal lord and bourgeois', wrote Miriam Beard in her *History of the Business Man*.[26] It was in the fourteenth century that the saying 'When Adam delved and Eve span, who was then the gentleman?' began to circulate; here the word 'gentleman' is used purely in a class sense; but, as time went on, personal attributes began to take precedence over the class element. By 1714 we find Steele demanding in the *Tatler* that not social position but personal behaviour should decide who is or is not a 'gentleman'; though the *Encyclopaedia Britannica* in its current edition does not find this criterion generally accepted before 1832.[27] Since then, education or self-education towards 'gentleman' status has continued to be under the influence of aristocratic models. In his book *In England Now* (1937), M. E. Chase asserts that the ideal towards which Englishmen have always been drawn is that of 'gentility'. Much the same conclusion is reached by Lewis and Maude in their monograph *The English Middle Class* (1949).[28] Clearly, the English court itself contributed much to keeping this ideal in force. In the years immediately preceding the last war, a visitor to England was bound to notice that the petty bourgeoisie was much given to wearing clothes of a bluish-grey colour, which was Queen Mary's favourite colour. Writing paper in this colour was very popular, and names given to children in the Royal Family immediately became the most popular names in Britain. If the exemplar of the 'gentleman' was particularly popular and widespread in Britain, this is due in part at least to the fact that Britain had a large colonial empire, in the exploitation of which the British working class willingly took part. This helped to blunt the class war, so much so that even the higher echelons of the proletariat tended to model themselves on the 'gentleman'. It was an exportable model as well, and it has even been said that the image of the 'gentleman' did as much for England's prestige in foreign parts as the export of coal. It is interesting to see how the word 'gentleman' itself was adopted in various countries, where it filled a gap in the indigenous lexicon. Thus while it was not accepted in Italy or Spain, it passed into general use in France and figures in *Larousse*.[29] This is a fascinating subject, which I treat elsewhere.

Had the aristocracy not continued to fascinate and attract the English throughout the nineteenth century, W. M. Thackeray could not have written *Vanity Fair* (1847) or the celebrated *Book of Snobs*. 'What Peerage-worship there is all through this free country!' he writes in the *Book of Snobs*. 'How we are all implicated in it, and more or less down on our knees.'[30] *Debrett's Peerage* is England's second Bible.

Everyone follows the doings of the upper classes, and the Court Circular is perused with avid interest. There is embittered competition for titles. Some 'snobs' go without food so as to be able to afford an additional lackey, and many do without things in private life so as to be able to appear in due style in public, that is, maintain their social standing. As Thackeray writes: 'Perhaps the best use of that book, the "Peerage", is to look down the list, and see how many have bought and sold birth – how poor sprigs of nobility somehow sell themselves to rich City Snobs' daughters, how rich City Snobs purchase noble ladies . . .'

Sons of titled people, says Thackeray, start off in life with every advantage over their non-aristocratic fellows, whom they soon leave far behind: 'Because a lad is a lord, the University gives him a degree at the end of two years which another is seven in acquiring.'

Snobbism is rife – not only in the universities but also in the liberal professions, where the wives of attorneys and lawyers vaingloriously compete for the best seats; it is rife in the Church and, obviously, in the Army. 'I would still like to know where, except in the United Kingdom, debts are a matter of joke, and making tradesmen "suffer" a sport that gentlemen own to.'

And here is Thackeray's classic account of social advancement:

> Old Pump sweeps a shop, runs off messages, becomes a
> confidential clerk and partner. Pump the Second
> becomes chief of the house, spins more and more money,
> marries his son to an Earl's daughter. Pump Tertius
> goes on with the bank; but his chief business in life is to
> become the father of Pump Quartius who comes out a
> full-blown aristocrat and takes his seat as Baron
> Pumplington, and his race rules hereditarily over this
> nation of Snobs.

The bourgeoisie has always been fond of its comforts, and English resistance to central heating has been seen (M. Beard) as class-based: an attempt to retain the upper-class image of tough austere aristocrats used to chilly castles, heavy armour and uncomfortable saddles. The great inventiveness which the bourgeoisie has displayed in the art of making life more comfortable, over the long period from Miletus to modern times – the inventiveness which Alberti shows in the Renaissance and Franklin in the Enlightenment – is alien to the aristocracy. Tocqueville warned that a fondness for one's material comforts is incompatible with a heroic attitude to life.

We come now to John Galsworthy and *The Forsyte Sage*. 'If the upper middle class,' we read in the preface, 'with other classes, is destined to "move on" into amorphism, here, pickled in these pages, it lies under glass for strollers in the wide and ill-arranged museum of Letters to gaze at. Here it rests, preserved in its own juice: The Sense of Property.' And, as we learn from the same preface, after the publication of *The Forsyte Saga*, Galsworthy received several letters from people who were convinced that he had portrayed their family: which says much for the accuracy with which Galsworthy has typified the class.

The first two volumes are set in the Victorian age, and therefore relevant to our present inquiry. The Forsyte family was not of very ancient ancestry. We first meet old Jolyon as head of the family in 1886. His father had been a bricklayer who had worked his way up to become a master builder; and his architectural ingenuity had contributed in no small measure to the defacement of London. The family background goes a long way towards explaining the Forsyte obsession with buying property, and, above all, with building themselves houses. The oldest stratum of Forsytes to whom the author introduces us is engaged in various fields of activity – merchants, notaries, brokers, industrialists, all of them very well off, which means that they are distinguished personages in London society. They are adept at picking the right addresses – after all, if one lives in Park Lane or at Hyde Park Corner, one is sure to have titled neighbours. Old Jolyon had not even been properly educated. 'He retained touchingly his attitude of admiration and mistrust towards a system appropriate to the highest in the land, of which he had not himself been privileged to partake.' His son, Jolyon, however, goes to Eton and thence to Cambridge. And although young Jolyon is no more than a modest insurance broker, he is accepted for membership of the Hotch Potch Club – an honour withheld from his father, who though rich was still a tradesman.

'Sixty-four years (i.e. of Victoria's reign – M.O.) that favoured property and had made the upper middle class, had buttressed, chiselled, polished it, till it was almost indistinguishable in manners, morals, speech, appearance, habit and soul from the nobility.' Swithin Forsyte, 'following the impulse which sooner or later urges thereto some member of every great family', betakes himself one day to the College of Heralds. Here he is assured that he has good reason to adopt a coat of arms with a 'pheasant proper' as the crest. Swithin does not take up the coat of arms as a whole, but he has the pheasant painted on his carriage doors and embossed on the coachman's buttons; and both crest and motto figure on his writing paper. The rest of the family follow suit.

The aristocratic veneer remains rather thin, however. The Forsytes observe the upper-class rituals of dressing and eating, taking care to have only what is distinguished and elegant; but underlying this veneer is a morality of the kind customarily described as 'bourgeois'. There is no place here for disinterested largesse and splendid foolhardiness. The family is characterised by its dispassionate and practical common sense and its careful conversion of everything into terms of money. Foresight is implicit in its very surname. This cautious farsightedness, bred by distrust, prevents the Forsytes from throwing themselves into anything. They never show their feelings. They never 'forget themselves', for this is to show one's cards and put oneself recklessly at the mercy of others. Property gives a sense of power and a feeling of security. Soames has a fine picture-gallery in his country house at Mapledurham, but he treats pictures as stocks and shares, trying to spot those which will appreciate in value and on which therefore money may legitimately be spent. The irreproachable wardrobe of the *grande bourgeoisie* not only serves the respectability to which it aspires but lends the requisite feeling of security. 'Impossible to conceive of him with a hair out of place, a tie deviating one-eighth of an inch from the perpendicular, a collar unglossed' – thus Galsworthy describes Soames. Aristocrats, of course, confident in the cachet conferred upon them by birth, do not have to keep up appearances to this extent. Describing a University ceremonial in his witty *Conseils à un jeune Français partant pour l'Angleterre*, André Maurois says that you can always tell the aristocrats by the holes in their socks.

The feeling of security pursued by the Forsytes is threatened by two wild assailants – love and beauty. Galsworthy himself says that the main purpose of the book is to show this threat in action. Old Jolyon's son is expelled from the family because he elopes with the governess and takes up painting. In keeping with the stereotyped view of the bourgeoisie we are familiar with, the Forsytes have little time for artists: they are 'idle rascals'. Soames's beautiful wife, Irene, leaves her rich husband for the architect Bosinney, an enthusiastic devotee of both love and beauty. As we see, the theoretical writers on the bourgeois ethos were not so far out when they asserted that the businessman cares nothing for beauty and is not interested in making love. The point is that neither of these pursuits was likely to further his career.

Other threats were looming up on the horizon, and Galsworthy uses the occasion of Queen Victoria's funeral to point to their social implications. Victoria's reign had seen such a massive accumulation of wealth that interest rates had fallen from 8 per cent to 3 per cent, and the country was full of Forsytes. In 1837 when Victoria came to the throne 'there were manners in the land and pigsties for the poor; unhappy devils were hanged for little crimes and Dickens had just begun to write. . . . It was an epoch which had gilded individual liberty so that if a man had money he was free in law and fact, and if he had not money he was free in law but not in fact.' It was an age that was passing – so Soames reflects – with the funeral procession of the Queen. Trade unionism was raising its head, there were Labour Party members in the House of Commons, men of property were threatened by socialists. 'Things would never be as safe again as under good old Vicky.'

If the bourgeoisie used the culminating phase of its great era to adopt certain traits specific to the upper classes, the latter, for their part, took over certain bourgeois features.

The commercialisation of aristocratic favours that was not uncommon in England before the Second World War had perhaps other causes in addition to the pauperisation of aristocrats, forced out of their family seats by progressively rising taxes. If a young lady of sufficiently distinguished birth wished to be presented at Court and curtsey to the Queen, thereby gaining a certain social distinction at least for the Season, she had first of all to find someone already accepted at Court who would agree to present her. Money seems to have changed hands on such occasions, but the transaction was not regarded as in any way infra dig. Similarly, people of good name were apparently paid (so I was assured in London) to grace social occasions with their presence. Perhaps bourgeois influence is also to be seen in the practice, allegedly prevalent in high social circles in England, of turning up at receptions at the precise time specified in the invitation: demonstrating thereby that one is aware both of one's obligations and of time; and satisfactorily methodical and precise in combining the two. It was in no way a reflection on the host's hospitality if the invitation, say, to a weekend at a country house, specified not only the moment of arrival but also that of departure, an arrangement which had the clarity and precision of a good business deal. And the leather patches protecting the elbows of young gentlemen at Oxford and Cambridge in the pre-war years struck many a foreigner as a sort of inverted snobbery. It looked as though they were playing at being thrifty.

5   A glance at Germany

If we can make certain broad generalisations about the part played by aristocratic models of behaviour in France and in England, this is not true of Germany. Here the situation is simply too complex. Much has been written on the social history of Germany, but not enough attention has been paid to the widely differing circumstances obtaining in the small states that came together to form the Reich, or to the individual characteristics of the free cities, for example, those in the once-powerful Hanseatic League. In *Buddenbrooks* Thomas Mann stresses the difference between the life-styles

of the Lübeck bourgeoisie and of their counterparts in
Munich. Their backgrounds were very different. For two
hundred years Lübeck had been at the head of the League,
and this was the factor that shaped its history. For reasons
of safety, the Hanseatic merchants travelled in large groups
from town to town over the large area extending from the
lower Rhine to Dorpat and Novgorod, and thus diffused
certain cultural traits which in the three hundred years of the
League's existence came to be stabilised and generalised.
There was one period when the morality of the Hanseatic
merchants was rigorous enough to anticipate the later
excesses of Puritanism. Strict rules governed the impeccable
quality of the merchandise and of the money printed for use
by League members. In their communal wanderings, a sort
of comradely bond was established among the merchants,
and this is probably the reason why they themselves were
strictly forbidden to advertise their goods. At the big fairs,
all League goods were displayed as a joint enterprise, and no
one merchant was allowed to extol his wares to the detriment
of his colleague's.[31] Thorough investigation of the development of bourgeois moral attitudes in the cities belonging to
the Hanseatic League is overdue – and this is only one of a
number of promising themes in connection with the development of bourgeois thought in the territory where a united
Germany was later to take shape.

Another factor that helped to give the German bourgeoisie
its peculiar character was the exclusiveness of the German
aristocracy: an exclusiveness outdoing anything known in
England or even in France, and which was particularly
marked in the case of the Prussian Junkers, who did not even
look like other people. Hence, the belief that in Germany
we find bourgeois culture in a purer form than anywhere
else has gained widespread credence. German bourgeois
tragedy of the eighteenth century shows us a bourgeoisie
which, far from imitating the nobility, sets itself up against
it. In Lessing's *Emilia Galotti*, Odoardo, Emilia's father,
harks back to a Roman exemplar when he stabs his daughter
to save her from falling victim to the wiles of a corrupt
prince. The princely court portrayed in Schiller's *Kabale und
Liebe* is equally corrupt, and it is offset by the simple, upright

family of the humble musician. If the German bourgeois tended to over-compensate, this was, according to some students of the subject, because they knew that more exalted social spheres were closed to them. Hence, too, the nineteenth-century cult of personality; the bourgeois who could not assume a feudal aura, became an 'individual', someone who mattered.[32]

For all the special nature of the German free cities, however, by the time we come to the twentieth century we can discern that same fusion of aristocratic and bourgeois elements which we find in the Forsytes. The classic example is provided by Thomas Mann in his great novel *Buddenbrooks*.

Since 1786 the Buddenbrook family has been running a grain business in Lübeck (Mann's home town). The family had profited richly from supplying grain to the Prussian army in 1813, and could thus move into a house grand enough to be worthy of the city-fathers of Lübeck (once the foremost city of the Hanseatic League). The cult of the family, which is at the same time the cult of the business, is deeply rooted in the Buddenbrook psyche, and again, as in the case of the Forsytes, the need for male heirs to carry on both family and business is felt as keenly as it would be in aristocratic circles. The family chronicle is solemnly recorded in an ornate volume which is taken with due reverence from its hiding place when required. The regular practice is for the eldest son to inherit the firm's seal. Any emotional attachment likely to lower the family tone is promptly stifled: thus, when Tonia has a harmless holiday romance with a medical student, she breaks it off, knowing that she is bound to put her family, and what they expect of her, first. Thomas Buddenbrook surrounds himself with everything that is aristocratic and elegant. In his desire for personal distinction he falls in no way short of the scions of aristocratic families; although, for Buddenbrook, 'distinction' is based on very different values. Like Soames Forsyte, he cannot bear to have a grain of dust on his clothes. His obsession with sartorial perfection serves to support his morale during a nervous breakdown. The senators of Lübeck value the charm and the aristocratic lightness of touch which he brings to business matters. This lightness of touch is very far removed from frivolity, but aristocratic models have not been without influence on its nurture in Buddenbrook circles. Thomas's sister, Tonia, has a hopeful eye firmly fixed on the aristocracy: 'What a stroke of luck – to be called von Schilling!' she exclaims about one of her school-friends, the daughter of a landed aristocrat. What Thomas Buddenbrook cannot stand about the aristocracy is its pride and arrogance, and he has nothing but contempt for the aristocrat's failure to manage money and stay out of debt. Faced with financial ruin, the aristocrat can think of nothing better to do than commit suicide, says Thomas derisively, when Ralf von Maiboom does away with himself, after being forced by his circumstances to sell Thomas his standing corn.

But the established bourgeois who resent the arrogance of the aristocracy behave with precisely the same arrogance towards bourgeois *nouveaux riches*. The Buddenbrook family looks down on the Hagenströms, who have come to town rather recently and have made their pile very quickly. Tonia barely acknowledges them in passing. In these bourgeois families a *mésalliance* can disrupt family bonds, for family solidarity is not so much a general obligation covering all the members of a family as a determinate obligation towards those members of the family who have not become *déclassé*. The marriage of Gotthold Buddenbrook to 'a shop-girl' excludes him from the inmost family circle, though even *déclassé* relations are invited on festive occasions.

The Buddenbrooks saga brings vividly to life some of the theories on 'the spirit of capitalism' discussed in Chapter 6 of this book.[33] When Tonia marries Permaneder and goes with him to the Catholic city of Munich, she is greatly struck by the totally different attitude to life she finds there. In Munich, it seems, people are not too concerned about making money, as long as they can enjoy themselves. Permaneder is a hop merchant: when courting Tonia he tells her: 'Munich is no commercial town. Everybody wants his peace and quiet and his beer; nobody gets dispatches while he's eating – not there.' Once they are married and Permaneder is safely in possession of Tonia's dowry, he horrifies his bride, who is still dreaming of social preferment, by telling her: 'I don't care about scraping money together. I want my comfort. I quit tomorrow and go into private life.' Here is the *rentier* spirit killing the capitalist spirit stone dead in a Catholic city! Grist for Weber's mill, with a vengeance. And elsewhere, as if at Weber's request, Mann writes: 'Thomas Buddenbrook had played now and then throughout his life with an inclination to Catholicism. But he was at bottom, none the less, the born Protestant: full of the true Protestant's passionate, relentless sense of personal responsibility. No, in the ultimate things there was, there could be no help from outside, no mediation, no absolution, no soothing syrup, no panacea.' According to Weber it was precisely such people who made lots of money!

In his *Zarys współczesnej literatury polskiej* ('Sketch of Contemporary Polish Literature'), published in 1951, which covers the years from 1884 to 1925, K. Wyka describes *Buddenbrooks* as a typical product of the twilight of the bourgeoisie, a funereal *roman fleuve* similar to Dąbrowska's *Nocy i dni* ('Nights and Days') which, as Wyka puts it, closes the tomb on the still warm cadavers. But the eclipse of one bourgeois family and its replacement by another was a phenomenon not entirely unknown in earlier centuries. In 1777 we find a citizen of Bordeaux in his *Apologie du commerce* bewailing the lack of commercial dynasties: the reason being that sons who inherit fortunes cease trading and lead lives of luxury and ease.[34] This is exactly what happens in *Buddenbrooks*. The Kröger dynasty to which Thomas Buddenbrook's mother belongs comes to an end with the son who is not interested in running a business and prefers to spend his money; while the elder Krögers are unable, because of their upper-class manners, to adapt themselves to a new situation. This is a danger threatening merchant families to which Defoe had already drawn attention. The place of the Krögers and the Buddenbrooks is taken by the *nouveau riche* Hagenström family, and it is they who move into the splendid residence built by Thomas Buddenbrook when the family home in the Mengenstrasse had ceased to satisfy him. Galsworthy could depict the Victorian era as a decline and fall; in Mann we are aware of a process of change, of shifting power, rather than of finalities.[35]

Gotthold Buddenbrook's marriage to 'the shopgirl', and

later, the somewhat dubious nature of Christian's emotional impulses, have let the family down socially and have impaired its unity and power; and the harm wrought by love (to use Galsworthy's idealist language) is taken a stage further by a novel attitude to the fine arts. Thomas's family falls apart after his sudden death in 1875 because his wife prefers playing the violin to bringing up children; and his only son, had he not been carried off by typhus, would have gone on listening to Bach fugues and hating with an innate hatred everything to do with his father's counting-houses. Many merchant families end up in similar fashion, and if we limit ourselves to the merchant's point of view we can see this as a decline and fall; though of course, from another point of view, composing fugues can be seen as a clear advance on selling corn.

When Thomas Buddenbrook comes to Ralf von Maiboom to buy grain, the nobleman receives this powerful city father, the senator of a great free city, with ostentatious discourtesy, not even asking him to sit down – which infuriates Thomas so much that he seats himself no less aggressively on the nobleman's writing desk. It is a scene that brings home to us the absolute nature of the German aristocracy: this could never have happened in the second half of the nineteenth century in England or France. But even then the barrier dividing the bourgeoisie from the aristocracy was being breached by the great industrialists of imperial Germany. The families of industrial barons were adorning their surnames with 'von' and maintaining costly castles in their country estates. Examples of these, looking like the strongholds of feudal princes, can be seen in the Recovered Territories (areas recovered by Poland after 1945 – Trans.).

Many an anecdote bears witness to the way in which the bourgeois colonists who went to build a new world in the virgin lands of America clung affectionately to tradition, and this is a subject which deserves special study. Miriam Beard says that since Americans cannot themselves have family trees, they like to be surrounded by pedigree dogs and cats which serve as mute courtiers. In 1898, 134 married couples descended from aristocratic forebears contributed to the export from America to Europe of the enormous sum of 170 million dollars in the form of dowries.[36] From Europe to America went antiques and the stones of ancient castles to be reassembled in their original form in the New World.

To sum up: as I said at the beginning of this chapter, there are theoretically two ways in which relations between a victorious and a vanquished class can take shape: (1) the victorious class may take over the models of the class it has supplanted; (2) the defeated class may reject its own erstwhile models. The examples I have given in this chapter (which, of course, need further amplification) seem to suggest a third possibility: the gradual fusion of the models of both classes, in which case the models proper to the supplanted class will continue to exercise a certain attraction. We find examples of this even in bourgeois France, where the supplanted class was in fact stripped of all political weight.

Chapter 11

Some thoughts on methodology: the social conditioning of theories

1 Two concepts of 'interest'

More than once in the foregoing papers I have had occasion to use the concept of 'interest'. For example, when dealing with moral directives of the Franklin type, I pointed out that, by helping to enrich those who applied them, these directives 'served their interests'. In the chapter on Defoe we saw how Defoe derided the idea of being 'born a gentleman' and stressed instead those personal values which can be acquired in life: a modification of the 'gentlemanly' paradigm which was very much 'in the interests' of Defoe and his class. Again when discussing the likely effects of a belief in predestination, we tried to find out whether such a belief was really conducive to economic success, or whether it merely served the 'interests' of those who wanted to defend their own privileged position against the claims of the oppressed classes, and to allay their own moral scruples. And finally I suggested in Chapter 9 that if the French moralists of the Enlightenment were so vociferous in their hedonism, this was mainly because it was a useful weapon in their struggle against a religion which they saw as a bulwark of the social and political system they were out to destroy.

These considerations, whether offered here as an original contribution to the subject or borrowed from other writers, turn on the word 'interest'. It is a theme I have already dealt with in my *Motywy Postępowania*, where I analyse the concept of egoism and the exact meaning of 'being guided by one's own interests'. What follows is largely a development of ideas advanced in this earlier work.

'Interest', says Bentham in his *Introduction to the Principles*

336

of Morals and Legislation, 'is one of those words which not having any superior *genus,* cannot in the ordinary way be defined.'[1] By this, Bentham means that it cannot be defined in terms of Aristotelian logic, which requires concepts to be defined in terms of their immediately superior categories. However, the Aristotelian system of definition is not the only one, and there is no reason why we should not seek a definition even in the absence of *genus.* The difficulty is not that theoretical analysis is unable to cope with this concept: the difficulty lies rather in attempting to define this term *in isolation,* since it belongs to the rather large group of words which become meaningful only when they are used *in context.* So, instead of asking what the word 'interest' means, let us inquire what people mean when they say 'Bringing about a state of affairs Y is in the interest of X.'

The word itself has been in circulation for a very long time, but probably nowhere and at no time was it used so widely as in the years of the Enlightenment in France. The word *intérêt* was on everyone's lips. For Helvétius, it is the concept underlying all others. 'In the last resort,' we read in *De l'esprit,* 'everyone follows his own interest' – apparently a state of anarchy which Helvétius resolves by leaving it to the legislators in their wisdom to coordinate people's interests. 'Interest governs all our judgments', we read in the same work. 'Interest alone decides whether people will have respect or contempt for their customs, fashions and ways of thought.'

Like other eighteenth-century thinkers, Helvétius has a psychological approach to the concept of interest: in other words, 'interest' is 'subjective interest'. The statement that bringing about the state of affairs Y is in the interest of X is more or less equivalent to saying that X wants Y. X wants Y because he hopes or believes that in this way he will experience pleasure, or, at least, avoid pain. Our interests are channelled by our wishes: in the final analysis, by our passions. The article on 'Intérêt' in the *Grande Encyclopédie* avoids those pejorative uses of the word which are bound up with 'des idées d'avarice et de bassesse'. Acting in one's own interests can lead to doing good as well as to doing harm. The same line is taken by Helvétius and other writers of the period. Helvétius writes: 'The commonality (*le vulgaire*) limits the use of the word "interest" to one thing alone – the love of money; the enlightened reader will realise that I use this word in a wider sense, and that I apply it in a general sense to whatever may afford us pleasure or spare us unpleasantness.'[2] Of course, such a theory must contain a streak of egoism; for if one is governed entirely by self-interest, then, in the event of a clash of interests, those of other people must be sacrificed to one's own.

The psychological approach underlies attempts – e.g. opinion polls and questionnaires – to ascertain what people do, in fact, want: that is, what their interests are. An opinion poll conducted in an over-crowded, stuffy and smoke-filled room would probably elicit the unanimous response that the window should be opened, and we could infer that it would be in the interests of the occupants to have more air. We have the same psychological approach in mind when we say that it was in the interests of the bourgeoisie to hoodwink the lower classes and justify bourgeois privileges *vis-à-vis* these classes and themselves. We say so on the basis of a certain tacit empirical generalisation which asserts that in a society where there are privileged classes and oppressed classes, everyone belonging to the privileged classes *wants* to retain these privileges, *wants* to feel secure in so doing and does *not want* to be troubled by any qualms of conscience in connection with them. In other words, interests are here ascertained on the basis of presumed wishes. These wishes are held to be normally stable, and the tendency to indulge in them forms part of human nature.[3]

The psychological interpretation of interest dominated the thought of the age of liberalism. Bentham advocated suffrage for all, including women, because he believed that all of us are equal in the sense that all of us are capable of experiencing pain and pleasure; and since each individual is the best judge of what gives him pain or pleasure, he is also the best judge of what is *in his interest* – so everyone should have the right to vote. The conviction that each individual knows best what he wants and what he needs, led to state interference in the life of the private citizen being reduced to a minimum. This *laissez-faire* policy went so far, that Spencer was able to voice his doubts as to whether the state had the right to decree compulsory schooling.

But another concept of interest makes its appearance in Bentham – the concept of enlightened interest which has come to be known as the concept of *objective* interest. According to this way of thought, people are often not clearly aware of what is in their interests and a decision has to be made on their behalf. The person qualified to do this is he who knows what is in their interests as *properly understood*. This approach, which is particularly characteristic of the decline of liberalism, opens the door to tutelary activity on behalf of others without consulting them, or even in flat contradiction of their wishes; the stock exemplar here is parental activity *vis-à-vis* children. The formula changes. The statement 'bringing about the state of affairs Y is in the interest of X' does not mean 'X wants Y', but rather 'Y is good for X': and furthermore, in this formula, 'for X' does *not* mean 'in the opinion of X', since there will be cases when the freely expressed opinion of X will not be available. In a backward country where women are degraded and exploited, the social reformer who is fighting *in their interests* for the right to vote, to be economically independent, and to choose the calling in life they wish to follow, does not do so after consultation with those concerned. He would continue to press for these reforms, even if it was made clear to him that most women in the country acquiesced in their way of life and were quite content to keep the home and look after the children, leaving the men to run other things. Similarly, we hold in general that learning to read and write is in the interests of the illiterate even if the latter do everything possible to avoid acquiring such skills. In such cases, X's wishes are neither necessary nor sufficient for the identification of what is in X's interests: the hierarchy of values to which appeal is made need not be checked against such factors. When we say that the right to elect and be elected, economic independence and free choice of vocation are 'in the interests' of women, all that means is that, with reference to the human exemplar we have in mind, women ought to have equal entitlement.[4]

It might be objected that this concept of interest is itself psychological, the only difference being that the wish signal-ling interest is now conditional. A woman *would want* the right to vote, etc., *if* she did not have a slave mentality, *if* she had self-respect and ambition. In this conditional framework, 'wishes' are imputed or presumed, in the light of a control system of values external to those to whom it is applied. The reformer who is fighting 'in the interests of women' may try to arouse these wishes in women, if only in order to secure their help in his efforts; but the crucial point is that he would continue his campaign even if he failed to open their eyes to values which are, in the final analysis, *his* values.

Disagreement may also arise with regard to the means employed to reach certain jointly agreed aims. For example, two workers may be agreed on the need to fight exploitation, but may disagree on the best way to go about this. In these circumstances the claim 'I know what to do in your interests' is a claim to deeper understanding of certain factual relations. If we are agreed on the factual relations, we may still disagree over values. For example, I may convince someone that smoking cigarettes is harmful to health, and that it will be in his interest to give it up. I am then expressing the value judgment that health is more valuable than the pleasure we get from smoking. But if the other person says, 'OK, so I'll not live so long but I'm enjoying myself,' there is really nothing I can say. All I can do is give the helpless shrug which is our customary response when we come into conflict with an alien system of values. It took a rise in wages to make the European who accepted the scale of values of the capitalist era work harder 'in his own interest'. How different from medieval man who, when he earned more, reduced his hours of work because, as he saw things, it was 'in his interest' to have, not more money, but more free time!

As I said, the concept of 'interest properly understood' runs parallel to the psychological concept of interest, though from time to time either may predominate. Bentham was sagacious enough to identify in morality those fictions created by man in order to invest himself with authority and the right to impose his will on others – such fictions as the word of God, revelation, natural law, moral sense, common sense, etc. – and it is instructive to find him adding a fiction of his own to this catalogue: 'interest as properly understood'.

I think we have to appreciate that both our psychological and our objective concepts of interest may prove to be too generalised to cover certain everyday intuitions. It is all very well to identify a congruence of interests and wishes; but can we ignore the object of these wishes? As I see it, if X desires a state of affairs Y, the realisation of that state of affairs is in X's interest. But suppose X wants Z to win the pools? Indeed, it would give X the very greatest pleasure if Z won the pools – but we do not then say that Z's win is in X's interest. In everyday usage, doing what is 'in one's interests' is bound up with concern for one's own self, and is indeed restricted to certain personal ends. I have dealt with this elsewhere[5] and do not propose to pursue the subject here.

It is worth our while, however, to consider certain distinctions which may help us to identify conflict of interests on the one hand, and agreement of interests on the other.

Linking interests with wishes, as the psychological concept of interest does, seems to founder in situations in which the wishes of two beings are in agreement while their interests are contrary, and vice versa. I am thinking of cases where an identity of wishes leads to a conflict of interests; or where concurrence of interests is bound up with disagreement of wishes. As an example of the former, let us imagine two dogs fighting over the same bone, or two rival suitors chasing the same woman. Or take the case of the crocodile which welcomes the bird that picks food from its teeth: their interests are the same, though their wishes are very different. The crocodile wants to get its teeth cleaned; the bird fills its stomach by playing the part of toothpick.

But a moment's reflection on these examples will be enough to restore the apparently disrupted parallelism of wishes and interests. Two dogs fighting over the same bone may appear at first sight to have the same wish – to get the bone. But Rover's real wish is that he, Rover, should get the bone, not Scottie: and vice versa. The same goes for the two rival suitors. Their wishes 'converge' as it were, by centring round one and the same object. This convergence makes it appear as though one and the same wish were present in both cases. In reality, however, these wishes are mutually exclusive as regards their simultaneous realisation; consequently, the parallelism between wishes and interests is preserved, and so is the possibility of defining the latter in terms of the former. In the case of the crocodile and the bird, the wishes are divergent, and the interests, while common, are also divergent – so once again wishes and interests are on the same track.

So a conflict of interests may on occasion be interpreted as a conflict of wishes; again, itmay represent the mutual exclusion of two non-psychological facts; at other times it may represent a combination of these two possibilities.[6] It is not difficult to find examples of this third type. Such a conflict arises, for example, between the tourist who has come to the mountains for a holiday and naturally wants fine weather, and the local farmers who are desperate for rain after a long drought. As I have pointed out elsewhere,[7] the factual conflict between the interests of X and Z is not necessarily linked to a conflict of wishes. Even if they both discern the factual conflict, one of them may be generous enough to render the psychological conflict avoidable. In the psychological sense, conflicts of interest may arise against a background of similar or dissimilar scales of value, of similar or dissimilar partialities. An example of this latter possibility arises in the case of two rivals for the hand of the same woman: they cannot both marry her. Here the conflict is decided, not by the nature of the desires involved but by the indivisibility of the object of these desires.

A coincidence of interests is also open to various interpretations. According to the psychological concept, interests are, as we have seen, not always in agreement when human wishes converge: that is to say, when they are directed towards the same object. So the argument that, because of the uniformity of human nature, there is a certain basic unity of interest among human beings, does not receive the support we might expect from such a uniformity. In the psychological sense, the interests of X and Z are in agreement when X's wishes do not include the wish that Z's wishes should *not* be fulfilled; and they are in agreement in the objective sense when the attainment of a certain object by X does not exclude, or even promotes, Z's chances of attaining some other object. The classical exponents of Liberalism believed in both of these forms of agreement of interest. Adam Smith saw this agreement as a gift from a beneficent nature, while others saw it as not always inborn but attainable thanks to the efforts of a wise legislator (Bentham). It has often been pointed out that belief in concurrence of interest serves to alleviate the consciences of egoists who are only too ready to subscribe to the doctrine that 'all will be well in the world when each of us sweeps his own backyard'. With reference to this concurrence, Spencer urged people to work for the good of others and not just for themselves, stressing that it is in everyone's interest to reduce the incidence of disease from which no one is safe; to increase human productivity so that each of us may gain thereby; to enhance people both morally and mentally, for how greatly do we all suffer from human perfidy and human stupidity.

Since goods can be arranged in various hierarchies – by subordination of means to ends, or by subordination of less important to more important items – conflict may arise on different levels, whereby disagreement on lower levels may coexist with agreement on more important things, and vice versa. The fight against exploitation in a capitalist society unites workers as their basic interest, but this does not exclude the possibility of conflict among workers on issues of less importance. For example, it is in the interest of miners to get more pay in their industry; but this involves a rise in the cost of heating and lighting which will adversely affect the rest of the working class, which is bound together by common interests of a higher order – the category to which class interests usually belong. It can also happen that the realisation of lesser and more ephemeral interests may obstruct the realisation of basic aims, as in the case of 'opium for the masses'. In general, it may be said that religion comforts the masses by promising them a measure of justice in the world to come; and this is *in their interest*, in so far as it is in anyone's interest to be comforted in hardship and suffering. Nevertheless, this extempore alleviation obscures and impedes the fundamentally important business of fighting exploitation.

2   Interest as a formative element in the shaping of social conditions

I remarked at the outset that if we describe an ideology as 'bourgeois' we may be referring to its origins in a bourgeois milieu or to its diffusion in such a milieu; and equally the adjective may indicate that the ideology in question serves the interests of the bourgeoisie, or is an expression of bourgeois attitudes. In what follows, we shall consider these last two cases. Exposure of the interests at stake has often served to identify a particular ideology as class-based; but there is more to it than that. The content of this or that doctrine has frequently been explained by appeal to the personal interest of the author, or to the interest of some grouping which is not a class in the strict Marxist sense. We may recall Callicles in Plato's *Gorgias*, who asserts that the weak have formulated the laws in their own interest. Realising that they must protect themselves against the strong, they have concocted the notion that it is 'bad' and 'unjust' to try to get more property than others, and that it is better to endure wrong than to inflict it. Thrasymachus in the *Republic* is guided by the same line of thought when he asserts that it is always the ruling party which decides in its own interests what is just and what unjust. 'Every government lays down laws for its own advantage . . . in laying down these laws they have made it plain that what is to their advantage is just. They punish him who departs from this as a law-breaker and an unjust man.'[8] In his *Fable of the Bees* Mandeville develops Thrasymachus' thesis, showing that morality is imposed on society by those who wish to govern it, the more easily to lead people by the nose. Making skilful use of human lethargy, they persuade citizens to perform various services for the state – even to sacrifice their lives for it. Scientific literature is full of unattributed observations of this sort: the claim, for example, that, in various cultures, models of feminine virtue – recommending purity, fidelity, submissiveness, industriousness, have served the interests of the men who propagate such models; or that the norms regulating relations between older and younger age groups are drawn up by the former in the light of their own interests.

The interests underlying the formulation and the promulgation of any particular doctrine have not always been recognised as economic in nature. Recognising man's urge for power as something fundamental and essential in his make-up, Hobbes writes: 'For I doubt not, but if it had been a thing contrary to any man's right of dominion, or to the interest of men that have dominion, that the three angles of a triangle should be equal to two angles of a square; that doctrine should have been, if not disputed, yet by the burning of all books of geometry, suppressed, as far as he whom it concerned was able.'[9]

Elucidation of a thesis and identification of its social genealogy in terms of 'interest' acquired particular force in connection with the interpretation of ideologies as superstructures for hidden economic interests of a class character. Lenin wrote: 'People always have been the foolish victims of deception and self-deception in politics, and they always will be until they have learnt to seek out the interests of some class or other behind all moral, religious, political and social phrases, declarations and promises.'[10] The principle of '*is fecit, cui prodest*' acquired a new lease of life.

Holding as it does that in the final analysis it is always economic interest that counts, Marxist exegesis does not always find it necessary to point this out *explicite* when analysing any given doctrine. The social dimension (function) of a doctrine is sometimes delineated with reference to the fact that such and such a class may find it of use in the takeover of power, or in maintaining itself in power; sometimes again with reference to the fact that it may be of help in the subjugation of oppressed classes or in stifling one's own moral qualms.

A favourite weapon in the armoury of those who actually hold power and intend to hold on to it is the notion of order. Those in power identify 'order' as the state of affairs obtaining under their rule; by the same token, those who oppose their rule are identified as 'trouble-makers'. Those in power are the custodians of 'public order'. Since any 'order' is order relative to the principles governing any given structure of relations, a *general* concept of order is not easily derivable from such contingent structures. In the cases germane to our thesis, the concept of order is absolutised by treating a contingent base as though it were invariant and permanent.

Kautsky treats the doctrine of free will as one proper to the privileged classes since, in his opinion, it bolsters up their rule by letting them sit in judgment on 'reprobates'. Kant opts for an intermediate position on the free will issue, allowing it in the noumenal realm but denying it in the phenomenal realm: a compromise which Kautsky dismisses as typical of Kant's intermediate social position.[11]

Perfectionist doctrines, again, as has often been pointed out, serve the quietism of the privileged classes very well by their inculcation of the notion that the best way to reform the world is to concentrate on self-improvement. By distracting attention from social reform, such ideologies help to consolidate the privileged classes in their bastions. At the same time, they help to salve the consciences of those who may well feel uneasy *vis-à-vis* social injustice, but who have no real reason to wish for any change in the situation.

The sermons of John Wesley, who founded the Methodists in England in the eighteenth century, attracted countless multitudes of the faithful; and reading these sermons today we can see very clearly how his doctrine of service helped the rich to salve their consciences and justify their privileges *vis-à-vis* the underdogs. True to the spirit of the age, Wesley urges people to make money, but at the same time reminds his listeners to see themselves as dispensers of a good which serves the general public – a doctrine of 'service' which big American industrialists had every reason to endorse.

Closely similar to theories which help to entrench privileged position and justify it both to oneself and to others, are theories which hold that the poor have always been with us, there will always be rich and poor, poverty is not shameful, the greatest good is a pure heart, man's happiness depends entirely on his spiritual values, etc., etc. In the same light we may see Spencer's theory which compares social life *per analogiam* with the life of an organism, in which every organ fulfils a specific function in its allotted sphere: a view which stabilises the existing order of things in favour of the privileged.

3   Human artefacts as pointers to their social matrix

'Depending on whether a given social class is in the ascendancy, at its peak or in decline, its moral teachings will express its rebellion, its self-justification or its regrets,' wrote Roger Garaudy in *Le Communisme et la moralité*.[12] In other words, we should be able to infer something about the nature of an ideology from inspection of its modalities, its ways of expression. Here again, we are dealing with something that has a long historical tradition behind it; and the contribution of Marxism has been simply to widen the field of reference by treating modes of expression as class-based rather than individual. Seneca's stoicism was formerly held to express an attitude which was natural enough at a time when Nero's tyranny spelled personal danger for anyone. Marxist analysis of Stoicism sees in it rather the expression of the pessimism and resignation that engulfed members of the Roman *nobilitas* in the days of its decline and fall.

Existentialism is usually seen as an ideology made to measure for quietists. The man who has no wish to get himself embroiled on either side of the barricades, who refuses to take any responsibility for the way things are going, will find it appropriate to proclaim the absurdity of all human action. But there is another way of looking at existentialism; it can also be seen as expressing the sombre mood of the declining bourgeoisie. The same goes for conventionalism in the theory of knowledge. As S. Żółkiewski wrote in *Kuźnica*: 'A lack of confidence in their knowledge was imposed on the middle class by their social position between pauperisation on the one hand and the prospect of a proletarian revolution on the other.' And further: 'The conventionalist attitude to general propositions is a metaphysical persuasion unsupported by reason; it is the expression of the agnosticism, the social and ideological helplessness of the middle classes in an age of imperialism. Conventionalism is an appropriate expression of their instability and indecision.'¹³ In Żółkiewski's opinion, it was in these circumstances that the culture of anxiety, despair, uncertainty and nescience was born.

Formalism in art has been often described as an expression of the dying bourgeoisie. Realising that their own demise is inevitable, they turn their faces away from reality; and painting without objective content is one result. In literature, we are asked to see the same tendency expressed in 'psychologism', the recollection of one's own sensations, the morbid dissection of subtle conflicts in one's own inner life.

We need not multiply examples. It is the form of reasoning that interests us, not the veracity or otherwise of the thesis. More than once in this book, I have used similar methods. Thus I have suggested that the Parnassianism of Matthew Arnold (see Chapter 2) was the expression of a tendency to screen oneself off from the lower social classes who were then gaining steadily in importance. And I agree with those who suggest that the nineteenth-century bourgeois drive for respectability was the expression of a need for prestige gained by means other than birth.

The human products, the artefacts which are the expression of certain attitudes and tendencies (as in our last example), also serve the interests of the producers (it is undeniable that prestige serves the interests of those who enjoy prestige). Accordingly, for any given doctrine, we shall find that its expressive functions (as thus construed) will mesh very closely with its functions as mapped according to the interest theory – after all, they are two sides of the same coin. The splendours of the Baroque churches may embody the triumph of the Jesuits; they also served as a means of impressing the masses. That is to say, the expression of an attitude served certain interests. On the other hand, the cosmopolitanism of the Greek Stoics, which is held to represent attitudes connected with the break-up of the old social bonds of the *polis*, served no explicit interest of the Stoics.

4 Difficulties besetting these methods

Methodologically, these arguments run up against certain difficulties, and in this final section we shall consider some of them.

(a) The methods we have been concerned with in this context are generally regarded as belonging to a sociological way of thought which seeks to assign any view or ideology under investigation to a temporally and spatially determined base. But we must not forget that all of the characteristics we have identified *assume* certain psychological premises which tend to be overlooked in the course of an elliptical argument. For example, we would not look for a hidden economic interest in the minds of those who, when they need labour, proclaim the virtues of industriousness, if we did not have a certain preconception of man as a being belonging to more than one category. Other examples are provided by the proposition that every normal man looks after his own economic interests, and the proposition that he does so at least in a class society.

Where interest is not explicitly economic interest, these propositions may take another form. We have seen the concept of order described as one serving those who hold power. This statement assumes the proposition that all men want power, and the proposition that when they have it they try to keep it. If we see opium for the masses in the teaching that happiness does not depend on money but exclusively on one's own spiritual values, or in the doctrine that economic success is the reward for one's own efforts, and the pauper has merely got what he deserves – in both cases we are assuming that all men share a tendency to entrench themselves in privilege. And if we see in the doctrine of social service espoused by so many big American industrialists nothing more than a way of allaying their own moral scruples, then we are assuming that people do not like their peace of mind to be upset by the hardships of others and therefore seek moral sedatives. Thus, while accepting as starting point the proposition that at any given time human attitudes and human products are conditioned by a concrete historical class milieu, we still have to make assumptions regarding the psychological concomitants: assumptions whose own social conditioning cannot be investigated beyond a certain critical point.

Theoretically, both the concepts of interest which were discussed earlier in this chapter – the psychological and the objective – can be used to track down the origins of such and such a doctrine. We reject the psychological one in favour of the objective one when, for example, we are persuaded that the theoretical or artistic work of such and such an author shows no trace of the wishes the former would ascribe to him. Anyone who thinks that Descartes's interest in mathematics is attributable to his preference for an infallible form of secular knowledge *vis-à-vis* revelation – a preference which would be in the interest of the up-and-coming bourgeoisie – will not relinquish this view even if the critics persuade him that no trace of any such wish is to be found in Descartes's works. The concept of objective interest allows us to identify the interests at stake without going into the question of the psychological concomitants. A reduction in, if not the total abolition of, the role of divine revelation was certainly in the interests of a bourgeoisie which was striving to rid itself of such remnants of feudalism as still barred its way forward. Descartes may have served these interests without being himself aware of so doing. Obviously it remains to be explained *why* one should act along the lines of one's own objective interests if one is not aware of them. This is a difficulty which does not arise when we operate with the concept of subjective interest which is always firmly underwritten in the shape of human wishes.

Psychological generalisations similar to those that turn up when we use the concept of interest to identify the social character of an ideology, reappear when we appeal to the expressive function of human artefacts for the same purpose. Those who see in the figure of the Renaissance *condottiere* the characteristic exemplar of the drive for expansion of the individual, are making an assumption which runs more or less as follows: people who have been tied down for a long time want to let off steam. Those who see in the Stoicism of Seneca not only insurance and comfort very understandable in the days of Nero, but also the expression of a pessimism characteristic of the twilight of Roman *nobilitas*, are assuming something which common sense puts as follows: people who are about to lose their social position are not exactly overjoyed. The same thing happens when we treat existentialism and conventionalism as philosophies of despair concocted by a moribund bourgeoisie. And when we construe the formalism of abstract art and the psychological fiction of the twentieth century as 'flight from reality' we are postulating that people who apprehend their approaching demise and don't know what to do about it close their eyes to the dangers looming up. This again is a psychological postulate of wide general application.

(b) Researchers have in general dismissed such psychological postulates as homespun truisms not worth mentioning in handbooks of psychology. They appear to be self-evident, as Engels's remarks on man in general appear to be self-evident: 'mankind must first of all eat, drink, have shelter and clothes before it can pursue politics, science, art, religion, etc.'.[14] In their general formulation they are, however, not always convincing. To say that people are 'always guided by self-interest' is to express an opinion which may well serve as a basis for discussion, as long as the word 'interest' is not interpreted in such a way as to reduce the whole proposition to a tautology. The same goes for the proposition that if you have been held in check for a long time, you will want to let off steam, let yourself go, when finally off the hook; it is very possible that after long suppression you are no longer capable of letting yourself go. If these propositions are formulated with the requisite precision to make them not general but particular propositions, it turns out that they are then applicable to specific sets of circumstances only. No one has taken the trouble to point this out because, as I said, no one seems to have noticed the elliptical nature of the argument and of the implicit propositions, mainly of a general nature, embedded in it.

These propositions tend as a rule to be extrapolations to classes and nations of observations made in the field of *individual* psychology. Thus, in a paper on 'Narodziny wielkiej kultury' ('The origins of great culture')[15] S. Czarnowski has contrasted the worldly civilisation of Greece with the religious culture of Israel, a culture completely taken up with the relationship between God and man; and has suggested that the Hebraic obsession with religion was bound up with their political situation. With their territorial independence threatened from two quarters, the Israelites enlisted Jehovah as an ally. The behaviour of a whole nation is here seen in terms of observations made in the field of individual psychology and summed up in such sayings as 'Seek God in your hour of need.' In this particular case, the transition from individual to national level is perhaps not too far-fetched; but in many cases the extrapolation is far more questionable.

(c) Let us accept that the general validity of a psychological assumption used with reference to a given ideology or doctrine is not in doubt. We have then to decide whether the assumption is properly used in the given case. This exercise is complicated by the fact that one and the same doctrine may serve different interests, and that identical human products may be the expression of differing attitudes and differing mental states.

The fact that one and the same doctrine may serve different – indeed, on occasion, mutually antagonistic – interests, is so well known that it hardly needs stating. 'The up-and-coming class sings the praises of progress', says Garaudy with reference to the eighteenth-century bourgeoisie.[16] But this same belief in progress is characteristic of nineteenth-century bourgeois ideology as well: that is to say, of a bourgeoisie which was no longer in its first flush of success. At times, doctrines serving different interests only *appear* to be identical. For example, the proletariat too started out with a belief in progress: but this progress was not based on the bourgeois scale of values. Not that such distinctions can be discerned in the concepts of progress entertained by the bourgeoisie, whether of the eighteenth or the nineteenth century.

The thesis that the development of societies is determined by certain laws has been used both by victorious classes to extinguish hope in vanquished classes (e.g. the French bourgeoisie proclaimed this doctrine after the Revolution) and, with equal success, to encourage the rise of the proletariat. Slogans about personal human rights are used by representatives of a threatened class in their own defence, and by those who are threatening them. A theory which appears to substantiate the inheritance of acquired characteristics may serve the interests of a dynamic class which wants to believe in the possibility of limitless transformation of its environment; but the same theory was used in the nineteenth century to stabilise a hierarchic social structure, by those who held privileged positions in that society. As then construed, the 'theory' laid down that the son of a manual worker had to be a manual worker instead of becoming a doctor, for example; while the doctor's son could reasonably hope to do better than his father in this calling simply because of his inheritance. Probably the most versatile of all theories has been that of evolution, variously drawn upon for their own purposes by people as different as *avant-garde* groups on the one hand and Adolf Hitler on the other.

The same sort of problems arise when we treat human products and artefacts as symptomatic of certain attitudes or frames of mind. The Biedermeier style in interior decoration is usually regarded as typical of cosy bourgeois quietism; the successful bourgeois could relax in domestic bliss in such surroundings, and this frame of mind was expressed in a liking for whatever was snug, personal and intimate. But people who feel threatened and insecure also long for secure and homely interiors. The stoicism of Epictetus was the expression of a slave's resignation to his fate – but it was with a copy of Epictetus in his hand that Toussaint l'Ouverture, the leader of the San Domingo insurgents, went into battle to win freedom for his people. So again we see that one and the same teaching may serve widely differing interests.

In the course of this book we have come up against all of these difficulties. The only way to avoid them is to restrict ourselves to talking in terms of concurrence and coincidence, and *not* in terms of necessary connection. When Czarnowski points out that the development of Greek culture *coincided* with the transfer of trade supremacy from Miletus to Athens, he is making no claim of a psychological nature: nor does he need to, as long as he restricts himself to talking in terms of coincidences. But when he tries to *explain* these coincidences, psychology rears its head. It is alleged, for example, that it is only possible for a wider interest in art and science to develop once a population's basic needs have been satisfied; and that as cultural horizons are widened by the expansion of trade, mental horizons are also widened.

In the same way, as long as Ranulf (see Chapter 7 above) posited no more than a concurrence between the petty bourgeoisie's assumption of political power and a marked tendency to be rancorous and find fault with others, he had no need to venture into the terrain of psychology. But as soon as he tries to explain the concurrence, psychological factors enter the argument, for example in the shape of the assertion that obligatory financial restrictions sour the petty bourgeois character.

Any attempt to go beyond the identification of concurrences and coincidences in the description of historical phenomena is fraught with difficulties, but this is not to say that these difficulties must always be shirked. In this book I have tried to establish in certain cases a dependence between historical phenomena. In spite of the risks involved, the attempt seems worth while.

Chapter 12

Concluding survey

1 The type concept as an instrument of research

In the course of this book I have selected certain control or standard concepts as being of use in the sort of comparative study which is necessary if we are to succeed in identifying the laws – assuming that such laws exist – informing the development of the moral life. It is clear, of course, that such comparative study cannot stop at analogous *content*, and that we must also look for *functional* analogy or discrepancy. However, this does not detract from the importance of the control concept for heuristic analysis of the test area. In the Marxist classics we find several references to the value of the control concept for scientific research. As I said in Chapter 1, Engels was fond of illustrating his arguments with examples from the history of France because he saw France as a country where various constitutional and social forms existed at different times in a typical or 'classic' character. And in the last, unfinished chapter of *Capital* Marx spoke of contemporary England whose economic structure (*ökonomische Gliederung*) was of 'classical' purity though it was not yet accompanied by a pure form of class structure (*Klassengliederung*).

Appeal in scientific research to what is typical or standard is as old as science itself. Conscious use of this method as a heuristic instrument, however, is of very much later date; and only very recently have attempts been made to elaborate some sort of methodology for typological research. In his work 'Über einige Kategorien der verstehenden Soziologie', Max Weber drew attention to the role played by types as tools in the hands of the sociologist. As he puts it, when we speak of 'feudalism', or when we say that such and such a system is 'bureaucratic', we are thinking of certain *types*. Perhaps we can never hope to isolate and identify these types in their exact quiddity, in their crystal state as it were, and must content ourselves with a more or less close approximation. Often indeed these types gain in clarity the further removed they are from reality. And as their clarity increases, so does their classificatory and heuristic value as analytical tools.[1]

Weber's short paper was published in 1913. Since then there has appeared the valuable book by C. G. Hempel and P. Oppenheim, *Der Typusbegriff im Lichte der neuen Logik* (1936). So far, logic had sought to operate in inflexible and clinically precise concepts alone: concepts which admitted or excluded, with no third possibility. In their book, Hempel and Oppenheim tried to expand this rigid system by pointing to scientific practice: scientists operate successfully with more fluid concepts – for example, in typological research. Typological classification gives us a new taxonomy of reality. Given a certain control type, we can arrange objects according to their proximity to, or remoteness from, this type. This is standard practice in science, where what cannot yet be measured has to be typologically ordered: for example, minerals are ordered by hardness, the hardest mineral being taken as the one which will mark others while itself remaining unmarked. This particular ordering may well run to infinity, but science has plenty of closed orderings, e.g. that between two poles. To this group belongs the ordering of psycho-physical types in Kretschmer's typology, into schizoids and cycloids. Both classification systems (operating in inflexible concepts) and typological research (using more elastic concepts) proceed on the basis of certain laws; and two of these laws are to be carefully distinguished – the empirical laws of classification and of ordering ('klassifizierende und ordnende empirische Gesetze'). As a rule, these laws are applied tacitly and are only rarely formulated *explicite*. In both cases – i.e. in classification as in typological ordering – attention to these laws will decide whether the taxonomy is artificial or natural. An ordering of people by their sensitivity to having the soles of their feet tickled would be regarded as artificial simply because, in the present state of our knowledge, this property throws light on nothing else and can therefore be disregarded. Our reflexes to a blow on the knee, however, come under an altogether different heading.

The Hempel–Oppenheim book is full of interesting detail and examples, but we cannot go into them here. In Poland, it has been mainly art historians who have shown some interest in the theory of types, and they will find much food for thought in this book. In the light of its conclusions, Tatarkiewicz's division of science into nomological and typological departments becomes questionable. According to Tatarkiewicz, the function of the nomological sciences is to identify and formulate laws; that of the typological sciences is to identify types.[2] But since neither the classification nor the typological ordering of reality can dispense with some sort of codification, that is, with the formulation of 'laws', this is not a distinction which will bear critical examination.

In his 'O pojęciu typu w architekturze' ('On the concept of type in architecture')[3] Tatarkiewicz defines 'type' as follows: 'The type is the aggregate of visible qualities common to a group of comparable works of art. If we wish to avoid abstractions, we can define it in concrete terms as the average specimen of the group.' And S. J. Gąsiorowski writes in his 'Metoda typologiczna w badaniach nad sztuką' ('The typological method in art research'): 'The artistic type is the formal principle, the aggregate of formal factors repeating themselves or recurring in stable form in a given art.'[4] Without going into the content of these definitions for the present, I think that in any attempt to define 'type' it would be a step forward if we remember that we are not dealing with a constant but with a variable which has to be defined in terms of a particular context. To put it another way, if we try to define, not the word 'type' but such propositions as 'Object O belongs to type P', we shall avoid such undesirable formulations as 'the type is the formal principle', 'type is the aggregate of qualities', 'type is the norm', 'type is the average', etc., etc.

Perhaps this is as good a place as any to take a closer look at the concept of 'type'.

The distinction made by Hempel and Oppenheim between two ways of ordering reality – by classification, and by means of certain model or control concepts – is a valuable step forward; and even if the authors do not expressly refer to control concepts, this is clearly what they have in mind. In the light of this differentiation, various typologies, hitherto found wanting because of their failure to comply with classificatory postulates, find new hope of survival. The Kretschmer typology, for instance, has been attacked on the grounds that it is not exhaustive, and that it admits various hybrid transitional forms. But typology is not constrained to comply with the postulates of formal classification. It does not have to be either exhaustive or disjunctive. Classification consists in reducing larger units to smaller units without remainder. Not so in the case of typology. Here, the construction of a type from among the phenomena under examination is no more than a heuristic tool in the hands of the researcher. Kretschmer could have confined himself to describing the schizoid type, and this would have been of service to science provided that the same tool was then found to be of use in further research. The success that attended Kretschmer's typology was in part due to the fact that it offered something more substantial than the artificialities of Spranger's '*Lebensformen*'. And a clear understanding of the tasks that may legitimately be undertaken by this typology cuts the ground away from under the feet of those who object that pure schizoids and pure cycloids are rarely met with, in that provision is made for a whole series of graduated transitional forms occurring between these two poles.

In everyday usage, the word 'type' is used interchangeably with the words 'sort' and 'kind'. Anyone engaged in comparing churches on the basis of the relationship between the height of the nave and the height of the aisles, can speak of two 'types' or two 'kinds' of church – the basilica, where the aisles are lower than the nave, and that where both are the same height. Similarly, following Wölfflin, we may distinguish in the graphic arts (a) linear art, which emphasises contour and draughtsmanship, and (b) painting, which covers over the construction with blobs of colour: and we can talk in everyday language of two types or two kinds of art. In the complex and highly differentiated classifications of the natural sciences, lexical needs for sectional labelling turned out to be so great that virtually every word capable of functioning here was called into service. But from 'type' we can form the adjective 'typical' and this gives the word a special status not shared by 'kind', 'sort', etc., and marks it as suitable for specific use with reference to paradigms, control models, and so on. There are certain characteristics by means of which we distinguish negroes from other human beings; and the typical negro is the negro who (a) exhibits these characteristics to a greater degree than other negroes, or (b) has more of them, or (c) combines in his person (a) and (b). The same applies to the typical aristocrat or to typical scarlet fever. In this usage, the word 'type' is connected with 'ideal' or 'classic'. Marx is said to have referred to typical capitalism as 'ideal' capitalism,[5] and when analysing the concept of 'type' Max Weber adds the adjective 'ideal' in order to stress the model or exemplary nature of the concept. Every object belonging to a certain type comes under a certain general concept; but not every general concept includes this model or exemplary element. In Weber's usage, an ideal type is such because it subsumes certain traits particularly fully and particularly distinctly; but one can imagine taking as model not something which is found only rarely and, in its pure state perhaps not at all, but something which is much more common (though this, it seems to me, happens very rarely, at least in the arts and humanities). The most explicit treatment of the 'ideal' type is to be found in Hempel and Oppenheim, since this is the concept they chose as basis for the ordering process which they see as the task of typology. We may note here that the actual use of some object as 'model' often leads to its being subsequently recognised as 'typical': for example, the Gesù church in Rome, which has been widely copied in other European countries.

As regards the gradation of characteristics by means of which the ideal type is delineated – a gradation which allows us to order objects according to their degree of departure from the model – we have to remember that this can take place in two ways. Accepting that woolly hair, thick lips and black skin go to delineate the 'typical' negro, we can arrange negroes either on the basis of a progressive intensification of these characteristics (a procedure which Hempel and Oppenheim seem to have in mind when they talk of 'abstufbare Eigenschaftsbegriffe') or on the basis of the presence or absence of any of these key features. For example, the 'regulation' thick lips and black skin may be present, but the hair is straight. The presence of a maximum number of regulation features may serve as basis for the establishment of a type, and an associated gradation becomes possible. The question whether Fascism is in power in a country, and if so, in what degree, is approached by G. Degré as follows: he first defines Fascism by four main indices: (1) racism; (2) ethnocentrism centring on the conviction that one's own group is superior to all others; (3) the 'leader' principle; (4) something which the author calls anti-pluralism in the structure of the state, i.e. centralisation. With Fascism thus defined, says Degré, in cases where some but not all of these indices are present, it is possible to talk of milder forms of Fascism – of proto-Fascism, for example.[6]

It is the gradation that interests us here, not the content; but the example does suggest some further considerations on the genesis of typological concepts. It is usual for a concept enjoying model status to be distilled from observation and comparison. For example, it has been observed that in certain religious denominations professed at a given time, a certain life-style, which is independent of doctrinal differences, imposes itself: a life-style marked by asceticism, disapproval of pleasure and amusement, and a tendency to extend strict control over the lives of others. To this kind of morality the name 'puritanism' was given; and the life-style thus designated came to figure as a standard or control model *vis-à-vis* which the morality of other countries and times could be measured. As long as it is not actually treated as a model, it remains no more than a general concept, not a type in my sense of the word. My terminology would, it seems, suit the needs of Hempel and Oppenheim, who make it very clear indeed that one and the same general concept can be treated as just that – a general concept – or as a type, depending on the use made of it. As they see it, the concept of a schizoid can be an element in a typology just as well as in a classification.

Types may be the product of comparison, or they may be set up on the basis of a single specimen – though this is hardly possible except where future comparison is envisaged, and where there is therefore reason to believe that the characteristics of the specimen are recurrent. Thus, one may visualise feudalism as a certain type of formation on the basis of the relations which obtained in France; or Fascism on the basis of the relations obtaining in Mussolini's Italy. Here, the choice of characteristics to delineate a type is not guided by an already observed reiteration factor, but rather, in view of an anticipated reiteration factor, by the selection of basic traits to the exclusion of ephemeral ones: since it is the basic factors that determine the reiteration of the whole complicated phenomenon. By this token we may question Ranulf's proposal[7] to add a fifth marker to the four proposed by Degré – namely, reluctance to agree that the pot should not call the kettle black. This is a general rather than a specific trait; and if it is particularly noticeable in Fascist practice this is simply because suppression of freedom of speech gave it a false isolation. Accordingly, this is a secondary characteristic, not something specific to Fascism.

Weber saw the 'ideal type' as a tool fashioned and used by the researcher. This does not seem to be true in all cases. Model concepts may take shape spontaneously. The concept of Christian morality is a case in point: as a typological concept it is the spontaneous fruit of manifold experience and comparison: it was not worked out in someone's laboratory. The same goes for that concept of morality which, in the nineteenth century, came to be called 'bourgeois morality' *tout court*, although it is in fact specifically linked with certain phases of bourgeois historical development.

2 Summing up

As I said in my Preface, I started to write this book as an exercise in the class differentiation of something which textbooks of ethics seemed to regard as an eternal and invariable entity – morality. I have concentrated on bourgeois morality, leaving feudal morality, with its aftermath in aristocratic morality, and proletarian morality to be considered at a later date. Bourgeois morality was very much a talking point at the turn of the nineteenth and twentieth centuries. It was at this juncture that whatever was 'bourgeois' began to be derided and decried by widely divergent protagonists of totally discrepant ideals. As the antagonisms deepened, their object remained more or less unchanged. The day of 'the peaceable, cautious man' (to use Marx's words in *The Holy Family*) 'who regulates his behaviour by rules dictated by fear and practical considerations' was over. No one wanted a society run 'in the interests of mediocrity, sentimentality and good business'. In sharp contrast to this smug and complacent bourgeoisie, the Communists put up the image of the militant worker who was to overthrow exploitation by revolution, and usher in the era of universal brotherhood. And Communism's most bitter enemy, Hitlerism, although it enjoyed the support of the petty bourgeoisie, also attacked pacifist bourgeois mediocrity, and propagated the 'Spartan' virtues of the Prussian Junkers in an effort to turn German citizens into a militant master race who would rule the world. Dazed by its dreams of power, the German petty bourgeoisie closed its eyes to the anti-bourgeois sentiments which proliferated in Nazi propaganda. Or at least these were not taken at their face value by the petty bourgeois, who saw himself in Siegfried's armour, or by his hitherto complacent wife, who had now been given her Valkyrie wings by Nazi ideologists.

I have singled out Benjamin Franklin as one of the apostles of this morality which found itself under such heavy attack at the turn of the century. He was the great advocate of the decent man, the respectable man: a model depending first and foremost on financial solidity, which is in its turn based on industry, thrift, orderliness, providence, caution, and on thinking in terms of cash. The practice of buying independence by means of money is no new thing. Seneca was far from despising independence gained in this way, though his Stoic faith required him to underwrite his independence by despising all goods, including riches. But intensive propaganda for a non-elitist and personal independence which could be gained by the daily saving of a penny or two through personal virtue, the constant caveat that an idle moment is money down the drain – this was all something of a novelty in its pre-capitalist setting. The slogan 'Time is money' had a very *avant-garde* ring to it in Franklin's day, which gave his homilies a special dynamism. Though they remained basically unchanged in content, these slogans gradually changed in social function, as we can see when we analyse twentieth-century bourgeois codes of practice in the USA. Franklinesque morality reached Poland after the loss of her independence, and was addressed (as the examples I have quoted go to show) to the small or medium craftsman, shopkeeper and peasant, or to the *déclassé* nobility. In the former case, the tone adopted was sober and cheerful; in the latter case, it was more pompous and bombastic.

What Franklin meant by thrift was very far from hoarding: he saved in order to invest. The same goes for Alberti (see Chapter 8), for whom 'thrift' consisted primarily in maintaining a balanced budget. In this, he was much assisted by the growth of accountancy. In Chapter 4 we looked at several variants of the concept of 'thrift' and found that this proverbial bourgeois virtue retains only a semblance of uniformity at the hands of various theoreticians. Today the whole concept of 'saving' has very largely moved into the public sector; and 'good husbandry' means adequate administration of the national resources. It behoves us therefore to examine these variants to see precisely what we are advocating and what we are rejecting. Similarly, we have to scrutinise the propaganda framework in which these virtues are presented, as it may well contain relics of bourgeois thought, formally persistent through inertia in a radically altered world.

Having presented Franklin's views as the exemplar for a certain brand of class morality – one which was mistakenly regarded at the turn of the century as 'bourgeois morality' *tout court* – we went back in history to look for Franklinesque attitudes in pre-Franklin days. We found something very similar in Daniel Defoe, whose works bear witness to his solidarity with the middle echelons of the world of commerce. It was precisely in this sphere that Franklin's teaching found its most receptive soil, and this is borne out by our analysis of Volney. Franklin had no social pretensions, nor did he assume any on the part of his readers. Aristocratic models were of little interest to the citizens of the New World. This cannot be said of Defoe, whose interesting and little-known works on the model gentleman and the model tradesman allow us to follow the metamorphosis of the 'gentleman' model *pari passu* with the ever more exigent claims made upon it by the ascendant bourgeoisie. Personal qualities, adequate education and decent manners would henceforth decide who was or was not a gentleman, and these qualifications were available to anyone who made enough money by applying the bourgeois virtues. These virtues were indispensable in the actual process of acquiring money, and of service thereafter in its retention and augmentation. And even if a man was unable during his own lifetime to breach the class barrier dividing the bourgeois from the upper class, his children, given the right start in life, would certainly do so.

The morality exemplified in this book by Franklin and Defoe developed *pari passu* with the Protestant sects, and many theoreticians have connected the two sets of events, by giving the sects a share in the emphasis laid upon certain virtues which in turn promoted the growth of capitalism. This is dealt with in Chapter 6, where we looked at different views of this alleged historical connection in the light of Max Weber's thesis concerning the Protestant ethic and its relation with the 'spirit of capitalism'. Weber's work is rich in content but far from systematic; and once the content has been systematised and critically analysed, not much of value remains. I have no difficulty in accepting the thesis that the Puritan ethic promoted the growth of capitalism, at least in England and the United States – a thesis which had in fact been advanced before Weber's statement of it. One may also accept without reservation the thesis that a certain life-style developed in association with Puritanism, and that the spread of this life-style among the masses was unprecedented. I do not, however, accept Weber's general thesis that wherever

Calvinism or a similar ethic makes its appearance, its adherents – i.e. those who adapt themselves to this new way of life – proceed to make their fortunes. It seems clear that the adoption of Calvinism can have various consequences, depending on who is adopting it and in what circumstances. In any case – and this is very important – the argument that the Calvinist dogma of predestination played a crucial role in the development of the drive to make money is not convincing; and the choice of Franklin to illustrate the alleged connection between Puritanism and the so-called 'capitalist spirit' is very questionable indeed. It is quite true that Franklin came from an ardently Puritan family, but he himself was a man of the Enlightenment rather than a Puritan. In sum, the role of the sects appears to me to be of far less importance in this context than certain other social factors which Weber fails to take into account.

In the earlier chapters of this book I was concerned primarily with an ideology as expressed in a set of maxims. In Chapter 7 I turn to moral practice, and concentrate on one trait which is constantly laid at the door of the petty bourgeoisie – a tendency to be nosy, to keep an envious and malevolent eye on what other people are doing, to be scandalised. The allegation is that these traits also go to mould bourgeois ideology. It was to such questions as these that the Danish sociologist Ranulf devoted long and careful study based on descriptions of the bourgeois way of life. His results seem to me to be questionable; but the problem is a fascinating one, and Ranulf's methods highlight all the difficulties bound up with induction in the social sciences. My main objection to Ranulf's thesis is this: if the envy and malice alleged to be typical of the petty bourgeoisie was due to enforced abstinence, how is it that the proletariat, which was much more deprived, did not react in equivalent fashion? Neither Ranulf nor any other researcher ever mentions the proletariat in this connection.

The next two chapters (8 and 9) are short monographs on two authors whom I have chosen as test cases in this context. The first of these is Leone Battista Alberti, who is regarded as the spokesman of bourgeois thought in the heyday of Florentine capitalism. The widely held notion that Florentine capitalism – at least as here expressed – was in any way similar to what Franklin believed and preached, will hardly survive study of his treatise on the family. When we compare Alberti's thought with the ancient classical treatises on the same theme, it soon becomes clear that Alberti belongs among those thinkers who are concerned with the good organisation and running of their own estate and household, rather than among those who teach the art of making money. His mental world is that of the Greek and Latin classics, not that of the Old Testament; his restraint is the Golden Mean, not the limitation and mediocrity of the petty bourgeoisie. In Alberti's works we can detect a fusion of feudal aristocratic elements with bourgeois traits, a fusion bound up with the gradual absorption of the aristocratic Alberti family into the ranks of the victorious bourgeoisie. A comparable fusion, but one proceeding from below upwards instead of from above downwards, is discussed in Chapter 10.

Chapter 9 is taken up with the moral teachings of Volney, the most 'bourgeois' of the ideologists of the French Revolution. The similarities between his teaching and that of Franklin go to show that these attitudes were not necessarily connected with Protestantism, nor were they the expression of an already victorious or nearly victorious bourgeoisie, as was the state of affairs in the United States; for in France, the same attitudes make their appearance while the protagonists are still locked in battle. Volney's highly successful career after the Revolution, and the agreement between his ideals and those of the industrialists of early nineteenth-century France, bear witness to the durability and continuity of certain bourgeois components which seem to have held their ground in spite of the horrors of the Revolution. Comparison of Volney's 'Catechism' with the other catechisms of the period shows that the one trait common to all of them was hedonism. This hedonism was used as a weapon in the anti-religion campaign, and it affords proof that an up-and-coming class does not always preach moral rigour and asceticism, though some scholars have made this generalisation from the special cases of the English bourgeoisie under Cromwell and the Italian bourgeoisie at the time of its fight for power. Of course, the anti-religion campaign was only one of the factors underlying the hedonism of the writers of the French Revolution; and as I said in Chapter 9, it would be interesting to know precisely why the French bourgeoisie on its way to emancipation chose this approach, while the English bourgeoisie made religion a cardinal point in its programme.

What Defoe had to say about the tradesman and the gentleman, and his attempts to adapt the gentleman exemplar to his own ends and uses and to those of his class, set the scene for Chapter 10, in which I discuss the superimposition, the overlapping and partial confluence of the bourgeois and aristocratic models in the nineteenth century. As I said in the Preface, the main purpose of this book is to differentiate between certain models of a class nature which have tended to be lumped together in an allegedly monolithic 'morality'. As the bourgeoisie was further differentiated, and as enormous fortunes were piled up in the age of imperialism, I note another component in the patchwork of morality, one representing the fusion of bourgeois and aristocratic elements. Of course it was no new thing for *nouveaux riches* to ape the nobility. In earlier periods of English and French history too, rich merchant families had lived in lordly style and had bought themselves coats of arms. However, the close of the nineteenth century saw this fusion become more general and more widespread. Even in Germany, where the nobility was particularly jealous of its exclusive status, the class barrier between it and the bourgeoisie was finally broken down. The economic successes of the industrial barons, particularly those in the armaments business, enabled them to acquire titles and take up residence in hitherto exclusive family seats.

Chapter 11 offers some reflections on the method used in this book – especially the technique (not exclusive to the author) of inquiring into and identifying the social conditions underlying a given theory or ideology. The pertinent questions here are: Whose interests did such and such a doctrine serve? And of what socio-economic structure was it an expression? This standard technique turns on the concept of 'interest'; and accordingly I spend some time defining this intricate concept, before proceeding to the main theme of the chapter. Various theorists have already worked out techniques for detecting these conditioning factors; here, my main concern is to supply them with a plausible *raison d'être*. On investigation, we find that arguments advanced in explanation of these conditioning factors are usually elliptical; that is, they depend on tacit assumptions. These are usually vague psychological generalities, which it is often very difficult to pin down in any precise fashion, and whose application in given historical circumstances is questionable to say the least.

This book has dealt with certain classic types of bourgeois moral thought as exemplified in the recent history of Europe and the United States; and this raises the whole question of how far the use of 'types' in scientific research is valid. The author's view is that the use of types as a research tool is not only generally accepted in practice but is also highly instructive. Thus, if we use the relations obtaining in medieval France to exemplify feudalism, we are using a *type* for instructive purposes. The researcher who asks himself, with French feudalism in mind, whether we can speak of 'feudalism' in Japan at a given moment in Japanese history, is using a classic type for heuristic purposes, a procedure which seems to me to be valid, as otherwise the quest for general scientific truths seems doomed to failure.

Whether the attempt made in this book to establish such general truths has been successful or not, the author hopes that the reader is now in a better position to judge what actually *does* take place in a field where it has been customary to consider only what *ought* to take place. By the same token, a belief in 'morality' as a constant may well yield to the realisation that many variants of morality may coexist – even in one and the same society.

Glossary of Polish authors

Boy-Żeleński, Tadeusz (1874–1941). Poet, translator, critic and publicist. His criticism was directed mainly at the stagnation in Polish literature round about 1900, academicism, and the complacency of the bourgeoisie in Kraków. His novel *Znasz-li ten kraj?* ('Knowest Thou the Land?') is a study of Kraków society in the Young Poland period. A superb translator from French (*c.* 100 volumes, ranging from Villon to Proust).

Breza, Tadeusz (1905–70). Novelist dealing with political and social problems. Became internationally celebrated for his two books on the Vatican and its problems: *Spiżowa brama* ('The Bronze Gate', 1960) and *Urząd* ('The Office', 1961) – the latter a novel.

Brzozowski, Stanisław (1878–1911). Novelist, philosopher and outstanding critic. His main works are *Sam wśród ludzi* ('Alone Among Men', 1911), a novel, and *Legenda Młodej Polski* ('The Legend of Young Poland', 1909), a work of philosophical criticism.

Dąbrowska, Maris (1889–1965). Novelist and dramatist. Her main work is the *roman-fleuve Noce i dnie* ('Nights and Days', 1932–4), a Tolstoyan picture of Polish society from the 1860s to 1914. Also known for *Ludzie stamtąd* ('The People from There') a realistic and gloomy picture of the Polish rural proletariat. Brilliant translation of Pepys's diary (1948).

Górnicki, Łukasz (1527–1603). Author of *Dworzanin polski* ('The Polish Courtier', 1566), an adaptation of Castiglione's *Corteggiano*. His prose style had a considerable influence on subsequent writers.

Kasprowicz, Jan (1860–1926). Lyric poet. Experimented with free verse in his best-known work *Ginącemu światu* ('To the Perishing World'). His themes are from Polish landscape and peasant life, and medieval imagery.

Kisielewski, Jan August (1876–1918). Made a great hit with his first drama *W sieci* ('In the Net', 1899), a study of teenage rebellion.

369

Kott, Jan (1914–   ). Marxist writer and critic. Celebrated for his very original approach to Shakespeare: *Szkice o Szekspirze* ('Shakespeare Our Contemporary', 1964).

Krasiński, Zygmunt (1812–59). Dramatist and poet. His main dramatic work is *Nieboska Komedja* ('The Un-Divine Comedy', 1833), a remarkable preview of revolution and class conflict. In later works, he was an eloquent exponent of Polish Messianism.

Mickiewicz, Adam (1798–1855). Poland's national poet. Born in the Lithuanian part of Poland; deported to Russia in 1823, in connection with political trial of Vilna students. From 1830 to his death, an exile in Paris. Main works: the romantic drama *Dziady* ('The Forefathers', 1832) and the epic poem *Pan Tadeusz* (1834), drawing on the Napoleonic campaign in Russia, and life in the Lithuanian countryside.

Orzechowski, Stanisław (1513–66). Polemicist, defending interests of Polish gentry. *Quincunx* ('Pyramid', 1564).

Orzeszkowa, Eliza (1841–1910). Populist novelist and writer of short stories on social themes: emancipation of women, social rights for Jews and peasants. *Nad Niemnem* ('On the Niemen', 1888), *Cham* ('The Boor', 1889).

Prus, Bolesław (1845–1912). Both as publicist and novelist, the leading Polish representative of positivism and realism. His main novel is *Lalka* ('The Doll', 1890), a realistic study of life in Warsaw in late nineteenth century, and of personal conflict generated by an obsessive love superimposed on successful business acumen. Also noteworthy is *Faraon* ('The Pharaoh', 1897), a study of a struggle for power in ancient Egypt.

Przybyszewski, Stanisław (1868–1927). Wrote in both Polish and German. His German works are in the spirit of *fin-de-siècle* decadence. In Polish, he produced the Manifesto (1899) launching the first phase of the 'Young Poland' movement. Art deified as an Absolute. Became notorious as a Satanist. Also wrote psychological dramas and an autobiography, giving a valuable account of literary life in Berlin and elsewhere: *Moi Współcześni* ('My Contemporaries', 1926–30).

Rzewuski, Henryk (1791–1866). Champion of Old Poland against the Enlightenment. Author of several works in novel form giving often humorous account of life in eighteenth-century Poland.

Sęp-Szarzyński Mikołaj (1550–81). Metaphysical lyric poet. Impressive sonnet sequence (1601).

Sienkiewicz, Henryk (1846–1916). Novelist, author of such enormously successful works as: *Ogniem i mieczem* ('With Fire and Sword', 1883/4), *Potop* ('The Deluge', 1886), *Pan Wołodyjowski* (1887/8). These three form a trilogy dealing with Poland's wars against the Cossacks, Swedes and Turks. Further, *Quo Vadis* (1896), *Krzyżacy* ('The Teutonic Knights', 1900), *Bez dogmatu* ('Without Dogma', 1891), *Rodzina Połanieckich* ('The Połaniecki Family', 1895).

Słowacki, Juliusz (1809–49). Romantic poet and dramatist. After Warsaw rising of 1830, in exile in Paris till his death. Travelled in Switzerland, Italy and the Mediterranean. Obsessed with hopes for salvation of Poland, he relapsed in his last years into a mystic Messianism: *Król-Duch* ('King-Spirit', 1847). His dramas include tragedy (*Lilla Weneda*, 1840), Romantic drama (*Kordian*, 1834, on the abortive rising) and satirical comedy (*Fantazy*, 1841).

Staff, Leopold (1878–1957). Poet and translator. Moved from Nietzschean mood of Young Poland to new realism and cult of simplicity.

Tuwim, Juljan (1894–1953). Joint founder of the 'Skamander' group of Futurist lyric poets. From 1939 to 1946 in America. Linguistically very gifted, endlessly inventive in the exploitation of linguistic resources and in formal experimentation. Some of his main collections are: *Czyhanie na Boga* ('Ambushing God', 1918); *Słowa we krwi* ('Words in Blood', 1926); *Biblia Cygańska* ('Gipsy Bible', 1933); *Bal w operze* ('Ball at the Opera', 1936); *Kwiaty polskie* ('Polish Flowers', 1949).

Zapolska, Gabriela (1857–1921). Known for two plays: *Moralność pani Dulskiej* ('Mrs Dulska's Morality', 1907) and *Panna Maliczewska* (1912), both savage attacks on conventional morality and bourgeois attitudes.

Żeromski, Stefan (1864–1925). Novelist. Best known for *Popioły* ('Ashes', 1904), a vast social panorama of Poland at the time of the Napoleonic Wars. *Przedwiośnie* ('Before the Spring', 1925) deals with the Bolshevik Revolution and the birth of the Polish state.

Notes

1 Introduction

1 J. Kott, 'Konfitury', *Kuźnica*, 1948, no. 142.
2 F. Engels, Preface to 3rd German edn of Marx, *The Eighteenth Brumaire of Louis Bonaparte*, in Karl Marx and Friedrich Engels, *Selected Works in Two Volumes*, London, 1950, vol. 1, p. 223.
3 R. Lewis and A. Maude, *The English Middle Class*, 3rd edn, London, 1950, ch. 1. (1st edn, 1949).
4 M. Ossowska, *Podstawy nauki o moralności*, Warsaw, 1947, pp. 323–4. Also the article 'Inteligent polski na tle grup towarzyskich Europy zachodniej', *Myśl Współczesna*, 1947. ('The Polish intellectual *vis-à-vis* Western European Social Groupings', in 'Contemporary Thought'.)
5 E. Goblot, *La Barrière et le niveau. Etude sociologique sur la bourgeoisie française moderne*, Paris, 1925.
6 S. Ranulf, *Moral Indignation and Middle Class Psychology*, Copenhagen, 1938.
7 R. Johannet, *Eloge du bourgeois français*, Grasset, Paris, 1924.
8 *Ibid.*, pp. 35–6.
9 Engels, *Ludwig Feuerbach and the End of German Philosophy*.
10 G. Degré, 'Ideology and Class Consciousness in the Middle Class', *Social Forces*, 1950, vol. 29, no. 2.
11 Quoted from Johannet, *op. cit.*, pp. 53–8.
12 Cf. the article by A. Meusel, 'Middle Class', in '*Encyclopaedia of the Social Sciences*'.
13 *Ibid.*

2 Bourgeois morality on the defensive

1 Marx, *The Eighteenth Brumaire of Louis Bonaparte*, in Karl Marx and Friedrich Engels, *Selected Works in Two Volumes*, London, 1950, vol. 1, p. 250.

2 See, e.g., Lenin, *The Task of the Russian Social-Democrats.*
3 Lenin, *Selected Works in Three Volumes*, Moscow, 1967, vol. 2, p. 194.
4 Lenin, *The Next Tasks of the Soviet Government.*
5 Lenin, *State and Revolution.*
6 Marx in letter to P. V. Annenkov, 28 December 1846.
7 Marx in letter to Schweitzer, 24 January 1865.
8 Engels, *Revolution and Counter-Revolution in Germany*, London, 1933, p. 14.
9 Marx, *The Poverty of Philosophy.*
10 Lenin, *The Task of the Proletariat in our Revolution*, in *Selected Works*, Moscow, 1967, vol. 2, p. 27.
11 Marx and Engels, *Communist Manifesto.*
12 Marx, *The Eighteenth Brumaire of Louis Bonaparte*, in Marx, Engels, *Selected Works in Two Volumes*, London, 1950, vol. 1, p. 252.
13 Marx, letter to P. V. Annenkov, 28 December 1846.
14 Lenin, *Left-wing Communism: An Infantile Disorder.*
15 Engels, 'Marx and the *Neue Rheinische Zeitung*', in Marx, Engels, *Selected Works in Two Volumes*, London, 1950, vol. 2, p. 333.
16 Marx, letter to Schweitzer, 24 January 1865.
17 See Lenin, *State and Revolution.*
18 Marx, *The Holy Family*, Moscow, 1956, p. 220.
19 Marx, *Early Writings*, introduced by Lucio Colletti, trans. R. Livingstone and G. Benton, Penguin Books, 1975, pp. 360–1.
20 Marx, *The Poverty of Philosophy.*
21 Marx, *Early Writings, op. cit.*, p. 362.
22 *Ibid.*, p. 377.
23 Lenin, *The Immediate Tasks of the Soviet Government.*
24 Marx, *On Proudhon.*
25 G. Sorel, *Matériaux d'une théorie du prolétariat*, Rivière, Paris, 1929, p. 129.
26 Engels, *Ludwig Feuerbach and the End of German Philosophy.*
27 Lenin, *Selected Works in Three Volumes*, Moscow, 1971, vol. 3, p. 218.
28 M. Gorky, *Les Petits Bourgeois*, Les Editions de la Nouvelle Critique, 1941. This is a collection of essays from different periods of Gorky's life. Inadequately documented with no indication of when or where published. Useful in present context, however.
29 Lenin, in *Selected Works*, Moscow, 1967, vol. 1.

30 Gorky, *op. cit.*

31 V. Mayakovsky, 'Harpagon'.

32 The word *filister* (Philistine) came to Poland and Russia from Germany, where it was used by students to denote ex-students or graduates. The word probably acquired its derogatory sense from the contrast between the lively and rebellious students of the day and their sober, settled elders – the ex-students. Before it acquired the pejorative sense in which we use it here, the word *kołtun* meant an urban Philistine and also a rural smallholder.

33 *Mayakovsky: Poems*, trans. and ed. Herbert Marshall, London, 1965, p. 138.

34 Balzac, *Le Père Goriot*.

35 Cf. Lenin, *A Great Beginning*, in *Selected Works in Three Volumes*, Moscow, 1971, vol. 3.

36 See Chapter 12 of Ptaśnik's monograph *Szlachta wobec miast i mieszczaństwa* ('The Nobility versus Towns and Town-dwellers').

37 *Policja Królestwa Polskiego na ksztalt Arystotelesowych Polityk wypisana i na świat dla dobra pospolitego trzema księgami wydana* ('The Polity of the Kingdom of Poland Fashioned on the Politics of Aristotle and Published for the Common Good in Three Volumes'), L. Merzbach, Poznań, 1859.

38 It is Bojanowski who hints at the possibility that some nobles may be less than blameless: but Kryski's view that a courtier is necessarily 'noble' wins the day.

39 Quoted from W. Smoleński, *Szlachta w swietle własnych opinii* ('Noblemen as Seen by Themselves'), Ateneum, 1880, vol. 3 (in vol. 29 of his works), p. 432.

40 See S. Starowolski, *Prawy rycerz* ('The True Knight'), Kraków, 1858; S. Starowolski, *Reformacja obyczajów polskich* ('Reformation of Polish Customs and Manners'), Kraków, 1859.

41 [H. Rzewuski], *Mieszaniny obyczajowe* ('Medley of Customs'), (published under pseudonym Jarosz Bejła), vols. 1–2. Wilno, 1841; 1843 (see vol. 2, p. 105).

42 *Ibid.*, vol. 2, p. 25.

43 *Ibid.*, vol. 2, p. 28.

44 *Ibid.*, vol. 1, p. 130.

45 *Ibid.*, vol. 2, p. 9.

46 *Ibid.*, vol. 2 (p. xxxi: preface).

47 Lenin, *A Great Beginning*, in *Selected works in Three Volumes*, Moscow, 1971, vol. 3, p. 237.

48 [H. Rzewuski], *Mieszaniny* . . ., vol. 1, p. 153.
49 As Stawar very aptly points out in his 'Studium o Sienkiewiczu' (see *Kuźnica*, no. 49) the women in *Bez Dogmatu* ('Without Dogma') and in *Rodzina Połanieckich* ('The Połaniecki Family') are the custodians of morality. Women can afford to represent an ethical or moral standard since they play no part in practical life, in the struggle for existence, from which it is man's duty to protect them. As Stawar very happily puts it, when women are glorified, it tends to be to the accompaniment of such insights as 'a foolish woman has as much sense as a hen; a wise woman has as much as two hens'.
50 Buying and hoarding grain in the hope that prices would rise as hunger increased came in for condemnation from Boy-Żeleński in his introduction to his translation of Balzac's *Le Père Goriot*. A similar attitude to Połaniecki's speculations was expressed earlier by Brzozowski who, in his *Współczesna powieść w Polsce* ('The Contemporary Novel in Poland') (Stanisławów, 1906) accused Sienkiewicz of failing to understand creative work, and said that *The Połaniecki Family* was a story, not about the Polish bourgeois but about 'a lot of tricky spivs out for what they can get'.
51 T. Boy-Żeleński, *Mózg i płeć. Studia z literatury francuskiej* ('Brains and Sex: Studies in French Literature'), vols. 1–3. Warsaw, 1926–8. See vol. 3, p. 336.
52 *Ibid.*
53 S. Przybyszewski, *Na drogach duszy* ('On Spirit Paths'), Kraków, 1902, p. 49.
54 T. Boy-Żeleński, *Znasz-li ten kraj?* ('Knowest Thou the Land?'), Warsaw, 1932, pp. 160–1.
55 Przybyszewski, *Szlakiem duszy polskiej* ('On the Path of the Polish Spirit'), Poznań, 1920, p. 66.
56 Przybyszewski, *Na drogach* . . ., p. 24.
57 Przybyszewski, *Szlakiem* . . ., p. 158.
58 Przybyszewski, *Na drogach* . . ., p. 75.
59 *Ibid.*, p. 74.
60 *Ibid.*, pp. 62–3.
61 Przybyszewski, *Szlakiem* . . ., p. 161.
62 L. Staff, *Mistrz Twardowski* ('Master Twardowski'), Lwów, 1902.
63 S. Kawyn, *Cyganeria Warszawska* ('Vie de Bohème in Warsaw'). The author develops his argument in *Zagadnienie*

grupy literackiej ('The Problem of the Literary Group'), Tow. Nauk. K.U.L., Lublin, 1946.

64 T. Boy-Żeleński, 'Okno na życie' ('A Window on Life'). Review of *Moralność pani Dulskiej* ('The Morality of Mrs Dulska').

65 *Ibid.*

66 Przybyszewski, *Na drogach* . . ., p. 49.

67 K. Wyka, *Zarys współczesnej literatury polskiej 1884–1925* ('An Outline of Contemporary Polish Literature 1884–1925'). Lectures published by Uniwersytet Jagielloński, Kraków, 1951, pp. 51–2.

68 Przybyszewski, *Na drogach* . . ., p. 53.

69 *Ibid.*, p. 15.

70 S. Brzozowski, *Współczesna powieść w Polsce* ('The Contemporary Novel in Poland'), Stanisławów, 1906, p. 161.

71 Cf. on this point the article by J. Strzelecki entitled 'Drogi i bezdroża polskiej intelegencji' in *Myśl Filozoficzna*, 1952, 1/3. Also, 'Materiały do nauczania historii literatury polskiej', *Wybór artykułów krytyczno-literackich*, vol. 2. Oprac. K. Budzyk and J. K. Jakubowski, Warsaw, 1950, pp. 15–16.

72 J. Kasprowicz, *Dzieła* (Works), vols. 1–22, pod. red. S. Kołaczkowskiego, Kraków, 1930. Zob. vol. 10, *O bohaterskim koniu i walącym się domu* ('The Heroic Horse and the Tumbledown House') (pp. 15–18: Modlitwa episjera).

73 K. Wyka, *Zarys* . . ., p. 54.

74 *Ibid.*, p. 63.

75 *Materiały do nauczania historii* . . ., pp. 24, 16.

76 See V. Leduc, Quelques problèmes d'une sociologie du Fascisme', *Cahiers Intern.*, 1952, vol. 12.

77 *Biuletyn Głównej Komisji Badań Zbrodni Hitleryzmu w Polsce* ('Bulletin of the Central Commission for the Identification of Hitlerist Crimes in Poland'), vol. 7, p. 124.

78 Erich Fromm, *The Fear of Freedom*, London, 1942, p. 183.

79 See Matthew Arnold, *Culture and Anarchy* (1869) and the essay entitled 'The Function of Criticism at the Present Time'.

3 The classical model: Benjamin Franklin

1 *The Life of Benjamin Franklin written by himself.*

2 *Ibid.*

3 Marx, *Capital.*

4 *Ibid.*

5 Quoted from B. Fay, *Franklin, the Apostle of Modern Times*, Boston, 1929, p. 164.

6 C. A. Helvétius, *De l'esprit*, Disc. III.

7 *The Life of Benjamin Franklin*, New York, 1956, p. 76.

8 The author of the short passage on Franklin in the *History of Philosophy* edited by C. F. Aleksandrov (vol. 2, Moscow, 1941) sees a common trait linking Franklin, Voltaire, Hume and Shaftesbury, in the combination of personal atheism with the conviction that religion is a good thing for the masses.

9 Benjamin Franklin, *Autobiography*, ed. W. McDonald. Everyman's Library, Dent, London, 1968, p. 60.

10 Benjamin Franklin, *Representative Selections*, ed. Mott and Jorgenson, American Book Company, New York, 1936, p. 176.

11 Aphorisms quoted from *The Way to Wealth*.

12 Thorstein Veblen, *The Leisure Class*, New York, 1899.

13 See Fay, *op. cit.*, p. 164.

14 *The Life of Benjamin Franklin*, *op. cit.*, vol. 1, p. 236.

15 See M. Weber, 'Die protestantische Ethik und der Geist des Kapitalismus', in *Gesamm. Aufsätze zur Religionssoziologie*, vol. I, Tübingen, 1920.

16 Benjamin Franklin, *Autobiography*, Yale University Press, 1964, p. 150.

17 *Ibid.*

18 Benjamin Franklin, *Representative Selections*, *op. cit.*, p. 196.

19 *Ibid.*, p. 176.

20 I quote from the Polish translation entitled *Nauki poczciwego Ryszarda*, Warsaw, (no date).

21 Here, Franklin might have found support from a most unexpected quarter. I refer to the praise of freedom as assured by capital voiced by Słowacki in a letter to Teofil Janiszkiewicz (Paris, February, 1849): 'As to the buying and further buying of land, in my soul I most resolutely oppose this. Every man needs to have a small piece of land so that in the worst case, he could feed himself by his own efforts and, literally, survive. But man's happiness that approaches most nearly to spiritual happiness, to the happiness of paradise, lies in freedom, in freedom connected with power. This freedom is in wings, and the wings that hold us above the earth are capital. The greatest landlords are paupers in comparison with me who have a few thousand francs ready and available so that I can use them any day for anything I like, and protect myself by

their agency from any force or compulsion.

'Wide lands make an egoist of you, caring nothing for people or for your nation. But if you possess forces far surpassing your bodily strength in the shape of capital, you must bethink yourself of your country which safeguards your capital. Willy-nilly you must wish all of your fellows well.

'If someone sets out to enslave you, capital will waft you to the very stars whence you can loose a thunderbolt on your would-be subjugator. And if you want to save someone you can rise equal to your love and give your all in one day.' See J. Słowacki, 'Listy do matki', in *Dzieła*, vol. 13, Wrocław, 1952. I am indebted to Dr. J. Kreczmar for drawing my attention to this letter.

22 Franklin, *Autobiography* (Yale), p. 164.
23 See Chapter 10, below.
24 Franklin, *Autobiography* (Yale), p. 99.
25 *The Way to Wealth*, quoted from the Polish translation, p. 36.
26 Franklin, *Autobiography* (Everyman), p. 35.
27 A. S. Lynd, H. M. Lynd, *Middletown: A Study in Contemporary American Culture*, New York, 1929, *idem, Middletown in Transition: A Study in Cultural Conflicts*, New York, 1937.
28 Page references are to the 1937 edition of *Middletown in Transition*.
29 I quote from the Polish translation of Dr K. Stanisławski.
30 C. Wright Mills, *White Collar: The American Middle Classes*, OUP, 1951. I know this work only from two reviews: one in the *American Sociological Review*, October 1951, and the other in *Cahiers Internationaux de Sociologie*, vol. 14, 1953.
31 Talcott Parsons, 'A Revised Analytical Approach to the Theory of Social Stratification', in *Class, Status and Power: A Reader in Social Stratification*, Glencoe, Illinois, The Free Press, 1953.
32 *Kolęda na rok 1793, czyli jak żyć na świecie*, Warsaw, 1793: *Uwagi i rady oparte na zasadach moralności i wolności. Kalendarz amerykański na rok 1794*, Warsaw, 1794; *Zdania polityczne i moralne na każdy dzień roku*, Warsaw, 1795. I am indebted to Dr A. Kadlerów for these bibliographical details.
33 C. B. Dunoyer, *L'industrie et la morale considérées dans leurs rapports avec la liberté*, Paris, 1825, p. 441.
34 I have to thank Prof. T. Kotarbiński for drawing my attention to these two booklets.
35 In the following quotes, C = *John Ploughman's Chats*; P = *John Ploughman's Pictures*.

36 A more ample dose of opium for the masses is contained in another book by Spurgeon which was translated into Polish under the telling title: 'The Book of Divine Promises; or, A Chequebook of the Faith upon the Bank of Eternal Treasure', B. Götze, Warsaw, n.d. The probable date is 1935. In content, this book is far more avowedly religious than the one I mentioned above. It takes the form of a sort of trade deal with God, based on the principle of reciprocity: 'Give so that you may receive – such is the way of the faith' (p. 17).

37 W. Berkan, *Życiorys własny* ('Autobiographical Sketch'), Poznań, 1924.

38 J. Kott, 'Konfitury', *Kuźnica*, 1948, no. 142. Reprinted with some alterations in the collective work *Pozytywizm*, vol. 1, Wrócław, 1950, and in *Kultura z okresu pozytywizmu*, vol. 1, *Mieszczaństwo*, Warsaw, 1949.

39 See *Kultura z okresu pozytywizmu*, p. 286.

4 Thrift as a virtue

1 Diary of Samuel Pepys, 2 May 1664.

2 J. Bentham, *Oeuvres*, vol. 4, Brussels, 1830, p. 71.

3 *Pracą i oszczędnością*, Bibl. Wydz. Ekon. PKO, no. 4, Warsaw, 1948.

4 T. Breza, *Mury Jericha* ('The Walls of Jericho'), Warsaw, 1945, pp. 194–5.

5 See the discussion of hedonism in my *Motywy postępowania*.

6 Breza, *op. cit.*, pp. 194–5.

7 Samuel Pepys, Diary, 28 September 1664.

8 Theophrastus, *Characters*, trans. J. M. Edmonds, Loeb Library, London, 1929, pp. 51, 65, 99, 121, 123, 125.

5 The merchant and the 'gentleman' in Daniel Defoe

1 Biographical details concerning Defoe are taken mainly from P. Dottin, *Daniel Defoe et ses romans*, Les Presses Universitaires, Paris, 1924. Where necessary, these have been amended in line with D. Marion, *Daniel Defoe*, A. Fayard, Paris, 1948.

2 E.g. on p. 224 Seneca figures among the Greek authors.

3 *The Complete English Gentleman*, David Nutt, London, 1890, p. 30.

4 H. Taine, *Histoire de la littérature anglaise*, 15th edn, Hachette, Paris, 1941.

5 Marion, *op. cit.*, p. 190.
6 Taine, *op. cit.*, p. 82.
7 Reference in what follows is to the 5th edition of *The Complete English Tradesman*, vols 1–2, J. Rivington, London, 1745.
8 *Moll Flanders*, Zodiac Press, London, 1962, p. 63. Further quotes from *Moll Flanders* are from this edition.
9 *The True-Born Englishman*, ed. L. A. Talboys, Oxford University Press.
10 *Robinson Crusoe*, Everyman's Library, London, 1945, p. 52. Further quotes are from this edition.
11 A. A. Elistratova, 'Defoe', in *Istorija angliskoj literatury*, vol. 1, 2nd edn, Akademiya Nauk SSSR, Moscow and Leningrad, 1945, pp. 330–54.
12 Taine, *op. cit.*, p. 83.
13 Marx, *Capital*, Lawrence & Wishart, London, 1970, vol. 1, p. 77.
14 Cf. Elistratova, *op. cit.*
15 Dottin, *op. cit.*, p. 480.
16 *Robinson Crusoe* (Everyman), p. 9.
17 Dottin, *op. cit.*, p. 796.
18 Marion, *op. cit.*, p. 128.
19 Taine, *op. cit.*, p. 80.
20 A similar verdict on Defoe, albeit in a different context, in Elistratova, *op. cit.*, pp. 350–1.
21 *The Complete English Gentleman*, p. 257.
22 R. Lewis and A. Maude, *The English Middle Class*, London, 1950, p. 23.
23 Ch. de Montesquieu, *The Spirit of the Laws*, trans. T. Nugent, London and New York, 1949, p. 30.
24 See my article 'Inteligent polski na tle grup towarzyskich Europy Zachodniej', in *Myśl Współczesna*, May 1947.
25 *Przegląd Nauk Historycznych i Społecznych* ('Review of Historical and Social Studies'), vol. 2, 1952.
26 *Ibid.*, p. 213.
27 J. Savary, *Le Parfait Négociant*, vols. 1–2, Paris, 1736.
28 G. Lefebvre, *Quatre-vingt neuf*, Paris, 1939, p. 48. Savary often seems to make a distinction between *marchand* and *négociant* but does not motivate it. See, for example, Vol. 2, p. 98.
29 *Ibid.*, part 2, book 1, ch. III.
30 Biographical details from preface to Savary's works, written by his son.
31 Savary, *op. cit.*, part 1, book 1, ch. 1.
32 *Ibid.*, ch. 5.

33 *Ibid.*, ch. 3.
34 *Ibid.*, chs. 3 and 4.
35 *The True-Born Englishman.*

6 The Puritan sects in the development of modern capitalism

1 W. Sombart, *Der Bourgeois*, Munich and Leipzig, 1913, p. 135.
2 L. Brentano, *Die Anfänge des modernen Kapitalismus*, Munich, 1913, p. 116. (This Brentano is not to be confused with Franz Brentano.)
3 M. Scheler, *Vom Umsturz der Werte*, Leipzig, 1919, vol. 2, pp. 247–79.
4 See Ossowska, *Podstawy nauki o moralności*, pp. 166–7.
5 E. Spranger, *Lebensformen*, 5th rev. edn, Halle, 1925. Page references are to this edition. The first edition appeared in 1914.
6 E. Power, *Medieval People: A Study of Communal Psychology.* Originally published in 1924. Here, page references are to the Pelican edition of 1937.
7 K. Kautsky, *Foundations of Christianity*, trans. H. F. Mins, New York, 1953.
8 *Ibid.*, pp. 167, 168, 169.
9 For a recent discussion of the psychoanalytic viewpoint, see R. Lewis and A. Maude, *The English Middle Class*, 3rd edn, London, 1950, pp. 296 ff.
10 M. Weber, 'Die protestantische Ethik und der Geist des Kapitalismus', in *Gesammelte Aufsätze zur Religionssoziologie*, Tübingen, 1920, vol. 1, pp. 1–236.
11 R. H. Tawney, *Religion and the Rise of Capitalism*, Pelican edn, London, 1942, (1st edn. 1926.)
12 Quoted on p. 175 of English edition of Weber, *op. cit.*
13 M. Weber, *Gesammelte Aufsätze zur Religionssoziologie*, vol. 2, pp. 203 f.
14 Further quotes from Weber are from vol. 1 of text.
15 See Brentano, *op. cit.*, p. 131.
16 *Ibid.*, pp. 151 ff.
17 Engels, *Socialism: Utopian and Scientific*, trans. E. Aveling, London, 1892, p. xxi.
18 Engels, *Ludwig Feuerbach and the Outcome of Classical German Philosophy*, Martin Lawrence, London, n.d., p. 68.
19 E. Westermarck, *Christianity and Morals*, London, 1939, p. 279.

20 S. Kot, *Ideologia polityczna i społeczna braci polskich zwanych arianami* ('The Political and Social Ideology of the Polish Brethren or Arians'), Warsaw, 1932, p. 28.
21 Quoted from S. Ranulf, *Moral Indignation and Middle Class Psychology*, Copenhagen, 1938, p. 40.
22 Brentano, *op. cit.*, p. 145.
23 Tawney, *op. cit.*, pp. 173–4.
24 *Ibid.*, p. 209 and n.
25 See W. A. Weiszkopf, 'Hidden Value Conflicts in Economic Thought', *Ethics*, 1951, vol. 61, no. 3.
26 Ranulf uses this parallel in another connection. More on Ranulf in the next chapter.

7   Resentment as a petty bourgeois trait

1 S. Ranulf, *Moral Indignation and Middle Class Psychology*, Copenhagen, 1938. Reviewed by M. Ossowska in *Przegląd Socjologiczny*, vol. 4. In what follows I make use of this review in somewhat amended form.
2 Cf. B. Groethuysen, *Die Entstehung der Bürgerlichen Welt- und Lebensanschauung in Frankreich*, vols 1–2, M. Niemeyer, Halle/ S. See also the article on Jansenism by the same author in *Encyclopaedia of the Social Sciences*.
3 V. Vedel, *By og Borger i Middelalderen* ('Town and Bourgeois in the Middle Ages'), Copenhagen, 1901.
4 V. Calverton, *The Liberation of American Literature*, New York, 1932.
5 Grønbech, *The Culture of the Teutons*, Copenhagen, 1931.
6 T. Sinko is of the opinion that, in praising the middle class, Euripides was following some treatise, no longer extant, which also influenced Herodotus and Aristotle in their attitudes to the middle class. See Sinko's *Literatura grecka*, Kraków, 1932, vol. 1, part 2, p. 310.
7 Quoted from T. Sinko, *op. cit.*, vol. 1, part 1, p. 252.
8 See T. Wałek-Czarnecki on Greece in the two-volume *Wielka historia powszechna*.

8   The early Italian Renaissance: Leone Battista Alberti

1 The biographical details are taken mainly from P. H. Michel, *La Pensée de L. B. Alberti*, Les Belles Lettres, Paris, 1930, p. 649. Also from R. Lang, *L. B. Alberti und die Sancta Masseritia*, Rapperswil, 1938.

2 In his *Ocherk iz istorii rannego kapitalizma v Italii*, Moscow and Leningrad, 1951, V. J. Rutenburg discusses the formation of the Alberti company in 1342 (p. 33).

3 M. A. Gukowski, *Mekhanika Leonardo da Vinci*, Moscow and Leningrad, 1947. Detailed account of Alberti's treatise on architecture, pp. 247–57.

4 W. N. Łazariev, 'Przeciw fałszowaniu kultury Odrodzenia', in *Materiały do Studiów i Dyskusji z Zakresu Teorii i Historii Sztuki*, 1951, pp. 7–8.

5 G. Vasari, *Le vite dei più eccellenti pittori, scultori e architetti*, Naples, 1876.

6 For the social and economic background to the period, see F. Antal, *Florentine Painting and its Social Background*, London, 1947. Antal investigates these matters in a very original and interesting manner.

7 In Italian: 'l'occhio del signore ingrassa il cavallo'. According to T. Sinko, this expression is of Iranian origin, and is used for the first time in European literature by Xenophon in the *Oikonomikos*.

8 The simile is taken from another of Alberti's works, quoted by Lang, *op. cit.*, pp. 41–2.

9 See Michel, *op. cit.*, pp. 207, 296–7, 580.

10 Xenophon, *Oikonomikos*, Loeb Library, London, 1959, p. 437.

11 The expression *oneste riccheze* means 'riches gained honestly'. When Alberti describes *onestà* as the choicest jewel of the married woman, he is thinking of her marital fidelity. Sometimes, *onestà* is taken to mean business reliability. See Michel, *op. cit.*, p. 268.

12 P. Hazard, *La Pensée européenne au XVIII siècle*, vols 1–3, Paris, 1954. See vol. 1, ch. 4. Other researchers take *humanité* to be part of the Roman heritage.

13 E. Goblot, *La Barrière et le niveau*, Paris, 1926. I dealt with this point at some length in *Myśl Współczesna* ('Contemporary Thought'), 1947.

14 *Odyssey*, trans. E. V. Rieu, Penguin Books, 1973, p. 128.

15 J. Burckhardt, *The Civilization of the Renaissance in Italy*, part II, section 1.

16 W. Sombart, *Der Bourgeois*, Munich and Leipzig, 1913, p. 149.

17 M. Weber, 'Die protestantische Ethik und der Geist des Kapitalismus', in *Gesammelte Aufsätze zur Religionssoziologie*, Tübingen, 1920, vol. 1, pp. 38–41.

18 M. Beard, *A History of the Business Man*, New York, 1938, p. 185.

19 Marx refers to this distinction in *Capital*.
20 T. Sinko, *Literatura grecka*, Kraków, 1932, T. 1, cz. 2, rozdz. XIX.
21 L. J. Columella, *Res rustica*, London, 1931. Latin text and English translation.
22 M. P. Cato, *De re rustica*.
23 It was not considered seemly for a woman to conduct business outside the house ('trafficasse con gli uomini fuori di casa in publico', p. 129, etc.)
24 Quoted from Michel, *op. cit.*, ch. 'La cité parfaite'.
25 A. v. Martin, 'Kultursoziologie der Renaissance', in *Handwörterbuch der Soziologie*, Red. Vierkandt, pp. 495–510.
26 St. François de Sales, *Oeuvres complètes*, Association G. Budé, Paris, 1930. *Introduction à la vie dévote*, vol. 2, ch. XIV. In ch. XV, Philothée is urged to take great care of her property 'car Dieu veut que nous facions ainsy pour son amour'.
27 *Ibid.*
28 Quoted from F. B. Kay, Introduction to Bernard Mandeville's *Fable of the Bees*, OUP, 1924, p. xcii.
29 Martin, *op. cit.*
30 Engels, Introduction to *Dialectics of Nature*, in Marx and Engels, *Selected Works in Two Volumes*, Moscow, 1962, vol. 2, p. 63.

9 Bourgeois moral catechisms and the French Revolution

1 Biographical data on Volney are taken mainly from the monograph written by Gaston-Martin, written as introduction to his edition of the Catechism, and from the biography of Volney by J. Claretie which precedes the text of Volney's *Les Ruines, ou Méditations sur les révolutions des empires*.
2 C. F. Volney, *La loi naturelle, ou catéchisme du citoyen français*, Paris, 1934. See introduction by Gaston-Martin, p. 17.
3 A. Mathiez, *La Révolution française*, Paris, 1930, vol. 1, p. 93. See also Gaston-Martin, *op. cit.*, p. 22.
4 Volney, *Les Ruines, ou Méditations sur les révolutions des empires*, Paris, 1869, p. 63. Further quotations from this edition of *Les Ruines* will be indicated by (R): quotations from the Catechism will be indicated by (C).
5 See Introduction to the 1826 edition of the Catechism, probably written by Volney himself.
6 See Morelly, *Code de la nature*, Paris, 1953, Introduction by

V. P. Volguine, p. 21. Volguine points out that in Morelly's usage 'egoism' acquires the meaning of a natural disposition towards the 'innocent desire to preserve one's own existence'.

7 The school of the Ideologists was formed under the influence of Condillac, and was so called because its members were mainly concerned with the rigorous analysis of ideas. The Ideologists continued the tradition of the Encyclopédistes, which is obvious in Volney's ethical precepts. See W. Tatarkiewicz, *Historia filozofii*, 2nd edn, Warsaw, 1949, vol. 2, p. 150. Gaston-Martin does not think Volney's participation in this group worthy of mention. There is no reference to the group in Volney's own work. The other thinkers belonging to the group were not interested in ethics.

8 P. H. D. Holbach, *Système social*, vol. 1, ch. VI, 'Le luxe'. Luxury, we are told here, is 'une émulation de dépenses et de richesses'.

9 C. A. Helvétius, *De l'esprit*, Mercure de France, Paris, 1909, p. 57.

10 C. A. Helvétius, *De l'homme*, Mercure de France, Paris, 1909, pp. 228 ff.

11 The phrase is taken from Duclos with whom we shall deal in a moment. For all the apparent similarity, there is a difference between this viewpoint and that of Socrates – that every evil action is at the same time an error. Socrates' point was that as soon as a man knows what is good he cannot help acting in accordance with this insight, so that wrongdoing always points to a mistaken judgment in the field of good and evil. Duclos is thinking of faulty assessment in the field of one's own personal interests.

12 Quoted from P. Hazard, *La Pensée européenne au XVIII siècle*, vols 1–3, Paris, 1946, vol. 3, p. 126.

13 G. V. Plekhanov, contributions to *The History of Materialism*.

14 D. Diderot, *Pensées philosophiques*.

15 Quoted from Hazard, *op. cit.*, vol. 1, ch. IV, 'La morale'.

16 *Ibid.*

17 Duclos (Ch. Pineau), *Considérations sur les moeurs de ce siècle*, Paris, 1798, p. 2.

18 Ibid., pp. 56–7.

19 Hesiod, *Works and Days*, trans. H. G. Evelyn-White, London, 1920, p. 29.

20 Duclos, *op. cit.*, p. 48.

21 Helvétius, *De l'homme*, ed. Keim, Paris, 1919, p. 257.

22 Hazard, *op. cit.*, vol. 1, pp. 230–1.
23 *Ibid.*, p. 364.
24 *Autrefois, ou le bon vieux temps. Types français du XVIII siècle*, Paris, n.d., pp. 217–25, 'Les Encyclopédistes'.
25 Duclos, *op. cit.*, ch. IX, 'Sur les gens des lettres'.
26 Hazard, *op. cit.*, pp. 361–2.

10 Bourgeois and aristocratic models in the nineteenth century

1 C. A. Helvétius, *De l'esprit*, Paris, 1909, p. 164.
2 See F. Antal, *Florentine Painting and its Social Background*, London, 1947.
3 Cf. N. Assorodobraj, 'Elementy świadomości klasowej mieszczaństwa (Francja 1815–1830)', *Przegląd Socjologiczny*, 1949.
4 T. Sinko, *Literatura grecka*, Kraków, 1932, vol. 1, part II, p. 310.
5 Aristotle, *Politics*, book IV.
6 Sinko, *op. cit.*
7 M. Beard, *History of the Business Man*, New York, 1938, p. 206.
8 Duclos (Ch. Pineau), *Considérations sur les moeurs de ce siècle*, Paris, 1798, p. 133.
9 Sédaine rose from being a manual worker to the post of secretary to the Academy of Architecture. The anonymous biographical note which precedes the play, ends with the interesting remark that 'all his contemporaries were agreed that in his person Sédaine combined "toutes les qualités essentielles de l'honnête homme".' The passage is worth quoting as it shows the phrase *honnête homme* still being used in a class sense.
10 J.-C. de la Métherie, *De l'homme considéré moralement, de ses moeurs et de celles des animaux*, vols 1–2, Maradan, Paris, 1802. De la Métherie, who was born in 1743, is not to be confused with Julien de la Mettrie (born in 1709).
11 *Ibid.*, vol. 1, pp. 270–2.
12 N. Assorodobraj, *op. cit.*
13 G. Lefebvre, *Quatre-vingt neuf*, Paris, 1939, pp. 51 ff.
14 Ch. de Méré, *De la vraie honnêteté*, Collected works pub. by Association G. Budé, Paris, 1930, vol. 3, pp. 69–70.
15 Ch. de Montesquieu, *The Spirit of the Laws*, trans. T. Nugent, London and New York, 1949, p. 24.

16 Beard, *op. cit.*, p. 414.
17 The link formed in England between nobility and bourgeoisie by the production of wool, is pointed out by Beard, and also by Christopher Hill in the first essay in his *The English Revolution of 1640* (1938).
18 Montesquieu, *op. cit.*, p. 24.
19 *Ibid.*, p. 29.
20 G. Lefebvre, *op. cit.*, p. 52.
21 Tocqueville quoted by André Maurois in *Histoire d'Angleterre.* See also E. A. Kosminski, *Issledovanija po agrarnoj istorii Anglii XVIII veka*, Moscow, 1947.
22 R. Garaudy, *Le Communisme et la morale*, Paris, 1945, p. 22.
23 See my article 'Inteligent polski na tle grup towarzyskich Europy Zachodniej' in *Myśl Współczesna*, 1947.
24 Locke, *Some Thoughts Concerning Education*, ed. Quick, London, 1892, p. 34.
25 *The Sir Roger de Coverley Papers. From the Spectator*, ed. Samuel Thurber. Boston, New York, Chicago, 1898. The figure of Sir Roger de Coverley is very reminiscent of André Maurois's Colonel Bramble in *Les Silences du Colonel Bramble*.
26 Beard, *op. cit.*, p. 568.
27 A. Livingston, 'Theory of the Gentleman', in *Encyclopaedia of the Social Sciences*.
28 R. Lewis and A. Maude, *The English Middle Class*, 3rd edn, London, 1950.
29 See Nyrop, 'Qu'est ce qu'un gentleman?' (trans. from Danish), in *Linguistique et histoire des moeurs*, Paris, 1934.
30 W. M. Thackeray, *The Book of Snobs*, in *Works of W. M. Thackeray in Thirteen Volumes*, London, 1894, vol. 9, pp. 11, 30, 31, 46, 80. On English snobbism and reverence for titles, see also E. A. Kosminski, 'K voprosu ob obrazovanii anglijskoj natsii', *Voprosy istorii*, 1951.
31 Beard, *op. cit.*, pp. 81 ff.
32 *Ibid.*, p. 448.
33 Quotes from *Buddenbrooks* are from the English translation by H. T. Lowe-Porter, London, 1962.
34 Beard, *op. cit.*, p. 411.
35 The fourteenth-century Arab writer Ibn Khaldun considered that nobility and prestige lasted at most for four generations in any one family. He used the terms 'founder, continuer and heir' to identify the first three generations, and described the fourth as that which dissipates what the first three have built up. 'The builder of the glory (of the family) knows what it

cost him to do the work, and he keeps the qualities that
created his glory and made it last. The son who comes after
him had personal contact with his father and thus learned
many things from him. The third generation must be content
with imitation and in particular with reliance on tradition.
. . . The fourth generation is inferior to the preceding ones
in every respect . . . this member actually despises these
qualities. He imagines that the edifice was not built through
application and effort . . . he sees the great respect in which
he is held by the people . . . (a respect which is not due to
his own merits and efforts)'. Quoted from Ibn Khaldun, *The
Muqaddimah*, trans. Franz Rosenthal, London, 1958, vol. 1,
pp. 279 f.

36 Beard, *op. cit.*, p. 705.

11 Some thoughts on methodology

1 J. Bentham, *Introduction to the Principles of Morals and
Legislation*, New York, 1948, p. 3.

2 C. A. Helvétius, *De l'esprit*, Paris, 1909, Disc. II, ch. 1.

3 One of the more recent statements of the psychological
concept of interest is to be found in H. D. Lasswell and A.
Kaplan, *Power and Society*, Yale University Press, New Haven,
1950. The definition given here is: 'An interest is a pattern
of demands and its supporting expectations' (p. 23).
According to the authors, any interest comprises
expectations and some form of conscious demand.

4 The concept of need is analogous to the concept of interest.
Loosely, one talks of 'needing' whatever one doesn't have,
whether it be bread or nylons. It is in this sense that we talk
of capitalism creating more and more needs, and it is in this
sense that the peasant who moves to town becomes more
demanding. In another sense, the lack of something is not
necessarily a 'need'; in this sense the term applies only to
shortages which are recognised as critical, and which it is
therefore legitimate to seek to make good. In this sense, the
satisfaction of hunger is a need; the desire to have varnished
fingernails is a whim. Legitimate needs are usually qualified
by such adjectives as 'elementary', 'fundamental', 'basic'.

5 See *Motywy postępowania*, pp. 154 f.

6 *Ibid.*, p. 152.

7 *Ibid.*

8 Plato, *Republic*, trans. Lindsay, Everyman Library, London, 1950, p. 15.
9 Hobbes, *Leviathan*, ed. Plamenatz, Fontana, London, 1962, p. 127.
10 Lenin, *Three Sources and Three Component Parts of Marxism*, in *Selected Works in Three Volumes*, Moscow, 1967, p. 45.
11 K. Kautsky, *The Origins of Christianity*.
12 R. Garaudy, *Le Communisme et la moralité*, Paris, 1945, p. 44.
13 S. Żółkiewski, *Kuźnica*, 30 January 1949.
14 F. Engels, Speech at the Grave of Karl Marx, in Marx, Engels, *Selected Works in Two Volumes*, Moscow, 1962, vol. 2, p. 167.
15 S. Czarnowski, *Kultura*, Warsaw, 1946.
16 Garaudy, *op. cit.*, p. 44.

12 Concluding survey

1 M. Weber, *Wissenschaftslehre*, 1913, pp. 520–3.
2 W. Tatarkiewicz, 'Nauki nomologiczne a nauki typologiczne'. Off-print from *Sprawozdań PAU*, vol. 46 (1945) nos 1–5, pp. 28–33.
3 *Przegląd Historii Sztuki*, vol. 2, 1930/31, pp. 1–2.
4 *Ibid.*
5 'Kautsky would have asked himself: "Are there historical laws concerning revolutions, which know of no exceptions?"', wrote Lenin in *The Proletarian Revolution and the Renegade Kautsky*. 'The answer would be: no, there are no such laws. Historical laws relate only to what is typical; to what Marx called, in a sense, "ideal" in the sense of average, normal, typical capitalism'.
6 G. Degré, 'The Fascist: An Operational Definition', *Social Forces*, vol. 24, no. 2, 1945. Quoted from Ranulf, who discusses Degré's work in his paper 'On the Survival Chances of Democracy', Copenhagen, 1948.
7 Ranulf, *op. cit.*

Index